D1540287

Cronbach, Lee Joseph, 1916–
    Psychological tests and personnel decisions ₍by₎ Lee J. Cronbach ₍and₎ Goldine C. Gleser. ₍2d ed.₎ Urbana, University of Illinois Press, 1965.

viii, 347 p.   illus.   24 cm.

Bibliography: p. ₍333₎–343.

    1. Psychometrics. 2. Decision-making.   I. Gleser, Goldine C., joint author. II. Title.

BF39.C7   1965   151.26   64–18667

Psychological Tests and Personnel Decisions

Psychological Tests and Personnel Decisions

**Lee J. Cronbach and
Goldine C. Gleser**

UNIVERSITY OF ILLINOIS PRESS
Urbana   Chicago   London

Originally published in a clothbound edition, 1965

Second Edition

252 00003 X

To the Memory of Nageswari Rajaratnam

PREFACE TO SECOND EDITION

This monograph was originally published in 1957 as the final report of a program of research supported by the Office of Naval Research under contract N6ori-07146. Because of continued demand for the monograph, particularly for use in graduate seminars, the publishers asked us to prepare a new, enlarged edition. We could not undertake a substantial revision of the manuscript, both because our time was committed to other projects and because our thinking on this problem has not departed in any significant way from that of the original edition.

Work since 1955 has reinforced our judgment that decision theory is more important as a point of view than as a source of formal mathematical techniques for developing and applying tests. The original chapters present that point of view in a form still valid today, though a current edition written *ab initio* would distribute its emphasis a bit differently.

While work on decision theory has not been lacking in the period since 1955 (when the earlier manuscript was completed), it has scattered over a broad front, and has not superseded the original line of reasoning. Rather than attempt to revise the monograph by scattered insertions of recent work, we decided to reproduce all the original material with minor editorial improvements, and to represent the more recent developments in the field by adding a bibliography, a chapter surveying recent trends and developments, and several pertinent papers by others. The papers by other investigators all fall within the general framework of decision-theoretic analysis, even though the several formulations depart in some respects from each other and from our own formal model. We have selected these papers from among the many available as those most likely to interest and to be understood by graduate students in psychology, education, and management; many valuable papers are mathematically quite formidable, and therefore unsuited to our typical reader. Two of the papers are based on theses not generally available; we thank Drs. Roche and van Naerssen for preparing their work in this form. We also acknowledge with thanks the permissions to reprint given by the following: The Royal Statistical Society, for the Finney selection from its *Journal* and the Birnbaum-Maxwell selection from *Applied Statistics;* The American Psychological Association, for our paper from *Journal of Educational Psychology;* the U.S. Air Force Personnel Laboratory, for the technical report by Ward and Davis; the Stanford University Press for material by Raiffa, from H. Solomon, ed., *Studies in item analysis and selection;* and *Educational and Psychological Measurement* for tables (Brogden, Ghiselli). We also thank Dr. van Naerssen's publisher J. B. Wolters of Groningen and his translator Mrs. J. Wassing-Hurst for their cooperation.

Some readers may note discrepancies between several figures in this edition and the first edition. Several erroneous figures were used in the original printing; the corrected figures appearing in this edition appeared also in later printings of the first edition.

Preparation of the second edition was carried out while the senior author was a Fellow of the Center for Advanced Study in the Behavioral Sciences, and while the junior author was supported by the Foundations Fund for Research in Psychiatry. Support for the original research was provided by the Bureau of Educational Research, University of Illinois, as well as the Office of Naval Research, and the revision was supported in part by grant M-1839 from the National Institute of Mental Health. It is a pleasure to acknowledge again the work of our associates on the original project, Eugene I. Burdock, Jack C. Merwin, Peter Erve, Jean Manis, Vera Strond, and Henry Plahn, and to acknowledge the work of Julie Raventos in preparing the present manuscript. In identifying recent developments we have been helped by several persons, including particularly Herman Chernoff, L. J. Savage, Milton Sobel, and Herbert Solomon.

LEE J. CRONBACH

GOLDINE C. GLESER

CONTENTS

Psychological Tests and Personnel Decisions
by Lee J. Cronbach and Goldine C. Gleser

List of Figures

1

THE TESTER AND DECISION THEORY

Our society continually confronts people with decisions for which they have inadequate information. It is for this reason that psychological and educational tests exist. Some of the problems on which tests are brought to bear are purely individual: the uncertainties of a boy trying to choose a career, or of a young couple trying to decide whether they are suited for marriage. Equally numerous are the occasions on which an administrator, teacher, or clinician turns to tests for assistance in making decisions about many people. The personnel manager wishes to know whom to hire; the military psychologist determines which men are adequately trained and ready for duty; the teacher inquires whether his class should be taught at a rapid or a slow pace. There is no end to such examples of the role of tests in decision making.

It is therefore desirable that a theory of test construction and use consider how tests can best serve in making decisions. Little of present test theory, however, takes this view. Instead the test is conceived as a measuring instrument, and test theory is directed primarily toward the study of accuracy of measurement on a continuous scale. Hull (1928, p. 268) voiced a principle that has been the root of nearly all work on test theory: "The ultimate purpose of using aptitude tests is to estimate or forecast aptitudes from test scores." It is this view that we propose to abandon. We acknowledge the usefulness of accurate estimation — but we maintain that the *ultimate* purpose of any personnel testing is to arrive at qualitative decisions such as those illustrated in the preceding paragraph.

The value of a test depends on many qualities in addition to its accuracy. Especially to be considered are the relevance of the measurement to the particular decision being made, and the loss resulting from an erroneous decision. Recommendations regarding the design, selection, and interpretation of a test must take into account the characteristics of the decisions for which the test will be used, since the test that is maximally effective for one decision will not necessarily be most effective elsewhere.

An appropriate test theory can evolve from a general and systematic examination of the decision problems for which tests are used and of the demands these problems place upon the test. In such a study of decision making and its implications for testing, we are fortunately able to draw on extensive mathematical contributions, many of them recent.

The following comment by a leading contributor to decision theory, M. A. Girshick (1954, pp. 448, 464), indicates the need for study of this sort and the difficulties:

> Statistical decision theory was originated some 15 years ago by Abraham Wald. In the past decade, great strides have been made in the field by Wald and others. However, so far these developments have had but little impact on experimental research in the social and physical sciences. There appear to be two basic reasons for this: one is the natural lag between theory and practice which so often occurs in science; the other, which in the present case may be more fundamental, is that decision theory to date has been too much concerned with the mathematical foundations of the subject and less with its immediate application. Curiously enough, here is a situation in which the foundational development, difficult as it is, is easier than the application to actual problems. . . .
>
> . . . Decision theory is in the process of development and is not yet a completed science. It takes for its domain the problem of rational behavior in the face of unknown states of nature. It gives a logical foundation and framework to mathematical statistics which it has never had before. It grapples with the problem of design of experiments in a manner never before attempted in statistics. It insists that cost considerations and consequences of decisions be taken into account in every statistical investigation. In doing so, it has brought sequential theory into the general framework and has made sequential decision procedures the rule rather than the exception. It bridges the gap existing in classical statistics between testing hypotheses and estimation by showing that the distinction lies mainly in [the collection of alternative actions that may be taken] . . . , which in one case is finite and in the other infinite. In its attempt to clarify the nature of the statistical decision process, it exposes the limitations as to what is attainable in the face of ignorance, and raises serious problems concerning rational behavior. . . . Finally because decision theory deals with the problem of decision making in its greatest generality, every particular statistical problem can be immediately placed in a general framework and thus exhibit its ramifications and implications.

ORIGINS OF DECISION THEORY

Despite the recency of its development, decision theory is closely related to long-standing problems in the social sciences, and is being used to some extent by psychologists, economists, and sociologists.

Within psychology alone, the theory has been brought to bear on problems ranging from learning experiments to studies of attitude measurement.

Economists have been concerned with decision processes for a long time. Businesses are continually faced with choices among alternative courses of action. Principles are needed that will assist managers in making the most profitable or most beneficial choices among products, among investments, etc. Serious limitations have been found in the theories of classical economics which emphasize the welfare of the individual entrepreneur. Most conspicuously, they fail to consider how decisions are reached by coalitions of individuals with different interests. This criticism led von Neumann and Morgenstern (1947) to study how an individual should make decisions when he is one of a group of participants in a game or a market. The resulting "Theory of Games" proved to have a great interest not only for economists, but also for military planners.

The work of Wald (1950), who extended the statistical theory of testing hypotheses into a general "statistical decision theory," paralleled and has merged with game theory. Wald's interest was partly instigated by problems of inspection and quality control in industrial production, where decisions to accept or reject manufactured articles are required. (Such inspection has an obvious similarity to one variety of personnel testing.) Both the statistician and the game theorist are concerned with decisions in the face of an uncertain future, but in game theory the uncertainty comes from the prospective selfish actions of competitors, while in statistical decisions the uncertainty comes from random variation in events.

Studies of decisions take into account the benefit or "utility" of various courses of action. Much thought has been given to problems of defining or estimating such utilities. Economists and mathematicians have tried, for example, to estimate what hypothetical utilities, attached to various consequences, could account for a person's decision to gamble even though he knows that the "house percentage" prevents his winning over the long term. Experimental psychologists have recently begun to study how people actually choose between courses of action, that is, what utilities are consistent with their actions.

Even where it is possible to determine what benefit each individual will receive from various courses of action, the best decision is hard to select if the interests of many individuals are at stake as, for example, in economic decisions of government (Arrow, 1963). One might assess the total effect of a decision by combining the benefits received by all individuals, but this can scarcely be done unless we can measure all persons' utilities on the same scale. Is the benefit rendered by reducing a rich man's taxes by $100 equal to the benefit when a poor man's taxes are reduced by $100? A whole body of theory referred to as "welfare economics" has tried to resolve dilemmas encountered in balancing the welfare of many persons affected by a decision.

A tremendous amount of knowledge has been developed around the general topic of decision problems. Since the tester is concerned with decision making, it is reasonable to expect significant understandings to result from restating testing problems in such a way that this knowledge can be brought to bear.

CHARACTER OF THIS REPORT

Our study did not begin as an attempt to translate utility and decision theories into psychometric terms. Rather, it began with recognition of certain questions about tests which we could not answer adequately under then existing formulations. One question, for instance, was how one might evaluate a test battery which measures several aptitude dimensions. Hitherto, testers have discussed only the validity of each single score or of the combined test against any single criterion. Except for Horst's recent work (1954), no effort has been made to consider the total contribution of the test in making decisions over all criteria. In trying to formulate theoretical models which would permit study of such questions, we were led inevitably to examine the utility of personnel decisions. It was at this point that we recognized our approach as a case within Wald's more general decision model. This comprehensive model, we found, clarified a wide variety of testing problems.

We have not drawn all possible inferences from decision theory. Indeed, we barely touch on some issues that patently lead to deeper and deeper inquiries. Furthermore, decision theory has been growing at a rate which has quite prevented us from exploring the significance for the tester of all new developments.

We have confined our own study to the simplest and most definite mathematical methods. No doubt some person with greater mathematical competence than ours can extract much further material for the tester from the mathematical literature.

The conceptual tools of decision theory make the tester aware of problems that have hitherto been minimized or overlooked. We believe that our restatement of testing problems in these new terms will assist all users of tests to understand what assumptions they are making and how adequate their procedures are.

At a more technical level, this report examines specific principles of test development and use. Some of the generalizations are restatements of results already in the psychometric literature, which take on new importance, new interrelations, and new meaning in the decision framework. Others are new developments entirely. We shall not list the contents of ensuing chapters here. The reader may obtain an idea of what is to be covered by examining the bibliography at the end of the book; the papers cited (excepting the mathematical sources) indicate the range of psychometric topics with which we deal. Our analysis will extend or reinterpret these papers, or integrate them with other parts of test theory. Since the topics include efficient design of tests, construction of selection batteries, interpretation of validity coefficients, and use of tests for individual assessment, we anticipate that the results will concern a large and diverse audience of test users.

The reasoning of this report is mathematical rather than empirical. A mathematical treatment has both advantages and hazards. The advantages lie in the precision with which conclusions can be stated, the finality with which they can be established, and the wide range of circumstances to which a derivation can apply. In contrast, an empirical study covers only a few particular circumstances and obtains results which are perturbed by various sorts of sampling error.

The disadvantage of the mathematical attack is that it involves assumptions that may not adequately describe real conditions. At times it is even necessary to make assumptions about postulated variables that have never been observed. In our model, for example, it is assumed that the contribution of a person to an institution, and the costs of testing, can be evaluated in some tangible, countable unit. Girshick's comments on this difficulty (1954, p. 463) are worth quoting:

Here again we see that decision theory demands a great deal of the decision maker. It demands that he be in a position to evaluate numerically for every possible state of nature in the situation under consideration the consequences of any of the actions he might take. It has been argued by many that no human being possesses the ability so to evaluate the utility of the various actions in all possible states. . . . The inability of the decision maker to formulate clearly the loss function is, in fact, a stumbling block in determining what a rational mode of behavior is for him. More bluntly, it is impossible to tell a person what is an optimal way for him to behave if he is unable to formulate clearly what he is after. . . . Decision theory acts as a gadfly to the research worker. It says to him: You cannot solve your problem unless you more clearly define your goal and the consequences of your decisions. Such a prodding is likely to be healthy.

Possibly a major contribution of the approach through decision theory is that it points clearly toward a variety of needed empirical studies. Thus our argument indicates that many *present* personnel procedures are based on assumptions regarding the interaction of the characteristics of the individual and the nature of the treatment to which he is assigned. These implicit, widely employed assumptions have been tested sketchily if at all. A similar finding is that tests used for placement of individuals (e.g., among various levels of instruction) should be validated in ways quite different from those in general use.

To provide the general reader with an overall grasp of concepts and results, the main body of this report contains a minimum of technical detail and mathematical reasoning. The detailed mathematical argument is found in a series of technical appendices.

This report does not attempt to present decision theory *per se*. A mathematical presentation of decision theory may be found in *Theory of games and statistical decisions* (Blackwell and Girshick, 1954). Girshick (1954) has presented an elementary survey of basic concepts in the field, and a popularized treatment is offered in Bross's *Design for decision* (1953). The subject of utility analysis has been reviewed by Adams (1960) and Edwards (1954), the latter review being particularly directed toward psychologists. (See also p. 159).

Decision theory is provocative, and forces one to alter his accustomed thought patterns. We anticipate that each reader will find a different facet of our argument important for him, and often his thoughts will veer off into pathways not covered by this investigation. The intended contribution of this monograph is, in a word, to stir up the reader's thoughts.

2

TYPES OF PERSONNEL DECISIONS

Any situation where a person is confronted with alternative courses of action is a decision problem. Applied psychologists encounter such problems daily in their work. The reference to "personnel decisions" in our title may suggest that we are concerned only with the decisions of industrial and military personnel management, but this is not the case. Our discussion embraces problems of guidance, clinical assessment, and teaching. We are concerned with the use of tests used in all these types of decision. While we speak of "tests," we are interested in all information-gathering procedures including interviews, biographical inquiries, and physical measurement.

A test theory should encompass in some manner all the various decisions for which tests are used. Indeed, it could be said that different test theories must be developed for each type of decision since each makes somewhat different demands upon tests. For theoretical purposes, however, it is not appropriate to separate guidance from clinical problems, or problems of teaching from those of industry. Instead, it is necessary to develop rubrics that classify problems according to the formal characteristics significant for decision theory.

INSTITUTIONAL VS. INDIVIDUAL DECISIONS

Institutional decisions such as selection of employees may be distinguished from individual decisions such as choice of a vocation. In the typical "institutional" decision, a single person makes a large number of comparable decisions. The "individual" decision is one in which the choice confronting the decision maker will rarely or never recur.

Examples of institutional decisions are classification of military recruits, screening of pupils to identify who should be studied by counselors, and determination of appropriate therapy for psychotic patients. In any of these instances, decisions are made regarding many people, using a constant philosophy or value system. The hospital wishes to use its therapeutic resources most efficiently; the industry wishes to choose employees who will in the long run contribute most to its balance sheet. One seeks the decision or policy which will yield as much benefit as possible to the institution. Individual interests may be taken into account, but only insofar as they affect the realization of the goals of the institution. From the viewpoint of an admissions officer, the best use of space in a medical school is to admit those who have the greatest probability of success, considering both motivation and ability. Between two candidates, the institutional value system would require impartial choice of the one with the better prognosis. Whether a decision is individual or institutional does not depend on whether persons are considered singly or in groups. A decision maker who considers one person alone (e.g., approving him for a driver's license after a road test), applying the value system of society, is making an institutional decision.

In an individual decision, the best course of action depends on the individual's value system and varies from one individual to another. A particular goal which would be worth any risk to one individual may have little value to another. Thus one boy applying for admission to medical school might value highly even a small chance of success, and would regard a shift from medicine into teaching or pharmacy as abandoning all his aspirations; another having comparable prospects of success might be contented or even relieved to abandon a medical career. Probability of success cannot be the sole consideration in the individual decision.

In the institutional decision, we may think of the decision maker as trying to maximize the benefit from a whole series of similar decisions. That is, he seeks the policy that will work best "on the average" over many decisions about admission or job assignment or therapy. Since each decision involves the same set of values, he can combine different decisions and strike some type of statistical balance that gives the best overall outcome.

The individual decision is often unique. The choice may occur only once in a lifetime. Even where the decision can be "remade" at a later time if the first course of action works out badly, the original decision has an uncancelable influence on the welfare of the individual. A poor choice of curriculum at the outset of a student's college education will continue to handicap him long after he has discovered his error and changed to a more suitable curriculum. It is meaningless to speak of an average outcome, since he makes only a few such decisions at most.

The insurance business is founded on just this distinction between institutional (or collective) decisions and individual decisions. The company can pool its decisions; it charges a premium such that the company's loss over all risks underwritten will be balanced by the totaled premiums. The premium is further increased by margins for safety, for administrative expense, and for profit. The purchaser is involved in only a few possible insurance transactions. In each, he decides to insure or not insure — that is, to incur a small and certain loss, or to risk a large loss at a low level of probability. If he insures, his premium is larger than his *pro rata* share of the risk. A man considering a large number of insurance transactions would find this course of action uneconomical because he loses on the average. He might more profitably make other financial provisions for covering possible losses. The man considering only a few insurance policies cannot expect that the outcomes for him will come close to the statistical average. He must evaluate the discrete alternative risks according to his personal scale of values.

Test theory, as it now stands, is relevant chiefly to institutional decisions. Regression formulas, for example, are designed to minimize the average squared error of estimate. Institutional decisions lend themselves to "strong" mathematical and statistical treatment, making generalizations possible. For this reason, our report deals almost entirely with institutional decisions. Many important personnel problems may require a decision theory based on the individual's value system. Counseling, for example, has moved more and more in the direction of encouraging individuals to make their own decisions. Some aspects of individual decisions will be discussed briefly in Chapter 10. (See also pp. 159-160.)

MAXIMIZATION AS A DECISION PRINCIPLE

Mathematical decision theory is highly general, encompassing many possible principles for arriving at a decision. In some situations a conservative principle which avoids any large loss is preferable; the purchaser of an insurance policy is following such a strategy. In other situations, choices are preferred which offer even a small probability of obtaining a large gain; many individuals seem to adopt this principle when gambling. In institutional statistical decisions, the most generally useful strategy is one which maximizes the average gain (or minimizes average loss) over many similar decisions. We shall employ the principle in developing test theory regarding institutional decisions. Even with this restriction, many important lines of attack are opened, indeed far more than we can exploit at present.

Assumption of a Cardinal Utility Scale

In order to define an expected gain and maximize it, it is necessary to make an important assumption about the utility scale on which the outcomes of possible decisions are evaluated. We must assume that the value of various outcomes can be expressed in "equal units of satisfaction" or the like, which are additive over many decisions. Where students are being selected for medical school, for example, an evaluation in terms of the average grade implies that admitting a group who will attain 30% A, 40% B, and 30% C grades is equivalent in value to admitting B students only. It is evident that such an assumption will not always be acceptable. One decision maker might prefer the former policy on the basis that it admits *some* highly superior students who will bring credit to the university. Another decision maker might prefer the second policy because the narrow range of ability makes the group easier to teach. The assumption of a cardinal scale of utilities is highly restrictive. Where it is applicable, it leads to relatively simple generalizations about best policies.

Much decision theory is based on the weaker assumption that outcomes may be evaluated on an ordinal scale. This requires simply that the decision maker be willing to order the expected outcomes in terms of his preference. Such ordinal utilities may not be averaged over decisions. Ordinal utilities, and problems associated with them, are under active study by many persons at present. One reason for this interest, apart from the purely mathematical attractiveness of the problems, is that ordinal utilities have been found a superior basis for economic theory (Adams, 1960). In psychology, Coombs (1953) has pointed out that the investigator who restricts himself to cardinal assumptions is unable to attack certain problems adequately. These include probability learning, level of aspiration, troubleshooting, preference among rewards or among wagers, etc.* Ordinal models are being used in some current

---

* Siegel (1959) uses cardinal utilities in a broader way than many other investigators. His work suggests that it may be possible to use such utilities in problems where they are not ordinarily considered appropriate.

research on these topics. Out of this work may come practical methods for dealing with ordinal utilities, and important insights for test theory. In our opinion, however, such developments will bear primarily on individual decisions rather than institutional decisions.

Assumption of a priori Knowledge

An investigator who wishes to maximize his expectations must have a firm basis for these expectations. An insurance company can successfully predict the net outcome of its wagers solely because of its accumulated experience with the distribution of losses for individuals grouped on the basis of age, occupation, state of health, etc. Knowledge of the expected distribution of outcomes (with and without information from testing) is likewise necessary in personnel decisions. Approximate knowledge of the joint distribution of tests and outcomes is ordinarily obtained by administering the tests to a sizable sample of individuals who are assigned to one or another treatment and then followed to determine the outcome. The distributions thus found form a basis for future policy. It is necessary to assume, of course, that the relevant features of the situation remain stable.

Two-Person Games

Much of the effort in decision theory and the theory of games has been to avoid assumptions such as those made above. Von Neumann and Morgenstern (1947) point out that many decision problems take the form of a "zero-sum two-person game," in which each person tries to increase his payoff at the expense of the other. The player cannot depend on statistical experience to predict his opponent's next move. When the opponent knows what move the player is making, he may be able to take advantage of this knowledge. A course of action that could have great value "if all goes well" is not a sound choice if it leaves a serious weakness for the opponent to capitalize on.

In such a case, it has been suggested that instead of trying to maximize expected payoff it might be better to follow a "minimax" principle. The minimax principle is to select always that course of action that will yield the least loss when one's opponent makes the least favorable response. The minimax principle is highly conservative, embodying the view that "if anything can go wrong, it will." Wald (1950) described statistical decisions as two-person games where the decision maker plays against Nature. The decision maker tries to guess (from partial information) what conditions exist in the particular situation that confronts him; Nature has chosen one from a wide range of alternatives. The minimax principle can be applied here also, but so pessimistic a view is doubtfully appropriate in statistical decisions, for Nature is presumably indifferent rather than antagonistic. Many attempts have been made to propose other decision principles (Thrall *et al.*, 1954), all of which aim to avoid assuming knowledge of an *a priori* distribution. No present alternative appears to be a better basis for making institutional decisions by means of tests than the assumption of a known joint distribution of test score and outcome.

CLASSIFICATION, PLACEMENT, AND SELECTION

Each decision in personnel work is an attempt to determine what should be done with one or more individuals. Sometimes the question is whom to hire and whom to reject. Sometimes the question is for what job a given recruit or applicant should be trained. Sometimes the decision is among educational or therapeutic methods. Letting the word *treatment* take a sufficiently broad meaning to cover all such examples as these, we may say that every personnel decision involves assigning each individual to an appropriate treatment. The number of individuals under consideration and the number of treatments available in any particular decision problem may be large or small.

In its most general form the decision problem is one of *classification*. Classification is thus understood to include guidance deci-

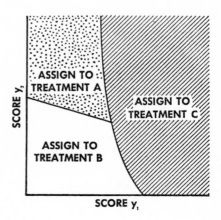

Figure 1. A classification procedure

sions as well as assignment to industrial jobs. It includes psychiatric diagnosis and similar discriminant problems involving no quotas, as well as classification to fill quotas. Information is used as an aid to classification; this information may be continuous or qualitative, and may involve one or several dimensions. Figure 1 illustrates schematically the general nature of the classification problem.

It is helpful to consider separately two special cases of classification that are much simpler to analyze than the general problem. The first case is that where information is univariate. Even when information is obtained in terms of more than one score or dimension, it is a common practice to combine such multivariate information into a single composite score before making decisions. If scores on the same composite scale are used in making all decisions between treatments, the classification problem may be termed a *placement* problem (Figure 2). The most common examples are dividing students among sections to be taught at different rates and using a trade test for coarse grouping of applicants. Use of a composite score to discriminate the brain-injured from the mentally deficient also exemplifies a placement decision. We shall see later that "measurement" problems can be considered as a particular variant of the use of tests for placement decisions.

Problems may also be differentiated according to whether or not rejection is allowed as one possible treatment, so that the person is eliminated from the institution. We can refer to these as *selection* problems; Figure 2 illustrates a selection strategy based on a nonlinear combination of two scores. We shall give particular attention to the relatively simple problem of selection on the basis of univariate information, where all accepted men are treated alike.

Constraints upon Decisions

Decision problems, whether concerned with classification, placement, or selection, may be distinguished on another basis: the

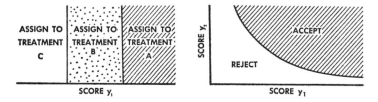

Figure 2. Placement and selection procedures

presence or absence of certain constraints. Two types of constraint are common: (a) number of treatments per man, and (b) number of men per treatment. The great majority of institutional decisions call for one treatment per man. The man is sent to one training course or to one job, or given one diagnosis. In individual decisions also, it is common to select one treatment at a time (e.g., in choice of curriculum). Some decisions involve multiple treatments, however, especially where specific duties rather than job classifications are assigned. In organizing a ship, for example, a man may be assigned to a combination of duties: radar watches, radio watches and maintenance, and lookout duty. Likewise a student may need to select five courses to fill a program of studies. When an individual may be assigned to more than one treatment, the decisions with regard to the several treatments are usually not independent. The problem then becomes one of finding the best pattern of treatments.

In institutional decisions the number of men per treatment may be constrained by a quota. Sometimes there is a definite number of vacancies, but in other situations the number of vacancies expected over a long period is to be considered. In the latter case, a minimal acceptance score may be determined that admits enough persons of good potentiality to maintain approximately the desired number of workers, students, etc. It is convenient to summarize a system of this character by translating the cutting score into a relative quota (one form of which is the familiar "selection ratio"). This quota states what fraction of a large population will be assigned to the treatment.

Not all institutional decisions are subject to a quota. Educational placement, in particular, may often be made without limiting the number of individuals who will receive any one treatment.

SEQUENTIAL AND SINGLE-STAGE STRATEGIES

We make a further important distinction between sequential and non-sequential strategies. The usual test theory assumes that a final decision is made on the basis of a battery of tests administered to all persons. This is a single-stage (i.e., non-sequential) decision procedure. It is possible, and probably more common in practice, to approach decisions sequentially. No irrevocable commitment of an individual to a treatment is made. Instead, after each stage of information gathering, the individual is sent on to some further experience where new information about him is obtained. This new information may modify his ultimate disposition. The decision to reject a job applicant is typically final and not to be reconsidered, but a decision to accept the man is really a decision to investigate him further. His work on the job provides further data, and if he proves unsatisfactory, he can be discharged.

Personnel decisions typically form a long chain. A student makes decisions about vocational choice in each successive year of schooling. Even after he has completed his training, he may shift into some other field or specialize within his field. Choice points where he altered his plan may be readily recognized; there are also less conspicuous points where he considered a change of goal but did not make one. The institution is likewise making a sequence of decisions about the student's acceptability in the chosen career. Each time grades are given or he is admitted to a new level of training, the institution chooses between eliminating him and "investigating further." The college admissions office may view a decision to admit a borderline student as ending the decision process; but from the perspective of a dean considering the student's poor marks a year later, it was a decision to gather further information by observing his college performance.

After a test is given, one either can assign the person to a treatment or can decide to administer further tests. Broadly speaking, those further tests may include job tryouts, education and training programs, or even initiating psychotherapy and observing the patient's response. A distinction between "tests" and "treatments" is a convenience, but one of doubtful logical justification. Choice of any treatment that does not remove the individual from the hands of the decision maker is to some extent an "investigatory decision," since new facts can always be used to modify an earlier plan. A decision-making procedure that permits information at one point to determine what information will be gathered next is called a *sequential* strategy. It will prove important and profitable to extend test theory to encompass sequential methods.

A TAXONOMY OF DECISION PROBLEMS

The foregoing distinctions suggest a possible taxonomy for decision problems. Problems similarly classified are describable within a set of general principles. While a taxonomy adequately covering the entire range of testing problems would be hopelessly complicated, a small effort in this direction will serve to summarize the present chapter and to indicate how broad is the domain that concerns the tester. This will make particularly clear the fact that subsequent chapters barely begin the needed exploration of personnel decisions.

To classify any decision problem, we ask these questions:

1. (a) Are the benefits obtained from a decision evaluated in the same way for each person? or
   (b) Are different values used in deciding about each person?
2. (a) Is the decision about each individual made independently? or
   (b) Are decisions about various persons interrelated?
3. (a) Is each individual assigned to just one of the available treatments? or
   (b) May he be assigned to multiple treatments?
4. (a) Is one of the allowable treatments "reject"? or
   (b) Are all persons retained in the institution?
5. (a) Is the information used in univariate form? or
   (b) Is it in multivariate form?
6. (a) Are decisions final? or
   (b) May one decide to obtain further information prior to final decisions?

These six questions define $2^6 = 64$ different patterns. While all of them might be described within one highly generalized model, such generality is likely to be confusing rather than clarifying. For this reason we shall discuss relatively specific problems within the 64 possibilities.

We can use a code pattern such as *aaaaba* to describe any decision problem in terms of the six questions. The symbol *aaaaba* would describe (1a) an institutional decision (2a) without a quota constraint, (3a) assigning a person to one treatment (4a) which may be "reject," (5b) on the basis of multivariate information (6a) obtained in a single stage of testing. The following chapters will be especially concerned with the patterns *aaa* . . . and *aba* . . . , that is, with institutional decisions where each individual is assigned to one treatment and where a quota may or may not be employed. Within *aaa* . . . or *aba* . . . there are eight possibilities:

. . . *aaa* Reject decisions allowed; univariate information; single-stage testing. This is the common selection problem, considered in Chapter 4.

. . . *aab* As above, with sequential testing. This is the concern of Chapter 6.

... *baa* No persons rejected; univariate information; single-stage. These placement and measurement problems are the concern of Chapter 5.

... *bab* Sequential placement, considered in Chapter 7.

... *aba*⎫ Multivariate information; single-stage; rejection may
... *bba*⎭ or may not be allowed. This is the classification problem considered in Chapter 9.

... *abb*⎫
... *bbb*⎭ Sequential classification, considered briefly in Chapter 9.

Even this tabulation does not indicate all the distinctions with which test theory may be concerned. Further distinctions remain to be introduced in later chapters.

In distinguishing between so many different decision problems, this chapter makes clear the need for broadening existing test theory. Any test theory well developed at present deals with only a very limited area within our category system. The classical measurement theory of Kelley, Hull, and Gulliksen deals entirely with pattern *aaabaa* (multivariate information, where considered, being reduced to a linear composite). Cases involving "reject" decisions present special characteristics. Some of these patterns (chiefly *aaaaaa*) have been treated in scattered papers, but only Brogden has done connected studies on them. We are forced to conclude that there is no "theory of mental tests" at the present time, although there are many fragmentary theories.

The present report shows some connections and differences between the various systems, and may therefore be regarded as a first step toward an integrated theory. There will probably always be a need for many alternative test theories covering different cases, however. While an abstract mathematical treatment can cover all or most of the range of personnel problems simultaneously, definite treatment of specific problems will usually be more comprehensible to the test user. The purpose of the overriding system is to make clear the differences among problems, so that misapplication of a subtheory will not lead to incorrect practices.

3

CHARACTERISTICS OF DECISION PROBLEMS

All personnel decision processes can be characterized in the same manner. There is, in the first place, an *individual* about whom a decision is required, and two or more *treatments* to which he may be assigned. The decision is to be made on the basis of *information* about the individual.

The information is processed by means of some principle of interpretation, or *strategy*, which leads to either a *terminal decision* or an *investigatory decision*. A terminal decision ends the decision-making process by assigning the individual finally to a treatment. The *outcome* is his performance under that treatment. An investigatory decision calls for additional information, dictating what test or procedure will be used to gather that information. This then leads to a further decision. The cycle of investigatory decision, information gathering, and decision making continues until a terminal decision is made. The decision process is illustrated schematically in Figure 3. As was discussed in Chapter 2, a decision is terminal only from the viewpoint of a particular decision maker. A treatment will often yield additional information about an individual that can serve to modify the treatment.

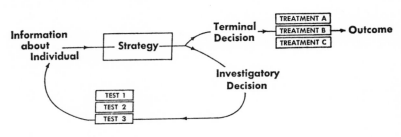

Figure 3. Schematic view of a decision process

STRATEGIES

A strategy (or decision function) is a rule for arriving at decisions. A strategy must state what the decision maker will do in any possible contingency (cf. Girshick, 1954). Thus a rule for college admission may say, "Any graduate of an accredited high school will be admitted; other applicants will be expected to pass certain tests of General Educational Development." This is equivalent to the following formal strategy:

Given information that individual i is a graduate, make the terminal decision "accept" with probability 1.

Given information that i is not a graduate, make the investigatory decision "Give GED tests" with probability 1.

At the second stage, given the further information that i's score on GED is *pass*, make the terminal decision "accept" with probability 1. Given information that i's score on GED is not *pass*, make the terminal decision "reject" with probability 1.

A strategy consists of a set of conditional probabilities. Probabilities employed in a strategy need not be restricted to 1 or 0. Given certain *information* about the individual, the probability of each *decision* is specified. The probabilities that constitute a strategy can be written as a matrix. Strategy matrix 1 describes each stage of the admission rule stated above, and strategy matrix 2 combines the two stages. Every entry is of the form $p_{d/y}$—the probability of making decision d, given information y. Matrix 2 makes clear that a strategy specifies the decision to be made in each possible contingency. Under the present strategy such a condition as "graduate, non-pass GED" cannot arise; if the test were routinely given to every applicant, however, the decision rule would need to provide for this contingency also.

STRATEGY MATRIX 1. PLAN FOR TWO STAGES OF DECISION REGARDING COLLEGE ADMISSION

INFORMATION CATEGORY (y)	DECISION		
	ACCEPT	REJECT	CONTINUE TESTING
First stage:			
Graduate	1	0	0
Non-graduate	0	0	1
Second stage:			
Non-graduate, pass GED	1	0	0
Non-graduate, non-pass GED	0	1	0

STRATEGY MATRIX 2. SAME PLAN, COMBINED FORM

INFORMATION CATEGORY (y)	DECISION				
	ACCEPT	REJECT	GIVE GED, ACCEPT	GIVE GED, REJECT	GIVE GED, CONTINUE TESTING
Graduate	1	0	0	0	0
Non-graduate, pass GED	0	0	1	0	0
Non-graduate, non-pass GED	0	0	0	1	0

The word *strategy* suggests that a conscious policy guides decisions. Even if choices are based on habit or some chance mechanism rather than policy, they can be described in a matrix. Each entry states what proportion of the time the decision maker makes each choice, under each set of possible conditions (information). The matrix describing a decision maker's practice must be based on tabulation of a large number of decisions. The probabilities recorded will often be other than 1 or 0. For example, suppose we examine recommendations of an interviewer for a private college where all applicants take a certain scholastic aptitude test. A tabulation of his decisions might report his decision pattern or "strategy" as this matrix:

INFORMATION CATEGORY (y)	DECISION	
	ACCEPT	REJECT
High school graduate, SAT above 70	.80	.20
Not high school graduate, SAT above 70	.80	.20
High school graduate, SAT below 70	.20	.80
Not high school graduate, SAT below 70	.10	.90

Every entry is a conditional probability. This interviewer evidently gives much more weight to SAT than to the fact of graduation. The table tells us that he accepts some graduates below 70; we do not know whether this is due to information not used in classifying entries for the table, or to sheer inconsistency in decision making.

A description such as this often reveals contingencies of which the decision maker himself is unaware. His strategy, that is, may be implicit rather than explicit, and may actually depart from some stated policy. Description of actual strategies is an important way to study industrial interviewing and rating, clinical diagnosis, and social perception. It is known, for example, that diagnostic teams in different hospitals report strikingly different proportions of certain pathologies among their intakes. This is apparently to be accounted for more by biases in the decision process than by differences in the intake populations. The overall proportions summarize some aspects of the "strategy" of the diagnostic team. More refined research would relate the probabilities to the categories of diagnostic information.

In any situation, some strategies are better than others. Just what constitutes a "best strategy" depends upon some subtle questions of evaluation, but once a way of evaluating outcomes is agreed on, the benefit from various strategies can be compared. If the decision maker aims to maximize expected utility, it is always better to assign persons in the same information category to the same treatment than to distribute them without further information. Sometimes a quota forces one to divide persons with the same observed characteristics, but otherwise in an ideal strategy matrix for institutional decisions the entries will always be 1 or 0.

Tabulation af actual strategy matrices reveals ways in which the decision-making practice departs from the ideal. Within a given category, the decision maker often differentiates, for example, recommending different treatments for persons whose score patterns are negligibly different. He may believe that this differentiation is based on additional information not represented in the scores, for example, impressions gained from interviewing. Unless such added information has considerable validity, the judge who differentiates within an objectively defined group may actually impair the utility of his decisions by introducing random variation (Cronbach, 1955; Meehl, 1954, p. 117). Once systematic errors in strategy are identified, they can be corrected by retraining.

EVALUATION OF THE DECISION-MAKING PROCEDURE

In evaluating a strategy for making decisions, one asks such questions as these:

1. Does this procedure arrive at the best decisions possible with this body of information?
2. Would gathering some other (or additional) information permit better decisions?
3. How much difference is there in the goodness of decisions arrived at by any two procedures?

Evaluation of a strategy involves evaluation of possible outcomes and the prediction of possible outcomes; these require separate consideration. First, it is necessary to state what value the decision maker places on each possible outcome. Then if the outcomes from a given strategy can be predicted, it is possible to evaluate the utility of the strategy.

Outcomes

The *outcome* consists of all the consequences of a given decision that concern the person making the decision (or the institution he represents). What outcome will result when the chosen treatment is applied depends on the characteristics of the individual and ordinarily on further unspecified situational variables. For example, the outcome of a decision to accept a student depends on unmeasured motivational factors on the one hand, and on the particular courses and instructors he selects on the other.

The decision problem would be enormously simplified if the decision maker could anticipate the actual outcome for each person under any treatment. A systematic comparison would establish the best assignment. Having only fallible information, the decision maker can at best predict the probability distribution of outcomes, or state the expected outcome over many similar decisions.

Prediction of Outcomes

An outcome is described in terms of some criterion or set of criteria. In industry, outcomes of hiring include the man's hourly production, his spoilage, his length of stay with the company, his effect on the morale and tenure of other employees, etc.

Empirical results from previous cases are required to determine how the information (y) is related to the criterion (c). This experience provides a validity matrix. There is one validity matrix for each treatment. In general form, it consists of a set of conditional probabilities $p_{c/yt}$. The criterion states may be simple judgments

VALIDITY MATRIX FOR TREATMENT *t*

INFORMATION CATEGORIES (y)	CRITERION STATES (c)		
	1	2	3
1	$p_{1/1t}$	$p_{2/1t}$	$p_{3/1t}$
2	$p_{1/2t}$	$p_{2/2t}$	$p_{3/2t}$
3	$p_{1/3t}$	$p_{2/3t}$	$p_{3/3t}$

("successful," "unsuccessful"), numerical scores, or complex categorizations of behavior. The validity matrix is like a contingency table, save that the latter is customarily stated in terms of joint probabilities or frequencies. In our computations, we shall assume that if the operational criterion is multidimensional it can be reduced to a single dimension by the application of appropriate weights. The validity matrix then takes the form of a bivariate distribution of test and criterion scores.

Valuation of Outcomes

Each information category leads to a different expected distribution of outcomes for a particular treatment. To compare alternative strategies for assigning individuals in a particular information category to a treatment, one must judge the desirability of each possible outcome. To evaluate outcomes cardinally requires assigning a value e_c to each possible criterion score. We shall assume here that such evaluations are expressed on an interval scale of utilities, but they may vary with c in any manner. To take a specific example, consider a criterion scale reporting the proportion of perfect objects produced by each machine operator. The higher this quality measure, the more valuable the operator is—but the benefit may not be a linear function. At the extreme upper end, a slight rise in quality of output may permit elimination of routine inspection. If so, a 2% rise in quality from 94% to 96% would represent a great gain. Where the quality is low, on the other hand, complete inspection is required, and the operator whose score is 76% yields negligibly more benefit than one at 74%. Practical difficulties of assigning values to outcomes will be discussed in Chapter 10.

The evaluated outcome may be referred to as a payoff. We can determine the expected payoff from an individual in a particular category y_i by weighting the value (e_c) of each outcome by its probability ($p_{c/y_i t}$), and summing over all outcomes. The cost of a test or any other procedure for gathering information must be expressed in utility units and deducted from the expected payoff.

Expected Utility from a Strategy

As we have formulated the problem, a strategy is only to be evaluated by its total contribution when applied to a large number of decisions. "Expected payoff from an individual" has little meaning unless one can average actual payoffs over a large number of individuals in the same information category. For this reason our model as developed here does not yield results interpretable with respect to individual decisions.

If we know the distribution of scores y_i in the population tested, the expected net utility for a large number of decisions is determined simply by adding the expected payoff for each y_i, weighted by the probability of that score. This can be stated algebraically, using the following symbols:

U = utility of the set of decisions
N = the number of persons about whom decisions are made
y = information category
t = treatment
c = outcome
e_c = value of outcome
C_y = cost of gathering information

$$U = N \sum_y p_y \sum_t p_{t/y} \sum_c p_{c/yt} e_c - N \sum_y p_y C_y. \quad [1]$$

The p_y describe the assumed y distribution, the $p_{t/y}$ are the entries of the strategy matrix, and the $p_{c/yt}$ are the entries of the validity matrix. C_y may or may not vary from score to score. Whatever strategy gives the greatest value of U is to be preferred.

PAYOFF FUNCTIONS RELATING UTILITY TO APTITUDE AND TREATMENT

If we are dealing with a single treatment, and prediction is based on continuous test scores, we may conceive of a function relating expected payoff e to score y. This payoff function states how much benefit a person with any given score is expected to contribute through production or learning or other outcome.

In selection there is sometimes only one possible treatment for accepted persons. More frequently, however, a variety of treatments might achieve the same ends. Thus, different curricula might be applied to attain certain educational objectives. Within an industrial organization, the responsibilities of various jobs might be modified.

Each treatment will have its own payoff function relating expected payoff to score. The payoff function, while presumed to be continuous, may take a variety of forms. Figure 4 shows possible payoff functions under different treatments, with univariate test information. According to the figure, very able men will perform best on treatment C, and least well on treatment A. With very low scores the situation is reversed, and A is the optimum treatment.

An illustrative situation is to be found in technical training. The curriculum could proceed at a rapid pace, assuming considerable knowledge of mathematics, technical vocabulary, and basic concepts on the part of the student. With a superior student such a method would produce rapid gains, but a weak student would progress slowly. More leisurely instruction which fills gaps in fundamentals and demands less mathematical understanding would permit the weak student to make maximum gains, but it would not develop the well-prepared student rapidly.

Little empirical information regarding payoff functions is presently available. For any single treatment, difficulties of prediction rarely permit us to fit any function more complex than a linear regression formula. Conventional comparisons of treatments show mean differences between payoff under two production methods or two instructional techniques. These results indicate only that one treatment yields higher outcomes for persons who are on the average like the experimental subjects and do not yield payoff functions. Such an experiment would indicate, regarding Figure 4, that treatment B is best. Significant interactions between ability and treatment are reported in some studies, but the data are generally inadequate to plot payoff functions. The scattered experimental evidence (see e.g., Anderson, 1949) warrants the belief that payoff functions for different treatments will differ in slope as well as in mean value.

Even more to the point is the fact that use of tests for educational placement implicitly *assumes* the existence of such different payoff functions. Our model therefore is merely a formal statement of what

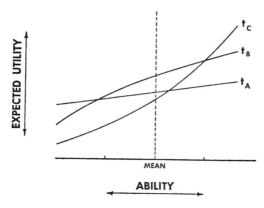

Figure 4. Three payoff functions

is everyday accepted without question, and examining its implications for testing is undoubtedly important. The realization that this assumption underlies practice is in itself an advance, because it makes clear the need for research on payoff functions. But let us first defend the claim that this assumption is currently made.

Dividing a group on the basis of some univariate information and assigning each segment to a different treatment must be justified by the belief that greater payoff will be obtained in this manner. With two treatments, there are three possibilities:

1. The payoff functions are identical, in which case placement is valueless since the treatment to which a man is assigned makes no difference in payoff.
2. The payoff function for one treatment is uniformly higher than the other for all score levels. In this event it is unwise to divide the group. All persons should be given the superior treatment unless institutional constraints require both treatments to be used (e.g., where there are too few therapists to give psychotherapy to all patients).
3. The payoff functions intersect somewhere within the score range. If this is the case, as in Figure 4, it is profitable to assign men to different treatments, so that each receives the treatment that "gets the most out of him."

Dividing students into sections to receive instruction at different rates clearly assumes the existence of condition 3, for there is no administrative necessity to vary the instructional pace from section to section.

The assumption that payoff functions do intersect, making placement profitable, is consistent with available theories about instruction. A person who lacks readiness to profit from one experience may be able to learn from another. Theories about response to therapy and about job performance likewise support an expectation that payoff functions will intersect. We therefore anticipate that empirically determined payoff functions will often be like those of Figure 4. Accepting the concept of intersecting payoff functions will allow us (in Chapter 5) to raise fundamental questions regarding the construction and validation of placement tests. We shall also use the concept as a base for studying certain selection problems.

Multivariate Response Surfaces

The problem of the tester may be further clarified if we think of the payoff function as a response surface in multidimensional space

(Box, 1954). Under any one treatment, the outcome for a given person might be presumed to be exactly predictable, if enough is known about his characteristics and the treatment is precisely controlled. Actually, some variance will always be unpredicted, and therefore one can only describe the expected payoff for a person having certain characteristics. It is convenient to think of the measured characteristics as expressed in terms of orthogonal factors $s_j = s_1, s_2. \ldots$ Any test score may be resolved by factor analysis into a linear composite of certain s dimensions. The person's characteristics are described by the pattern $\tilde{s}_i$. For each pattern $\tilde{s}_i$ there is an expected payoff e_{it}. The payoff function is a response surface continuous in the s_j. A different surface is expected for each treatment.

In any decision problem, we are actually concerned chiefly with a subset of the various s's, those which are related to payoff. For any set of treatments under consideration, the test scores may be so factored as to extract those dimensions that account for variance in payoff under at least one treatment. Payoff under any treatment depends on one or more of these *aptitude* dimensions. Any other of the test-score dimensions will have zero coefficients in payoff functions for all the treatments. Our argument to this point has emphasized that one may choose that one of several distinct treatments for which $e_{\tilde{s}_i t}$ is greatest, as estimated for an individual from whatever test information is available.

Quite a different response surface may be considered if we regard treatments as varying continuously. Treatments may vary along a large number of dimensions, which might be designated $w_1, w_2, \ldots$ The classic example is found in chemistry, where temperature, pressure, and concentration of some reagent may be varied. The yield of the reaction will vary accordingly, and a continuous response surface may be fitted to observed points. Experimental psychologists likewise are accustomed to think of factors in a treatment as continuous variables; time between trials, proportion of reinforcements, amount of ego-involvement, and discriminability of cues, for example, affect various forms of learning in a presumably continuous manner. In personnel psychology, precise control of treatments is difficult and very often the decision maker is confined to a few alternatives. But in principle the treatments given a student may vary in a continuous manner. Such variables in an instructional situation may include the amount of supportiveness of the instructor, the pace of instruction, or the extent to which the instruction demands mathematical ability. In psychotherapy, the treatment may vary in warmth, depth of interpretation, and extent of medical supplementation. If the concept that treatments vary continuously is accepted, for individuals having the characteristics $\bar{s}$ there is a response surface $e_{\bar{s}t} = f(\bar{w}_t)$. This surface presumably has an absolute maximum (and perhaps local maxima).

If the relation of payoff to the treatment parameters were independent of the person's characteristics, then such parameters would be of little interest to the personnel tester. The same treatment would be best for all individuals. There is often an interaction, however, among individual characteristics and treatments, so that the location of the maximum payoff differs for different patterns $\bar{s}$.

The personnel worker is usually concerned with choosing individuals to fit a fixed treatment. In clinical and guidance testing, however, it is the individual that has been fixed and the treatment is to be selected from many possibilities. The task of the clinician appears to be to adjust the treatment as nearly as possible to the optimum for the individual. He can ordinarily use his information to select from among an almost infinite variety of treatment conditions that one pattern which seems best for the person. It is true that present sources of information are a poor basis for making such adaptations, but this indicates only that gains from adaptation are likely to be limited at present. Certainly the physician does not hesitate to compound drugs, rest, exercise, diet, and bedside encouragement in an individualized formula. The same flexibility is ultimately open to the teacher and the psychotherapist, but their supporting science is less adequate at this time.

The response surface linking payoff to treatment factors has been ignored in test theory because it plays little part in traditional personnel decisions. Assigning men to fixed categories, or predicting their scores under a single treatment, is all that the industrial and military psychologist has attempted. But even in personnel classification adaptation may be possible. One may vary such important conditions of a job as amount of on-the-job instruction, amount of supervision, and pacing of work. Introducing radical changes in degree of responsibility or amount of automatic control makes changes in payoff even more likely. So long as one can expect to employ men of a given quality, one should set the treatment so as to maximize their payoff. Within the limits of practicality, a change in quality of men calls for adaptation of treatment. Thus in all personnel testing there may be need to consider payoff as a function of treatment variables.

Considering both types of variables affecting payoff, we see that

$e_{it} = f(\bar{s}_i, \bar{w}_t)$. Since both s and w are (in principle) multivariate, the problem cannot be easily represented geometrically. Algebraic analysis is complex but not impossible. Rather than attempt a comprehensive study of such payoff functions, we shall mainly examine problems involving a single aptitude dimension s. We shall restrict ourselves also to a subset of treatments whose payoff functions with respect to s vary in a continuous manner. These radical restrictions permit exploration of only a corner of the total problem, but a great deal is to be learned even from such a limited case.

The foregoing considerations lead us to make a distinction between decision problems involving "fixed-treatment" and "adaptive-treatment" conditions. In the former, the treatment is specified *a priori*, without regard to information from the particular persons tested. For example, a job or curriculum is defined and an attempt is made to select the individuals who will perform best in it. In adaptive treatment, however, the choice of men and choice of treatment are both made in the light of test data. Thus the personnel manager may be allowed to reduce the difficulty of a job when he has to fill vacancies with a poorer quality of applicant. Speaking generally, the aim of adaptive treatment is to choose the treatment for an accepted person in order to fit his aptitudes as well as possible, or to fit the group of accepted persons as a whole if all must be given the same treatment. So long as the payoff function for any admissible treatment is linear and positive in slope, the same men will be selected under either fixed or adaptive conditions. As Chapters 4 and 5 will show, however, the contribution of testing is different in the two conditions. Chapters 7 and 8 will demonstrate that the testing procedure itself may profitably be altered as one shifts from fixed- to adaptive-treatment assumptions.

Assumption of First-Degree Payoff Function

In the mathematical developments of the following chapters, we shall assume first-degree functions relating expected payoff to aptitude under any treatment. When a single aptitude is involved (as when a single test score is used), there is a linear payoff function. This simple relation has been used by many previous investigators (e.g., Brogden, 1946; Cochran, 1951; Richardson, 1944).

If one wishes instead to consider payoff functions of higher degree, a very large number of possibilities would be available, and present empirical knowledge gives no basis for choosing any one of these as especially realistic. Fortunately, a linear relation serves as a good approximation to many functions of higher degree, especially when there is considerable unpredicted criterion variance.

4

SELECTION DECISIONS WITH SINGLE-STAGE TESTING

Chapter 4 examines the most familiar of personnel decisions, selection on the basis of a single test or composite score. The most common examples are industrial selection, admission of students, and psychiatric screening of recruits. Typically, a constraint is placed on the number or the minimum quality to be accepted.

A discussion of selection decisions at this point has many advantages, even though not all the results to be presented are new. Stating a familiar problem in terms of our model will clarify utility analysis, and lay the groundwork for the consideration of other personnel decisions.

THE INTERPRETATION OF VALIDITY COEFFICIENTS: EARLIER WORK

Evaluating the benefit obtained from tests is of considerable practical interest. Many of the studies have been stimulated by the "public relations" problem of convincing business management or military authorities that the benefits from testing programs justify their cost. Professional workers, in planning testing programs, must decide which tests to use, and how many; and this requires balancing costs against estimated benefits.

The contribution of a testing program depends on the importance of the decisions to be made, the selection ratio, and possibly other characteristics of the situation. The situation being fixed, the cost and validity of the test determine whether it should be used and how much is gained by using it. Thus assessing the value of the testing program requires a study of the benefits associated with any level of test validity.

The relation of benefit to validity has long been regarded as an important question. Interpretation of validity coefficients is an important topic in the training of test users, as is evidenced by its ubiquitous appearance in professional texts on testing and also in literature on testing aimed at a more general audience. As at least four different formulas for interpreting the validity coefficient have been given, we face the problem of choosing between them or of reconciling them.

The validity coefficient is usually defined as the correlation of test score with outcome or criterion score. We shall use r_{ye} in our discussion because the decision maker is interested in predicting the *evaluated* outcome, that is, the outcome expressed in utility units.

The rule having the longest history translates the validity coefficient r_{ye} into the "index of forecasting efficiency," $E = 1 - \sqrt{1 - r_{ye}^2}$. The prominence of this index and its close relatives is attributable to the emphasis placed upon them by Truman L. Kelley in his *Statistical method* (1923a) and by Clark L. Hull in *Aptitude testing* (1928). The index compares the standard error of scores predicted by means of the test to the standard error when there is no information on the individual and the group mean is used as an estimator of his score. The proportionate reduction of the standard error is taken as a measure of the value of the test.

The "coefficient of determination" r_{ye}^2 provides a second scale for evaluating a test. This coefficient expresses the ratio of predicted variance in payoff to the total variance. Although it appeared in Hull's book (p. 267), it has become prominent only much more recently.

According to the customary interpretations based on these formulations, a high validity coefficient is necessary to obtain substantial benefit from testing. The index of forecasting efficiency describes a test correlating .50 with the criterion as predicting only 13% better than chance; the coefficient of determination describes the same test as accounting for 25% of the variance in outcome.

Such generalizations do not recognize that the value of a test varies with the particular decision for which it is to be used. This point was first emphasized by Taylor and Russell in 1939, following an earlier statement by Thurstone (1931, p. 59). They examined what proportion of employees are likely to be "satisfactory" before and after selection by means of a test. This proportion depends on the percentage of applicants accepted (selection ratio). A test with validity .30 permits substantial improvement when the selection ratio is low, and under some conditions a test with validity .80 gives virtually perfect selection. The Taylor-Russell report challenged conservative traditions in the measurement field: "The wide-spread acceptance of such measures [as E and r^2] as the correct way of evaluating correlation coefficients has brought about a considerable pessimism with regard to the validity coefficients which are ordinarily obtainable when tests are tried out in the employment office of a business or industry or in an educational institution. . . . Very considerable improvement in selection efficiency . . . may be obtained with small coefficients."

Brogden (1946) evaluated decisions directly on a utility scale to interpret the validity coefficient, and concluded that in selection the gain from use of a test is linearly related to the validity, regardless of the selection ratio. He argues that a test of validity .50 gives 50% of the improvement that would result from using a perfect test. This result is contrasted with an interpretation based on the coefficient of forecasting efficiency which Brogden quotes from an outstanding text on measurement published in 1936: "Tests with a coefficient of validity less than .5 are practically useless except in distinguishing between extreme cases." The linear relation has also been discussed by Cochran (1951), and in modified form by Richardson (1944), Jarrett (1948), and Brown and Ghiselli (1953).

The Brogden generalization, like that of Taylor and Russell, encourages far more extensive use of tests than do the interpretations in terms of r^2 or E. Wesman (1953) rationalizes this seeming discrepancy by pointing out that in selection an error of prediction regarding a superior man who is accepted does no harm. So long as it is wise to hire both A and B, it does not matter that the test overestimates A's production, and underestimates B's. Only errors which "cross the borderline" so that a man is hired who should not be, or vice versa, impair the utility of the decisions. The analyses disagree because the coefficients E and r^2 assign evaluations differently than do the more recent analyses. In computing E and the coefficient of determination, the loss to the institution is taken to be a function of the discrepancy between predicted and actual performance. But once a man is selected, his contribution depends on his actual performance, not on the prediction made about him. Errors in prediction are costly only when they cause errors in decision. This is recognized by the Taylor-Russell treatment and, in slightly different ways, by its successors.

The value of a test can be stated only in terms of the specific type of decision problem, the strategy employed, the evaluation attached to the outcome, and the cost of testing. We shall use the utility model to derive this relationship for simple selection decisions, and later for a variety of other conditions. It will be increasingly clear that the linear interpretation of the validity coefficient, or some minor departure from it, is appropriate for simple selection, but that other indices must be chosen in other decision problems. Brogden (1949b, p. 170) indicates why interpretation of validity coefficients presents so much difficulty.

In general, it is probably true that statistical formulas are not developed with the primary objective of providing interpretations most meaningful for a research worker having problems peculiar to a given area of research. The formula is more apt to be developed as an expression of certain mathematical relationships. In the derivation, assumptions—often highly limiting in nature—are introduced as necessary to the development of a given formula. Applications are sought at a later date. Very often it is found that the assumptions are so restrictive that the coefficient can legitimately be used in only a small proportion of certain types of application. In other instances the coefficient may have legitimate application but may not provide the interpretation needed.

BASIS FOR JUDGING GAIN FROM TESTING

It is customary to interpret the value of tests in terms of improvement over chance. "Percentage of possible improvement" is frequently reported, the maximum possible improvement being the gain that would result if a test of validity 1.00 were used. This is a relative measure of gain. Occasionally writers have examined absolute gain, using some utility unit such as the Brogden-Taylor "dollar criterion" (1950). Richardson (1944) introduced still a third variant, obtaining an efficiency ratio by dividing the absolute utility after testing by the absolute utility from unselected men.

Chapter 2 suggested that expected outcome under any strategy should be evaluated on an absolute utility scale. The value of a strategy involving a test can be compared to the utility from the best strategy not using the test ("best *a priori* strategy"). The difference is the gain from testing, and is positive or negative depending on the cost of the test. We shall not translate this difference into a ratio.

The proposal to consider the "best *a priori* strategy" as a baseline may appear to be only another way of referring to "improvement over chance." But this rephrasing will perhaps significantly alter judgments about the value of a particular test. Most important, it leads to the conclusion that the test-criterion correlation based on a population of completely unselected applicants is often *not* the proper validity coefficient for judging the value of testing.

A priori Population

The usual validity coefficient reported for a test is the zero-order correlation relating test to criterion in an unselected group of applicants. It has perhaps been insufficiently recognized that the Taylor-Russell paper and others subsequent to it do not necessarily interpret *this* validity coefficient. The Taylor-Russell discussion presupposes a validity coefficient based on present employees. This population is likely to have been screened using information other than the test. It is to this population that the selection ratio will be applied. Jarrett requires that the validity calculation be based on individuals who "would have been put to work," that is, who would have met any requirements already in use. This definition is consistent with the Taylor-Russell argument, and we also adopt it.

We use "validity" subsequently to refer to a correlation computed on men who have been screened on whatever *a priori* information is in use and will continue to be available. This pre-screened group is referred to as the *a priori* population. Such a validity coefficient is lower than that based on all applicants, the reduction being due to truncation of range through selection. Any zero-order coefficient based on unselected persons must therefore be reduced before applying the interpretations derived below.

Best a priori Strategy

Even when the *a priori* population is defined as suggested by Jarrett, chance selection is not necessarily the alternative strategy with which testing is to be compared. The decision maker who does not test may use interviews or other available information to provide some basis for a decision. Thus, military recruits could be screened with better-than-chance efficiency by utilizing recorded information about civilian job experience and grade of school completed, instead of tests. Tests will improve decisions, but not as much as is implied by the phrase "improvement over chance." Similarly, if testing were impossible in educational placement or selection, one would not fall back upon a chance decision, because previous school records could be used with substantial predictive validity.

Tests should be judged on the basis of their contribution over and above the best strategy available that makes use of prior information. The manner in which this comparison should be made depends on our contemplated use of that information. At least three possibilities should be considered:

1. All prior information is used and will continue to be used for pre-screening of applicants. In this case, validity coefficients should be calculated on the pre-screened group. The *a priori* strategy would be chance selection from this group to fill the quota.
2. Decisions will be based on the test or on certain other information such as school records. One or the other will be used, not both. In this case, the difference in utility between the two strategies, taking cost of each into account, would indicate the advantage of testing.
3. Previously available information and testing information will be combined into a single score or pattern of scores on which decisions will be based. In this case, the gain due to testing is the difference between the utility obtained by the composite scoring technique and the utility obtained using only the previously available information.

Contribution of Various Types of Tests

Evaluating a test in the light of its independent contribution to utility might reshape many of our present testing policies. Conrad (1950, p. 65) makes this demand regarding validity information in test manuals:

> . . . we ought to know what is the contribution of this test over and beyond what is available from other, easier sources. For example, it is very easy to find out the person's chronological age; will our measure of aptitude tell us something that chronological age does not already tell us? It is also easy, in some cases, in a local community, to obtain a person's school record. If that is so, then the question is, Does the intelligence test or the measure of aptitude tell us anything that is not already told by the previous information? The *independent contribution* is certainly something which should definitely be known, but very seldom is it revealed to us in the information which test publishers provide.

High validity coefficients have most often been attained for tests which are essentially work samples of their criteria. A typing test given an applicant, a test of mathematical ability given a prospective engineering student—these tests offer good validity because they reproduce the criterion situation in miniature. Where such a work sample might be used, a record of past performance is also a valid basis for decisions, and is often routinely available. Because school marks are a good predictor of subsequent school marks, a scholastic aptitude test contributes much less to decisions than its validity coefficient suggests.

Per contra, tests having rather low zero-order validities often deal with attributes that are hard to test, and also hard to assess from any non-test data. Tests of leadership, social and emotional adjustment, or creativeness rarely boast validity coefficients beyond .30. But they predict qualities where useful alternative evidence is almost never available. Their contribution to utility in these situations might therefore be higher than the contribution of, say, the group intelligence test in decisions where it is relevant, after due subtraction in both cases for overlap with *a priori* information.

Many other examples may be given. In the classroom, growth in some types of skill and knowledge can be assessed by the teacher in her daily contacts with pupils through assignments, class discussion, and observations. These data, if cumulated with reasonable care over several months, will have sufficient validity that a test can improve the teacher's decisions by only a small increment. Other objectives of considerable importance are quite difficult for the teacher to judge, partly because opportunities for observation are scattered and partly because the criteria for judgment are difficult to formulate. These objectives include reasoning habits, attitudes, creativity, and application of knowledge. A test in one of these areas, even though it has severely limited validity, may yield more insight than a traditional achievement test which largely confirms what the teacher already knows. Generally, the more difficult it is to prepare a valid test for an objective, the more difficult it is for the teacher to make judgments about it without the test. Here also, then, the contribution of the test over and above available bases for the same judgment should be the criterion of its worth, rather than some measure of its accuracy, standing alone.

FIXED-TREATMENT SELECTION

In selection one decides between accepting an individual into an institution and rejecting him. The institution may be a university, an industrial plant, a military service, etc. In general, the aim of the decision maker is to accept those individuals whose expected payoff is highest, within the limits placed upon him by the available information and by whatever quota he must fill. In fixed-treatment selection, individuals are chosen for one specified "treatment" which cannot be modified.

For men accepted, a certain payoff accrues to the institution. We shall assume that this payoff has a linear regression on test score. A decision to reject a man will mean in most instances that he has no further contact with the institution. We may therefore regard the outcome of such a decision as having a value of zero. We shall also assume that test scores are normally distributed, with zero mean and unit standard deviation. This implies that the expected payoffs for randomly selected men are normally distributed.

This assumption of normal distribution of payoff is unrealistic in some situations. Standards set by management often place a lower limit on production which would cause the distribution to be skewed positively. Voluntary limitation of output in a work group skews the curve in the opposite direction. And thorough standardization of a task eliminates variability entirely among those who remain on the job. Specifying a particular distribution permits a more complete exploration of functional relations, but generalization to other distributions is hazardous. Formulas derived under the normal assumption would need to be modified for any specified nonnormal distribution of payoffs. Our general conclusions regarding the relationship of validity to utility depend only on the nature of the hypothesized payoff function. Many conclusions regarding particular optimal strategies, however, depend in addition upon the normal assumption. Brogden (1946, 1949a) has examined thoroughly the effect on utility of departures from normality.

Linear Relation of Utility to Validity

The net gain in utility per man tested from selection for a fixed treatment is linearly related to the validity of the test, under the assumptions stated above. As Appendix 1 demonstrates,

$$\Delta U = \sigma_e r_{ye} \, \xi(y') - C_y. \qquad [2] \ (1.8)*$$

C_y is the average cost of testing one person, r_{ye} is the correlation of the test with the evaluated criterion in the *a priori* population, and σ_e is the standard deviation of this payoff. y' is the cutting score on the test, and $\xi(y')$ is the ordinate of the normal curve at that point. In this expression, $\sigma_e r_{ye}$ is the slope of the payoff function relating expected payoff to score. It would be possible to employ here, as we do later, the concept of an aptitude s intervening between score and payoff, such that $r_{ye} = r_{ys} r_{se}$. This would make the development more closely comparable to that for adaptive treatment, but the argument would be less straightforward.

It is particularly important to note that the slope of the payoff

---

* Where double numbers are provided, the former is the identifying number of the equation in the text, and the second locates it in the Appendix. (1.8) indicates the eighth equation in Appendix 1.

function is influenced by several factors, since conventional methods place almost exclusive emphasis on the test-criterion correlation. An increase in correlation leads to an increase in slope, but slope also depends on the spread of criterion scores (which may vary for different treatments) and on the value associated with one unit on the criterion scale. The relation of gain in utility to selection ratio and validity is shown in Figure 5. On the vertical axis of this and subsequent figures $\Delta U/\sigma_e$, which is dimensionless, is plotted rather than ΔU. This does not distort the relations depicted. For this illustration, C_y is set equal to $.05\sigma_e$. This cost is probably unrealistically large, but such a cost aids in depicting relationships clearly. The shape of the various curves would change only slightly with smaller values of C. In no case can $\Delta U/\sigma_e$ become larger than $.399$ as r increases and cost decreases.

Most of the conclusions implicit in equation [2] were originally pointed out by Brogden (1946, 1949a, 1949b). Utility is a linear function of validity, and if cost is zero, is proportional to validity. With fixed-treatment selection and linear payoff function, we may reject the interpretation of the validity coefficient in terms of r^2 or

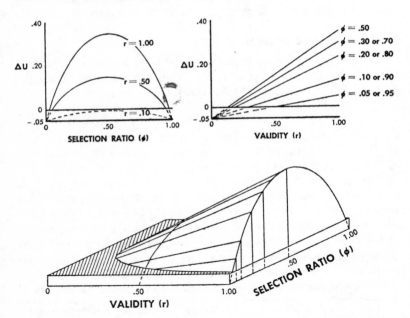

Figure 5. Relation of gain in utility to validity (r_{ye}) and selection ratio in fixed-treatment selection

$1-\sqrt{1-r^2}$. Contrary to the Taylor-Russell results, the linear relation holds at all selection ratios.

Effect of σ_e on utility. A utility model brings in the important parameter σ_e. For any one treatment σ_e is constant, and indicates both the magnitude and practical significance of individual differences in payoff. A decision maker selecting men for many different assignments is frequently able to test for only a few of them, and must decide where tests can make the greatest contribution. The importance of an assignment can justify using a test of low validity (Brogden, 1946, p. 71). Gain in utility depends on the product $\sigma_e r_{ye}$. Therefore a test of validity .30 for one decision may be more beneficial than a test having validity .60 for some other selection decision, if σ_e for the former decision is at least twice as large. A large σ_e is an indication that individual differences on the criterion in question have large practical importance. Tests for important decisions which fall far short of the ideal predictor may be much more worth using (and improving) than tests which give excellent guidance in making minor decisions.

Effect of cost on utility. Cost of testing should be taken into account along with validity and σ_e in deciding which test to use for a particular decision. The utility contributed by test 1 is greater than that from test 2 whenever

$$\sigma_e r_{y_1 e}\, \xi(y') - C_1 > \sigma_e r_{y_2 e}\, \xi(y') - C_2.$$

Test 1 is preferable whenever

$$r_{y_1 e} - r_{y_2 e} > (C_1 - C_2)/\sigma_e\, \xi(y').$$

The difference in costs between two competing tests will not often be large enough to justify use of the less valid test, but at some point (see Chapter 7) increases in test length can increase cost enough to offset accompanying gains in validity.

Effect of selection ratio on utility. With a fixed number of applicants, total gain in utility is greatest when 50% of these men are to be accepted. That is to say, tests make the greatest contribution to the selection decision for which 50% of the *a priori* population can be utilized, other parameters being equal.

At extremely high or low selection ratios, gain in utility drops below zero, because the benefit from selecting superior men cannot compensate for the cost of testing. At these extremes the decision maker who tests is worse off than the one who fills his quota at random. Testing is unprofitable whenever y' becomes so extreme that $\xi(y') < C/\sigma_e r$; the location of this limit is shown in Figure 6. No matter what the selection ratio, testing is unprofitable if $C/\sigma_e r > .399$. In general, the limiting selection ratios are symmetric about .50; thus if $C/\sigma_e r = .05$, it is unprofitable to test if $\phi > .98$ or $< .02$.

Further insight into the role of selection ratio can be gained from a consideration of the average gain in utility *per man accepted*. This measure depends on r and σ_e in the same manner as total gain. Analysis of average gain shows that one may profitably alter the selection ratio if this is allowable. The relationship of average gain to ϕ, for a given r, has been described by Brogden, and is shown in Figure 7 (see eq. 1.10). Average gain increases to a maximum as selection ratio decreases and then drops rapidly, falling to $-\infty$ as selection ratio approaches zero. The average ability of individuals increases if selection is made more severe, but the proportionate cost of testing per man accepted increases. Varying the selection ratio (or cutting score) in a particular problem, we can arrive at an optimal strategy. The selection ratio that yields greatest average gain in utility depends on the ratio of C to $\sigma_e r$ as shown in Figure 6 (cf. eq. 1.13).

In many selection situations, the decision maker has a fixed quota to fill, but may vary the number to be tested. The industrial tester, for example, may have a certain number of vacancies in a given period, but be able to alter the number of persons screened to

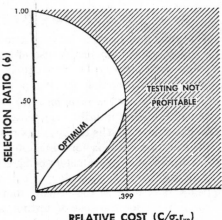

Figure 6. Utility as a function of selection ratio and cost

fill these positions, reducing the selection ratio correspondingly. In this case the selection ratio of equation 1.13 can be interpreted as indicating the *number* of people to test relative to the number selected. The smaller the cost of testing, the larger the number of applicants it is profitable to test to fill the quota. *It is always desirable (assuming fixed quotas and linear payoff) to test at least twice as many men as will be accepted* if the test is worth using at all. At the low costs most likely to be encountered in practice, the number of individuals tested should be large relative to the number to be selected.

SELECTION WITH ADAPTIVE TREATMENT

It is reasonable to suppose, as Chapter 3 pointed out, that the decision maker often will be allowed to adjust the treatment according to the quality of the men he accepts. Such "adaptive treatment" should yield greater benefit than is obtained under fixed treatment, save where by good fortune the fixed treatment happens already to be optimal for the accepted men.

A General Payoff Surface

The first step in undertaking a study of adaptive treatment is to introduce a general payoff surface linking payoff functions for different treatments.

A postulated aptitude factor. When only one treatment and one test are under consideration, the contribution of testing can be studied adequately in terms of the relation of test score to criterion. The payoff function is the regression of the evaluated criterion on

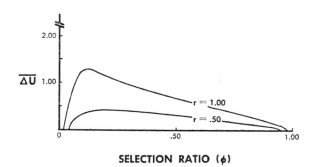

Figure 7. Average gain in utility per person accepted

the test score. To deal with competing treatments, it will be convenient to postulate an aptitude factor s.

The advantage of the intervening variable s is that it permits us to separate aspects of the decision problem chiefly associated with the differences between treatments from those chiefly associated with the test. Where several tests measure the same underlying variable, and we wish to consider their relative effectiveness, the introduction of s permits us to invoke the same payoff function with relation to all tests. Each treatment has its own payoff function; but if all the treatments under consideration depend on the same aptitude, it is much simpler to describe the relation of payoff to this aptitude than to have a separate payoff function for each test-treatment pair.

As explained in Chapter 3, test scores may be factored, and among those factors the ones that account for variance in payoff under any of the treatments being considered are referred to as aptitude factors. That is to say, any factors that, when removed from the matrix of r_{ye_t}, reduce all residuals to zero constitute a set of s dimensions. There will not in general be a unique set of s's for a given body of data, since these factors may be rotated in various ways. One would ordinarily rotate in one of the ways that minimize the number of s dimensions.

In studying selection and placement, we restrict ourselves to the case where only a single aptitude dimension is required to account for all communality between test scores and payoffs. If we are dealing with a single test, as we do in most subsequent chapters, the "true score" on the test may be regarded as such an s dimension. It is assumed that the test and payoff under any treatment have no common variance save that accounted for by s, so that $r_{ye_t} = r_{ys}r_{se_t}$. We shall not extend our analysis of adaptive treatment to the classification problem, where multivariate information is employed and more than one s dimension is involved in decisions. The study of adaptive selection and placement requires assumptions going some distance beyond presently available data, and it appears wise to delay extension to more complicated cases.

The function relating expected payoff to aptitude s is

$$e_{st} = \sigma_{e_t}r_{se_t}s + e_{ot}. \qquad [3] \quad (2.1)$$

Admissible treatments. As indicated in Chapter 3, treatments may conceivably vary continuously with respect to many dimensions. For a general theoretical survey it is convenient to assume that the decision maker can draw the final treatment from among such an infinite array of possibilities, rather than from a few alternatives.

Since we assume that the payoff for any treatment is a linear function of s, it is possible to classify all conceivable treatments with respect to only two parameters, the slope and the intercept of this function. Furthermore, one and only one treatment with any particular slope need be considered. This is possible because, of two treatments having the same slope, the one with the higher intercept is uniformly preferable at all levels of aptitude. Only this treatment is admissible. For convenience, we write m_t for the slope instead of $\sigma_{e_t} r_{se_t}$.

Equations relating e, s, and t. To relate e to s and t, we employ the simplest mathematical function that covers a reasonable variety of non-trivial relationships. Appendix 2 states the specific assumptions leading to the following equation:

$$e_{st} = m_{st}s + c + bm_{st} - am_{st}^2. \qquad [4] \quad (2.3)$$

We may substitute $r_{ys}y$ for s where desirable. This surface, depicted in Figure 8, is a hyperbolic paraboloid with these properties:

1. There is a saddle point where $s = -b$. Through this point pass two straight lines that lie in the surface.
2. All horizontal cross-sections (equal payoff) are hyperbolas asymptotic to these lines.
3. All cross-sections where t is a constant are straight lines.
4. All cross-sections where s is constant are parabolas. This implies that there is a best treatment for each value of s, and that

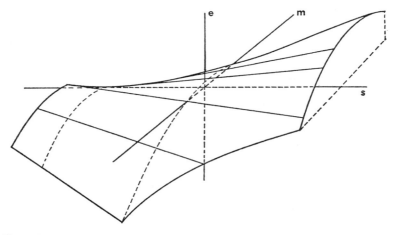

Figure 8. Expected payoff as a function of aptitude and treatment

the loss from assigning a person to treatment t rather than the t_s optimal for him is equal to $a(m_t - m_{t_s})^2$.

The parameters a, b, and c depend upon the particular s linking treatments and tests.

This "saddle" surface is unfamiliar to most readers, and may seem highly arbitrary, but it is in fact a function of great flexibility, capable of fitting a great variety of response surfaces. It is the only interesting function that could be considered without either going to an equation of degree higher than two or abandoning the assumption of linear regression, within treatments, of outcome on aptitude. The surface fits data in which the regressions have positive slope for some treatments and negative for others; in such data, b will be low in value, so that the saddle point falls within the aptitude distribution. For the perhaps more common case where all slopes are positive, but vary in magnitude, the surface can also fit the data. The value of b will be large, placing the saddle point far to the left of the score distribution and toward the positive end of the m scale. The model implies that in principle one might determine the difference in treatments which causes some to have relatively small slope, and exaggerate that difference experimentally to produce treatments with zero or negative slope. This supposition may or may not be true; in the use made of the model here, what is of importance is the goodness of fit within the region occupied by actual values of s for existing people and of m for existing treatments.

Utility in Adaptive Selection

The formulas for estimating gain in utility are developed in Appendix 3. In evaluating the benefits gained from selection with adaptive treatment, and contrasting them with fixed-treatment benefits, one must reconsider not only the relation of payoff to score, but also the entire definition of gain in utility. In fixed treatment, *a priori* utility and *a posteriori* utility are simply the benefits when selected and unselected men are given the same treatment. But now the *a priori* treatment and the *a posteriori* treatments can be different.

The best *a priori* treatment is t_o, a treatment suited to the average unselected man. Assuming a quota $\phi(y')$, the *a priori* utility per man tested is

$$U_{ot_o} = \phi(y')(c + b^2/4a). \qquad [5] \quad (3.2)$$

The parameters are those of the utility surface (eq. [4]).

So long as we confine ourselves to tests measuring a single aptitude s, the choice of treatment to be given after testing depends on r_{ys}. The more valid the test, the more the aptitude of the selected men will depart from the average and the farther the selected treatment t_s will depart from t_0. The *a posteriori* utility per man tested is

$$U_{yt_s} = \phi(y') \left[\frac{1}{4a} \left(r_{ys} \frac{\xi(y')}{\phi(y')} + b \right)^2 + c \right] - C_y. \quad \text{[6] (3.13)}$$

The striking feature of this equation is the introduction of an r^2 term in addition to a linear term. In effect, by raising the quality of the men and simultaneously changing the treatment to take full advantage of this quality, adaptive treatment "compounds" the gain from any improvement in test validity.

The average gain in utility

$$\Delta U = U_{yt_s} - U_{ot_o} = \frac{r_{ys}^2}{4a} \frac{\xi^2(y')}{\phi(y')} + \frac{b r_{ys}}{2a} \xi(y') - C_y. \quad \text{[7] \quad (3.8)}$$

With adaptive treatment, the benefit from testing is a *parabolic* function of r_{ys}. We will arrive at a fuller understanding of why the gain from adaptive selection takes this form after examining adaptive placement in Chapter 5.

Equation [7] permits us to generalize only about the relation of utility to the validity of the test as a measure of aptitude s. The usual validity coefficient r_{ve_t} is equal to $r_{ys} r_{se_t}$ under our assumption, and this value may be expected to vary from treatment to treatment even when only one aptitude is involved. Since the slope of the pay-off function $m_t = \sigma_e r_{se_t}$ is different for each treatment, it follows that the value r_{se_t} will also in general be different so that there can be no single validity coefficient in an adaptive-treatment problem.

If two or more tests are under consideration which measure different aptitudes, their relative value in adaptive selection (or placement) is difficult to describe. For each aptitude there will be a different payoff surface, involving new values of a and b. All subsequent statements in this chapter referring to the relation of utility in adaptive selection to "validity" are *restricted to the case where the aptitude linking test to treatments is the same for all tests compared.*

Comparison with the Fixed-Treatment Case

To compare fixed with adaptive treatment, we rewrite equation [2] in this manner:

$$\Delta U = m_{t_A} r_{ys} \xi(y') - C_y. \quad \text{[2]}$$

In order to examine a specific case, let us assume that the treatment originally in use is that best suited to the average man, that is, $m_{t_A} = b/2a$ (cf. eq. 3.1). Such a situation could arise if previous selection policy had been fairly satisfactory, but it is thought that greater benefit will result if men of even higher quality are obtained. Using the *same* treatment after testing and a fixed-selection ratio, the gain in utility is

$$\Delta U = \frac{b}{2a} \, r_{ys} \, \xi(y') - C_y. \qquad [8]$$

If, however, the institution were now to change the treatment to that optimally suited to the average ability of the selected men, the gain in utility is increased by $\frac{1}{4a} \, r_{ys}^2 \, \frac{\xi^2(y')}{\phi(y')}$. This additional gain might be obtained, for example, when tests are introduced into a school selection program and subsequently teaching methods are adjusted to the higher level of ability of the accepted students.

When the *a priori* treatment is *not* that best suited to the average man, comparison between fixed and adaptive selection becomes more complicated. One must fix in mind the levels of utility obtainable by the following strategies:

1. Random selection, fixed treatment t_A U_{ot_A}
2. Random selection, treatment t_o suited to average men U_{oto}
3. Random selection, treatment suited to aptitude level s U_{ot_s}
4. Selection by test, treatment t_A U_{yt_A}
5. Selection by test, treatment t_o U_{yto}
6. Selection by test, treatment t_s U_{yt_s}

For the sake of illustration (Figure 9) we assume that the treatment t_A originally in use is that suited to very superior men whose average aptitude is s_A. Treatment t_o is the best of all treatments for a group of men whose average aptitude is zero. Finally, if the men actually selected have the average aptitude s (in the figure, $0 < s < s_A$), the payoff function for the best *a posteriori* treatment is that marked t_s. In addition to the payoff lines for three treatments, the figure shows a curve to which all such functions are tangent (eq. 2.6). The tangent to the curve at any value of s shows the payoff to be obtained by giving the optimum treatment to men having that average level of ability. On this diagram, the six levels of utility are indicated.

The gain in utility with fixed-treatment t_A is represented by the difference between U_{ot_A} and U_{yt_A} (cost of testing here being disregarded). The final utility is, in this instance, distinctly less than may be attained with a less demanding treatment. If one were to change from t_A to t_O without selecting men, a benefit would accrue that is actually nearly as large as the benefit (ΔU fixed) reportedly attainable by testing. The gain due to testing should be considered as the gain beyond the best *a priori* utility, and is represented by ΔU adaptive ($U_{yt.} - U_{oto}$). Other diagrams can be examined where the fixed treatment is located so that $s_A < s$, or even $s_A < 0$. The following generalizations apply to all such combinations.

Even though adaptation of treatment is common in practice, discussions of the value of testing in selection have overlooked this possibility, clinging to fixed-treatment assumptions. The *utility* from selected men is always greater with adaptive treatment than with fixed treatment, save at that one value where $s = s_A$. To a certain extent, therefore, these discussions have underrated the utility that can be obtained using the test. On the other hand, the *gain* due to testing with adaptive treatment is often less than the gain under fixed treatment, because the *a priori* utility can be much higher under adaptive conditions. By including a component that could be achieved by altering the treatment to use *un*selected men more profitably, these discussions *over*rate the contribution of testing. Which effect is the larger would depend on the particular utility surface, the location of s_A, and also on the cost of adaptation. If practical conditions make it unreasonable to adapt treatments to men of average ability, then testing does have the value claimed

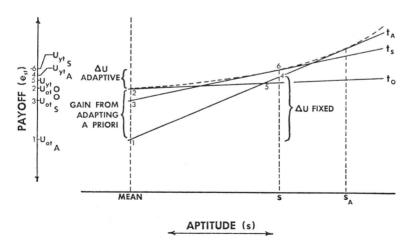

Figure 9. Comparison of gains from fixed and adaptive selection

for it in equation [2] where utility is linearly related to validity. But if treatment is "fixed" only because the question of adapting it has not been raised, the advantage claimed in the linear relation is much too great and the test is being credited with contributions that could be obtained in another manner, perhaps less expensive in the long run.

The amount the test adds to the best *a priori* utility is described by the surface shown in Figure 10. All cross-sections with selection ratio constant are parabolas. Since we are comparing tests involving the same aptitude, validity is here represented by r_{ys}, not r_{ye}. With r_{ys} constant, the cross-section is asymmetric, having a maximum at a selection ratio somewhat less than .50. The surface plotted is based on these parameters: $a = 1$, $b = \frac{1}{2}$, $C = .05$.

Implications for Choice of Tests

Persons validating selection tests should consider explicitly what might be achieved by adapting treatments. It is necessary to determine empirically the shape of the payoff surface wherever adaptation is allowable. Such investigations might well begin by comparing payoff functions for only two alternative treatments aimed toward

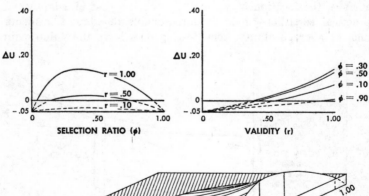

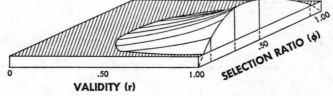

Figure 10. Relation of gain in utility to validity (r_{ys}) and selection ratio in adaptive-treatment selection

the same goals, but ultimately it will be necessary to consider cases involving several continuous treatment dimensions.

The traditional sequence of industrial selection research has been to establish a job and associated training procedure, and then to seek predictors that will weed out applicants likely to perform poorly. It is appropriate to fix production goals without reference to the available selection tests, but there is no reason at all to regard the job organization or training methods used to attain those goals as being independent of such predictors. If payoff functions differ when different training methods are used, and these functions intersect somewhere in the range of ability, then it may be possible to modify the training with advantage. Determining objectives is the first step in selection research; after that, the research should seek to identify *the best combination* of tests, training method, and job organization.

Testing can bring about two types of change: an increase in the average quality of accepted men; and a further increase in benefits when treatment is adapted to fit this new level of quality. When treatment can be modified, it is possible that much of this increase in utility can be attained by adapting treatment to fit the level of ability of unselected men. The relative advantages of selection without adaptation, adaptation without selection, and adaptation with selection depend on the parameters of the postulated payoff surface (and on the cost of adaptation). No unqualified generalizations as to proper practice can be made without considering particular surfaces established empirically.

In a sense, adaptation permits one to trade increased training cost for attrition in screening. If one insists on utilizing only the cream of the applicants, the training can be less costly or can attain a higher terminal level. If a lower grade of applicant is accepted, one takes best advantage of his ability with a longer and less demanding training program. The quality of men selected depends on many things: on the social conditions which make the applicant pool larger or smaller, on the personnel requirements of other programs, and on the validity of the relevant tests. If two aptitudes are relevant to the same job, adapting treatment to fit men near the average on one aptitude would permit more severe screening on the other. The optimal strategy would be a complex mixture of adaptation and selection.

Recognizing the possibility of adaptive treatment provides a new way of looking at virtually every problem of test utilization. It seems likely that new results will emerge whenever this hitherto suppressed consideration is brought into test theory.

THE INTERPRETATION OF VALIDITY COEFFICIENTS IN SELECTION

The preceding pages deny the possibility of any simple answer to the query, "How valuable for selection decisions is a test with validity r?" Neither the index of forecasting efficiency E nor the coefficient of determination r^2 is directly related to utility when payoff functions are linear. Neither, therefore, seems appropriate as an index of selection efficiency. Moreover, our utility functions bear only a limited resemblance to those of Taylor and Russell. And while utility is linearly related to validity in fixed-treatment selection, we find that the linear relation does *not* apply in selection with adaptive treatment. We may now integrate the various approaches to the interpretation of validity coefficients in selection, and point to some differences in the various rationale.

The Linear Relation

Brogden's linear relation between validity and utility describes the usefulness of a test (or composite score) under the following conditions:

1. Persons are divided into an accepted and rejected group. The rejected group is eliminated from the institution, while persons in the selected group are given uniform treatment.
2. The proportion of persons to be accepted is specified.
3. The treatment to be applied to accepted men is fixed *a priori*.
4. Payoff from accepted persons has a linear regression on test score. The utility of a decision to reject is the same for each individual. This implies that decisions are evaluated in terms of institutional utilities.

The Taylor-Russell Results

The relation between validity and utility reported by Taylor and Russell is rather similar to the linear relation under many conditions. The chief differences are that (i) they report different shapes for the validity-utility relation at different selection ratios, and (ii) the relation becomes decidedly non-linear at high validity or when a high proportion of unselected men are judged successful.

The Taylor-Russell approach assumes fixed treatment and is otherwise like the Brogden analysis, except that outcomes are evaluated differently. Taylor and Russell ignore rejected men, in effect assuming their contribution to be zero. Accepted men are classified into "successful" and "unsuccessful" groups, and all men in each group are regarded as making equal contributions. Thus, while Brogden assumes a continuous equal-interval scale for payoff at different levels of criterion performance, Taylor and Russell assume a discontinuous two-valued payoff. The two scales are related in such a manner as this:

c	20	25	30	35	40	45	50
e_c (linear assumption)	−1	0	1	2	3	4	5
e_c (Taylor-Russell)	0	0	0	0	1	1	1

The Taylor-Russell approach resembles that used in acceptance testing of industrial products. In that field, inspection plans are described by various tables indicating the efficiency with which each plan protects the purchaser against defective objects. The Taylor-Russell tables indicate the "average outgoing quality (AOQ)" for a personnel inspection plan, and are therefore comparable to the AOQ tables for industrial inspection. Each table indicates what proportion of "defective individuals" will be passed by a particular selection ratio, knowing the frequency of such individuals in the population.

Where unsuccessful men are discharged or removed from their assignments or fail to complete the training, the difference in utility between a successful and an unsuccessful man is likely to be great. Training effort is wasted; morale of all employees suffers; management time is consumed in making the decision to discharge. Such costs may be far more significant than the differences among the workers retained. Under some conditions, moreover, differences in ability beyond the minimum needed to perform the job do not lead to differences in benefit. If production is standardized either by job definition or by voluntary restriction of output, then benefits will depend little on ability. In these instances, evaluation by the proportion of successful workers among those accepted may be fully appropriate.

Sometimes differences in output are believed to occur, but are presently unmeasurable. Thus teachers who fail as instructors or class managers are discharged, but no agreement can be obtained on relative evaluation of the teachers retained. Likewise, in evaluating psychiatric screening a person who breaks down must be counted as markedly different in value from those who do not, but it is difficult to sustain any quantitative comparison of contribution among those who remain above the level of overt disturbance. This situation too justifies a stepwise evaluation.

Examination of the number of "hits" is sometimes accompanied by an examination of the "misses," or number of persons rejected who were of acceptable quality. The best-known discussion of this approach is Berkson's "cost-utility" paper (1947). He defines "utility" as the proportion of unsuccessful men eliminated, and "cost" as the proportion of successful men rejected. In any selection scheme, raising the cutting score increases the Berkson "utility" with a corresponding increase in "cost." The decision maker seeks a strategy that balances these two risks most satisfactorily. A group of sociologists (Duncan et al., 1953) has described several distinct formulas for evaluating hits and misses, which need not be reviewed here. Our thinking is most consistent with the plan that assigns particular values to "hits" and "misses," and adjusts the cutting score to maximize expected utility. In institutional selection with fixed quota where men rejected leave the institution, it is not meaningful to consider misses, however. Rejection of men of good quality does not decrease the output of the institution; their frequency bears only on "what might have been." Two-sided evaluations are appropriate only when the screening test divides men into two groups who remain within the institution but are treated differently. An example is the use of a test to predict parole, where both the parolee and the man held in prison affect the "balance sheet" of the correctional system. These, however, are placement rather than selection decisions.

Parabolic Relations

Like others who have investigated the selection problem, we find no basis for interpreting the usefulness of tests in terms of the coefficient of forecasting efficiency or the coefficient of determination. These indices should not be employed in evaluating tests for selection purposes. Chapter 5 will consider the appropriateness of these indices for certain other decisions.

Paradoxically, having dismissed two traditional parabolic functions, we find that another parabolic relationship is appropriate for evaluating tests in selection. Where adaptive treatment is allowed and all tests being compared measure the same aptitude, equation [7]—or some similar function based on a payoff surface of degree higher than two—is the most adequate statement of the relation of utility to validity. When the selection ratio is moderate to high, this parabola has little curvature and the linear relation approximates it fairly well. At low selection ratios, concave curvature may be appreciable (quite contrary to the Taylor-Russell picture of convex curvature at low selection ratio).

By neglecting the possibility of adaptation, some discussions of the linear relation between utility and validity tend to give a misleading picture of the value of testing *per se*. If the treatment presently in use is fixed, as it is in some industrial situations, small increases in validity of selection procedures will result in considerable benefit. If adaptation of the treatment is possible, however, and selection ratio is low, much of the gain can be achieved by adjusting the treatment to the average man and thus raising the utility of the *a priori* strategy. If selection is then employed, the increase in utility that results is linearly related to validity, but it is possibly quite modest in amount. Further adaptation of treatment to the selected group brings additional gains that are parabolically related to validity.

Our analysis of adaptive selection surely calls for a reconsideration by those who have used the linear relation to "prove to management" that tests are beneficial. The "profit" they have piled on the scales includes a substantial bag of gold that might be earned by another branch of the business if testing were abolished. Testing is usually beneficial under adaptive conditions, but not as beneficial as has been claimed when only fixed treatment is considered.

"What is a test of given validity worth?" is a complicated question. The total benefit achieved through use of a test is of more concern to the institutional user than is the proportion of possible benefit or improvement obtained. This total benefit is increased, generally speaking, with increases in the number of persons to be tested, the importance of the criterion performance to the institution, and the extent of individual differences in performance. The benefit decreases with greater cost of testing. Therefore a test of validity .20 in one situation may be more beneficial than a test of validity .60 in another. The characteristics of the specific decision determine "what the test is worth."

5

PLACEMENT DECISIONS

In placement, persons are divided among two or more groups who remain within the institution and receive different treatments. Division of a group between two treatments has often been spoken of as screening or selection (e.g., "selection of students for an accelerated program," "screening of emotionally disturbed cases for individual examination," "selection of prisoners for parole," etc.). In each of these instances, the "selected" group is given one treatment while the others remain within the institution (broadly defined) and are given some other treatment. Therefore, these are placement decisions. Although placement may be considered as a special case of classification, it is of importance in itself because most measurement and prediction by means of tests can be interpreted in terms of the placement model.

In fixed-treatment placement with a limited number of categories, the score scale is divided into segments, and persons in each successive segment of the scale are assigned to a different treatment. Sectioning of students into classes according to learning ability is a prototype placement problem. Illustrations are also found in some types of job assignment, for example when a proficiency test is used to determine the level of responsibility (pay grade) to which a typist will be assigned. Each level has its corresponding duties and pay, and is characterized by a different function relating utility to aptitude. These placement decisions involve a rather small number of alternative treatments. An indefinitely large number of alternatives may be used, however, persons being located within smaller and smaller intervals on the scale. In the limit, the placement problem thus becomes a problem in measurement or estimation.

Even though an institutional decision maker thinks of his task as "prediction" or "measurement," he may use only a few discrete categories. An example is the fitting of teaching methods to the pupil's estimated IQ. One would not treat those with IQ 109 differently from those with IQ 110, but one could modify the treatment to take account of grosser differences. Such use of measurements is ordinarily better described as a problem in placement with adaptive treatment than as placement with fixed treatment, because past experience has determined what treatment is most suitable at each IQ level and the decision maker is free to use that best treatment.

It is appropriate in this chapter to consider a second type of adaptation, namely the altering of quotas on the basis of test information. For instance, three rather different levels of training may have been developed, each involving its own course outline, test materials, and instructional aids; these programs would be difficult to change, and so treatments would be fixed. But the proportion assigned to each treatment could be altered. Improvement in test validity would warrant assignment of more persons to the extreme categories. Adjustment of quotas may also be beneficial when treatments are adapted, if the maximum number of treatments is fixed. The discussion in Chapter 4 regarding the optimal selection ratio deals with a rather similar problem.

RELATION OF UTILITY TO VALIDITY

Fixed-Treatment Conditions

To examine what utility results with fixed treatments and fixed quotas, we employ assumptions similar to those used with selection. Appendix 1 presents the detailed mathematical argument. There are n different treatments, fixed a $priori$, and we assume that for each treatment there is a linear function relating payoff to test score. The score continuum is divided into n intervals each bounded by y_t' and y_t'', which are fixed so that the proportion of the distribution falling in each segment equals the quota set for the corresponding treatment t. With each treatment is associated a value of $\sigma_{e_t} r_{y e_t}$, the slope of the payoff function. The gain in utility per man tested is

$$\Delta U \text{ (fixed)} = \sum_t \sigma_{e_t} r_{y e_t} \Delta \xi_t - C_y. \qquad [9] \ (1.19)$$

Here, $\Delta \xi_t$ stands for $\xi(y_t') - \xi(y_t'')$; below, we shall also write $\Delta \phi_t$ for $\phi(y_t') - \phi(y_t'')$. At some points it will be helpful to write B_{yd} for $\sum_t \sigma_{e_t} r_{y e_t} \Delta \xi_t$.

It is possible to rewrite equation [9] in terms of the differences between validity coefficients for adjacent treatments:

$$\Delta U = \sum_t \xi(y_t') \left[\sigma_{e_t} r_{ye_t} - \sigma_{e_{t-1}} r_{ye_{t-1}}\right] - C_y. \quad [10]$$

The bracketed term is the covariance of score y with the difference in payoff under two adjacent treatments; these covariances are weighted by $\xi(y')$ to obtain the total benefit. Clearly, since the test may have a different validity coefficient for each treatment, utility is not a simple function of any single validity coefficient. However, the greater the correlations of the test with the *differences* in payoff between treatments, the greater is the utility from using the test for placement.

It will simplify some of our discussion to express utility in terms of an underlying aptitude s as was done in connection with adaptive selection. Since we are restricting ourselves to a single test score y, we can without further loss of generality introduce an s such that for every treatment $r_{ye_t} = r_{ys} r_{se_t}$. Since $m_{st} = \sigma_{e_t} r_{se_t}$,

$$\Delta U = r_{ys} \sum_t m_{st} \, \Delta \xi_t - C_y. \quad [11]$$

In placement with fixed treatments and fixed quotas, utility is linearly related to the component r_{ys} of validity.

Adjusted quotas. Total utility is increased by adjusting the quotas even when treatments are fixed in advance. Strategy should ideally be adjusted so that each person receives that one of the treatments for which his expected payoff is greatest. The most profitable cutting scores are determined, for particular values of $\sigma_{e_t} r_{ye_t}$ and e_{ot}, from equation 1.22. The cutting scores are related to r_{ys}. As r_{ys} approaches zero, the optimal cutting scores depart from the mean; an increasing proportion of the cases are assigned to the particular fixed treatment that is best suited to average men. This treatment is also the one to which all persons should be assigned for the optimum *a priori* strategy; we designate this treatment as t_o. (This is not necessarily the t_o discussed in adaptive selection.)

$$\Delta U = r_{ys} \sum_t m_{st} \, \Delta \xi_t + \sum_t (e_{ot} - e_{ot_o}) \, \Delta \phi_t - C_y. \quad [12] \ (1.23)$$

The second term here is less than zero. As in selection, the simple formula for gain in utility with fixed-treatment placement (eq. [9]) includes a component that could be obtained merely by *a priori* adaptation, giving the treatment best for unselected men to everyone. For that reason, the gain from testing expressed in equation [12] is less than the gain with the same treatments and fixed quotas. The total utility including *a priori* utility is, however, greater with adjusted quotas than with fixed quotas.

In equation [12] the values of $\Delta\xi$ and $\Delta\phi$ depend on r_{ys}, and therefore ΔU with adaptive quotas is not a simple linear function of r_{ys}. The function depends on the particular treatments to be used.

Benefit compared to selection. Fixed-treatment selection is obviously a special case of fixed-treatment placement in which there are just two treatments, for one of which $m_t = 0$. Making this substitution reduces equation [9] to equation [2]. There may be combined selection-placement problems such that one group of men is rejected while the others are assigned within the institution on the basis of the same test. These too can be treated as special cases of equation [9].

When just two treatments are in use, equation [10] becomes identical to equation [2], save that $\sigma_{e_t} r_{ye_t}$ is replaced by $\sigma_{(e_t - e_{t-1})}$ $r_{y(e_t - e_{t-1})}$. Figure 5, presented in our discussion of selection (p. 38), therefore also applies to the relation of utility to validity in placement with two fixed treatments. It is also to be noted that the discussion of two-stage sequential selection in Chapter 6 and Appendix 4 applies to sequential placement into two categories, since the covariance of y with differential payoff may be substituted for $\sigma_e r_{ye}$ in all equations. It is important to emphasize that this paragraph refers to the *gain* in utility with testing.

Validation of Tests for Placement with Fixed Treatments

Utility depends on the *differential payoff* of the treatments as a function of aptitude. If all m_{st} were equal, the gain in utility as a result of placement would be zero regardless of r_{ys}. (See eq. [11].) Placement using a univariate score is profitable only when the slope of the payoff function is different for different treatments. This does not necessarily mean that the test-criterion correlation r_{ye} must differ from treatment to treatment, since the slope m_{st} depends also on σ_{e_t}.

Although the implications of this fact for placement have not to our knowledge been discussed, a comparable result established in connection with differential prediction, that is, classification, problems is well known (see, e.g., Brogden, 1951; Wesman and Bennett, 1951). A test of general intellectual ability having equal validity for predicting success in engineering and in liberal arts does not predict in *which* field a student will do better. A test of mathematical ability which may be a poorer predictor for either curriculum assists in differential prediction because it is more closely related to engineering than to liberal arts. This relationship has been widely discussed in recent years in connection with both classification of workers and differential diagnosis of patients.

Differential payoff, rather than predictive validity as usually measured, is similarly important in placement. This implies that tests intended for placement purposes in schools may have been validated in the wrong way. Where two or more treatments depend on the same aptitude, testers have generally been satisfied to examine the validity of a test for predicting criterion differences *within* treatments instead of examining how well it predicts payoff differences *between* treatments, that is, the interaction of outcome and treatment.

Use of a test in placement rests on the assumption that no one treatment yields greatest payoff over the entire range of scores in the population. Numbering the segments of the y continuum in order from 1 to n, and numbering the treatments correspondingly, we may rewrite equation [10] thus:

$$\Delta U = r_{ys} \left[(m_{st_2} - m_{st_1}) \, \xi(y_1'') + (m_{st_3} - m_{st_2}) \, \xi(y_2'') + \ldots \right.$$
$$\left. + (m_{st_n} - m_{st_{n-1}}) \, \xi(y_{n-1}'') \right] - C_y. \quad [13]$$

The bracketed term summarizes the differential contribution of a perfect measure of s to placement, taking into account the particular treatments and the quotas for each treatment. This is multiplied by r_{ys} to determine the differential contribution of the test itself. Thus utility in placement depends on two things: the power of the test to measure the aptitude dimension s, and the power of s to predict differential payoff.

An aptitude dimension that is strongly related to criterion differences within treatments (all m_{st} being large) may have no relation to differences between treatments (if the m_{st} are equal). Consider a set of treatments for which two aptitudes are relevant, aptitude s_1 being estimated with validity 1.00 by test y_1, and aptitude s_2 being estimated with validity .10 by test y_2. This information alone does not permit us to say that test y_1 is superior. Even adding the fact that within all treatments s_1 is a much better predictor than s_2 does not settle the question. If $m_{s_1 t}$ is a constant for all treatments, y_1 has no value for placement. The importance of an aptitude for placement depends on the change in m_{st} over the treatments under consideration.

Publishers of scholastic aptitude or achievement tests frequently recommend those tests for sectioning students. The claim of empirical validity is supported by giving the correlation of the test with a criterion of success within some treatment, or occasionally within a pooled group from several treatments. *It has not hitherto been recognized that what the consumer needs to know are the slopes of the payoff functions or other data on the interaction of test and treatment.*

Tests presently used may be ineffective for placement even though they are good predictors within a treatment. Possibly quite different types of items would make superior placement tests, because qualities that determine *differential* response to various treatments are not generally those which best predict criterion performance within one treatment. General mental ability, for example, is likely to be correlated with success in mathematics no matter how the subject is taught. If the alternative teaching procedures are an abstract deductive method and an applied inductive method, the brighter students should do better with either approach. Payoff functions for both treatments against general ability will have positive slope, and may or may not intersect within the ability range. On the other hand, there may be other qualities of the individual (say, interest in abstract problems, or liking for rigorous reasoning) that would have quite different relations to the two treatments. A measure that predicts success under one treatment and not the other would be a much better aid to placement than a measure that predicts both.

Adaptive-Treatment Conditions

Where allowable, adapting the treatment to the persons assigned to it is expected to have advantages in placement as in selection. *A priori,* the best adaptation is to assign all men to the treatment best for the average man. *A posteriori,* the best treatment is determined from the general utility surface. Appendix 3 demonstrates that gain in utility is a function of the *square* of the validity with which the test measures the s dimension:

$$\Delta U = \frac{r_{ys}^2}{4a} \sum_t \frac{\Delta^2 \xi_t}{\Delta \phi_t} - C_y. \qquad [14] \quad (3.6)$$

The parameter a reflects the curvature of the general utility surface for s.

Figure 11 shows the relation of ΔU to validity and quota, in an adaptive placement problem with two treatments. Here we assume that $a = 1$ and $C_y = .05$. Restricting the problem to two treatments means that there is a single cutting score y' between treatments, and

$$\Delta U = \frac{r_{ys}^2}{4a} \frac{\xi^2(y')}{[1 - \phi(y')] [\phi(y')]} - C_y'. \qquad [15]$$

Here, $\phi(y')$ is the proportion of men given one of the two treatments, arbitrarily designated.

It is of interest to compare equation [15] with the corresponding equation [7] applying to adaptive-treatment selection. Equation [7] contains a term in r_{ys}. The reason is that "adaptive-treatment selection" is actually a mixture of fixed and adaptive placement: one group of men are given the treatment best suited to their average aptitude while the other group are given a fixed treatment (reject) for which $m_{st} = 0$. As a matter of fact, many mixtures of fixed and adaptive placement can be envisioned that are of practical importance. It is common practice to use a fixed treatment for the "normal" pupils in a school, for example, but to segregate handicapped pupils and give them a treatment adapted as well as possible to their capacities. Utility functions for such mixed situations will contain both r and r^2 terms.

Adjusted quotas. In Appendix 3 it is demonstrated that, with a specified number of treatments, cutting scores should be located so that for any pair of adjacent treatments

$$2y_t' = \frac{\Delta\xi_t}{\Delta\phi_t} + \frac{\Delta\xi_{t-1}}{\Delta\phi_{t-1}}. \qquad [16] \quad (3.15)$$

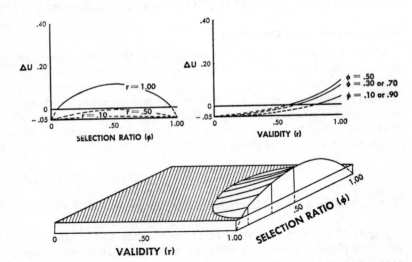

Figure 11. Relation of gain in utility to validity (r_{ys}) and selection ratio in adaptive-treatment placement

The cutting score should be located halfway between the means of the groups assigned to adjacent treatments. If we plan to divide the group among n treatments, equation [16] provides $n-1$ simultaneous equations. Since y'_t is included in the argument of $\Delta\xi_t$ and $\Delta\phi_t$, the equations are not readily solved. It is of particular interest to note that in adaptive treatment the optimum cutting scores do not depend on r_{ys}. When there are just two treatments, the optimum procedure is to divide the group at the mean. With three treatments, the optimum cutting scores are $+.65$ and $-.65$. This allocates 26% of the cases to the two extreme groups, and 48% to the middle group. The optimum cutting scores can be determined for any value of n by successive approximations. These are indicated in Figure 12 for various numbers of treatments; the proportion of cases assigned to each treatment can be read from the percentile scale.

Desirable difference between treatments. When choosing treatments from a large number of possibilities, one can use similar or markedly different treatments for persons having a specified difference in aptitude. Differences of the form $m_{st_1} - m_{st_2}$ will be smaller in the former case than in the latter. For a fixed number of treatments, equation [16] defines the range of test scores within each treatment group. The expected average aptitude in each group can then be determined. The optimum value of m_{st} for the group is then determined from equation 2.5. This implies that there is an optimum separation of treatments for any given problem.

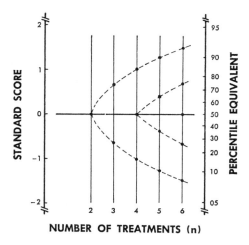

Figure 12. Optimum cutting scores for adaptive placement

The greater r_{ys}, the more may adjacent treatments differ. With three adaptive treatments, 26% of the men (average test score = 1.20) should be assigned to the "upper" group. The treatment used should be that suited to men whose average aptitude is $1.20r_{ys}$. With low validity, all persons are assigned to treatments very similar to t_o. When y is a good measure of s, treatments may differ to a much greater degree.

When raters, assessors, or other judges estimate individual differences, they tend to overdifferentiate. For example, counselors tend to predict that more students will earn grades of B or better than actually do so. They ordinarily make insufficient allowance for error, and therefore recommend differentiating treatment more than their predictors warrant. In the language of Chapter 2, the assessor does not use the optimum strategy, which (for adaptive treatment) is indicated by equation [16]. This inefficient strategy is one factor contributing to the frequent finding that psychologists applying clinical judgment to objective data make poorer decisions than a statistical formula applied to the same data. Both empirical and mathematical aspects of such judgments have been discussed elsewhere (Cronbach, 1955).

Effect of Increasing Fineness of Discrimination

We next inquire how utility varies when a test is used for a larger number of discriminations. When the number of different treatments n is increased, the decision maker faces a more difficult decision. It has generally been believed that a higher standard of validity is required for a test to be useful in making fine discriminations.

Fixed treatments, fixed quotas. An analysis of the change in validity for fixed-treatment placement can be made only under fairly specific assumptions. Suppose, for example, that our test is a measure of aptitude s and that we employ those n treatments from the general surface that would be optimal if r_{ys} were 1.00. Then, using equation 2.5 and substituting in equation [11],

$$\Delta U = \frac{r_{ys}}{2a} \sum_t \left[\frac{\Delta \xi_t}{\Delta \phi_t} \right] \Delta \xi_t - C_y. \qquad [17]$$

Now if we also assume that the same proportion of persons is assigned to each treatment, $\phi_t = 1/n$ and

$$\Delta U = \frac{r_{ys}}{2a} \, n \sum_t \Delta^2 \xi_t - C_y. \qquad [18]$$

If some other set of fixed treatments were used or some other quotas, the function would have a somewhat more complicated form. With uniform quotas, the product $n \Sigma \Delta^2 \xi$ increases with n as shown in Figure 13. In the limit, as $n \rightarrow \infty$, $n \Sigma \Delta^2 \xi$ approaches 1.00.

Adaptive treatment. When equal numbers of persons are assigned to all treatments, and treatments are adapted to fit the group, equation [14] reduces to

$$\Delta U = \frac{r_{ys}^2}{4a} \, n \sum_t \Delta^2 \xi_t - C_y. \qquad [19]$$

Figure 13 also indicates the relation of n to benefit from adaptive placement with fixed equal quotas.

When both treatments and quotas are adapted, ΔU is related to n by a curve almost identical to Figure 13. With very fine division of the scale, that is, as we approach continuous measures,

$$\lim_{n \rightarrow \infty} \Delta U = \frac{r_{ys}^2}{4a} - C_y. \qquad [20]$$

Under the conditions studied, the gain in utility as a result of increasing the number of treatments is small. After the first few treatments, benefit increases only very slightly with increased fineness of discrimination. With only two treatments, $n \Sigma \Delta^2 \xi$ equals .64, with four treatments, .86. Since the limit is 1.00 as n increases, the further increase is necessarily very gradual.

Everyone agrees that accuracy of measurement is advantageous, but three rather different types of advantage have been discussed in the literature. We have already established that, as measurement

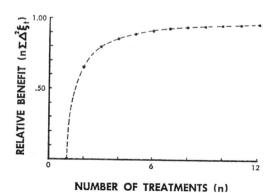

Figure 13. Increase in benefit from placement with increased number of treatments

improves, the resulting assignments achieve more nearly the maximum payoff from each individual (number of treatments being fixed). Second, we have seen that better measurement permits greater separation of treatments, with accompanying gains in utility. A third benefit sometimes expected is that better measurement warrants dividing persons among more categories; it remains to determine whether this is the case.

It has generally been believed that there is a strong relation between the accuracy of a test and the fineness of discrimination for which it may be used. The error of estimate based on r_{ys} specifies limits within which s will be expected to fall, and a more valid test estimates performance within any treatment more accurately. For this reason it has been suggested that greater accuracy permits one to place persons among a greater number of treatment categories. Bloom (1942), for one, has interpreted test reliability in terms of placement decisions, requiring that frequency of erroneous placement shall not exceed 0.1%. By this reasoning, a reliability of .56 justifies use of three categories, .84 justifies five, and .96 justifies ten. The same approach could be applied to r_{ys} (which equals the square root of the reliability if s is equivalent to the "true score" on the test). The required coefficients would then be .75, .92, and .98 respectively, for three, five, and ten categories.

Our results do not support the conclusion that greater reliability or validity justifies division into more groups. Under the conditions leading to equations [18] and [19], finer differentiation results in the same proportional increase in benefit no matter what the value of r_{ys}. For example, the gain in utility with four treatments, disregarding C_y, is always 7.5% above that with three treatments. Our result differs from Bloom's because he evaluated decisions by the number of erroneous placements rather than by the magnitude of errors. We have counted gross errors of placement which lead to large changes in outcome as more serious than fine ones, whereas he has counted all errors as equal. Bloom's method of evaluating outcomes does not seem realistic for the educational placement problems he discusses. The allowable number of subdivisions has nothing to do with the accuracy of the test.

The value of increasing the validity of the test as a measure of the s continuum is that it permits greater separation of treatments. With a good test people may be divided into ten groups and given ten sharply distinct treatments, that is, treatments suited to quite different levels of aptitude. With a poor test people may still be divided into ten groups, but the ten treatments should not be extremely different. The conventional view is close to ours only when fixed treatments and adaptive quotas are involved. Suppose that there are six treatments, for example, those appropriate respectively where $s < -2$, $-2 < s < -1$, $-1 < s < 0$, $0 < s < 1$, $1 < s < 2$, $2 < s$. If quotas may be adapted, an increase in r_{ys} warrants placing more persons in the extreme categories. For r_{ys} below .40, the optimal strategy is to assign about 99.5% of the cases to the middle two categories, because that proportion of persons will have an estimated s_i between $+1$ and -1. Practically speaking, only two categories are used. As validity increases, more persons should be assigned to the second and fifth categories. When $r_{ys} = .60$ about 5% of the cases will go into each of these groups. Ultimately, with $r_{ys} = 1.00$, about 2% of the cases will go into the first category, 2% into the sixth, and about 15% into the second and the fifth. Thus the number of fixed treatments to which persons are assigned with appreciable frequency does increase with r_{ys}.

Under adaptive conditions, accuracy of measurement bears on the number of treatments used only as the decision maker may decide that small amounts of differentiation are not worth bothering with and combines two similar treatments into one.

THE INTERPRETATION OF VALIDITY COEFFICIENTS IN PLACEMENT AND MEASUREMENT

When Chapter 4 examined the relation of test validity to utility of selection decisions, the evaluation of the validity coefficient in other uses of tests was held in abeyance. We may now summarize relations encountered in both selection and placement.

In placement, a test is used to locate the person among several treatments, and no one coefficient can be identified as *the* validity of the test. The test is likely to have a different correlation with criterion for each treatment. We have therefore distinguished three elements that determine payoff when prediction is made from a single test, namely σ_{e_t}, r_{ys}, and r_{se_t}. The variable s is common between a particular test and all treatments. So long as all tests under consideration are linked to the treatments through the same s, we can develop a general function relating utility to the validity of the tests as a measure of s, that is, in terms of r_{ys}.

In this case, gain in utility in placement with fixed treatment and fixed quotas is a simple linear function of r_{ys}. This conclusion depends on the assumption that there is a linear relation of expected payoff to test score. Assuming in addition a second-degree surface relating e, s, and t, the benefit in adaptive placement with fixed or adjusted quotas is a function of r_{ys}^2. The results for fixed quotas apply to placement into any number of categories. Even if n becomes infinite, the linear or r^2 function applies, according to whether treatments are fixed or adaptive.

Typical decisions involving measurement are best interpreted as adaptive-placement problems. The person who "measures" in order to apply the treatment optimal for the obtained score is engaged in adaptive placement with an (hypothetically) infinite number of alternative treatments to be considered. Therefore the coefficient of determination r_{ys}^2 appears to be the proper index for evaluating the usefulness of a test in personnel decisions calling for numerical measurement.

The coefficient of forecasting efficiency has a long history, and has been widely used as an index of test merit. But in the light of these results we must now ask whether it has any proper place in test theory. If it is a proper index of test efficiency, there must be some decision problem and associated payoff function such that the coefficient is proportional to benefit from testing. The coefficient of forecasting efficiency evaluates a test by the absolute error of estimate, relative to the error of a chance estimate. This evaluation would be appropriate only in a problem where payoff declines linearly with error. One type of payoff surface (and to the best of our knowledge only one) can be described for which this is true, namely a ridge-shaped surface, formed by the intersection of two planes. In such a surface, the payoff function for any single treatment is like that in Figure 14, where the treatment shown is that optimal for aptitude s. The coefficient of forecasting efficiency can be justi-

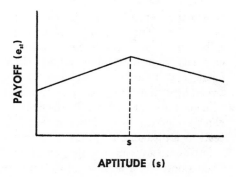

Figure 14. Possible payoff function for a single treatment

fied in a decision problem where the payoff function takes this shape, and the question therefore is whether such a function would occur in practice.

Outside the personnel field, measurement problems can be imagined where this function might apply. Suppose nails are sorted by size into bins, by a process involving some error. Then the carpenter who reaches for a certain size of nail for a given job will perhaps get one of incorrect size. The more the nail deviates in either direction, the worse suited it is: too small a nail will not hold the work firmly, too large a nail is ugly and risks splitting the wood. Perhaps the payoff function is neither linear nor sharply discontinuous, but over a range of sizes Figure 14 might be a reasonable approximation. Similar functions might be involved in the payoff from, say, various sizes of clothing allotted to a person, or various concentrations of electrolyte in a plating bath. Therefore we can argue that absolute error of estimate is a suitable loss function for some measurement problems.

But does it apply in personnel testing? We think not. Overestimating a score leads to assigning a person to a treatment he may be unable to profit from. But underestimating aptitude seems unlikely to have consequences like those of underestimating the size of a nail. The man who is placed in a treatment "too simple for him" will ordinarily outperform the man of lesser ability. The loss lies in the failure to assign the man to a treatment where he could do even better. In some situations boredom might cause inferior performance on the part of "excessively able" men, but we have not identified a situation where the payoff function seems likely to be sharply ridged; instead, the rising-then-declining function is likely to be a smooth, gradual curve. We therefore conclude that the coefficient of forecasting efficiency is not a suitable index for describing the value of a test in personnel decisions. We may have overlooked some type of decision which has a payoff function justifying this index, but it is surely not appropriate for typical selection and placement decisions. The person who proposes to use $1 - \sqrt{1 - r^2}$ as an index must bear the burden of proof, showing that this index is proportional to gain in utility for some particular decision.

Recent writings have distinguished the value of a test for screening or selection from its value in other uses. The Brogden linear relation and the Taylor-Russell function were connected specifically to coarse screening, and have been regarded as inapplicable to precise decisions or prediction for an individual (see, e.g., Wesman, 1953). The coefficient of forecasting efficiency or the standard error of estimate is ordinarily invoked for these latter cases. The coefficient of determination r^2 is not often mentioned directly as an index of efficiency, although it is prominent in test theory.

Our results, taken all together, lead to the following quite different views:

1. There is no single "validity coefficient" on which the contribution of a test depends, save in the case of fixed-treatment selection. In a placement problem, a measurement problem, or an adaptive-selection problem, we can only compare the contributions of various tests measuring the same aptitude continuum. Statements can then be made about the value of the test as a function of r_{ys}.

2. In selection with treatment and quota fixed *a priori*, utility is a linear function of the correlation between test score and evaluated outcome, that is, of the validity coefficient. In fixed-treatment, fixed-quota placement, utility is a linear function of the several validities corresponding to the various treatments. It is also a linear function of the validities of the test for predicting the differences in payoff between pairs of treatments. Finally, utility may be interpreted as a linear function of r_{ys} in fixed-treatment selection and placement.

3. When we may regard all successful men as making equal contribution to the institution, the Taylor-Russell tables are more appropriate for evaluating selective efficiency in fixed treatment than the linear function. Otherwise, the Taylor-Russell results are best regarded as a rough approximation to the linear relation.

4. In placement or measurement with adaptive treatment, utility is a function of r_{ys}^2, which has the form of a coefficient of determination. To compare tests measuring different aptitudes, the parameter a of the payoff surface for each aptitude must also be taken into account.

5. Selection with adaptive treatment combines the features of fixed and adaptive placement. The relation of utility to validity involves both r_{ys} and r_{ys}^2 terms.

6. Where treatments are fixed, but quotas may be adapted according to the value of r_{ys}, the relation of utility to validity becomes too complex to be described in a simple index.

7. No case of practical importance has been found where the coefficient of forecasting efficiency is a suitable index of test efficiency.

6

TWO-STAGE SEQUENTIAL SELECTION

The preceding chapter assumed that the selector would make a single terminal decision. The use of investigatory decisions, mentioned in Chapter 2, will now be considered. Efficiency of testing is often improved by a sequential plan allowing the decision maker to continue testing whenever he is in doubt about acceptance or rejection of an individual.

POSSIBLE USES OF SEQUENTIAL METHODS

Sequential Acceptance Testing

Sequential methods were first developed to meet the requirements of industrial inspection, but their scope has been extended to cover all testing of statistical hypotheses. The quotation from Girschick (see p. 2) indicates that they are now "the rule rather than the exception" in statistical decisions. The original industrial inspection problem is remarkably similar to personnel selection. Either the manufacturer or the consumer inspects samples of products to determine whether a given lot is of acceptable quality. This is precisely analogous to deciding whether an applicant is of acceptable quality on the basis of a sample of his behavior, and one may therefore anticipate gains from transferring the inspection methods to personnel work.

Sequential plans are strategies in which investigatory decisions are allowed. In two-stage plans, a terminal decision is required after the second testing. Multi-stage plans are also possible, investigatory decisions being allowed after every stage; some terminal decisions are made after each test, but a steadily decreasing fraction of the cases are carried through subsequent tests.

Sequential plans are beneficial because it costs something to gather information. Obviously, if observations cost nothing, it would always be better to administer the full series of tests, whatever its length, to every person. As was pointed out in the preceding chapter, test theory has generally ignored costs of testing, but even quite small costs affect choice of testing procedure. We may anticipate economies from adoption of a sequential plan in personnel selection.

Considering only cost of testing, maximum benefit would always be attained by multi-stage testing. Administering a sequential selection plan, however, involves costs that would not arise in single-stage testing. A sequential plan requires intelligent administration; in individual processing of recruits or applicants the smooth flow of the processing line would be disrupted if time for a certain examination were to vary substantially from person to person. Where a complete sequential plan would be awkward to administer, a two-stage plan is frequently a satisfactory compromise. It retains much of the efficiency of the multi-stage plan, yet is relatively easy to administer.

The present chapter explores the characteristics of two-stage sequential sampling plans for personnel selection. This analysis will not *per se* indicate just when sequential plans should be used, since the cost of administering the plan is not included in the mathematical specifications. (In this, we follow the practice of statisticians.) While our analysis will show benefits from the adoption of sequential procedures, these benefits must always be weighed against the unspecified administrative costs.

Experience in other fields suggests that sequential procedures attain a given level of accuracy of decisions with about half the amount of testing required by a single-stage plan. Arbous and Sichel (1952) have studied a two-stage "pre-screening" procedure for personnel testing. Although their procedure is not the optimum sequential plan, they report noteworthy savings in testing time. A similar pre-screening plan was developed independently by Cochran (1951). He points out that in a great variety of situations it is advantageous to reduce the original group by stages. He gives as one example the selecting of hogs for breeding, where some of the original group can be dropped because of inferior weight. Final selection among those who pass the weight test is based on the quality of their first offspring (a test which is expensive because it requires long delay). Sequential methods are especially beneficial when testing cost is high, as when costly radar equipment is used in a proficiency test (cf. Evans, 1953). Sequential testing is also advantageous when subjects are tested individually, since cost of testing is then relatively large.

Other Sequential Decisions

Our interest in sequential methods is not confined to a literal application of the acceptance-testing methods of industry. Sequential approaches to many other problems may be equally important, as Fiske and Jones (1954) demonstrated by their review of psychological applications.

The sequential method departs from the traditional psychometric procedure of standardizing test questions so that all persons are tested in the same way. Questioning is pursued only until the required decisions can be made; testing time can therefore be used more efficiently. Many forces appear to be compelling increased concern for efficiency in testing. For one thing, the identification of more and more aptitudes relevant to various occupations or job assignments means that thorough testing over all significant fields will henceforth require more time than is usually available. In proficiency and achievement testing also, it is increasingly recognized that a very large number of outcomes need to be measured in order to assess the individual and his instruction. A further reason for highly efficient testing is that tests are being introduced where only very small amounts of testing time are available. This is notable in military research where it is desired to test men on active duty in advanced areas. Such pressures already confront psychologists with demands to produce a test to measure this or that ability in five minutes of testing time.

Frequently the tester is required to decide among several treatments for each individual. Job classification is an example. In clinical testing also, one ordinarily has many hypotheses about the individual which he may accept or reject. In these instances, the problem at the first stage of testing is to divide the *alternatives* (rather than the people) into three classes: those accepted, those rejected, and those to be studied further. What alternatives remain to be considered will determine the character and length of the subsequent tests. Present procedures in guidance and clinical testing are obviously sequential in nature; this provides considerable motivation for developing adequate theory regarding sequential testing. Such a theory not only can clarify what is now going on, but should ultimately lead to substantially better procedures for "sequential analysis within the individual."

DETERMINATION OF OPTIMUM STRATEGY

The two-stage selection procedure involves two tests y_a and y_b, which may be correlated. One test is administered to every man; the second test is given only if the decision maker wishes further information before making a final disposition of the individual. The first test may be one of a group of dissimilar tests or it may be a short test made up of representative items from the complete battery, the remainder of the battery being considered as the second test. As a matter of convenience, we express the scores on the two tests in terms of independent components, y_1 being the standardized score on the first test and y_2 being the standardized score on the other test after the first test is partialed out.

Alternate Testing Plans

At least five different selection strategies are available (without considering the possibility of altering the lengths of tests y_a and y_b):

Non-sequential battery. Administer the total battery to all men, and accept those having highest scores on an optimally weighted composite. This is the conventional selection method, and we shall hereafter refer to it as the "Battery" procedure.

Single-screen. Administer either test alone, and base all decisions on it.

Sequential. After the first test is given, divide the group into three portions: those accepted, those rejected, and those to be given the second test. Base final decisions for the last-named men on the composite of both tests. We hereafter refer to this as the "Sequen-

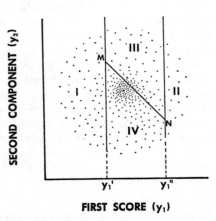

Figure 15. Sequential selection procedure

tial" strategy even though Pre-reject and Pre-accept are also sequential devices.

Pre-reject. After the first test, reject some men and continue to test all others. For these others, base final decisions on the composite of both tests.

Pre-accept. After the first test, accept some men and continue to test all others. For these others, base final decisions on the composite of both tests.

Figures 15 and 16 will aid in distinguishing these procedures. Figure 15 shows the joint distribution of y_1 and the independent second variable y_2. Three lines are located in this figure. The line at y_1' is a cutoff below which persons are rejected after the first test. The line at y_1'' is a cutoff above which persons are accepted on the basis of the first test alone. The slant line cuts off persons whose weighted composite score $Y = f(y_1, y_2)$ is above a certain level. Any person is accepted whose composite score on both tests is above the line, and vice versa. The lines divide the distribution into areas I, II, III, and IV. Each strategy represents a different treatment of these areas, as shown in Figure 16.

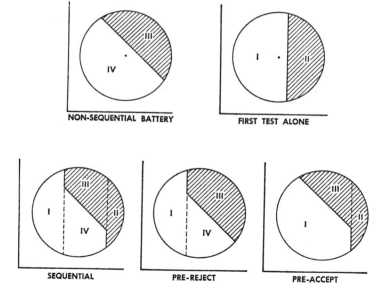

Figure 16. Alternative methods of selection

The Pre-reject strategy is a version of the Arbous-Sichel method. They propose that an inexpensive portion of the battery be used as a first screen to eliminate those men who have very low probability of passing on the battery as a whole. Their method is not optimum, since it neglects the possibility of accepting some men on the first screen and does not allow for adjusting risks according to the cost of the second test. Cochran's method also is a Pre-reject procedure, but one that does not take cost of testing and selection ratio formally into account.

Evaluation Assumptions

At least three different methods of specifying evaluations are available, any one of which leads to a somewhat different location of the cutoff points y_1' and y_1''. The first is the use of a continuous scale for evaluating outcomes in utility units and specifying a relation between payoff and test information. If the *a priori* distribution of test scores and payoffs is known, and if fixed treatment is used, the strategy which maximizes payoff can be determined for a given cost of testing. This method is employed in Appendix 4, using a linear relation of payoff to test score and assuming a normal distribution of scores and payoffs. While such a system of cardinal utilities is mathematically satisfying, it requires difficult computations. Procedures based on Neyman-Pearson risks (see below) have therefore very often been used to study practical problems. We shall use such a method to study multi-stage sequential procedures in Chapter 7 and Appendix 6.

Neyman-Pearson risks were introduced into general hypothesis testing as a modification of the confidence-level system of Fisher. While Fisherian analysis reports the risk of rejecting a null (or other *a priori*) hypothesis when it is true, the investigator wishes also to consider the risk of accepting this hypothesis when some alternative hypothesis is true. Neyman and Pearson drew attention to these two kinds of "errors," and used them to compare the power of various statistical tests. A decision maker is required to indicate the errors he wishes to avoid and to state what risk of each error he is willing to tolerate. (Unless he can tolerate some degree of error, he cannot use a sampling plan to get information.) In a selection plan, the decision maker might wish to eliminate men whose true aptitude is below a standard score of $+.5$, for example. It would not ordinarily be a matter of concern if the plan admitted some men at .48 or rejected some at .52, but there is some magnitude of error which would be serious. The decision maker is perhaps willing to admit some men as low as .35, on the theory that they can be discovered and eliminated, and wishes to minimize the risk of missing men of aptitude .55. Thus we have two tolerance limits, .35 and .55. He now specifies the risk for each error, perhaps stating that he is willing to tolerate admitting 10% of the men at aptitude .35 (the risk will be less than .10 for men below .35), and will tolerate a risk of missing 2% of the men at .55 (less above that point). In the language generally used for this system, the α risk is said to be .10, and the β risk, .02. Once these are specified, the selection procedure requiring the minimum amount of testing can be readily determined. This strategy is not dependent on an assumed *a priori* distribution. To compute the expected net utility it would be necessary to make such an assumption, however, since different distributions result in a different total frequency of each kind of error.

A selection plan based on Neyman-Pearson risks does not weight costs of testing explicitly. Instead, the decision maker is required to take them into account implicitly in setting tolerances and risks. Determination of a sequential plan and study of its performance characteristics has been reduced to a simple routine procedure (Freeman *et al.*, 1948; Statistical Research Group, 1945) by studies performed during World War II by the Statistical Research Group at Columbia University (referred to below as SRG), working under the leadership of Wald. It is generally believed that the methods based on risks are an adequate approximation to the procedures based on a cardinal utility scale, for those cases to which they apply. The evaluation of strategies in terms of the number of "hits" and "misses," discussed above in connection with the work of Taylor-Russell and Berkson, might also be applied to sequential problems. Indeed, Arbous and Sichel employ this evaluation to describe the efficiency of their plan even though they employ risks in developing it.

Location of Cutoffs

In our treatment of the two-stage sequential procedure, the cutoff scores on the first test and on the total battery (the lines y_1', y_1'', and MN in Figure 15) are to be located so as to maximize utility for any selection ratio and strategy, assuming linear regression of payoff on battery score and taking into account cost of testing. The mathematical solution is presented in Appendix 4. The same cutoff

y_1' is associated with a particular MN for both Sequential and Pre-reject strategies, and the same y_1'' for Sequential and Pre-accept. Whichever test is designated y_1 will be given to all men. Persons falling into any score array on y_1 are accepted or rejected at once if screening on the second test will not raise their total contribution enough to compensate for the cost of testing.

There is no simple formula by which y_1' and y_1'' may be located directly, but the *vertical* coordinates y_2' and y_2'' of points M and N depend on only two parameters, C_{y_2} and r_{y_2Y}. These represent the cost of the second test and its correlation with the total battery (remembering that any component correlated with the first test has been removed from y_2). The following relation specifies y_2':

$$y_2' \, \phi(y_2') = \xi(y_2') - C_{y_2}/\sigma_e r_{Ye} r_{y_2Y}. \qquad [21] \ (4.18)$$

y_2'' is equal to y_2' and opposite in sign.

The foregoing equation is very much like equation 1.13, which expresses the optimum selection ratio in single-stage selection (Figure 6). An analogous cost-benefit ratio dictates the selection ratio within the array for the two-stage problem. The lower boundary is set so that the second test is not used to select among men in any y_1 array where the battery cutting score (line MN) would accept fewer persons in the array than the optimum selection ratio for a test used singly that has cost C_{y_2} and validity equal to the independent validity of the second test. The upper boundary is set so that the second test is not used if the battery cutting score *rejects* fewer persons than the optimum selection ratio for maximum *gain per man rejected* when the second test is used singly.

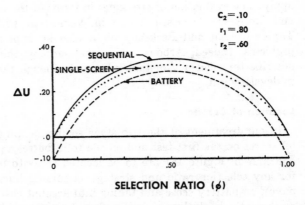

Figure 17. Gain in utility with Sequential and non-sequential strategies

In order to specify the sampling plan, we choose a cutoff value $Y = Y'$, where Y represents the best weighted composite of y_1 and y_2. The cutoff YY' accepts a different percentage of the subjects under each of the strategies. By the method described in Appendix 4, y_1' and y_1'' are computed. The utility for any strategy is a function of the expected payoff of the men selected (summed over the shaded areas of Figure 16) less the cost of testing. The cost of testing is C_{y_1}, plus C_{y_2} times the proportion of persons given the second test. From equation 4.8 one can calculate the utility for any strategy and, from equation 4.9, the selection ratio corresponding to Y'. By taking a series of values for Y', we generate a curve showing utility as a function of selection ratio.

Comparison of Sequential and Non-Sequential Strategies

Curves for these and other various sets of parameters were obtained by programming* the equations of Appendix 4 for the Illinois Automatic Electronic Computer (ILLIAC), Figures 17, 18, and 19 are based on three sets of parameters, chosen to illustrate several conclusions. An examination of Figure 17 will acquaint the reader with the type of information to be obtained. Utility per man tested is plotted as a function of selection ratio for three testing strategies. The figure is based on two parameters, r_1 (written $r_{y_1 Y}$ in Appendix 4) and C_2 (elsewhere written $C_{y_2}/\sigma_e r_{Ye}$). Fixing r_1 determines the contribution of the second test to the battery, since the sum of squares of the independent contributions must be 1.00. Dividing cost by $\sigma_e r_{Ye}$ (and also dividing ΔU by $\sigma_e r_{Ye}$ before plotting) has no effect on the shape of the functions to be discussed and makes it simpler to compare various strategies since it reduces the number of parameters to be considered. In a practical problem the validity r_{Ye} of the total battery is fixed by the choice of tests.

The cost C_1 of the first screen does not enter into the comparison of strategies *per se*, since it is charged against utility equally in all strategies. Thus for the purpose of comparing various strategies after a first test has been designated, no generality is lost by setting C_1 at zero. In general the cheaper test should be used as the first screen, but if the more expensive test is the more valid, the choice of first screen depends also on the selection ratio. In our analysis we tacitly assume that the test chosen as first screen is preferable at all selection ratios. In Chapter 7 we consider how to adjust the length of the first test when both tests measure the same thing.

---

* With the assistance of Jack C. Merwin.

The dotted line in Figure 17 indicates the utility obtained by administering the first test alone (Single-screen). This curve is similar to the cross-sections in Figure 5. The broken line indicating utility under the Battery strategy is likewise consistent with Chapter 4. In this figure, the cost of the second test is so great that Battery is never as profitable as Single-screen.

The solid line describes the utility yielded by the Sequential procedure at each selection ratio. At extreme selection ratios, Sequential comes close to the curve for Single-screen. At all selection ratios, Sequential is equal or superior to either of the other strategies. We shall find that this is a general conclusion.

Figure 18 employs tests with the same relative validity as Figure

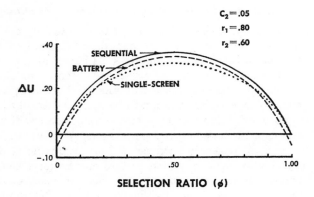

Figure 18. Gain in utility with Sequential and non-sequential strategies

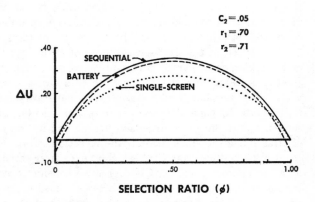

Figure 19. Gain in utility with Sequential and non-sequential strategies

17, but the cost of the second test is lowered. This raises the utility for Battery at all selection ratios so that it is now superior to Single-screen at intermediate selection ratios. Sequential also yields more benefit than formerly, but its advantage over Battery has declined. Figure 19 retains the same cost, but raises the contribution of the second test and correspondingly decreases the contribution of the first. Comparing this to Figure 18, we find that the change has lowered the value of Single-screen, giving Battery greater superiority. But Sequential, which uses the second test only in relatively doubtful decisions, is still superior to both the other strategies.

In the subsequent illustrations pointing out various trends in the computed results, the parameters of the decision problem are generally taken to be $\phi = .50$, $r_1 = .70$, $r_2 = .71$ (which values would be equal save for the necessity of rounding in computation) and $C_2 = .10$. The values ΔU and C_2 are defined as in Figures 17-19. It should be noted that the vertical scale in Figure 20 is different from that of the previous figures.

The advantage of Sequential over Battery and over Single-screen is shown in Figure 20. At extreme selection ratios the advantage over the conventional Battery procedure equals the cost of the second test. At selection ratios near .50, Sequential has relatively little superiority. The figure emphasizes the comparison of the Sequential strategy to the *better* of the two non-sequential procedures. At extreme selection ratios it is compared to Single-screen, and at intermediate selection ratios, to Battery. As expected,

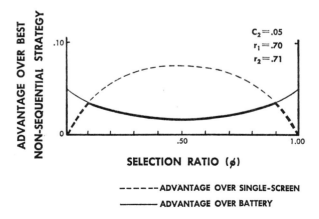

Figure 20. Comparison of Sequential and best non-sequential strategy

Sequential is consistently superior by some slight amount, but its most striking advantage occurs neither at extreme selection ratios nor where $\phi = .50$. Battery and Single-screen yield equal utility at two selection ratios where cost and contribution of the second test are exactly balanced. Sequential always offers its maximum advantage at these selection ratios.

Effect of Variation in Cost

The cost of the second test obviously determines which of the strategies should be used. When a person is given the second test more information is obtained, but if cost of testing is high, the decision maker should seek this information only for the most doubtful decisions if at all. The change of utility with cost is shown in Figure 21, with r_1 and selection ratio held constant. The following points should be noted. As cost increases (or $\sigma_e r_{Ye}$ decreases), Battery becomes less and less beneficial. At some point Single-screen becomes superior to Battery. At low cost, Sequential is slightly better than Battery; at high cost, slightly better than Single-screen. The greatest difference occurs, as before, where the Single-screen and Battery lines cross. The pictured relationships are typical, although the magnitude of differences depends on the parameters. It should be realized that if C_2 becomes very low, the test now given second would be the better first screen.

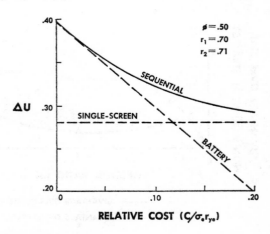

Figure 21. Utility as a function of cost of second test

Effect of Variation in r_1

The greater the weight of y_1 in the composite the greater the benefits from both Single-screen and Sequential (Figure 22). At low values of r_1, Battery is about as good as Sequential. (Here it would perhaps pay to give the second test only.) As r_1 increases, the advantage of Sequential over Battery increases, but its advantage over Single-screen diminishes and finally becomes negligible. More extreme selection ratios or higher costs of second test would enlarge the region of r_1 in which Sequential is only slightly better than Single-screen.

PRE-REJECT AND PRE-ACCEPT STRATEGIES

Under all conditions of testing, the utility from the Pre-reject strategy lies between that of Battery and Sequential (Figure 23). When selection ratio is high, very few people will be rejected at the first stage and Pre-reject has negligible advantage over Battery; when selection ratio is low, Pre-reject is nearly as advantageous as Sequential. Pre-accept has a similar relation, approaching Sequential at high selection ratios and approaching Battery at low selection ratios. The curves for Pre-accept and Pre-reject are mirror images.

Improvement in utility for these incomplete sequential procedures,

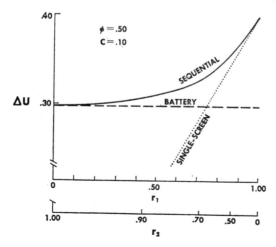

Figure 22. Utility as a function of relative validity of tests

over the best non-sequential, is plotted in Figure 24 as a function of selection ratio. Pre-reject gives only half the advantage of the full Sequential method when selection ratio is .50, and gives much less advantage at higher selection ratios. It is, however, as good as Sequential at low selection ratios.

We conclude that under our assumptions the proposal of Arbous

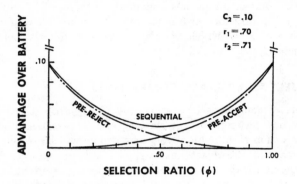

Figure 23. Utility with Pre-accept and Pre-reject strategies

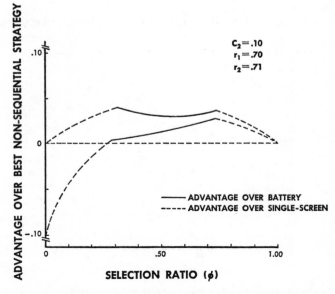

Figure 24. Comparison of Pre-reject to Sequential and best non-sequential strategy

and Sichel, and the complementary Pre-accept method are not superior to Sequential. There are, however, practical situations where a complete sequential strategy cannot be considered. For example, if the second "test" consists of admitting men to the training course and weeding out those who do poorly, "pre-acceptance" is meaningless since all men accepted have to go through the training. Cochran's breeding experiments are similar, in that second-screen data (quality of first litter) are necessarily obtained for all subjects not rejected.

AMOUNT OF TESTING SAVED

The core of the Sequential strategy is the correct determination of the cutting scores y_1' and y_1''. Arbous and Sichel provide charts to indicate optimum cutting scores in their method, for various selection ratios and r_1. In lieu of such charts or tables for our strategy,

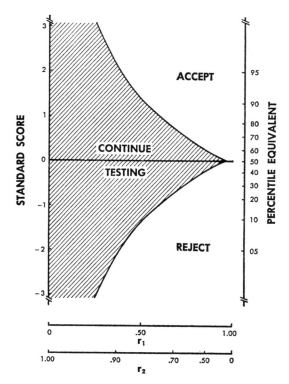

Figure 25. Cutting scores on first test when $Y' = 0$

Appendix 4 outlines a procedure by which the tester may readily compute the desired cutoffs, knowing the parameters of his decision problem.

Typical results are plotted in Figures 25 and 26. In each diagram, the cutting scores are shown as a function of r_1, assuming a cost of .10 units for the second test. Setting $Y' = 0$ (Figure 25) will yield a selection ratio of .50 regardless of the value of r_1. When the first test accounts for nearly all the battery variance, the two cutting scores coincide at zero, and no one is given the second test. As the contribution of the second screen increases, more and more persons are given the second test. When $r_1 = .80$ and $r_2 = .60$, the second test is given to persons with y_1 between $-.46$ and $.46$, that is, to about 35% of the applicants. The Sequential strategy saves 65% of the second-screen testing ordinarily required.

One would be interested in the relation of first-screen cutoffs to

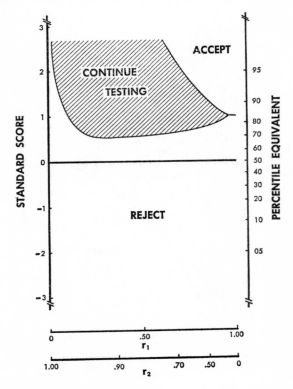

Figure 26. Cutting scores on first test when $Y' = 1$

r_1 for selection ratios other than .50, but to determine this relation would require a very large number of computations. Any given Y' yields a different selection ratio depending on r_1; to obtain a desired selection ratio, therefore, one must choose a value of Y' depending on r_1. It is not too difficult to compute first-screen cutoffs for a particular value of Y'. This has been done for $Y' = 1$; the results are plotted in Figure 26. When $r_1 = 1.00$ a selection ratio of .16 is obtained, but as r_1 decreases the selection ratio very rapidly decreases. One can see from Figure 26 that as the contribution of the second screen increases the proportion of persons given the second test increases and then decreases. This is not particularly meaningful, however, since when the battery score is determined almost entirely by the second test the selection ratio approaches zero for this value of Y'.

Figure 27 shows the proportion of the total group given the second test at each selection ratio, for one set of parameters. Also plotted is the proportion who would be given the test if Pre-reject strategy were used. A sequential procedure greatly reduces the amount of testing when the selection ratio moves toward either extreme. The striking advantage of Sequential over Pre-reject in terms of testing effort saved confirms our earlier conclusion.

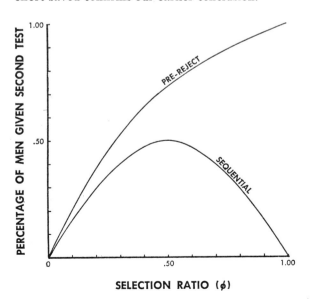

Figure 27. Proportion of persons given second test

7

EFFICIENT TESTING PROCEDURES

Among the chief problems of the decision maker is the efficient design of testing procedures. The time he can devote to testing is often severely limited, and how to use that time efficiently is a matter of concern.

ADJUSTMENT OF TEST LENGTH

One way in which the efficiency of testing can be increased is by adjusting a test or battery to the length that would yield maximum gain in utility for the decision problem in which it will be used. When a particular collection of items is used, gains in efficiency can be obtained by altering the number of items. With a battery of tests treated as a composite it may be desirable not only to alter the lengths of the separate tests, but also to omit some tests entirely despite the fact that they improve the multiple correlation.

Optimum Length for a Single Test

The validity of a test rises as it is lengthened, the increase being gradual unless the units forming the test have low intercorrelations. Since validity does increase indefinitely, there might seem to be no limit to the desirable length of test. A utility analysis, however, demonstrates that there is an optimum length, beyond which increases in cost outweigh benefits from greater validity. This point was recognized by Hull.

Speaking of a battery composed by adding units with validity .40 and intercorrelation .20, he wrote (1928, p. 262): "The tenth [unit] adds only 1.2 points to the correlation yield. The question inevitably arises whether an increase of a single point or so in the correlation yield is worth the extra time and labor involved in giving and scoring an entire additional test unit. In any case it must be perfectly obvious that because of this law of diminishing returns a place must be reached sooner or later where the addition of a new test will not contribute enough to the prognostic value of the battery to justify the incidental expense involved." Despite this early statement, the validity-cost balance has generally been ignored in discussions of test design, and has never been reduced to a definite function.

To study the effect of lengthening a test we express the general equation for placement or selection as follows:

$$\Delta U_k = B_{y_k d} - C_{y_k}. \qquad [22] \quad (5.3)$$

Here the subscript k indicates that we are considering a test of length k. B_{yd} is the benefit from using test y in a particular decision problem d, and has been defined for each type of decision so far considered.

The cost of a unit test may be divided into two portions, C_0 and C_1. The first element C_0 is an initial cost of testing which may be assumed to be constant, regardless of length. This "setup" cost takes into account assembling subjects, giving directions, etc. The marginal cost C_1 of a unit test may be assumed proportional to length, and includes examiner time, time of men tested, scoring costs, etc.

When k similar units are combined to form a test, benefit from testing is an increasing negatively accelerated function of k. Cost increases linearly and must eventually exceed benefit. The difference between benefit and cost is the net gain in utility.

The benefit must be specified for a particular unit test and a

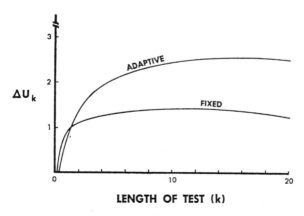

Figure 28. Utility as a function of test length

particular decision problem. As Appendix 5 shows, somewhat different equations (5.4 and 5.13) describe the increase in benefit with length in fixed-treatment decisions and in adaptive-placement decisions. Figure 28 shows the change in utility with length for both types of decisions. While these curves are based on a particular set of parameters ($B_{y_id} = 1$, $r_{y_1y_1} = .30$, $C_0 = .05$, $C_1 = .02$), the general shapes of the curves would be similar for other parameters. Change of parameters would shift the maxima and alter the curvature. No direct comparison of the curves for fixed and adaptive treatment is warranted, and no meaning is attached to the fact that the adaptive curve is higher in the figure, since the parameter B_{y_id} is defined differently in the two cases.

For any test, there is some one best length (unless the test is too invalid to ever repay its cost). If the test is shorter than this optimum, the tester is not attaining full utility. As a test is lengthened beyond the optimum value, ΔU declines and eventually becomes negative. The utility curve is fairly flat over a large range of k, and it is therefore not critical to determine *precisely* the best k for a given situation. The left portion of Figure 29, based on equation 5.6, shows the optimum k for fixed treatment as a function of other parameters. The right portion (from eq. 5.16) shows the optimum for adaptive placement. In both cases, the optimum length of test increases as cost C_1 decreases, benefit B_{y_id} increases, and/or intercorrelation $r_{y_1y_1}$ decreases. In selection, shorter tests should be used as the selection ratio departs from .50. The optimum length does not depend on C_0, the "setup cost." An optimum length of test for adaptive selection also exists (eq. 5.19). Adequate cost estimates are not available to indicate the range of B/C in typical practical

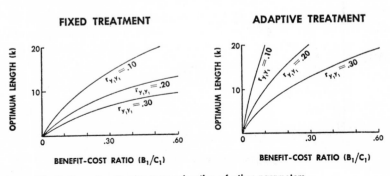

Figure 29. Optimum length of test as a function of other parameters

situations. If the parameters employed in Figure 29 are realistic, many present tests are too long for greatest efficiency.

Optimum Battery Length

A similar effect occurs when tests are combined into a composite predictor, as is usual with test batteries. The multiple correlation rises slowly as the battery is augmented. In fixed treatment, the gain from adding the vth test is $\Delta R - C_v$, where ΔR is the resulting increase in the multiple correlation and C_v is the cost of the vth test. A test which, used as a sole predictor, contributes sufficient validity to be worth its cost may not add enough in a battery to be profitable (cf. eqs. 5.10, 5.11).

Previous writers have suggested ways of determining optimum composition of a battery of fixed length. Long and Burr (1949) consider the case where tests have fixed but not uniform lengths. The conventional procedure for choosing tests to form the battery should then be modified. They indicate how to select the best combination of tests for any specified testing time. Horst (1949) goes further, altering the lengths of tests in order to maximize the multiple correlation for any fixed total testing time. His argument is parallel to ours save that he does not introduce a setup cost for each new test. Taylor (1950) provides a clear discussion of the Horst solution, with examples.

While these solutions consider the design of a battery with a specified length, they do not take the further step of determining the optimum length. As we have indicated above, the cost of additional testing at some point outweighs benefit from improved prediction. Using equations 5.10 and 5.11 in an iterative procedure similar to that of Horst, it is possible to build up a battery approaching the optimal as closely as desired both in length and composition for a fixed-treatment selection problem. Probably one could devise a more direct method, taking into account the type of decision problem, the cost of each test, its benefit at unit length, and all test intercorrelations.

The problem of maximizing the efficiency of a battery of tests can be further generalized to situations where many decisions are to be made from the obtained information. Such cases have been treated by Horst and others and will be discussed in the following chapter.

Distribution of Effort in Two-Stage Sequential Testing

The tests used in a two-stage sequential plan should also be designed for maximum efficiency, the lengths of the first and second tests being adjusted according to their unit validities and costs. We deal with distribution of effort within a battery of fixed total length and cost; the optimal length of a two-stage battery has not been studied. No comparable problems arise in the usual multistage plan, where the tests used at successive stages are identical in validity and cost.

The ideal distribution of effort can be examined by computations similar to those in Chapter 6. These computations are practical where the battery may be divided into units of equal validity and cost, but not for heterogeneous combinations. A given homogeneous battery may be divided in any proportion between the two stages of testing. For purposes of illustrating the effect of various divisions on validity, we have divided the battery into 20 identical units. Any number k of these units may be employed as the first screen. In this example, the intercorrelation of units is set at .10, C_1 at .005, and C_0 at 0. (As in Chapter 6, utility and costs are relative to $\sigma_e r_{Ye}$.) Figure 30 shows how the gain in utility from Single-screen, Battery, and Sequential procedures is altered by changes in k, with selection ratios .50 and .10. The utility from Battery is constant, since the cost of the battery and the validity do not depend on the way it is divided. Utility from Single-screen increases with length

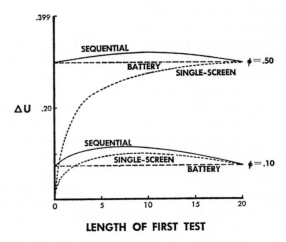

Figure 30. Utility in two-stage selection with varying distribution of effort

in the manner of Figure 28. With the parameters here assumed, the first screen would profitably be lengthened beyond 20 units when the selection ratio is .50. The optimum length for the first stage of a two-stage battery, however, is about ten units—much less than the optimum length for the same test used as a single screen. For a selection of .10 (or .90), the optimum single screen is one with k approximately 9, and the optimum length of first stage is about 8. If the first stage of testing is much shorter than this optimum, Battery is nearly as good as Sequential. If the first stage of Sequential procedure is much longer than the optimum, Sequential offers little advantage over the Single-screen. The proportion of the battery assigned to the first stage should decrease, other things being equal, when the selection ratio becomes more extreme, the intercorrelation of unit tests becomes higher, and cost per unit test becomes higher, or the product $\sigma_e r_{Ye}$ becomes less.

MULTI-STAGE TESTING

A type of sequential testing more general than we have hitherto considered employs a large number of stages for individuals whose assignment is difficult to determine, but for other individuals makes terminal decisions after one or a few stages. Such a multi-stage sequential testing process distributes effort very efficiently. The length of test is adjusted to the individual on the basis of the information about him as it is received.

Wald and the SRG have developed multi-stage sequential strategies for a great variety of problems, including some of those that concern us. In early studies, multi-stage procedures were given detailed attention only under the condition that the same test is used at every stage, that is, when the decision maker continues at every stage to collect further samples of the same sort of information (but see p. 169). Wald (1950, pp. 114ff.) developed a "recursion" formula that specifies the ideal sequential procedure and permits determination of the benefit from such a procedure, provided one knows the *a priori* distribution of aptitudes and the cost of testing. This method is laborious to treat computationally, and the older SRG methods may be regarded as an adequate approximation. The SRG methods are designed for situations where one lacks prior knowledge of the distribution of true scores, and where outcomes are specified in terms of risks of various sorts of errors rather than in terms of utility units. We have been able, however, to adapt the methods to certain of our fixed-treatment problems. For those readers interested in the procedures, we summarize the SRG methods in Appendix 6 and indicate how the optimal multi-stage strategy can be determined for any specified parameters. The present discussion confines itself to presenting typical results.

Where persons are to be divided into two groups, each to receive a fixed treatment, a desired division point y'_∞ is established. Then, on the basis of the information y available after any stage of testing, one can estimate the probability that an individual is above y'_∞. When this probability approaches one or zero, one can confidently make a terminal decision regarding the individual. The optimal strategy provides two scores for each stage of testing which constitute the boundaries of the region in which testing continues. As soon as an individual crosses either of these boundaries, testing for him ceases. A person attaining the higher of these scores is assigned to one treatment, and a person falling at or below the lower score is assigned to the other treatment.

The utility from a multi-stage test depends on the cost of the unit test, the intercorrelation of unit tests, and the relevant payoff functions. To study the gain in utility from a multi-stage procedure, benefits and amounts of testing required were computed, using an ILLIAC program for multi-stage testing devised for us by Kern Dickman. The program applies to decisions with two categories. Here we discuss the results in terms of selection rather than placement.

As a matter of convenience, we have defined the unit test as one for which $r_{y_1 y_1} = .10$. In practice, one might employ larger or smaller

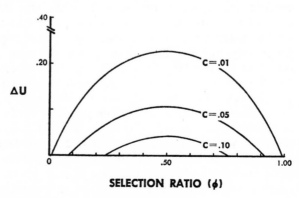

Figure 31. Utility in multi-stage selection as a function of selection ratio

units, with correspondingly larger or smaller intercorrelations, but this change would affect results very little. Cost and utility are expressed relative to $\sigma_e r_{y_\infty e}$. At each true score total cost is proportional to the number of stages of testing, and net utility is determined by subtracting cost from benefit. For any cost of unit test and selection ratio, there is an optimum strategy. When persons are selected by this strategy, the utility varies with selection ratio in the manner shown in Figure 31. These curves are rather similar to those found for two-stage sequential testing. The relation of utility to cost of the unit test is depicted in Figure 32.

The advantage of sequential testing over non-sequential testing is demonstrated in Figure 33. Here, one curve shows the gain from sequential testing assuming $C_1 = .01$. The other curve indicates the utility to be expected if every man were given a test of uniform length, the length of test used at any selection ratio being exactly equal to the average length of test for the sequential procedure. Calculations for the non-sequential curve are only approximate. The sequential plan where the same total amount of testing is distributed unequally over the men tested is superior at any selection ratio to the conventional procedure. More than this, because the lengths of the non-sequential tests are very near the optimum in each case, it is not possible by any adjustment of length to increase the utility of the non-sequential plan to the point where it equals the sequential procedure. That is to say, with this test the utility

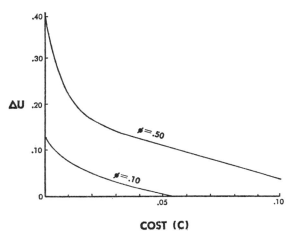

Figure 32. Utility in multi-stage selection as a function of cost

reached by sequential selection is unattainable by a non-sequential method.

Sequential Testing for Placement Purposes

Sequential methods of obtaining information can be applied to placement decisions other than the two-treatment case discussed above. Sobel and Wald (1949) describe a procedure for deciding which of three intervals along a continuum a parameter falls into. They employ assumptions such as those discussed in Appendix 6. This method can be applied directly to placement decisions in personnel work (see also p. 168).

No study has been made of the contribution of sequential placement for more than three treatments where payoff under each treatment is a linear function of score. The strategy specifies that testing will continue only if the total score after any stage of testing falls between certain values. A terminal decision is made for each person as soon as the risk of error is reduced to tolerable size. Testing is most extensive for a person whose true score falls near one of the boundaries. It is evident that considerable time can be saved in testing persons far from any borderline, but the saving will be small for persons near the borderline. As the number of treatments increases, there are more borderlines and more persons must be given long tests. Sequential testing for placement into many categories, therefore, appears likely to have limited value as the number of categories becomes large. Indeed as $n \to \infty$, that is, in a measurement problem, it has been established that the sequential method has no advantage, where parallel tests are used at all stages (Stein and Wald, 1947; Wolfowitz, 1950).

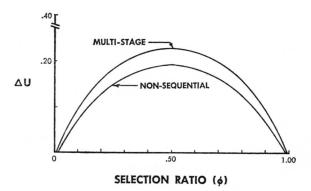

Figure 33. Utility from comparable non-sequential and multi-stage procedures

Designing tests according to a sequential pattern can perhaps improve their efficiency for other uses than selection or placement (see also p. 171). While most test theory assumes the test to be identical for everyone, some individual tests require decisions at one stage as to what questions will be administered next. Thus the Stanford-Binet Scale employs the vocabulary score to determine a trial basal age. In measurement of sensory thresholds, the ascending and descending trials of the Method of Limits are similarly sequential in nature. Recently developed answer sheets which permit immediate scoring of responses open up the possibility of sequential procedure in group tests.

One situation where such a procedure promises to be valuable is in analytic proficiency or achievement measurement. Here, many different types of attainment need to be checked so the subject can be given further training where necessary. If a minimum performance standard can be established for each type of attainment, a short test can be administered for each. When these tests are scored, decisions can be made at an acceptable level of confidence regarding those dimensions where the person's score is extremely high or low, and he can be asked to take a further test on each dimension where his score is less extreme. This procedure is repeated until a decision has been made regarding every dimension. The total amount of testing required for any individual is considerably less than would be needed if sufficient items were administered non-sequentially to make sure that every decision reaches the same minimum level of confidence. Somewhat more complicated variants of the procedure can be used for multidimensional tests where the tester is interested in identifying the person's highest aptitude or his salient personality characteristics, etc.

Attention may be drawn to a paper by Somerville (1954) which appears to represent a first step toward the mathematical study of sequential processes where each stage of decision making indicates what hypotheses should be tested next. Somerville studies a two-stage sampling problem where the first stage obtains data on many dimensions, and only the dimension with the highest estimated mean is to be tested in the second stage. In this problem, he is able to determine the optimum length for the first stage.

There is another possible use of sequential technique in designing single-score tests. In two-category placement, it has sometimes been found desirable to use a "peaked" test where the difficulty of all items is chosen so as to be maximally discriminative at the critical aptitude level. With more categories, the efficiency of testing could perhaps be improved by adjusting the difficulty of items according to the person's performance on the preceding items. For example, if there are three categories, separated by aptitude s' and s'', there could be two levels of item difficulty. Level 1 would be such as to discriminate most sharply between persons above and below s'; level 2 would discriminate at s''. The test might begin with five items at level 1, which would be scored immediately. Persons who pass, say, three or more would be directed to try a group of items at level 2, while the remainder would take further items at level 1. At the end of this stage, those successful at level 1 (all items considered) would move to level 2. Those who had attempted level 2 would be divided, some moving back to level 1, others remaining at level 2. Those who, in the end, succeed at level 2 are assigned to the top category, and those who fail at level 1 to the bottom category; the remainder go into the middle category. Such a procedure can be varied by introducing more categories and more levels of difficulty, by altering item intercorrelation, by altering the number of items at each stage, and so on.

We have made only a sketchy exploration of this procedure. It appears that such a sequential procedure is advantageous only when the items of the test are highly homogeneous in content, that is, have high tetrachoric intercorrelations. Then, if the items are sufficiently homogeneous in difficulty within levels, and sufficiently widely spaced between levels, the various subtests will discriminate between individuals on the basis of their position on the aptitude continuum. In general, the higher the tetrachoric correlations, the greater the number of levels which may be used and the closer together may be the division points. It is well known (Lord, 1955) that item intercorrelations in educational and psychological tests are rarely high enough to yield "difficulty factors," unless they are applied to a group having an exceptional range on the attribute measured. Very high intercorrelations are presently encountered only in a few unusual instruments, such as Guttman-type attitude scales. These devices would seemingly be benefited by further development of sequential test designs. (See p. 172.)

8

THE BANDWIDTH-FIDELITY DILEMMA

In deciding whether to use a test, the practical worker considers not only its validity but also its range of applicability. There is an obvious difference between the value of a measure of mathematical proficiency, used in several decisions about a student by his teachers and counselors, and that of an equally valid measure of drawing ability applied to only one or two decisions. The way a test is scored affects its value; a single overall score will usually have a narrower range of application than a pattern of subscores on the same test. *Utility analysis suggests that the contribution of a test be judged over all decisions, rather than in terms of validity for any one decision.* It is this total contribution to the institution that determines which tests, or which scores, should be used.

An example will show the significance of this argument. Instruments available to classroom teachers for evaluating pupil adjustment, such as questionnaires, sentence completion tests, and sociograms, have limited but positive validity. A pupil's poor score on such an instrument can influence many of the teacher's decisions: decisions regarding how to discipline him, how much pressure for greater achievement to apply, what social activities to suggest, and whether to make a diagnostic case study of him. Although the adjustment inventory improves any single decision much less than a test of, say, spatial ability improves the decision to which *it* is relevant, the former test, applicable to many important decisions, is likely to be more beneficial.

Working with a person over a period of time, a teacher or therapist applies a great variety of treatments. Each time, he classifies the person as requiring (ready for) the treatment or not. We may regard the test interpreter as having many hypotheses of the form: "Treatment t_A is suitable for this individual." A decision to accept or reject is made regarding each hypothesis. These are typically placement decisions, since the person not given the treatment remains within the institution. These decisions are independent whenever one decision does not affect the others. We shall term a set of such independent decisions, a *compound decision*. Our consideration of the contribution of a test over decisions will be limited to this case.

A model involving independent decisions is admittedly oversimplified, since decisions about a person are likely to be integrated rather than independent. The decision of a counselor to recommend remedial reading for a student may be independent of his decision to try to broaden the student's participation in social affairs, but it is more likely that recommending remedial reading will dictate postponing the expansion of the student's social life. This example might be regarded as allowing four alternative treatments (modify reading and social program, modify reading alone, modify social program alone, modify neither). If the probabilities that a person will be given the four treatments are predictable from the probabilities that he will be given reading and social treatments, considered separately, we have a compound placement decision (i.e., two independent placement decisions). If decisions are not independent, the problem involves four categories. While these categories might all be predicted from a single test, it is much more likely that the appropriate predictors will involve at least two factors, and therefore this problem is no longer one of placement. Such general classification problems are more common in industry and military personnel work than are compound placement decisions. Even where decisions are not strictly independent, however, the compound placement model may be a useful approximation.

Our inquiry involves two subquestions. First, it is necessary to find an expression for the value of a test or battery used for compound decisions. Second, we employ this expression to identify general principles regarding the optimum design of the testing battery in problems involving compound decisions.

UTILITY OF A TEST IN COMPOUND DECISIONS

We recall that the gain from making any one decision d is

$$\Delta U_d = B_{yd} - C_y. \qquad [22]$$

B_{yd} is the benefit obtained when test y is used as a basis for this decision, and depends on the character of the decision problem, the treatments, and the location of cutoffs, as well as on the validity of the test for whatever aptitudes are involved.

If the same test, scored in the same or a different manner, is used for several decisions about the same persons, further benefit is obtained without further cost. The grand total contribution of testing is

$$\sum_{d} \Delta U_d = \sum B_{yd} - C_y. \qquad [23]$$

The contribution of the test is more or less proportional to the number of decisions for which the set of scores can be used. A test which applies to v similar fixed-treatment decisions contributes the same net utility as another test having v times as much validity which applies to only one. In adaptive treatment, where B_{yd} is a function of $r_{\bar{y}s}^2$, a test must apply to v^2 similar decisions before it is as profitable as another test having v times as much validity for one such decision.

One must be cautious in implying that tests can compensate for poor validity merely by being used repeatedly. When the validity of a test is near zero, multiplication is most unlikely to raise the total utility to a satisfactory level. Moreover, a positive validity coefficient computed on one sample does not guarantee usefulness for a test. Sampling error of low correlations is substantial, and our argument is based on coefficients established for the population.

DISTRIBUTION OF EFFORT IN A MULTI-SCORE BATTERY

The test designer and the user of tests frequently have to choose between careful estimation of a single variable and more cursory exploration of many separate variables. Tests may be constructed to yield separate scores on a number of diverse, internally homogeneous scales, or to provide a single measure loaded with the general factor underlying items. Particularly where the test is to be used in a variety of decisions rather than to predict one single criterion, questions arise as to whether to establish independent part scores or to obtain a careful measure of a single attribute (Loevinger et al., 1953). The person choosing published tests for a testing program faces similar questions, since he can use available time to measure one or two variables by means of long tests, or employ a much larger number of short tests measuring a variety of characteristics.

This dilemma may be described in the language of the communications engineer as a choice between "wideband" and "narrowband" tests. In using a particular channel, such as a telegraph wire, one may either crowd many messages into a period of time, or give a single message slowly and repetitively. The former, more varied message has greater "bandwidth." The wideband signal transmits more information, but the clarity or dependability of the information received is less than for the narrowband signal except under ideal communication conditions. Random errors can seriously confuse the wideband signal; this is spoken of as a lack of fidelity. The tester's situation is analogous. If he concentrates on facts relevant to a single decision, he gets a much more dependable answer than if he spreads his effort. But by concentrating, he leaves all his other questions to be answered on the basis of chance alone.

This suggests that in any decision situation there is some ideal compromise between variety of information (bandwidth) and thoroughness of testing to obtain more certain information (fidelity). For the purposes of designing electronic communication circuits, such ideal compromises have been worked out within the Shannon mathematical theory of communication (1949). Because of its close analogy to testing problems, we once expected the Shannon theory to provide a basis for test design. Upon close examination, the Shannon model proves not to fit the tester's problem (Cronbach, 1953, 1956). Though information theory is suggestive, the tester's problem must be treated within the more comprehensive mathematical structure of decision theory.

Previous solutions. We wish a maximally efficient strategy for gathering information when a large number of decisions are to be made. These decisions depend on various aptitudes, which in the general case may or may not be correlated. Some relatively general mathematical solutions have been offered, but none of them leads to easily comprehended or communicated results. Certain restricted solutions have appeared in the literature. Elfving (1952) and Chernoff (1953) suggest a way to determine the optimal distribution of effort which minimizes the total squared error of estimate. Chernoff shows that this least-square index leads to the "locally optimum" division of effort under a wide range of conditions, provided error of estimate is small. The Elfving-Chernoff method assumes that all decisions are equally important, and does not make allowance for a setup cost C_0. Horst and MacEwan (1956) have employed similar assumptions to obtain an optimal battery for fixed total testing time, where the battery is to predict various criteria.

These investigators have assumed that the tests are intended to estimate the standard score on each criterion as accurately as possible, there being a different criterion for each decision. The index used is the sum of the squared errors of estimate for the various criteria, or what is equivalent, the sum of R^2_{yc} over criteria, where R is the multiple correlation of the test scores with the criterion. Such an index clearly applies to measurement problems where treatments will be adapted to the estimated criterion scores of the individual (cf. eq. [21]).

Placing its entire emphasis on the validity coefficients as it does, this index is not a fully satisfactory basis for judging the contribution of a test. When all criterion measures are reduced to standard scores, they are in effect assumed to be equally important. Second, the index leaves quotas or cutting scores out of account. While these are irrelevant in measurement with an infinite number of categories, the quotas become an important factor in utility when tests are used to select among a few alternative treatments. Finally, it is to be noted that the least-squares criterion is relevant to adaptive-treatment decisions, but according to our previous chapters is not a suitable index for fixed-treatment decisions. This index would, however, agree with our analysis in warning against judging test merit by the validity coefficient against each single criterion considered separately.

We shall take into account the parameters of the decision problem. In so doing, however, we find it necessary to impose other serious restrictions so that we deal with only certain special cases.

Equivalent decisions and tests. The first special case to be considered is that where each of a set of terminal decisions depends on a different aptitude, and there is a test which measures each aptitude. We assume that B_{v_id}, $r_{y_iv_i}$, C_0, and C_1 are the same for every test, that is, that the decisions and the unit test relevant to each are similar. The correlations among tests and among outcomes are zero. Both setup and marginal costs are assumed to depend entirely on time, but setup costs are independent of the length of the test. Bandwidth is described by v, the number of dimensions to be tested.

The question is: If the tester has T units of testing time available, is he wiser to divide that time over all decisions or to concentrate on measuring one variable? Or is his best choice intermediate between these? When he lengthens one test, he improves its contribution, but is left with many decisions to be made on a chance basis; if he uses many short tests, he can cover all his decisions, but with highly fallible information.

With equivalent tests and similar decisions, the tester should divide his time equally among whatever number of tests he gives. This is true because the relation of benefit to length (eq. 5.1) is convex, and therefore the contribution corresponding to length $\frac{1}{2}(k_1 + k_2)$ is always greater than the average of the contributions at k_1 and k_2. The problem reduces to determining the optimum number of tests of uniform length. (If decisions and tests were not uniform, it would be desirable to use tests of different lengths and no simple statement about bandwidth could be made.)

In fixed treatment, the contribution of any test as a function of length is as was indicated in Figure 28. The constraint on testing time fixes a total allowable cost C_T. Appendix 7 demonstrates that the contribution from a battery of v uniform tests, each of length k and each used for a separate fixed-treatment selection or placement decision, is

$$\sum_d \Delta U_{kd} = vB_{y_1d}\sqrt{\frac{r_{y_k y_k}}{r_{y_1 y_1}}} - C_T \qquad [24] \quad (7.2)$$

where

$$v = \frac{C_T}{C_0 + kC_1}. \qquad [25] \quad (7.9)$$

If C_0 is zero, $v = C_T/kC_1$. Substituting this value of v in equation [24], it can be seen that utility is a monotonic decreasing function of k. Utility then increases indefinitely as v increases (although v could never increase beyond the point where each test contains only one item). If there were no initial cost it would be profitable to increase bandwidth up to the limit of the number of decisions to be made.

Where there is an initial cost, there is a limit to how short the tests can be because extremely short tests cannot repay the setup cost. The relation of gain in utility, for all tests combined, to the number of tests has the general form shown in Figure 34. (As a matter of convenience, ΔU and v are both expressed relative to C_T in this figure. C_0, C_1, and B_{y_1d} are set at .05, .02, and .2 respectively.)

If the uniform decisions involve adaptive-treatment placement, the equation analogous to equation [24] is

$$\sum_d \Delta U_{kd} = vB_{y_1d} \frac{r_{y_k y_k}}{r_{y_1 y_1}} - C_T. \qquad [26] \quad (7.14)$$

This function also is shown in Figure 34.

The optimum length of any one test (which, substituted in eq. [25], gives the optimum bandwidth) is obtained by maximizing equation [24] or equation [26] with respect to k. For fixed treatment under the specified conditions the optimum length is

$$k = \frac{1 - r_{y_1y_1}}{4\,r_{y_1y_1}} \left[-1 + \sqrt{1 + 8\,\frac{C_0 r_{y_1y_1}}{C_1(1 - r_{y_1y_1})}} \right]. \qquad [27]\ (7.13)$$

For adaptive-treatment placement, the optimum is located where

$$k = \sqrt{\frac{C_0(1 - r_{y_1y_1})}{C_1 r_{y_1y_1}}}. \qquad [28]\ (7.25)$$

It is to be noted that with the postulated uniform decisions the optimum bandwidth does not depend upon B_{y_1d}, but only on the cost and intercorrelations of unit tests. Even more important, the optimum number of tests has no relation to the number of decisions to be made (save as this provides an upper limit). If the optimum v is five in a given situation the decision maker should measure five dimensions, whether he is concerned with 5 decisions or 100. Moreover, we can arbitrarily define the length of a unit test, say, by adjusting it to make $r_{y_1y_1} = .10$. The optimum therefore depends entirely on the ratio C_0/C_1 for the tests under consideration.

Such exploration as this demonstrates that it is frequently profit-

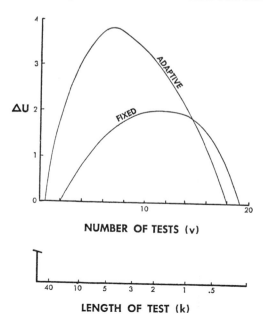

Figure 34. Relation of utility to bandwidth

able in making independent decisions to divide time among several tests rather than to devote all time to a single test. Too great a dispersion of effort, however, is just as unprofitable as too great a concentration. With uniform tests, greater bandwidth is profitable for independent, uniform decisions when there is low initial cost C_0 relative to C_1. This condition will obtain when the introduction of new dimensions can be accomplished without allowing time for new directions to the subject, practice items, etc. Personality questionnaires and interviews meet this requirement and therefore can increase bandwidth profitably; in ability measurement, setup time for new dimensions is sufficient to place greater restriction on bandwidth. The foregoing analysis assumes, however, that we cannot single out certain dimensions as being particularly important, an assumption which is contrary to fact in most selection and guidance.

Non-equivalent independent decisions. The values of $B_{y_i d}$ vary from test to test if the unit-test validities differ, or if the decisions to be made from the tests are not equally important, or involve different cutting scores, different numbers of treatments, etc. It may be seen from equations 5.6 and 5.16 that the optimal k_d increases as $B_{y_i d}$ increases, other parameters being equal, for either fixed or adaptive treatment. In general, the greater the disparity in values of $B_{y_i d}$, the more time should be given to the tests with larger B even though this reduces bandwidth. This principle requires further qualification, however, when $r_{y_i y_i}$ or the ratio C_0/C_1 changes from test to test.

Appendix 7 indicates a general solution for the optimum distribution of effort in adaptive placement which takes into account all parameters of the unit test provided one defines the unit test by fixing C_1. Then, designating the length of any one test as k_d, the gain in utility over a set of v tests is

$$\sum_{d=1}^{v} \Delta U_d = \sum_d B_{y_i d} \left[\frac{r_{y_k y_k d}}{r_{y_1 y_1 d}} \right] - \sum_d (C_{0d} + k_d C_1). \quad [29] \ (7.14)$$

The total number of test units $K = \Sigma k_d$ is defined by

$$K = \frac{C_T - \sum C_{0d}}{C_1}. \quad [30]$$

A composite parameter $D_{y_i d}$ is introduced:

$$D_{y_i d} = \frac{B_{y_i d}(1 - r_{y_1 y_1 d})}{2 C_1 r_{y_1 y_1 d}}. \quad [31] \ (7.17)$$

Then, for any specified set of v tests, the optimum length of the test for the decision d' is given by

$$k_{d'} = 1 - \frac{1}{r_{v_1 v_1 d'}} + \frac{D_{v_1 d'}}{\sum D_{v_1 d}} \left[K - v + \sum_1^v \frac{1}{r_{v_1 v_1 d}} \right]. \quad [32] \ (7.21)$$

There is a similar equation for each other test. Appendix 7 discusses an iterative procedure for comparing the utility achieved using one set of tests, with their optimal lengths, to that from another set of tests. No comparable explicit formula for k_d can be obtained for fixed treatment, because the system of equations 7.6 of the appendix has not been solved.

Horst's procedure for finding the optimal group of subtests and their appropriate length is also an iterative method, but allows the tests and criteria to be correlated so that a change in length for one test may affect the utility for all decisions. With this added complication, the optimum lengths cannot be expressed by an explicit formula such as equation [32] and must be determined by successive approximations.

Our special case gives a somewhat clearer picture of the factors affecting distribution of effort. Increase in $B_{v_1 d}$ (relative to C_1) for one particular decision increases k_d. Increase in $r_{v_1 v_1 d}$ for any d markedly decreases k_d. When tests are alike with respect to these parameters it is best to divide time evenly among them. As one test takes on greater validity or importance, other things remaining equal, it is better to give more time to that test. As the benefits from the unit tests become more unequal, a point is reached where it is more profitable to spend *all* available time on one test. For a dimension where unit tests have low intercorrelations, benefit increases greatly with length; but where the intercorrelations are high, there is little value in lengthening the test.

Koopman (1953) has made a general study of distribution of effort between two experiments. He introduces an exponential "return function" relating benefit to length of test, which is comparable to our function based on the Spearman-Brown formula. Despite this difference, his conclusions are consistent with ours.

We present a hypothetical numerical example in order to illustrate our conclusions. Suppose that there are five tests, with these respective values of $B_{v_1 d}/C_1$ and $r_{v_1 v_1 d}$ at unit length: 5, .30; 1, .30; 0.5, .30; 0.5, .10; 0.1, .10. We assume C_0 to be negligible and let $K = 20$. Computing from equation [32] gives these respective lengths: 11.2, 3.7, 2.0, 5.6, and -2.5. The negative value implies that test 5 yields insufficient benefit to be used when $K = 20$, so it must be dropped from the set. When the optimum lengths are recomputed, with $v = 4$, the values become 10.3, 3.3, 1.7, and 4.6. The values of the parameters in this example were deliberately made markedly unequal. At unit length, test 1 gives ten times as much benefit as test 3, and five times as much as test 2. In this situation their optimum lengths have the ratios 6:1 and 3:1. Test 4 and test 3 contribute the same benefit at unit length but because the unit-test intercorrelations of test 4 are smaller, it has a much greater optimum length. The lengths of the tests are ordered according to the ratio of B/C_1 to r.

Generalizations. In establishing generalizations, we pool the information derived from our analysis with that from the work of Horst and Koopman. These results apply to a single-stage battery used as a basis for terminal decisions.

1. It is generally profitable to divide testing time among many tests rather than to concentrate on a single test, when many decisions are to be made regarding the same persons.

2. Using fewer tests than there are decisions may be preferable to dividing time over all decisions. Such restriction on bandwidth becomes important under any of the following conditions: (a) the initial costs of the tests are unequal and not all negligible, (b) the contributions of the tests at equal length are markedly unequal, or (c) intercorrelations of unit tests (units being defined by equal cost C_1) are higher for some of the tests than for others.

3. For any given problem there is an optimal distribution of effort, both with respect to number of tests to be given and amount of time to be devoted to each test. Where the tests are uniform, it is wise to divide time equally among the tests given. Where the tests are not uniform, it is profitable to allow time to the tests roughly in the order of the ratio of their contribution per unit cost to the intercorrelation among unit tests.

4. It is not critically important to employ precisely the optimum length of test. Minor departures from the optimum reduce utility very little in the cases we have examined.

Our analysis confirms that there is indeed an optimal compromise between "bandwidth" and "fidelity" in testing for compound placement decisions. Similar results are to be expected for classification decisions. The validity coefficient of a test relative to a particular decision describes only one aspect of its usefulness. Where it is in competition with other tests, the amount of time to be given to it depends upon its contribution per unit cost and the correlation among units. The cumulative benefit from a series of moderately valid tests may outweigh the benefit to be expected from a smaller number of more dependable tests.

9

CLASSIFICATION DECISIONS

Classification decisions, unlike those previously discussed, are necessarily based on multivariate information. The problems associated with classification are considerably more complex than those encountered in selection and placement, and our treatment is consequently much more limited.

At present, one of the most crippling difficulties is that the ideal strategy for a classification decision involving quotas cannot be determined. A strategy has two aspects, the information-gathering procedure and the procedure for allocating men after the information is obtained. A truly optimal strategy can be designed only by considering both aspects simultaneously, and this presents mathematical difficulties of a high order, as Dwyer (1953) has pointed out. The sequential methods of Magwire which we shall discuss below offer an appropriate strategy for classification except when there are numerical quotas to be satisfied exactly in a given sample. Where sample quotas are fixed, it is presently possible to describe an ideal allocation strategy only after the test battery has been specified.

While the classification problem for fixed treatments can be described in algebraic terms, the formula describing utility contains an expression which cannot be integrated and is therefore not simply comprehended. Numerical substitution may be used to explore the functions relating utility to characteristics of the test battery, but so many parameters are involved in even the simplest classification decisions that little clarification is gained thereby.

We have therefore limited our discussion to an interpretation of previous work on classification in the language of decision theory. Our discussion brings together a variety of hitherto isolated results and raises important questions. We first describe the fixed-treatment classification problem in a form comparable to that for selection and placement, in order to examine what factors affect utility. The adaptive-treatment problem is discussed in a less technical fashion, our aim being to examine the meaning of adaptive treatment in a classification problem. The proposals of Horst (1954, 1956) regarding the design of classification or differential-prediction batteries are then considered in terms of the assumptions about the decision problem that they appear to invoke. Finally, we consider possible development of sequential methods in classification.

CLASSIFICATION WITH FIXED TREATMENTS

The most common classification problem is one in which certain fixed treatments are available, and each man is to be assigned to one of them. Each man i yields a certain payoff e_{it} under whatever treatment t he receives; with n treatments, there are n values of e_{it} for him. Some writers formulate an assignment strategy in terms of operations upon the n by n matrix of estimated e_{it}. We, however, shall consider the test scores rather than the estimated payoffs as the starting point, to obtain a formulation readily applicable to large samples.

A set of tests $y_a, y_b \ldots$ is available. We assume that payoff is a first-degree function of scores on these tests. For each treatment t, there is a linear combination of scores Y_t, determinable by multiple-regression methods, which best predicts the payoff under that treatment. The adequacy of this prediction is indicated by the multiple correlation $R_{Y_te_t}$. The several Y_t need not be uncorrelated. (For the reject treatment, payoff is assumed to be zero regardless of the test scores, but this function is merely a degenerate case of the ordinary regression equation.)

A vector notation ($\tilde{y}_i$ or $\widetilde{Y}_i$) is used to indicate the particular pattern of scores belonging to person i; for each $\tilde{y}$ there is a corresponding $\widetilde{Y}$. When treatment t is applied to a man having a given pattern of predictor scores, the estimated payoff is

$$e_{\tilde{y}_it} = e_{\widetilde{Y}_it} = \sigma_{e_t}R_{Y_te_t}Y_{it} + e_{ot} - \sum_y C_y. \qquad [33]$$

Any strategy for assignment states a complete set of values of $p_{t/\widetilde{Y}}$ or $p_{t/\tilde{y}}$. Regardless of whether the strategy employed is optimal or not, we can express as follows the total utility which is attained by using it:

$$U = \sum_t \sigma_e R_{Y_te_t} \int_{\widetilde{Y}} p_{\widetilde{Y}} p_{t/\widetilde{Y}} Y_t d\widetilde{Y} + \sum_t p_t e_{ot} - \sum_y C_y. \qquad [34]$$

The integration is over all values of $\widetilde{Y}$. In the second term, p_t is the proportion of persons assigned to the treatment. This equation applies to either fixed or adaptive quotas. In an optimal strategy, all persons having the same $\widetilde{Y}$ are assigned to the same treatment; $p_{t/\widetilde{Y}}$ is 1.00 for one treatment and 0 for all others.

For each treatment there is a payoff function having the form of equation [33]. These equations describe hyperplanes that intersect pairwise in hyperplanes of one less dimension. The intersections divide the space defined by the $\widetilde{Y}$ dimensions into regions such that for each region there is one particular treatment that gives the highest obtainable payoff for every person in the region. Where there is no quota constraint, these intersections therefore indicate the optimum strategy.

Where quotas must be satisfied, the hyperplanes must be shifted parallel to themselves in such a way that the adjusted regions contain the desired number of persons. Cardinet (1959) has developed a procedure for graphic determination of this strategy where there are just three treatments. From the estimated payoffs for the three treatments, the first centroid factor is extracted. The scores for each person on the two remaining orthogonal components are plotted. Three lines in this space indicate the locus of points where two of the estimated payoffs are equal. These would serve as boundaries of regions in the quota-free case. If fixed numerical quotas are to be satisfied, one counts the number of persons in each region. After observing which regions have too many persons and which have too few, one shifts the boundary lines in the appropriate direction parallel to themselves; to facilitate this step, Cardinet draws the lines on a plastic overlay which slides to the new position. A count is made of the number of persons added to or subtracted from each region by each shift. The position of the lines that satisfies the quotas is quickly located. This visual method will not serve where the number of treatments and the number of information dimensions are both greater than three.

Cardinet's method is particularly helpful when quotas are stated in terms of the proportion of a population to be assigned to each treatment. If the procedure is once applied to a large sample from the population, the lines that cut off the desired proportions specify the strategy to be used on all further samples, so long as the nature of the population remains constant.

The strategy assigns all persons in a certain region to t and the integral in equation [34] is equivalent to the integral of $p_{\widetilde{Y}} Y_t d\widetilde{Y}$

over that region. Y_t will not in general be normally distributed within this subgroup even when Y_t is normally distributed over all individuals. The reader may confirm this by considering the very simple case of three treatments, the third being reject and the composite scores Y_{t_1} and Y_{t_2} being uncorrelated. Suppose further that $\sigma_{e_{t_1}} R_{Y_{t_1}e_{t_1}} = \sigma_{e_{t_2}} R_{Y_{t_2}e_{t_2}}$ and that the quota $p_1 = p_2$. Then to treatment t_1 will be assigned those persons at the upper end of the y_{t_1} distribution, excepting those for whom $Y_{t_2} > Y_{t_1}$. Because of this last requirement, the distribution of Y_{t_1} for those assigned to t_1 will not be normal. The lack of normality of the Y_t distribution makes it impossible to simplify the equations for utility in classification.

To study the gain in utility and the factors that determine it, we now restrict ourselves to the fixed-quota case. The *a priori* utility is $\Sigma\, p_t e_{ot}$ and the gain in utility from testing is

$$\Delta U = \sum_t \sigma_{e_t} R_{Y_t e_t} \int_{\tilde{Y}} p_{\tilde{Y}} p_{t/\tilde{Y}} Y_t d\tilde{Y} - \sum_y C_y. \quad [35]$$

Writing $\bar{Y}_t$ for the average value of Y_t among those assigned to treatment t,

$$\Delta U = \sum_t \sigma_{e_t} R_{Y_t e_t} p_t \bar{Y}_t - \sum_y C_y. \quad [36]$$

Equation [9], which described utility in placement with fixed treatment and fixed quotas, is a special case of equation [36], since $\Delta \xi_t$ in [9] equals $p_t \bar{y}_t$. Whereas equation [9] could be evaluated directly from the tabled normal distribution, it is difficult to evaluate equation [36]. For three treatments it is possible to make use of the Pearson tables of the bivariate distribution, but the computations for even this limited case are laborious. We have not evaluated equation [36] for various values of the parameters, but we may review some of the findings of Brogden (1951) who computed, under certain special assumptions, the average utility per man selected. (See also p. 163.)

Brogden considers the selection-classification problem where some men are to be rejected and the remainder are divided among several treatments. He determines the value of decisions based on a single "general" predictor (equally correlated with outcome under every treatment) and compares this to the value obtained by using a separate "differential" predictor for each criterion. The general predictor permits rejection of the poorest men, but the men it accepts can be allocated to treatments only by chance. The differentially scored battery predicts the outcomes for the person under the several treatments and therefore, insofar as quotas permit, one can assign him to the treatment which promises the largest outcome from him. Brogden assumes zero intercorrelations among the predictor scores Y_t obtained from the differential battery, and assumes that the correlation $R_{Y_t e_t}$ between an outcome and its corresponding predictor score is the same for all treatments. Other assumptions include first-degree payoff functions, equal σ_{e_t}, and a normal distribution of Y's. The quotas are equal for all treatments other than reject.

The value of each type of battery is determined for varying numbers of treatments. Figure 35 shows the benefits obtained when the number of treatments for accepted men varies from one to five, the number of predictors in the differential battery increasing accordingly. The quota for each treatment other than reject is fixed at 20%. The validity for the general predictor with respect to each treatment is taken as .50, and each validity coefficient $R_{Y_t e_t}$ of the differential battery is .50. Where just one treatment is available for accepted men, the differential predictor is identical to the univariate one. With two treatments in addition to reject, 40% of the group is accepted. The average quality of men accepted is necessarily lower than in the first case, but the decline in ΔU is much less serious with the differentially scored battery than with the single predictor. As the number of treatments is further increased, the advantage of the differential battery becomes even more apparent. Brogden's example, one should note, assumes that differential predictors have the same level of validity as the general predictor, which is not true for differential batteries so far developed. These mathematical results, however, encourage efforts to improve differential predictors, since their potential advantage is great.

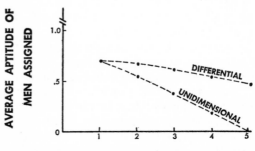

NUMBER OF TREATMENTS FOR ACCEPTED MEN (n)

Figure 35. Quality of men assigned with unidimensional and differential information

In Brogden's results it is notable that gain in utility has no simple relation to the predictive validity of the tests. The univariate predictor has the same validity as any of the differential predictors, yet the differential battery yields the greater gain in utility. Equation [34] indicates that, as we have previously found for other fixed-treatment, fixed-quota decisions, utility is a linear function of the validity coefficients. This relation, however, holds only when the assignment strategy is fixed independently of the test validities. If the validity of the battery with respect to any one treatment is altered, the payoff surfaces intersect at new positions. This should lead to a change in the assignment strategy and thus change the value of $\bar{Y}_t$. The net change in utility is therefore a quite indirect function of the change in validity.

To clarify the relation of utility to differential validity, we can express equation [36] in terms of orthogonal variables. The tests $y_a, y_b, \ldots$ may be resolved into orthogonal components $y_j = y_1, y_2, \ldots$ While any set of orthogonal components can be used for mathematical purposes, it is perhaps worthwhile to think of extracting first those components that account for the r_{ye_t}. Any components of the test battery that are uncorrelated with outcome will then disappear from the estimation equations. Equation [36] holds when the Y_{it} are predicted from the estimated y_{ij} instead of from the original test scores.

Under the assumption of a first-degree payoff surface,

$$e_{\bar{y}_i t} = \sigma_{e_t} \sum_j r_{y_j e_t} y_{ij} + e_{ot} - \sum_y C_y. \qquad [37]$$

We may introduce a special notation for the purpose of considering differential validity. Let t' be the treatment to which the man is assigned and $\bar{y}_{j(t')}$ be the average y_j among those assigned to t'. Then, by a development analogous to that for equation [36], we find that if each man is assigned to the treatment optimal for him, subject to the fixed quota constraints,

$$\Delta U = \sum_{t'} \sigma_{e_{t'}} \sum_j r_{y_j e_{t'}} p_{t'} \bar{y}_{j(t')} - \sum C_y. \qquad [38]$$

We propose to put this into another form, and in order to do so consider what the payoff would be if the persons assigned to t' were redistributed at random among the treatments t, in the proportions p_t. The fraction $p_t p_{t'}$ of the original sample would then have been assigned to t, and since their average score is described by the set of $\bar{y}_{j(t')}$ the payoff is $p_t p_{t'} e_{ot} + p_t p_{t'} \sigma_{e_t} \sum_j r_{y_j e_t} p_{t'} \bar{y}_{j(t')}$.

Summed over t, this is the *a priori* utility that would result from random assignment of this subsample. Taking all t' into account, we have in effect a random assignment of the whole population. Hence summing over all t and t' gives us the *a priori* utility

$$\sum_t p_t e_{ot} + \sum_t p_t \sigma_{e_t} \sum_{t'} \sum_j r_{y_j e_t} p_{t'} \bar{y}_{j(t')}. \qquad [39]$$

But the first term alone then represents *a priori* utility and hence the second term equals zero—as it should, since with random redistribution of the several groups of men the average of each y_j among the men assigned to each t is zero. We now alter the form, and only the form, of equation [38] by subtracting from its right member this second expression whose value is zero. After rearranging, we obtain

$$\Delta U = \sum_{t'} \sum_j p_{t'} \bar{y}_{j(t')} \sum_t p_t(\sigma_{e_{t'}} r_{y_j e_{t'}} - \sigma_{e_t} r_{y_j e_t}) - \sum_y C_y. \qquad [40]$$

This equation is analogous to equation [10] for gain in utility in placement. The term in parentheses is the difference in the slopes of the payoff functions for the specified pair of treatments with respect to a particular y_j. This equation demonstrates again the well-known fact (Wesman and Bennett, 1951) that the value of a measure for classification depends not on its ability to predict outcome within treatments, but on its interaction with treatment. We remind the reader, however, that the hyperplanes bounding the region where persons are assigned to t' shift as the validity shifts; therefore, even when the quota remains constant, $\bar{y}_{j(t')}$ varies with the validity. This complicates the relation between utility and validity.

The discussion of implications on pages 57-59 applies to classification as well as to placement. As was mentioned there, the importance of differential validity has been discussed previously, but the role of σ_e has been too little recognized. For a test (or a factor) to be used in dividing men between two treatments, it is necessary that $\sigma_e r_{ye}$ for treatment t_1 differ from the corresponding product for t_2; inequality of the correlations does not suffice. For example, suppose one predictor dimension has validities .20 and .60 for two treatments. This might seem to promise differential value, but if the respective σ_e are 3 and 1, the predictor is not useful for making assignments. Conversely, we might have thought that a factor has no differential value if its correlation with outcome is .40 for each treatment. If the variance of the two payoffs is different, however, making assignments on the basis of this factor may yield appreciable gains in utility. Analyses of outcomes expressed in standard-score form have led to oversimplified discussions of the value of a classification test solely in terms of validity coefficients. In a given practical situation, a difference of one standard deviation in outcome will not have the same value for every treatment. The importance of considering the slope of the payoff function in utility units is therefore obvious.

It will be noted that the estimation of payoffs in this section has been based on regression formulas, and that the intersection of regression surfaces has been used to determine the boundaries of assignment regions. We have avoided use of the well-known Fisherian discriminant functions because the underlying model of the discriminant function appears unsuitable for personnel decisions. The basic concept underlying the discriminant function is that a number of classes exist, to each of which a particular individual "belongs." Differences among members of a given class are disregarded. This function divides the score space into regions so as to maximize the probability of "correct" classification of each individual. It is possible to weight errors of a given type or to specify acceptable Neyman-Pearson risks for each of the possible types of misclassification. The regression model, on the other hand, is consistent with the view that there is no uniform cost of assigning a person "belonging in category A" to category B. Instead, the cost depends upon the pattern of scores. The theory of the geneticist is based on discrete classes such as species, and it is meaningless for him to speak of different payoffs from allocating different members of the same class in the same way. Here, the discriminant function is fully appropriate. The model is much less appropriate in personnel decisions where there is no theory of qualitatively different types of persons. Even in clinical diagnosis where categorical labels are commonly used, the discriminant function is probably unsuited. Calling a person "schizophrenic" means that a certain treatment will be applied. One expects variation in the response of these "schizophrenics" to the treatment, a variation that is in principle predictable by means of a payoff function. This variation should be taken into account in developing the classification strategy.

The foregoing section may be summarized as follows. By assuming that payoff under any treatment is a first-degree function of test scores, we arrive at an equation for gain in utility which shows that the value of a testing procedure depends in a complex manner on the quotas, the several validity coefficients for each test, and the dispersion of payoffs under each treatment. This relationship is a general one, of which the expressions relating gain in utility to validity in selection and placement are special cases. The general case is far too complicated to justify the generalization that increases in validity bring proportionate increases in benefit from testing. Laborious calculations for specific sets of parameters would be required to establish the true shape of such functions in classification.

CLASSIFICATION WITH ADAPTIVE TREATMENT

In both selection and placement, the concept of adaptive treatment led to significant findings. We therefore have inquired how adaptive-treatment classification could be defined, even though we do not go on to develop formulas for this case.

It has been customary in job classification, clinical diagnosis, etc., to think of each treatment as discrete and qualitatively different from the alternatives. While qualitative differences distinguish such pairs of treatments as lobotomy and psychotherapy, in many other personnel decisions we may think of a continuous multidimensional manifold of treatments (cf. pp. 27-29). Thus, while parole and continued imprisonment seem at first glance to be qualitatively different, one may conceive of a continuum between strict incarceration and freedom. Intermediate stages include relaxation of supervision in prison, furloughs, and parole with mandatory reporting. The full range of possible treatments can be characterized only by considering many dimensions; besides degree of liberty, there can be variation in the amount of education and rehabilitation offered, the degree of sympathy displayed by supervisors, and other aspects of the treatment.

This concept of adaptation is relevant to most areas of applied psychology where treatments have hitherto been viewed as discrete and unordered. Teaching methods certainly may vary by degrees along such continua as amount of active practice, rapidity of pacing, and amount of explanation. Between jobs there is often a similar series of intermediate possibilities combining the features of the several jobs in various degrees. In the Strong Vocational Interest Blank, for example, chemist and author-journalist seem like divergent vocational paths, but there exist intermediate opportunities such as science reporter or editor of chemical reports. Strong's factor analyses of interests indeed may be regarded as identifying some of the continua along which occupations (i.e., treatments) differ.

Whether treatments can be adapted will depend on the situation. Often, although it is impossible to adapt treatment to each individual, it is possible to adapt to the average level of aptitude in each group. Therefore, as in selection (see p. 49), the ultimate aim of research becomes the discovery of the best combination of treatment categories and classification procedures, within whatever practical constraints exist.

In order to examine adaptive classification formally, it would be necessary to introduce aptitude dimensions s_1, s_2. . . . This could be done simply by defining each s as the "true score" on one of the orthogonal y dimensions previously discussed, so that $r_{ye_i} = r_{ys}r_{se_i}$ for each corresponding y and s. A person's pattern of s scores is independent of the lengths of the tests used to measure his y pattern. In placement, the treatment was characterized by the slope of the payoff function with respect to a single s dimension. When there are several s dimensions, the payoff function for each treatment has a slope with respect to each of these dimensions. The nature of the continuous payoff surface involving all treatments and all dimensions is therefore much more complicated than in placement. Since at present we have no empirical facts about even the simple surfaces involved in adaptive placement, it would be unduly speculative to consider what form the surface for a classification problem might take. Ultimately it should be possible to choose reasonable assumptions and to derive the relations between utility, the characteristics of the decision problem, and the tests employed.

DESIGN OF TESTING PROCEDURES

Single-Stage Batteries

How to design a test battery that will be maximally efficient for the classification of personnel is a problem of great importance, for which only Horst has offered solutions. By examining what assumptions about the decision problem his model entails, we can provide a partial basis for evaluating them. His two proposals deal with constructing the best batteries for "multiple absolute prediction" (Horst and MacEwan, 1956, 1957) and "differential prediction" (Horst, 1956). We have already seen (p. 100) that the former procedure is designed to select the subset of tests that will maximize $\sum_t R^2_{Y_t e_t}$. This is an appropriate index of gain in utility in compound adaptive placement, where several treatments will be given to each individual, each treatment being adjusted to his ability on one dimension. Horst's other proposal is to select tests which maximize the sum of the squared "differential validities" of the test battery. A differential validity coefficient indicates how well the given tests can predict differences in payoff between two treatments, that is, it is the correlation between the difference in payoff and the best "least-square" estimate of that difference obtained from a test battery. Horst shows that for standardized criterion scores, this index of differential prediction is equivalent to maximizing the difference between the average predicted variance and the average predicted covariance of criterion scores. By simple analogy to the compound adaptive placement problem, we can immediately place one interpretation on the Horst "differential-prediction" procedure. This procedure minimizes the sum of squared errors of estimates of criterion differences, whereas the "absolute-prediction" procedure minimizes the same errors for the original criteria. This formula then does arrive at the best battery for a series of compound decisions, where each decision depends on the measured difference between two criterion scores. Every pair of differences is taken into account successively in determining the series of treatments for the individual.

This does not appear very similar to the usual classification problem. Only in quota-free adaptive placement (measurement) was the gain related to the squared error of measurement of a single variable; Horst's index therefore appears most likely to apply to adaptive classification where every person can be treated differently. Certainly his procedure does not provide the ideal battery for fixed-treatment classification. In this case, as equation [36] makes clear, utility is a function of the R_{Ye} rather than their squares, and the boundaries between regions must enter into the determination of utility. The Horst solution, moreover, makes no adequate provision for a reject group who receive no courses, job assignments, etc. Thus his analysis would apply only when all individuals tested are to be utilized.

Perhaps a generalized payoff function for an adaptive-treatment problem could be found such that gain in utility would be proportional to the sum of squared errors that constitutes Horst's index. This would require that the payoffs under various criteria have equal variances, that the criterion dimensions have equal weight, and that the summed cross-products of errors be unimportant. It appears that only in a very special case will Horst's index be exactly proportional to gain in utility.

Horst has offered the only systematic procedure for maximizing the efficiency of a classification battery, and thus has taken an important pioneering step. The function used to define efficiency does not correspond clearly to any common type of decision problem, and it is demonstrably not the correct function for the fixed-treatment example to which Horst applies the method. Further work may show that Horst's method is a useful approximation for cases where some other efficiency index would be preferable on logical grounds.

Sequential Testing

Sequential methods should be especially advantageous in classification because a large number of dimensions are usually involved and exhaustive measurement is out of the question. Often a limited amount of information will serve to eliminate a number of treatments from consideration, and to indicate one or two of the dimensions as especially critical in choosing among the remaining treatments. If, for example, a general aptitude battery consisting of a series of short tests shows that person i stands high on the aptitudes required for jobs A and B, the next stage of testing can concentrate on whatever aptitudes differentiate A from B. For another person having a different pattern on the general battery, quite different tests would be relevant to the final decision. Such sequential testing in which the second stage is tailored for the individual should be more efficient than a non-sequential plan.

Some of the basic theory for multidimensional sequential testing can be derived from an unpublished paper by Magwire (1953). He was investigating "the sequential choice of experiments," but his methods appear to be directly applicable to testing of individuals. He states the decision problem in a general form. A number of tests are available. After any stage of testing, the individual may be assigned to a fixed treatment or may be held for further testing. At each stage of testing the person's expected payoff under each treatment can be estimated. If the payoff under one treatment is greater than would probably be obtained by testing him further, thus arriving at a more certainly correct decision but incurring additional costs of testing, a terminal decision is made. Wherever it is profitable to test further, Magwire's procedure indicates which test should be given next. The procedures developed are a generalization of Wald's recursion formula (1950), and take into account the payoff functions and the cost of testing.

From Magwire's work it appears possible to develop an ideal sequential strategy for the quota-free fixed-treatment case which is often encountered in guidance or diagnosis. A strategy can also be developed for the case where population quotas are fixed, provided that the population distribution is known. Where a finite numerical quota must be exactly satisfied in a particular sample, however, Magwire's solution would not apply. No use of Magwire's formula in actual computations has been reported, and the computations may prove far too laborious for practical use. Even so, the theory opens the way to generalizations regarding the design of sequential procedures and may serve as a base for computational shortcuts and approximations.

10

EVALUATION OF OUTCOMES

The assignment of values to outcomes is the Achilles' heel of decision theory. Once outcomes have been evaluated, one can proceed in a fully rigorous fashion to compare particular decisions or general strategies. The evaluation of outcomes, however, seems often to be arbitrary and subjective, leading one to question whether any of the conclusions from decision theory can be trustworthy if the starting point itself is open to dispute.

The most telling answer to this objection is to point out that decision theory invokes no more subjective evaluation than does any method of arriving at courses of action. Every choice between actions involves evaluations, and every doctrine or set of principles embodies value judgments. Decision theory is no more dependent on evaluation than is traditional measurement theory or discriminant analysis. The unique feature of decision theory or utility theory is that it specifies evaluations by means of a payoff matrix or by conversion of the criterion to utility units. The values are thus plainly revealed and open to criticism. This is an asset rather than a defect of this system, as compared with systems where value judgments are imbedded and often pass unrecognized.

It is always difficult to set down a payoff matrix assigning comparable values to all the consequences of a decision, as those who have applied game theory to military strategy have discovered. Comparing the value of bombing an enemy city to the value of preventing a flood at home seems absurd because, at first glance, these events are incommensurable. The comparison is required, however, by the fact that a single act (e.g., shifting engineers from dam construction to airfield construction) enhances the probability of one outcome at the expense of the other. Whoever decides on such an act is weighing the "incommensurables" on the same balance, whether he does so consciously or not. Personnel decisions likewise require a balancing of seemingly non-comparable outcomes. The personnel manager may let a humanitarian outcome such as the self-respect of an aging worker offset tangible losses in production. A school may select students on the basis of factors (e.g., religion, social class) that have no relation to probable academic achievement; in so doing, the policy maker is allowing outcomes other than achievement to compensate him for the fact that he is not securing the best possible students.

In clinical decisions, the outcomes include the duration of treatment, the amount of staff effort absorbed, and the contribution (or cost) of the patient to the community after release. It is at this point that the "balance sheet" concept seems discordant with the humanitarian purpose of the institution. The decisions made, however, must consider the community welfare. "We had better take this patient in, to relieve strain on his family"; "We had better use our space on cases where there is greater prospect of recovery"; "We cannot invest this much therapeutic time on a single patient"; "This treatment does not cure, but it makes the patient more manageable"—all these statements reflect an intention to obtain maximum advantage for minimum cost. Nor is this incompatible with concern for the patient's welfare. If it wishes, the institution may include the patient's expressed feeling of well-being in its evaluations. The critical point is that the institution must still balance this against other outcomes; cheerfulness purchased at the price of delaying the patient's becoming independent may be a bad bargain.

Much attention has been given to the logic of evaluation and to procedures for making estimates of value (see Adams, 1960; Arrow, 1963; Smith *et al.*, 1953; see also p. 159), but these difficult problems have not been handled as successfully as the choice of strategy once values are assigned. The progress to date consists largely in defining the problem of evaluation and distinguishing among different approaches to the problem. We shall review these possibilities as they might be applied to personnel decisions.

Attention was drawn in Chapter 2 to differences between "institutional" and "individual" decisions. In the former, a single decision maker is concerned with a large number of decisions of the same sort, and a reasonable meaning can be given to the concept of the total utility of a set of decisions, since all the decisions are evaluated by the same payoff matrix. The individual decision, on the other hand, must be evaluated by the individual's personal payoff matrix, and the same person rarely confronts the same decision repeatedly. There have been attempts to formulate strategies that take into account simultaneously the welfare of many individual decision makers. Such "welfare economics" cannot be developed save by the introduction of some superevaluation which provides a rule for balancing one man's satisfaction against another's dissatisfaction (Arrow, 1963). Any one such rule can be defended against another only in terms of the judgment of some superordinate decision maker. It follows that the individual decision can be considered only as an isolated event, for which any concept of "averaging outcomes" over many decisions is inappropriate. Since additive utilities have been assumed throughout our previous chapters, it is most important here to consider evaluation for institutional decisions.

INSTITUTIONAL EVALUATION OF OUTCOMES

Comprehensiveness of Evaluations

Although it is a truism to say that in evaluating a decision all outcomes must be taken into account, the principle is deserving of some discussion. Employment decisions are commonly validated solely against some measure of the proficiency or rate of performance of the men accepted. There are, however, many other consequences: some number of beneficial suggestions or acts of leadership, some costs of training and supervision (see Doppelt and Bennett, 1953), some degree of absenteeism and some spoilage of materials.

The variety of consequences of a decision is well illustrated by the studies of Raines *et al.* (1954), who attempted to determine the value to the Navy of a neuropsychiatric screening program. Among the consequences for which actual criterion data could be obtained were frequency of subsequent psychiatric discharges, frequency of bad conduct discharges, amount of time spent in hospital, and frequency of disciplinary offenses. In addition, they point out (pp. 820-821) that there are probable differences between screened and unscreened men in proficiency and efficiency of job performance:

> In estimating the cost to the military services of utilizing marginally adjusted men, the assumption is sometimes made that this cost involves solely those men who are discharged before they complete their required period of service. It is taken for granted that, if a marginal recruit manages to complete his enlistment and to receive an honorable discharge at the end of his term, his service is *ipso facto* successful and he has demonstrated his worth to the service. Unfortunately, completion of service without discharge is no guarantee of the quality of the service rendered.
>
> . . . These results . . . show that such [marginal] men are more "expensive" to the services, and that when their utilization is demanded by manpower needs it will be necessary to make provision for the added

demands they will entail upon medical and disciplinary facilities. They also confirm the clinical picture of the maladjusted individual as one who, even when he is meeting the formal adjustment standards of his group, is doing so at a greater cost to the group's medical facilities and with greater friction upon its social organization than is his adjusted compatriot.

It is important to note how this detailed analysis differs from the evaluation employed by Taylor and Russell, or others who count hits, misses, and false positives. In this situation, the data clearly indicate wide differences in the quality of service among successful men, and since these differences are predicted by the screening procedure they have to be given a place in the evaluation system.

Goodman's discussion of the parole situation (1953) exemplifies an even more comprehensive consideration of outcomes. The purpose of the prison system is to benefit society as a whole, and the parole board must take into account all the social consequences of its decision. If the man is paroled, he contributes to the community economy through his work, his supervision by a probation officer costs so much, he perhaps commits a new crime that has both direct and indirect costs, his children are better (or worse) citizens by virtue of his presence in the home, etc. For the man not paroled, the above outcomes arise with some altered probability when his term ends, and there is in addition the cost of his longer imprisonment to consider. To such direct outcomes must be added the indirect effect of a parole decision on the conduct of the remaining prisoners and on potential criminals in the community. Finally, the parole board gives some weight to purely human sympathy for the prisoner and his family.

It is not easy to place a value on all these consequences of a decision, especially as the effects extend indefinitely in time. In practice, it is necessary to simplify the problem. One possibility is to drop from consideration any consequences of minor importance to the institution before proceeding to more systematic evaluation. If various desirable outcomes are correlated substantially with each other, one need be little concerned to observe all outcomes since a decision rule which maximizes one of them would tend to maximize the others, and a simple weighting can account for the value of those not observed.

In many situations, however, some of the important outcomes have low intercorrelations. Amount of production per hour may be negatively related to job tenure, if there are ample opportunities for able people to find better-paying jobs. There may be a zero correlation between production and promotability, if supervision calls for different talents than routine operation. For this reason one cannot be satisfied with validating testing procedures against a single production criterion, nor with the assumption that perfect prediction of such a criterion would by itself provide the basis for an ideal selection system.

Combination of Outcomes by Empirical Analysis

Data from multiple criteria must be reduced to a single cardinal or ordinal scale to permit decision making. That is, the various patterns of outcome must be arranged to indicate, between any two possibilities, which is preferred. Sometimes one can identify an obvious reference scale that represents the aims of the institution and can reduce other data to it. Brogden and Taylor (1950) argue that in most business management the ultimate standard for judging decisions is the "dollar criterion" of the balance sheet. Some firms might deny this, insisting that preservation of certain traditions or of harmonious relations with the workers comes ahead of profit considerations. Even in these cases, however, the balance sheet provides a convenient yardstick, since there is undoubtedly some point short of bankruptcy where the firm would become concerned with income even at the sacrifice of "intangible" values, and thus the exchange rate for these intangibles can be inferred. It is not necessary that an actual criterion be accepted as primary; some abstract scale of utility may be the common metric to which all outcomes are commuted.

Value judgments are inevitable at some point in the statement of payoffs, but the number of judgments employed should be as small as possible to avoid inconsistencies in the system. Often the number of judgments can be reduced by accounting procedures, that is, by careful empirical observation. If the sole reason for concern with spoilage, for example, is the cost of reworking or discarding the material, then a careful record of such costs indicates the seriousness of the spoilage. Brogden and Taylor describe in detail the logical and observational steps required to locate other outcomes on the "dollar criterion" scale. Military personnel decisions perhaps allow for similar accounting, since one might hope to translate certain proficiency standards into their consequent contributions to fighting power. The important outcomes of combat morale and combat efficiency are difficult to observe even in wartime, however, and cannot be studied empirically during peace. Comprehensive empirical accounting is likewise impeded by the geographical spread of military operations. It is therefore apparent that judgment will play a greater part in military than in business evaluations. The difficulties become even more overwhelming as we turn to educational and clinical institutions that seek to create long-lasting changes in people, changes of diverse kinds and with diffuse effects.

The outcomes of personnel decisions are often expressed on arbitrary scales (e.g., ratings or standard scores on proficiency measures). For evaluation it is necessary to interpret these in relation to units of production or some other absolute scale. A man's contribution depends on the quality of his performance summed over the duration of that performance. A statement in such absolute terms is required not only to take into account differences in job tenure, but also to provide an absolute estimate of benefit against which to weigh the absolute costs of the information-gathering procedure.

At first glance costs of testing and interviewing appear trivial when compared to gains in production over an extended period. More careful reasoning indicates that these costs cannot be disregarded. Experience from detailed accounting in connection with industrial inspection procedures is relevant (Freeman *et al.*, 1948). The cost of an act of inspection is very small, and the benefit from improved quality is substantial. Nonetheless, the costs of 100% inspection frequently outweigh the benefits. It was to restore this balance that sequential methods were invented, and they were regarded as having such great dollars-and-cents value that for several years they were classified as a military secret. Common sense itself provides an argument for considering costs of tests carefully. Since testing procedures do improve the quality of workers assigned to jobs, and since validity rises with length, if cost were truly negligible we would be wise to lengthen tests indefinitely. The absurdity of this proposal implies at once that there is a point of diminishing returns where costs begin to outweigh increases in quality. The best strategy for gathering information can only be determined by precise data on costs of testing.

Inferring Values from Decisions

The theory of utility scales has been built up from two somewhat different points of view, one concerned with eliciting direct statements of values from the decision maker, and one concerned with inferring his values from the decisions he makes. Either of these approaches can be applied to the study of personnel decisions.

The inferential approach employs the decision model in an inverse fashion. If one knows what decision a person has made in a great number of instances, then it is possible to determine what set of values is most consistent with these choices. Logically, this requires the assumption that the decision maker is following the correct strategy (except for random variation) for some set of values. A simple example of such reasoning may be taken from a study of a screening test presented elsewhere (Cronbach, 1953). This test was evaluated by its authors on the basis of the proportion of persons at each score who later succeeded or failed; the limitations of that procedure may be disregarded for the purposes of the present example. Their tabulation, after smoothing, indicates that in the recruit population the probability of success at certain score levels is as follows: at 4, 95%; at 7, 88%; at 9, 70%; at 10, 50%. Then if a given user of the test who is not subject to quota constraints applies a cutting score of 10, rejecting men with that score and above, we observe that he will accept a subgroup with a success rate of 70% but not one with 50% successes. For him, the balance point is somewhere around a success rate of 60%. Since, for him, 60 successes balance 40 failures, we can say that the value of a success (relative to the zero value obtained from the rejects) is two-thirds of the cost associated with accepting a failure. For a decision maker who applies a cutting score of 9, this fraction is about one-third. He regards acceptance of a man who will fail more seriously than the decision maker who sets a higher cutting score.

This method, of course, does not establish what the relative values of the outcomes ought to be; it says only that the decision maker is acting *as if* he accepted those values. The decision maker, confronted with this information about his operations, is free to deny the appropriateness of these values. If he does, the next step is to obtain a statement of his values and translate this into a strategy which will differ from the one now in use.

A posteriori interpretation of the values which are consistent with an action sometimes throws an interesting light on decisions. Sarbin (1942), in a well-known study, reported the predictions of student grade averages made by college counselors. One important finding was that these counselors consistently overestimated the students' probable grades; Sarbin regards this as a constant error or bias. This interpretation is sound if the quality of a judgment is evaluated by the absolute error of estimate. But if we hypothesize instead that the judgments are rational, we seek the evaluation system within which such "biased" judgments maximize utility.

Assuming that the counselor may expect to have a symmetrically distributed error of estimate, it is sound strategy to have a mean error greater than zero if he regards overestimates as less serious than numerically equal underestimates. It is indeed possible to calculate a set of values for over- and underestimates which would in this way rationalize any particular "constant error." It then remains to inquire whether one could reasonably regard underestimates as more serious. A counselor might contend that the underestimate has serious social consequences: it discourages the student and causes him to expect a lower standard of achievement from himself, perhaps to try less hard and to earn lower grades, perhaps even to drop out of school in view of his unsatisfactory prospects. The overestimate leads to false hopes, but the student will remain in school and obtain a valuable education even if his ultimate grades do disappoint him. Having read this casuistry (see Smith *et al.*, 1953, on the application of this term), the reader has perhaps already developed for himself a counter-argument to defend the greater seriousness in college counseling of overestimates. This is precisely the point of the example. If one judge prefers to emphasize one outcome and a second prefers to emphasize another, there is no scientific or logical basis to defend one emphasis over the other. The "obvious" assumption that overestimates are equal in seriousness to underestimates, that is, that the numerical magnitude of the error is the criterion of cost, is itself based on value judgments and has no special justification over the other possibilities. This reiterates one of our fundamental theses: when mathematical formulas are used as guides to policy making they carry hidden value judgments that the decision maker might be unwilling to accept if he considered them explicitly.

Extensive laboratory experiments have been made to infer value systems from behavior, chiefly in gambling (Edwards, 1954; see also p. 159). These studies support the view that individuals or cultural groups have characteristic patterns of action that are consistent with different systems of values. All of these studies may be regarded as developing techniques that could be applied to important institutional decisions. At best, however, inferential procedures merely distill out values for examination. To provide a basis for future conduct, an explicit acceptance or revision of these values by the decision maker is required.

Explicit Value Judgments

Explicit judgments might be obtained by asking the person to state how many utility units each outcome is worth on his personal value scale. These judgments are, however, quite difficult to make and if the judgments are obtained repeatedly there will be variation in the evaluation of an outcome and inconsistency in the information about different outcomes. The most common procedure to improve the estimation of values is to employ some method of psychophysical scaling. These methods give a satisfactory degree of reliability, although it is often necessary to suppress certain inconsistencies in the data by describing them as "error" (Coombs, 1953). Churchman and Ackoff (1954) report the use of such techniques to arrive at statements of institutional values in business; each of the examples has its parallel in personnel decisions. One firm required a quality control strategy for inspection of penicillin packages. There were eight possible types of defects, and a comparison of their seriousness was required to specify the inspection procedure so as to minimize overall risk for a given expenditure of effort. Nine persons carrying responsibility in the corporation (i.e., institutional spokesmen) participated in a scaling experiment, and from their responses a composite evaluation was established. Precisely comparable questions are involved in planning a personnel testing program where a decision must be made as to the relative importance of such various aspects of the criterion as carefulness, speed, ingenuity, stability, and leadership. A second firm described by Churchman and Ackoff was engaged in long-range planning, and used scaling methods to compare various "intangible" objectives of company policy. There is considerable similarity between this problem and that of comparing educational methods whose outcomes differ both quantitatively and qualitatively.

The problem for which comparison of outcomes seems of most immediate importance is that of classification. All schemes for differential assignment assume at some point that the outcomes for the various jobs are evaluated on the same scale. Sometimes as a stopgap all criteria are reduced to standard scores, but, as we noted in the previous chapter, this is unsatisfactory. Before such methods as those of Dwyer, Cardinet, or Votaw and Dailey can be applied, then, it will be necessary to obtain judgments of the importance of the jobs to the institution. Attention will also need to be given to the scaling of any single criterion. The assumption regularly made, that equal units on a criterion scale represent equal increments of value, is demonstrably false in some instances and open to question in all.

EVALUATION FOR INDIVIDUAL DECISIONS

Where a decision has a single definite outcome or configuration of outcomes, the decision maker has only to compare that result with the result of alternative decisions. No logical distinction need be made between the individual and institutional decision. Where a series of decisions is to be made, the problem becomes one of finding the correct general decision rule or strategy. The institution will evaluate each of these decisions on the same scale of values, and if that scale is one of equal intervals, the value of the set of decisions may be obtained by summation. This procedure for comparing one set of decisions to another has been the basis for all mathematical studies in the preceding chapters. In the individual decision, it is not possible to choose between courses of action save on the basis of the values of the one to whom the decision pertains. In a group of students seeking vocational counseling, the decision for each must be evaluated on a different scale of values. Since the student will make a particular choice only once, it is manifestly impossible to seek a strategy that is superior on the average, for the average has no meaningful definition. A particular decision must be evaluated on the basis of the expected outcome and its value for this individual.

One might ultimately evaluate a decision by its actual outcome, but this appears inappropriate since factors beyond the ken of the decision maker influence the ultimate event. He might make a quite correct judgment in terms of his values and all ascertainable facts, which would nonetheless prove to be "wrong" when examined with hindsight. One's theory must make a place for the fact that the consequences of a given decision are almost never certain. Instead, with each decision is associated a certain probability distribution of expected consequences. Of two decisions, that one is preferable for which the total distribution is preferable. Since we deny the possibility of repeating the decision many times, it is meaningless to inquire which policy would lead to the greatest total utility over many applications. The judgment must be made on the distribution, not on its average.

This is a point worthy of some emphasis, because here again the transfer of statistical concepts developed for testing scientific hypotheses to decision making has led to some misconceptions. In the literature on counseling, one finds numerous references to the responsibility of the counselor for helping the client make the right decision. The "right decision" is almost invariably interpreted as being that course of action in which his mean expectancy of success is greatest. This viewpoint has two faults. One is the implicit assumption that one particular decision is best for all persons having the same pattern of test scores. Our discussion of individual evaluations implies that two students might draw different conclusions from the same data and both be correct. Second, the assumption that the mean of the distribution of outcomes is the proper index must be questioned.

This problem may be considered most satisfactorily if we restrict ourselves to the simple problem of choice of curricula, where success is to be judged by grade average. Test scores might predict that a student's most probable grade average is 2.5 in curriculum A and 3.0 in curriculum B, 4.0 being the highest grade attainable. Since a choice of one curriculum may involve denial of important elements in his self-concept, or may lead toward a career which the student believes he would not enjoy, it is clear at the outset that success is unlikely to be the only criterion. When the student's values are taken into account, we may find that a 2.5 average in A will actually be more rewarding to him than a 3.0 average in B. But assume for the moment that these averages *qua* averages are equally appealing; there still remains the question of the probability distribution. Suppose that the grade average in curriculum A is difficult to predict, so that there is a large standard error of estimate. Then perhaps there is a probability of .10 of grades in the interval 3.25-3.75 in curriculum A, along with an equal probability of grades in the interval 1.25-1.75. On the other hand (to simplify), the probability may be 1.00 of a grade between 2.75 and 3.25 in curriculum B. With these alternatives, one student may prefer the former alternative, having confidence in his ability to take advantage of the one chance in ten which would give him a very good record. Another, wishing to avoid risk, would prefer curriculum B. The choice between distributions, that is, between hazards, rests on personality factors and affective responses. In a choice such as this, it is impossible for anyone save the decision maker himself to determine the "correct" conclusion.

This was recognized some time ago in the influential statement of Bordin and Bixler (1946). They point out that the counselor, equipped with facts, can help the student recognize the probabilities attendant upon each choice. In contrast to predecessors who spoke of the counselor as telling the student the correct course of action, they left the full responsibility for choice upon the student. While their argument was based on a theory regarding the way a person learns about himself, and perhaps on a view regarding the ethics of interpersonal relations, we now supplement their reasoning with the mathematical argument that "the correct course of action" can be defined only by the person whom the decision affects.

Viewing the decision process formally as one in which information is combined with an evaluation system and knowledge of probable outcomes leads to another suggestion regarding counseling. The literature on counseling has placed great emphasis on the collecting of information and the statement of probable outcomes. However important it is to correct the client's misconceptions regarding the probable outcomes of various decisions, this is just one side of the decision process. An equally important determiner of the utility of the decision is whether the client brings to bear a consistent and fully acceptable value system. By "fully acceptable," we mean fully acceptable to himself—consistent within itself and consistent also with his hidden, even repressed attitudes toward the world. A great deal has been written on the counseling process as a realistic self-examination, a disclosure of aptitudes and weaknesses. Clearly, it must be equally concerned with bringing the person to full awareness of his own true values.

Those who have proposed follow-up studies to evaluate the counseling process have been most concerned with the client's growth in "objective self-knowledge" (i.e., knowledge of the probable outcomes of his decisions) and with the "success" of those decisions as judged by some objective standard. But one of the main contributions of the counseling process may be to alter the person's verbalized value systems, particularly by eliminating contradictions between various wishes and hopes. It seems worthwhile therefore to study how the client's evaluation system itself changes during counseling. No one can say whether a given change is "good" or "bad," since a person is the judge of his own values. In view of the central place they play in the decision process, however, any knowledge of the nature and development of such personal evaluation systems could be helpful.

11

THE IMPORTANCE OF DECISION THEORY

The applied psychologist may regard test theory as but a means to his ends, a series of mathematical rules which help him to refine his procedures. Although test theory does have this function in psychology, it plays a far more important role as a sort of Gray Eminence, constantly and silently shaping the ends themselves. For test theory is both a source and an embodiment of the values that direct operations involving tests.

THE PRACTICAL POWER OF TEST THEORY

It is not too fantastic to regard test theory as exercising a control over its field comparable to that of an economic theory or a religious code over the institutions of a culture. Institutions are formed by the daily transactions of the culture, and in these transactions the participants act first of all to satisfy their needs and values. But the code they accept brings certain values strongly to mind and thus has a deciding influence in many choices. Institutions consistent with the ostensible values receive steady encouragement, and institutions that serve other values are viewed with suspicion. Institutions for relieving needs that the code ignores can emerge only by fighting their way against the current, as it were.

A theory or code, setting forth values and assumptions explicitly, makes conformity easy. But it also displays these assumptions in full light where their inadequacies and inconsistencies can be seen and repaired. It is the task of the philosopher, economist, or political theorist to clarify issues and expose fundamental faults in the cultural system. All great historical reforms have stemmed from such revision of value assumptions. A fundamental revision of test theory will affect testing practice in the same manner that a fundamental change in political theory affects daily life in the nation that adopts it.

Test theory exercises its strongest effect by censoring new test offerings. A new clinical technique may have a dazzling debut, arousing all manner of fluttering hopes among the young clinicians who flock around her. But off in the corner of the ballroom are the test critics, severely observing the goings-on and grimly preparing their report on the young darling's character and accomplishments. Only recently have the chaperons been armed with an "official" statement of technical recommendations by which a young test is to be judged, but these standards merely formalize what has long been conveyed in books on testing, in test reviews, and in training courses. This code has made and broken reputations. While a particular test frowned on by the reviewers may attain great popularity and prosper for a time in a demimondaine existence, such popularity is transient. A stable place in society is awarded only to tests that have the critics' sanction.

To speak of social and philosophical aspects of test theory, and to question the objectivity of test criticism, must astonish those who regard test theory as but a special type of mathematics. Mathematics we esteem as eternal and impeccable, one of the few embodiments of universal logic. But all mathematics rests on postulates, and while the deductions have a universal and objective character the postulates do not. Postulates are only a formal description of a situation, and in an applied problem they describe the situation as perceived by a particular observer. If we can find a satisfactory description which differs from the traditional one, mathematics permits us to erect a new theory contradicting the old at many points.

A new test theory will have numerous practical consequences. It may, for example, ultimately offer a different formula or procedure for determining which items should be retained in a test. It will certainly modify the evaluation of particular testing instruments. But what is of far greater significance is that it may channel testing effort in new directions and open new areas of psychology to cultivation. Traditional theory has encouraged those types of tests which meet the traditional criteria, and as a result the possibilities of general intelligence tests and of achievement tests have been exploited to a high degree. Other types of tests have performed badly by the classical criteria, and psychologists have been discouraged from developing further tests of these types. At present, for example, there is great skepticism in certain circles regarding the practical usefulness of personality tests of every description, and of many types of specialized aptitude test. The development of a new variety of test drags to a halt when it proves unable to satisfy the demands of measurement theory. Any alteration in those demands may lower the esteem in which the previously successful tests are held, and raise hopes for some varieties which could not meet the old criteria. To forecast what new measurements may result from adoption of decision theory is impossible, but we may hope for such developments just as we would hope for new crops to flourish in a region where the climate changes.

DECISION THEORY COMPARED TO ALTERNATIVE MODELS

Since the beginning of the mental testing movement, the psychologist and educator have relied on one particular description of the testing process. The classic presentations of this theory are Kelley's *Statistical method* (1923a) and Gulliksen's *Theory of mental tests* (1950). These volumes offer a whole series of techniques of test construction, formulas for combining test scores, and theorems regarding the value of tests singly or in combination. Improvements in test technique during the past 50 years have been victories over defects exposed by this theory—over subjectivity in scoring, over inadequate sampling of an ability domain, over excessive overlap between tests, etc. These important advances demonstrate the merit of this theory. Since any theory must emphasize some values at the expense of others, however, it may not give the appropriate answers to all testing problems, and our alternative theory has drawn attention to several such inadequacies.

The traditional theory views the test as a measuring instrument intended to assign accurate numerical values to some quantitative attribute of the individual. It therefore stresses, as the prime value, precision of measurement and estimation. The roots of this theory lie in surveying and astronomy, where quantitative determinations are the chief aim. In physical science, in the biometrics which was the forerunner of differential psychology, and to an increasing degree in contemporary psychological research, instruments are used for estimating quantitative variables. In pure science it is reasonable to regard the value of a measurement as proportional to its ability to reduce uncertainty about the true value of some quantity. The mean square error is a useful index of measuring power. There is little basis for contending that one error is more serious than another of equal magnitude when locating stars or determining melting points; measurement theory is unobjectionable when applied to such appropriate situations. (But see p. 153 ff.)

In practical testing, however, a quantitative estimate is not the real desideratum. A choice between two or more discrete treatments must be made. The tester is to allocate each person to the proper category, and accuracy of measurement is valuable only insofar as it aids in this qualitative decision. This view of testing as an aid to decision making is not unique to psychology. When a physical measuring instrument is used to control an industrial process, decision theory is more satisfactory than measurement theory for its evaluation.

Attention in traditional test theory has centered on a particular measuring instrument which is applied in the same manner to all persons. One speaks, therefore, of the validity or error of measurement of a test. When testing is seen as an aid to decision making, one recognizes that different information may be required for different individuals. The conventional questions about "a test" do not apply to a sequential procedure. Since we cannot speak of the validity of a test that differs for every person, we must speak of the efficiency of the entire decision-making procedure.

The unsuitability of measurement theory for practical psychological testing was hinted at as long ago as 1928, when Hull noted inconsistencies between measurement theory and the logic of selection problems. This discrepancy has repeatedly returned to attention, notably in the writings of Taylor and Russell and Brogden. They considered the selection problem as a choice between two alternative treatments, and arrived at conclusions inconsistent with the classical theory. Although these papers dealt with selection as an isolated problem, we may see it as one special type of personnel decision. These papers, challenging widely held beliefs as they did, may be regarded as the first ripples in a cascade of developments that follow when we consider the test in relation to the decision for which it is used.

Our formulation does not discard measurement theory. On the contrary, we have identified the circumstances where it applies rigorously and where it may serve as an approximation to the ideal solution. But the nature of every decision problem must be specified and these specifications must be used to determine the appropriate mathematical model. The most important parameters involved are the payoff functions for alternative treatments and the constraints upon decisions (e.g., the selection ratio). These parameters, together with the parameters of the tests (validity, reliability, intercorrelation, and cost), determine the value of the testing procedure to the decision maker.

Measurement theory has neglected the decision itself because it developed in the context of pure science. A meter stick or a thermometer is used in a particular experiment to obtain a number. Over the life of the instrument, all parts of the scale will be used, in connection with a great variety of reasoning processes. The scale is used for compound independent decisions, and it is reasonable to regard error at every point as equally serious, on the average. The psychological tester often has to decide which of several attributes to measure in a short time, but the physical scientist has not had to choose between measuring temperature and velocity or some other attribute. It is this type of choice—which now also confronts the physicist packing measuring instruments into the limited space of an artificial satellite—that makes it necessary to consider the importance of measurements for decision making. Measurement theory appears suitable without modification when the scale is considered in the abstract, without reference to any particular application. As soon as the scale is intended for use in a restricted context, that context influences our evaluation of the scale.

In the absence of an explicit concept of payoff for the decision maker, psychological measurement has probably been subtly influenced by quite another value consideration. It seems to us that an abstract conception of "justice" lies behind much of the concern about error of measurement. An ability test is expected to rank persons from best to poorest, and error distorts the ranking. Since such distortion is "unfair" to the individuals who are ranked lower than they deserve, testers want to reduce error of measurement. But from a utilitarian point of view, these errors can be ignored unless they alter the goodness of whatever decisions are to be made. An attribute that is, in the abstract, deserving of reward has no bearing on allocation to treatments if it does not predict differential payoff.

A test designed to be maximally efficient for a particular decision will freely allow errors to enter if they are irrelevant to that decision. The test designed on the basis of pure measurement theory devotes testing effort to irrelevant information, and thus is not as efficient. We would expect, for example, that a test battery developed by Horst's extension of measurement theory would not be optimally efficient for classification decisions, since the theory gives no consideration to quotas and payoff functions. To date the only attempt to develop tests for a specific decision problem is the work on "peaked" tests for selection decisions. For selecting persons above a particular level of ability, it has been proposed to restrict test items to one level of difficulty. Lord (1955) has recently summarized this work; the tests so designed are indeed a bit more efficient than those designed in the classical manner, but the difference is trivial in magnitude. Sequential procedures also sacrifice accuracy at some places in order to have greater accuracy where it most affects decisions; when costs of testing are appreciable the sequential method has clear advantages.

Just as the measurement model is not the only possible starting point for test theory, so the decision model is not the only alternative that might replace it. One prominent and rather well developed alternative is the discriminant function. The discriminant model recognizes that discrete alternatives may confront the tester, who regards his basic task as the allocation of each individual to the proper one of several categories. It differs from our approach chiefly in the way payoffs are specified. Each person is said to "belong" in a particular treatment, and the evaluation of a strategy consists of some suitably weighted function of the number of erroneous assignments. Sometimes this way of formulating a problem will be ideal, although it is then possible to regard it as a special case within decision theory. Another evaluation is, we believe, more often suitable in personnel classification. We may consider payoff within a treatment as varying continuously with score, and allocate people so as to maximize total payoff. This avoids any assumption that persons fall into homogeneous types, or that payoff is the same for all "correct" decisions. To put it differently, the discriminant function is concerned entirely with between-groups variance in test score, whereas our model takes into account the fact that predictable variance in payoff *within* groups dictates information-gathering and assignment strategies.

Another alternative to traditional measurement theory stresses the fact that test data are qualitative rather than truly quantitative. Ferguson, Guttman, Loevinger, and others view the test as an instrument for locating persons in categories. This theory recognizes that the overall validity coefficient of a test is a less important quality than its power to discriminate at the boundary lines where decisions are to be made. Each author has proposed an index of the goodness of a test as a categorizing instrument, and these indices could be used in place of the error of estimate or the validity coefficient. Test construction could point toward maximization of such indices. Again, the decision model provides a vantage point for inspecting the proposal. In a discussion of the Ferguson-Thurlow approach reported elsewhere (Cronbach, 1953), we show that this method of describing the testing process has two defects. It treats all errors of discrimination as equally serious, even when the order of categories makes some errors far more serious than others. Second, it compares the decisions made by the test to chance decisions, instead of to the best *a priori* strategy. Since the decision model permits us to use the strategy and payoff matrix required by a given practical problem, it is more flexible than these alternative proposals, but will lead to the same conclusions in the limited situations where their assumptions apply.

As compared with the alternative theories, decision theory has one distressing characteristic. Instead of the definite formulas and procedures for test construction that other theories offer, decision theory is a general model for stating any particular testing problem. With certain commonplace assumptions we can generally derive formulas expressing the value of a test and principles for designing efficient tests. The formulas, however, involve so large a number of parameters that they are difficult to comprehend, and many of them can be evaluated only by numerical integration. As compared with the algebra of measurement theory or the discriminant function, the mathematics of decision theory is involved and laborious. This is the price paid for bringing in the parameters required to describe a problem rigorously. Where this price is too high, the tester can make simplifying assumptions to obtain approximate answers to his questions. Decision theory states the questions comprehensively, and thereby reduces the likelihood that an inadequate approximation will be taken as an exact and final answer.

THE VALUE OF GENERAL ABILITY TESTS

If test theories gild or blemish reputations, the clearest way to see the consequences of a new theory is to apply it to particular types of tests. The application does more than improve our understanding of the test discussed. It makes the important concepts of the theory more meaningful, and spotlights the factual and theoretical questions to which research must be directed. We begin by discussing the general ability test, which of all tests is the most successful by the standards of measurement theory; in the subsequent section, we turn to some of the procedures such as the interview and projective techniques which have been especial targets of criticism.

By general ability tests, we refer particularly to measures of scholastic or intellectual ability of the type widely used in predicting school and job performance. Such tests are general because the attribute they measure is related to success in a great number of undertakings.

In the prevalent theory, the validity coefficient is the cachet of test nobility. The coefficient of determination looks scornfully on any test that cannot account for 20% or more of criterion variance, and the coefficient of forecasting efficiency sets even more haughty standards. The general ability test is virtually the only test whose coefficients consistently come within the range from .40 to .80, and this fact has made it the most universal of procedures for psychological assessment. No new theory alters the empirical fact that this type of instrument has high technical quality; does decision theory, however, modify the way the instrument is judged?

For some tests, perhaps, taking into account the importance of a decision as we do by means of σ_e would cause us to lower our estimate of the value of the test. But the criteria on which the general ability test bears are often of the highest importance, and indeed are closely related to the person's success and adjustment in his entire life. Furthermore, decision theory argues that a test bearing on many decisions makes far more contribution than a test that bears on only one, and this is where the general test excels. A single IQ for a high school student tells teachers of a dozen subjects whether or not to press for higher accomplishment, tells what occupational range the student may properly aim toward, helps in decisions about college education, and so on without end. From this point of view, the traditional theory seems if anything too restrained in its enthusiastic appraisal of the general ability test.

Other aspects of decision theory, however, temper this enthusiasm. We need not dwell on the finding previously summarized (pp. 65-68) that utility is most often proportional to validity, and that the coefficient of forecasting efficiency sets indefensible standards. While this result does alter the way we judge a test of validity .40 as compared to one of validity .20 or .30, the change is rather minute as compared to other consequences of our theory.

The argument that a testing strategy must be compared to the best *a priori* strategy applies with particular force to general tests. If valid decisions can be made using information already at hand or cheaply obtainable, the test should be judged by the increase in validity it offers. The zero-order validity coefficient is relevant only if, without the test, the decision maker would be forced into chance decisions. Just because the general test deals with qualities required in a wide range of performances, information on those qualities can be obtained from past performances. We are told by Professor P. E. Vernon that in England success in grammar school has been predicted from properly scaled primary school ratings with validity coefficients as high as .80 (for the total range of talent). In a typical study, the best test battery raised the multiple correlation by less than .05. A validity coefficient of .82 for a general ability test makes it appear spectacularly valuable, but its true contribution to decision making is scarcely a 5% improvement over non-test decisions. In view of the importance of the decision, even this gain very likely repays the effort of testing. (But see our further discussion below.) When the estimated value of the test is deflated to proper proportions, however, one immediately wonders whether tests of rather low validity, bearing on decisions where substitute data are not available, might have greater social importance. It is only speculative to suggest that such importance might be found in predictors of delinquency, emotional disorders, or vocational interests; for a test to be valuable as a screening device, it must not only predict with some accuracy, but there must be beneficial treatments available for those singled out by the test.

In academic decisions, treatments in which payoff is closely related to test score are certainly available. Yet that very success of the general ability test as a predictor may imply that the tests are not right for the uses to which they are put. This question was first raised by the realization that in counseling of college students the most common problem is a choice between curricula or vocations. Since the general test predicts grades in every curriculum to about the same degree, it sheds no light on the decision of the typical student. For this reason, differential tests of abilities and interests have been sought which would predict between-treatment differences. The same argument has been applied to military classification, with a resultant increase in use of differential predictors.

Decision theory has formalized the concept of payoff in differential decisions, and extended it in two ways. First, it has been shown that in classification the value of measuring a dimension depends in a complex manner on the payoff functions relating outcome to the various dimensions and on the quotas for the treatments (Brogden, 1951). These relations have to date been studied only superficially, but the results tend to devalue the general test. Second, a previously unrecognized type of decision has been identified, namely the placement decision. Placement decisions are a subspecies of classification decision and the same principles apply.

Since only one score continuum is involved, the factors affecting utility can be thoroughly traced. Moreover, this special case covers many of the important applications of tests.

A placement decision is involved when persons are grouped on the basis of their scores in a general ability test, and each group receives a different treatment. Now for each treatment there is a relation between payoff and score, which for simplicity we assume to be linear. The slope is determined by the variation of payoff σ_e and the validity coefficient r_{ye} for that treatment. The contribution of the test to a placement decision depends on the differences between slopes for the several treatments, and therefore the value of a test for sectioning students will be zero if the slope of the payoff function is the same for all treatments. A general test is, by its very nature, positively correlated with success in a great variety of treatments, and its value for placement is limited by that fact.

The correlation of .85, more or less, between prediction and grammar school success in England is far less significant than it seems at first glance, because a very large correlation would surely be found also in the "modern secondary" school to which most of the rejectees go. From the viewpoint of national policy, the aim is to maximize total output. The present scheme does this only if the slope $\sigma_e r_{ye}$ is greater for grammar schools than for modern secondary schools. The facts to determine this are not available, simply because it has previously been thought that predictive validity alone is required. Very likely, σ_e for an unselected range of talent is greater in grammar schools than in modern secondary schools, and if so the allocation procedure would be profitable. But the profit is less than the r of .85 suggests. Moreover, better bases for decision could be invented if differential payoff were held in mind as the goal. The general ability predicts success in both treatments. There must be attributes (methods of problem solving? preference for abstract thought? character traits? interests?) which are more relevant to one mode of instruction than the other. The slopes of payoff functions for these qualities will be less steep than for the general test, but the difference in slope from treatment to treatment and the benefit from testing will be greater.

British secondary school allocation has afforded a useful example of a placement problem, but it is not unique. Nearly all the everyday uses of ability and achievement tests in American schools are for placement rather than selection decisions; our observations apply there as well. And the observation that applies with greatest force is that the basic data required to determine the worth of placement tests have never been obtained.

A decision model has forced us to formulate one more concept which bears on the reputation of ability tests, and that is the notion of adaptive treatment. American testers have placed themselves at the disposal of institutions wishing to assign men to predetermined treatments, and have pointed with pride to the fact that they often can raise the average output by careful selection. But nearly equal gains can often be attained by another branch of personnel technology which refuses to accept the treatment as given. The job simplification expert and the human engineer seek to fit the job to unselected men. The greater their success the less the value of selection. The tester has failed to realize that he is competing with the treatment simplifier. And the latter's method is often the more economical, for his changes may be made permanent while the tester must evaluate new employees forever.

The true problem is to find the optimum combination of adaptation of treatment and selection of persons. This calls, not for rivalry between engineering psychologist and tester, but for intimate cooperation. As we have stated the problem abstractly, one can attain a given goal (e.g., training of radar operators) by an infinite variety of treatments that vary continuously over many dimensions. For every person there is a best treatment, and for every treatment a best type of person. Only by a study of the payoff surface linking treatment dimensions and payoff dimensions can one arrive at the best combination. This calls for a combination of the experimental methods of the job designer and the differential-correlational methods of the tester. The vast problem thus posed is impossible to cast in concrete terms at present, but if we look at just one aptitude at a time, we can make some progress.

For any one type of score such as general ability we have a family of straight lines relating score to payoff for various treatments which in its simplest form is characterized by its envelope, a second-degree curve (Figure 9). The greater the curvature of this line, the greater the value of adaptation. If the curvature is great, adaptation to unselected men gains much of the value testers have been claiming for selection. Adaptation may be accomplished by routinization, reduction of the verbal components of training, and other means. Even in schools and universities, elimination of intellectual hurdles that are irrelevant to the person's later performance could reduce the importance of selection on general intellectual characteristics. There are practical limits to modification of treatment, but these limits are astonishingly remote.

Putting all the foregoing argument together, we can neither exalt nor abase the general ability test. We form a rather favorable impression of its value from its usual validity coefficients, and this impression is enhanced when we recognize the number and importance of the decisions on which it bears. But we overrate the test if we do not recognize that it duplicates information usually at hand; it improves the best *a priori* decision much less than the customary comparison with a chance decision implies. And as an aid to placement decisions, the test has surely received much too much credit; it may even have been used where its true value is negligible.

This analysis makes clear that the question whether a given test is profitable or unprofitable is meaningless. The value of a test is great for one decision and small even for other decisions involving the same treatment. A generalized study of payoff functions for a type of test can tell us far more than we now know regarding its usefulness. But it has no universal value. Its contribution must ultimately be judged in terms of the particular decision problem the decision maker has before him.

THE VALUE OF WIDEBAND PROCEDURES

Of all the implications of decision theory, perhaps the most dramatic is the new interpretation it offers for wideband procedures. In counseling and guidance, one must ordinarily help the person answer several questions at once, and each answer involves somewhat different types of information. The counselor may obtain information narrowly focused on one dimension, or may use a procedure which covers many areas. Bandwidth, that is, greater coverage, is purchased at the price of lowered fidelity or dependability. For any decision problem there is an optimum bandwidth. This conclusion departs from conventional theory, which assumes that it is always desirable to maximize dependability.

Among the important wideband procedures are the interview, the projective technique, the essay examination, and analysis of patterns of successes and failures on ability tests. Each of the wideband devices is unsatisfactory, by the usual standards of predictive efficiency and reliability. Our work suggests, however, that the negative evidence may not bear on the usefulness of the procedures for the function they best fulfill.

Let us begin with the interview, a technique which is universally accepted by those who make personnel decisions. No matter how elaborate a testing program may be, it is supplemented by an interview wherever the cost of interviewing permits. Indeed, some of the very psychologists who report negligible validity for interview judgments themselves insist on interviewing the prospects when they have a vacancy to fill in their own offices. The evidence, however, is preponderantly negative. Interviewers' judgments disagree with each other and with objective criteria. Why, in the face of such evidence, does the interview retain its popularity?

If the interview were omitted, estimates of intelligence and other qualities appraised objectively would be more valid than when contaminated by interviewers' impressions. By omitting the interview, however, the employer would give up the possibility of obtaining information on characteristics that formal measurement procedures do not reveal. An interview permits the decision maker to cover the length and breadth of the subject's history and character. "How did you get along with your last employer? What aspects of your work interested you most? Tell me about your family. . . ." In this varied conversation, significant facts can come to light which no structured test or questionnaire could reveal. A reluctance to talk about a particular job experience perhaps discloses a failure. Other remarks hint at a competitive attitude that would be an aid in one job and a hazard in another. The personality traits that receive chief attention as one interview develops may only be glanced at in an interview with another person. The virtue of the interview is that it can turn in any of hundreds of directions, following leads in a way that the structured narrowband procedure cannot.

Quite similar comments could be made regarding the projective technique, which touches on abilities, interests, social relations, sexual attitudes, methods of thinking, and so on through hundreds of characteristics. Any given record says next to nothing about some of these areas, but each record presents a few striking individual features of undoubted importance to the clinician. The essay test has a smaller range. As a measure of factual knowledge a history paper compares more or less unfavorably with an objective test in the same area. The essay test, however, gives information on spelling, organization of ideas, manner of attack on a problem, imagination and originality, special biases, and so on. The teacher scoring such a paper has a better chance to "get to know" the student than does the teacher scoring an objective test.

The wideband procedure sheds light on many different decisions. The employment interview does not bear only on whether to hire the person. It suggests how to assign him, how to supervise him, what weaknesses must be allowed for, what are his prospects for promotion, and so on. The projective test helps the clinician to decide regarding dozens of steps of treatment. And the essay test may provide numerous suggestions about educational procedures.

One may contrast two aspects of any information source: exhaustiveness and dependability. Exhaustiveness is the extent to which the information offered covers the ground we wish to know about. Dependability is the extent to which the information offered is true. Only a precise evaluation of a given procedure can indicate whether it strikes the proper balance between the two desirable qualities. Though any one fact or judgment from a wideband procedure is undependable, the procedure as a whole contributes more in some circumstances than a narrowband procedure. The wideband procedure can perhaps improve every decision that is to be made. The narrowband procedure gives accurate information with respect to one decision, but provides no guidance at all for the remaining decisions, leaving them to be made on *a priori* grounds.

Even where a wideband technique does contribute more than a precise narrowband instrument, the decision maker should be reluctant to rely on untrustworthy information. Usually it is practical to make the wideband instrument the first stage in a sequential process, arriving at reversible rather than terminal decisions. A sequential process makes ideal use of fallible data, trusting them only to the extent that they deserve. Actually, in most present practice, wideband devices are used sequentially rather than for final decisions.

The interview is used to identify questions that need to be considered and facts that need to be obtained. In vocational guidance, the client mentions activities which have interested him, and the counselor notes that all of them involve detailed stereotyped work. This leads, first, to further questions about interests to see whether the hypothesis of preference for stereotyped activities is sound. Second, it suggests the possibility of underlying emotional insecurity that can be investigated by intensive interviewing, a personality test, or information from acquaintances. For another client, the salient observation is a strong artistic interest coupled with poor grades in art courses. The next steps are to verify the genuineness of the interest by questions as to *what* about art he likes, to determine the reasons for his poor grades by questioning his instructors, and perhaps to apply tests of artistic talent. In counseling of a student referred for low grades, the interview would suggest whether the critical questions relate to lack of interest in his curriculum,

poor study methods, an undesirable attitude, poor reading, an emotional problem, or something else. Dependable measuring instruments exist for several of these areas, and would form the next stage
in fact-finding. It would be possible to describe in similar detail
the sequential nature of employment interviewing, clinical diagnosis,
or educational diagnosis.

In the ideal situation, the decision maker comes to no conclusion
on the basis of the wideband procedure. It directs his subsequent
observations, and perhaps suggests a tentative treatment that will
enhance his opportunity to observe what is pertinent. Ultimately,
he hopes to obtain enough data for a highly dependable terminal
decision.

The merit of the broad survey as a first step in decision making is
obvious. In a hundred counseling interviews attention is directed to
a hundred different questions, each of which appears salient in only
a fraction of the cases. All this ground could not possibly be covered
by systematic, precise techniques. The survey is fallible; it misses
some points, and opens up false leads. But the subsequent questioning reveals the false leads as false, and there are fewer missed points
than there would be if a narrowband procedure had been used.

The wideband procedures, though condemned on the basis of validation research, have won a large and loyal following who claim to
have had satisfactory experience with the methods. We submit that
the enthusiasm of their users is the result of satisfactory experience
with them *in their sequential application.* The critic, on the other
hand, has most often applied standards appropriate for evaluating
terminal decisions. The interview gives an undependable impression
of intelligence. Judgments of aggression based on the Rorschach
disagree too often with observed social behavior. Psychiatrists interviewing the same person frequently arrive at quite different estimates of emotional stability. Qualitative analysis of Binet or
Wechsler protocols is a poor way to measure flexibility or creativeness. The evidence is that estimates from wideband techniques are
rather unreliable and have low validity. Used sequentially, however, they draw attention to facts which would otherwise be missed.
The price of pursuing false leads is one the decision maker is often
willing to pay.

In recent years controversy has centered on projective methods,
which have been an active subject of research. The proponents of
these methods have tended to reject the negative evidence, claiming
that the techniques permit highly valid judgment. There is no objective support for the claim that projective data are a valid basis

for terminal decisions. Supporters of projective tests have seemingly rested their case on the wrong grounds. We suggest that they have argued for the conventional validity of their tests because that has been the only passport to respectability in test theory. Decision theory points out the existence of quite another virtue in tests and the available evidence is not inconsistent with the claim that projectives have this virtue.

We believe that proponents and critics of projective tests could agree on the following statements: Inferences from projective tests are often wrong, but right more often than chance would allow. Projective techniques frequently suggest hypotheses about the individual that, when confirmed, have great practical importance. Many of the suggestions and hypotheses about idiosyncratic characteristics of the individual are subsequently proved baseless. The theory and technique of projective testing and interpretation can be greatly improved.

Reconciliation of the objective evidence with the clinician's enthusiasm is made possible by the fact that the evidence disproves claims that should never have been made, but supports claims consistent with much clinical practice. Our argument should be compared with Meehl's discussion (1954) of the value of clinical judgment in diagnosis. His conclusion that clinical methods are chiefly useful for constructing hypotheses to be confirmed by further investigation is strikingly similar to ours.

Placing wideband techniques in a logical framework encouraging to their advocates does not absolve them from all criticism. There is some risk that our clarification of logical possibilities will be taken as an endorsement of present practices. Nothing could be farther from our intentions. Projective and other wideband methods are used in indefensible ways which should be criticized and corrected. We hope that our theoretical analysis directs criticism toward the essential points and away from false issues.

Recognizing the much greater value of wideband techniques when used sequentially will, we hope, discourage the use of these methods for terminal decisions. Research on these methods should consider their usefulness as a way of focusing investigation. It is necessary to determine how often the leads suggested by a given wideband procedure are fruitful. Considering this along with the importance of the findings and the cost of the procedure is the only legitimate basis for evaluating the method. A low "validity" is acceptable if the cost of separating the true leads from the false is tolerable.

There is a continuum from great to narrow bandwidth. The tester can spread himself too far, just as he can confine himself too narrowly. By structuring the interview or the projective technique one can reduce the bandwidth with a corresponding gain in fidelity. The fact that the bandwidth of current projective methods is almost unlimited suggests that it would be profitable to restrict them to some degree. In the TAT, for example, better information about relations with parents would presumably be obtained by increasing the proportion of plates involving parent figures. In many diagnostic problems the attendant sacrifice of information about other aspects of the person would surely be justified.

The true issue is not whether wideband methods are good or bad. The question is, for any given decision problem what is the best information-gathering procedure? If a projective technique would be useful, just how should it be designed and interpreted to give the greatest help? Nothing in our argument leads us to think that any procedure can conceivably give an accurate analysis of "the whole personality." Instead, it is necessary to distill from a limited quantity of information the most intelligent possible decision. The problem is to find the procedure which, in the time available, offers the greatest yield of important, relevant, and interpretable information.

A FINAL WORD

Our search for a coherent theory of decision making on the basis of test information has led in many directions. Wherever we turn, we find unanswered questions. Research of many types is needed, ranging from simple fact-finding to major inventions. Mathematical studies of test design and allocation strategies, new types of empirical studies of payoff surfaces and of validity, and even philosophical studies of evaluation problems have a part to play in extending test theory. Along with these theoretical developments we perceive many possibilities of replacing present measuring instruments with new ones: placement tests of superior differential validity, personality surveys with appropriate bandwidth for particular tasks, collections of brief tests for sequential classification, and so on. Our final conclusion may be optimistic or pessimistic, but it is inescapable. The test theory developed to date covers only a small corner of the domain within which the decision maker operates, and in only a few specialized instances have we discovered the testing practices that will most increase the utility of personnel decisions.

SUPPLEMENT

A GUIDE TO RELEVANT LITERATURE / 1955-63

Our intention in this supplement is to inform the reader of trends in the research literature so that he can locate whatever materials are pertinent to him. While the ingredients represented in our survey might conceivably be combined into some great new insight, we cannot yet report that we or others have made any such advance over our first edition position. Rather, we see recent writings as pushing ahead toward more definite applications of certain principles in actual situations, and, in another vein, toward extremely abstract analyses of various problems that move farther and farther from application.

Many readers of the first edition have reported that their greatest need is not for further elaborations but for a readily comprehended presentation of the original material. We have not found it possible to satisfy the demand, as the material is technical and requires a somewhat formal presentation if detailed results are to be examined. Among the brief presentations of the theory that have appeared, Wickert's presentation (1962), originally written for West African educators and managers, is particularly well suited to a general audience. The basic text *Elementary decision theory* by Chernoff and Moses (1959) covers lucidly and at a rather simple level the mathematics of decision making and choice among strategies, and the concept of a utility scale.

THE IMPORTANCE OF DECISION THEORY

In the years since 1955, there has been considerable interest in the various philosophical, statistical, and practical problems associated with decision making. A whole new methodology has begun to take shape, under such names as operations research and dynamic programming. In theoretical statistics the basic premises of Fisher have been challenged and those of Neyman and Pearson greatly extended by the so-called Bayesian position that has developed from decision theory.

The vigor of these developments itself attests to the value of a decision-theoretic approach. But, while many of the publications present elaborate mathematical solutions or data-processing methods, the consensus of specialists today is that the merit of decision theory lies more in its power "to stir the reader's thoughts" than in its yield of algorithms and formulas. Thus Wagner (1962), reviewing Churchman (in Ackoff, 1961) on "decision and value theory," remarks: "Having read this fine survey, one is left in awe at the intrepidity of business men in carrying out their complicated daily tasks. . . . An executive tottering at the brink of undertaking an O.R. [operations research] approach should be advised that O.R. is a matter of substituting one set of problems for another, and he had better decide early which set he would rather face." The problems to which Wagner refers are the need to specify, in a highly explicit form, the payoffs from the possible outcomes and the various other parameters of the decision situation. Lindley (1961) comments similarly about dynamic programming, stating that it becomes directly useful only when one has an exceptional amount of information on the parameters of the practical situation.

There is a paradox here. Decision theory is distinguished from simpler models by the fact that it is built of concepts that are often neglected: the set of alternative treatments, the costs of experimentation, the possible outcomes and the payoffs associated with them, etc. Yet when one seeks to make use of decision theory, he almost invariably sets a number of these key concepts aside, so as to make the model tractable. It makes sense in certain problems of sequential test design, for example, to assume the cost of collecting data to be negligible; to bring in such costs explicitly makes the problem much harder to think about. On the other hand, the *concept* of cost is indispensable, since, if cost were truly negligible, it would never be advantageous to terminate data collection.

There are two levels at which decision theory is to be comprehended. It is, on the one hand, a set of notions, all of which are to be kept in mind in formulating questions. Second, it is a formal machinery for determining optimum strategies. In working out formal solutions it is invariably necessary to neglect certain of the key concepts, to introduce strong assumptions, or to ask for detailed information that cannot practically be supplied. Even when one is using decision theory in only a "notional" way, it is often necessary to simplify the model to keep the discussion within bounds.

This is illustrated in our paper (Cronbach and Gleser, 1959) which we reproduce below (pp. 291-293). This study originated in the proposal of certain testers to use confidence bands in reporting score profiles so that, given two scores, x and y, the test user would interpret the difference $x - y$ only if it were at least $\sqrt{2}$ times its standard error. Lord (1958) had evaluated this procedure by examining the α risk of interpreting an observed difference when the true difference is in the opposite direction; he reached conclusions generally favorable to the proposal. Our interest in decision theory led us to consider various ways in which the interpretative strategy might be evaluated, and our reanalysis led to somewhat less favorable conclusions. We did not attempt to introduce a formal payoff function (i.e., to assign losses to errors of different magnitudes). Instead we relied on loose statements such as "When a terminal [individual] decision is under consideration it appears reasonable to set the maximum [acceptable] risk at .10 or .05." Speaking of risks rather than expected utilities simplified the discussion sufficiently so that we could place proper stress on a distinction between average risks and individual risks, each of which is pertinent to certain practical uses of difference scores.

Similarly, in our main work of the past five years on reliability or generalizability theory (with Rajaratnam), we have been helped by decision-theoretic concepts to understand the problem, yet have been quite unable to make use of the full machinery of the theory. In studying errors in data collection, one should, according to decision theory, weight the errors according to their effect on the decision for which the data will be used. In our reformulation of reliability theory (Cronbach *et al.*, 1963), we omitted weights and fell back upon appraising the mean square error. Our formulation introduces so many complications, even without considering alternative treatments and payoffs, that a fully decision-theoretic account is unmanageable and will remain so, at least until the remainder of the structure is more familiar. We did, however, consider the test as an aid in decision making, and this formulation clarified reliability problems. Once we distinguished the data on which decisions are based ("decision data") from the possibly different set collected to study the accuracy of the test ("generalizability data") longstanding ambiguities and confusions vanished. In particular, it became immediately clear that the choice between two intraclass correlation formulas rests on the proposed experimental design for the decision study (and, indeed, that a new formula is required for a certain exceptional experimental situation). Another aspect of the theory, not yet prepared for publication, distinguishes "comparative decisions" from "absolute decisions." The former are concerned with individual differences in the sample of persons being considered simultaneously (as in a competition or a decision with quota constraints) ; in the latter, decisions are made about each person independently. We find that errors must be examined differently in these two cases; the conventional reliability coefficient is appropriate, at best, only for the rather limited class of comparative decisions. In this work also, the contribution of decision theory was one of perspective rather than of mathematical machinery.

BAYESIAN STATISTICS

The statistical theory most familiar to the present generation of behavioral scientists assumes, in effect, that the investigator must reach conclusions entirely on the basis of the data in the present investigation. A decision to accept the null hypothesis on the basis of an F-test, for example, is based entirely on the present data. Obviously, the investigator somehow brings to bear his past experience and theoretical knowledge in judging the acceptability of the hypothesis, but to the orthodox statistician any such wisdom is "outside" the statistical problem.

A large number of statistical theorists now advocate extending the formal statistical model so as to encompass all the steps in reasoning: the set of alternative decisions, the risks or losses associated with each type of error, the beliefs held—prior to the experiment—about the alternatives, and the appropriate conclusions in the light of the added information from the experiment. Though acknowledging that the estimates of risks are somewhat arbitrary and that the prior beliefs of the consumer for whom the statistical study is made are subjective and hard to determine, Bayesians defend their inclusion in the theory on much the same grounds as we defend the inclusion of payoffs in analysis of decision problems. Even if not formally represented in the theory, payoffs actively influence decisions (e.g., whether to repeat an experiment when the observed difference is "non-significant"). Only by giving payoffs and prior probabilities a formal representation can one examine the extent of their influence.

Bayesian statistics have aroused no little controversy. The reader is referred to the summary paper by Edwards *et al.* (1963) and its excellent bibliography, and to a statement of the Bayesian position by Savage (1961). Among the several papers skeptical of the attempt to give prior probabilities and payoffs a formal place in statistics, perhaps the most interesting to the non-specialist is that of E. S. Pearson (1962). The flavor of the controversy is best exhibited in the reaction to Anscombe's 1961 paper. Replies and rejoinders by Bross, Birnbaum, Schlaifer, and others—both in short articles and in letters to the editor—echo through issues of the *American Statistician* down to the present moment.

The use of prior information in the Bayesian fashion is illustrated in one commonplace psychometric practice. A regression estimate of a person's true score, given his test score, combines this new experimental finding with the expected score in "the group to which he belongs"; the weight for the former increases, relative to the latter, as the accuracy of the test increases. Knowledge that John, who is applying for college admission, is a senior from Central High School where the mean score of seniors taking the College Board Test is 650 is "prior knowledge" in the sense of the Bayesian analyst, and basing decisions on the regression estimate of true score is a rudimentary Bayesian strategy (Chernoff and Moses, 1959, pp. 136, 201). We make a better inference about John when we take this prior information into account than when we make predictions from observed test score alone.* This argument is in close accord with our position (see pp. 34-36 above) that the value of a test must be judged by how much the test improves decisions over those that would otherwise be based on prior information, rather than by "improvement over chance." The concept has been further discussed by Sechrest (1963) under the happily chosen name of *incremental validity*.

Edwards, Savage, and other Bayesians advocate their methods both in applied work and in scientific research. But the argument that decision theory is appropriate for scientific reasoning encounters strong opposition. The late R. A. Fisher (1956), for one, was vehemently opposed to representing the benefit or loss from a scientific conclusion on a utility scale. The key objection is that the benefits from a bit of knowledge stretch far into the future and its economic value cannot be foreseen. Tukey (1960) sets up a contrast between decision theory and "conclusion theory." A decision, he says, leads us to act *as if* some state of affairs existed; it does not involve a belief that the hypothesis on which we act is "true." The decision is often tentative and is always *ad hoc;* it is frankly

---

* It is interesting that Robbins (1960), reaching precisely this conclusion from a mathematical analysis, finds the conclusion intuitively unacceptable because it is "unfair" to regard one student as a better prospect than another when both have the same observed score but are identified with different parent populations.

a gamble. But the scientist seeks to draw a conclusion that can stand as true for a long time to come. Conclusions, therefore, are commitments to believe until strong counterevidence appears. Tukey proposes to confine each type of statistical theory to its own province. While he admits the logical integrity of the decision-theoretic view of experimentation, he regards decision theory as an inappropriate guide in the scientist's statistical activities. Argument about the logical basis for scientific conclusion drawing is more likely to increase in vigor than to abate.

VALUES IN THEORY AND PRACTICE

Assessment of Criterion Performance in Utility Units

The notion of a "dollar criterion" based on a careful determination of benefits and costs—even though elaborated with some care by Brogden and Taylor—remained a hypothetical proposal until a few recent investigations developed personnel evaluations in dollar terms. Roche (1961), in a thesis of which a condensed version is reproduced below (pp. 254-267), appraised the performance of radial drill operators in a manufacturing plant and derived a cents-per-worker-per-hour measure of the benefits of selection. Van Naerssen (1963; see below, pp. 273-290) made a similar analysis of benefits in the selection of drivers for the Dutch Army. Myers and Forgy (1963) studied the screening of loan applications, which is an accept-reject decision formally analogous to hiring, but one where the dollar payoff is very readily examined.

Myers and Forgy, by conventional empirical procedures, identified facts on the application blank (e.g., "now has a telephone") that could be included in a scoring system to predict whether a prospective loan will be paid off or defaulted. Using a high cutoff score, the company makes relatively few loans, with a high degree of safety; a low cutoff accepts risks that, on the average, lose money for the company. The study is necessarily confined to persons already given loans on the basis of a credit investigation, rather than an unselected population of applicants. Such a study shows the incremental validity of the scoring technique, but does not indicate what would be expected if the technique were used *in place of* the customary but expensive investigation. The published evaluation stops with a discussion of the number of good and bad accounts eliminated by each cutting score.

A private report prepared for a second finance company (Myers, personal communication) carried the analysis of loan experience considerably further. Myers makes use of the base rate of good accounts, 98.55% of applications surviving the credit examination. This is an important addition to the technique of the Myers-Forgy paper which, in ignoring base rates, invites an interpretation on the assumption that good and bad risks are equally numerous. The figures in Table S1 consider only the lower score intervals that contain a large number of bad risks. The net profit in any interval is based on an estimated average profit of $145 on a paid-in-full account and a loss of $480 on a charged-off account. (Determining loan sizes, terms, and payment histories as a function of score level would give a more precise estimate of payoffs.)

The obvious decision rule is to reject persons at 21 or below, since good and bad loans balance at a score just above 21. The break-even point could be determined somewhat more securely if calculations were made from smoothed frequency distributions rather than raw frequencies, so that fluctuations in the sample would not distort results.

The payoffs calculated in Table S1 show the benefit from using the scoring procedure following preliminary acceptance on the basis of a credit investigation. Data are not available to determine the surely greater benefit that would result from using the scoring procedure alone. Myers points out that the greatest benefits are to be expected by using the scored application as a first screen, rejecting

TABLE S1. BENEFIT (ANNUAL RATE) FROM USING VARIOUS DECISION RULES WITH MYERS' CREDIT SCORING SYSTEM

(unpublished data supplied by Myers)

SCORE INTERVAL	NUMBER OF APPLICANTS ACCEPTED*	PER CENT BAD IN VALIDATION SAMPLE	NET PROFIT IF ALL LOANS MADE	CUMULATIVE NET GAIN	BENEFIT IF PERSONS AT OR BELOW THIS LEVEL ARE REJECTED
26–27	3,384	2.6	$ 435,680	$585,030	$ −585,030
24–25	835	10.3	67,325	149,350	−149,350
22–23	952	5.6	104,915	82,025	−82,025
20–21	40	100.0	−19,200	−22,890	22,890
18–19	170	11.8	12,150	−3,690	3,690
16–17	24	100.0	−11,520	−15,840	15,840
14 and below	9	100.0	−4,320	−4,320	4,320
All applicants	45,000	1.45	$6,117,500		

* Distribution on estimated base of 45,000, extrapolated from proportions in validation sample.

very low scorers and possibly accepting high scorers without the credit investigation. He calculates that the saving to the company in investigation fees would be in excess of $40,000 per year, since the scoring procedure costs next to nothing whereas the investigation costs $5 per man.

If one wishes literally to know the benefit from testing in industry, a careful cost accounting is necessary. Roche's pilot study (1961) on radial drill operators was carried out with the assistance of accountants at the Caterpillar Corporation in Peoria, Illinois. As can be seen from Roche's report (pp. 254-267), assessment of the profit attributable to each worker requires a complex allocation of overhead and labor charges, as well as an evaluation in dollars and cents of his production. It is evident from the difficulties Roche encountered that investigators doing validation research can rarely afford accounting studies of this nature.

Van Naerssen, at the end of a study of ways of predicting various criteria of driver success in the Dutch Army, translated into monetary terms the data on validity. Of particular interest is the fact that quite different answers were obtained, depending on the criterion considered; indeed, a somewhat different logic was required for translating different criteria into utilities. Reducing accidents might be an important benefit from selection, but there seemed to be no rational basis for making a monetary calculation to represent lives saved. Although the battery in use could predict accidents, there were so few accidents in the military situation that the criterion became unreliable and the validity dropped to .20. Hence van Naerssen's analysis suggested that testing did not pay for itself in accidents prevented. Training cost, on the other hand, could be very much reduced by testing, within a pool of recruits who lacked driving experience. Finally, an attempt to represent in utility terms ratings made by superiors indicated that testing was highly advantageous.

This draws attention to the marked difficulty of a dollars-and-cents analysis where selection affects several diverse criteria. Our model calls for reducing all criteria to a common scale, rather than considering the criteria separately. But van Naerssen's criteria are very nearly incommensurable, and it would be extremely difficult to work out the optimum selection ratio, for example, considering all information.

An analysis having some resemblance to van Naerssen's but narrower in scope was made by Harding and McWilliams (1957), who compared the cost of selecting airmen for a six-month Russian course by two methods, the Carroll-Sapon test and a four-week tryout course. The two methods had more or less equal validity, but the test cost was figured to be $800 less, per man selected, than the cost of the tryout. This figure cannot be taken too seriously, both because the tryout seems to have been handled in an uneconomical way and because there may be a validity advantage for the trial-course method. These figures, however, for cost of testing are worth noting:

Time for testing (300 men, 4 hours each)	$2,293.50
Time for administration and scoring personnel	109.20
Cost of test materials	62.25
Per man tested	$ 8.22

Laboratory directors in the pharmaceutical industry must decide which of many proposed investigations that might lead to marketable drugs should be pursued. This is a tactical decision like that required regarding a proposal to develop a new test battery or a new educational procedure. Davies (1962), in a paper logically similar to that of Brogden and Taylor, illustrates how costs and prospective benefits may be weighed systematically even though the ultimate outcome of any one line of research is unknown. Here again, decision theory helps to state a problem in formal terms that make it more likely that all relevant facts will be taken into account by the decision maker. Davies' analysis does not rebut the charge of Fisher and others that decision theory is ill-suited to guide scientific strategy; he succeeds because he is considering scientific studies in an applied setting where one *can* take the corporate balance sheet as a sufficient criterion.

Blumberg (1957) discusses public health screening where one may apply an inexpensive but not highly valid test to decide who should be given a precise diagnostic test. He displays, using data on diabetes, the usual function relating hits, misses, and false positives to score on the screening test, and shows how the optimal cutting score and the utility depend on the weights assigned to these. He examines bases on which such weights may be more rationally determined, and compares the expected-value formula with other ways of evaluating the screening procedure. Somewhat similar considerations enter the less mathematical discussion of parole decisions by Mannheim and Wilkins (1955, esp. pp. 216-217).

The Utility Scale of the Decision Maker

The decision theory on which we have relied is a theory of *ra-*

tional decision making. It takes certain stated values as a starting point, and examines how a man holding those values should act or, more basically, how he should proceed to select an action. But one can use the decision model in the reverse way, to study *actual* decision making. Knowing that a man acts in a certain way, what can we infer about either his values or his decision-making strategy? This is the problem to which behavioral research on decision making addresses itself. A recent summary of such work, which has been flourishing in experimental laboratories during the past several years, is provided by Edwards (1961). A review and bibliography on the general theory of utility by Adams was given limited circulation in 1954; it is now more readily available (Adams, 1960). Arrow (1958) reviews, from the standpoint of the economist, much of the literature in behavioral decision theory and in mathematical models for choice. A second edition (1963) of his *Social choice and individual values* has now appeared. Restle (1961) deals with such models and applies them to the measurement of utility and other experimental questions.

As we pointed out earlier (pp. 122-123), a rational individual decision should be based on the individual's utilities, rather than on some postulated common scale for converting outcomes to utilities. Moreover, producing changes in the individual's utilities might be as significant a function of education or guidance as producing changes in the probabilities he associates with various possible outcomes of his decision. Some studies have assessed individuals' utilities for grades by experimental techniques (Becker and Siegel, 1958; McDaniel *et al.*, 1961*). No studies of individuals' evaluations of outcomes other than grades have been reported.

Blau *et al.* (1956) offer an important heuristic scheme in which occupational choice is seen as the resultant of an extended process of change in the individual's expectations and preferences, these being shaped in part by the various selection mechanisms that limit occupational entry. The scheme is decision-theoretic in a general sense, though not at present mathematical; it directs attention particularly to the variables that need to be appraised at crucial points in the train of vocationally significant experiences and choices.

The psychology of the decision maker is a proper problem for personnel psychology. What strategies, combining weights, risks, etc.,

---

* McDaniel *et al.* claim that the utility measures predict grades, but this is questionable since their multiple correlation capitalizes on chance.

are used by persons engaged in student admissions, counseling, and making clinical diagnoses? This can be investigated by techniques similar to those used in the experimental laboratory. Churchman (1961) develops at length the argument that the values of the institutional decision maker can be inferred from the decisions he actually makes under a sufficiently large variety of circumstances. N. M. Smith, Jr. (1961), however, expresses a strong dissent.

Very little has been done to investigate the decision maker, though a pilot study on vocational choice was reported by Ziller (1957; see also the work of Ward and Davis, 1963, p. 16). One superficially appealing technique that some investigators have tried leads to dubious interpretations. It is sound enough to correlate the decisions made by a clinician with the available predictor variables, and to compute the beta weights that predict his decisions; these weights usually differ from the weights that best predict whatever criterion the decisions are relevant to. But—for reasons pointed out below (p. 180)—two superficially different sets of weights may lead to almost equally large multiple correlations. The discrepancy in weights by no means implies that bad decisions are being made by the clinician.

SINGLE-STAGE DECISIONS

Selection Theory with Rectangular Distributions

The most direct development from our 1957 work is the study of van Naerssen (1963), some portions of which are produced below in translation (pp. 273-290). He examines the consequences for the theory of assuming a rectangular distribution in place of the normal distribution assumed for test scores in the original monograph. He finds that the rectangular assumption gives quite similar results. In particular, when the optimum selection ratio to fill a fixed quota is determined, the rectangular and normal solutions are nearly the same; this makes it possible to generalize over the considerable variety of distributions intermediate between normal and rectangular.

Two other studies are not covered in our translation. The first deals with decision rules for the case where subjects come from two populations having different aptitude-payoff distributions (e.g., experienced drivers and novices, both considered for training as Army drivers). The second deals with two-stage selection in the manner of our Chapter 6, but with an assumed rectangular distribution of first-stage and second-stage scores. The cutoff scores describing the ideal strategy may be calculated more simply than those from the normal model. Van Naerssen suggests that his simpler equations may serve adequately to determine strategies even when distributions are more or less normal.

Selection with Restriction

Several papers deal with the selection situation in which there are multiple criteria with low or negative intercorrelations. This might occur, for example, where criteria of employee performance include precision of work, speed of work, and length of work before voluntary termination. In Rao's (1962) formulation, one of these is the primary target, and the selection battery should predict it. If, however, the battery score proves to be negatively correlated with any other criterion, selection on the battery score will impair the average performance in that respect. Rao modifies the usual multiple-regression solution so as to make sure that no such deterioration takes place on any dimension, accepting a somewhat lower average for the selected men on the primary criterion than would be obtained using the conventional regression formula. The situation might be handled in another way, by assigning a payoff value to each combination of criterion scores and using the regression formula that best predicts payoff. This more directly considers how much performance on the primary dimension the decision maker is prepared to sacrifice in order to avoid any specified loss on another dimension. Both approaches are illustrated in a paper of Kempthorne and Nordskog (1959) on the selection of poultry for breeding, where the breeder is concerned with egg production, egg weight, body weight, and other criteria. Elston (1963) discusses the possible advantages of forming a weighted composite of the several criteria.

Placement

Johns (1961) treats the theory of decision rules in placement problems where the rule is derived on the basis of information from a sample of the population, and therefore is subject to error. The decision rule derived by his recommended procedure approaches— as the sample size increases—the rule that would be derived from complete population information. Of particular interest is his use of a loss function that is midway between the "hits and misses" count of the usual analysis of discrimination, and the linear payoff of our placement model. He assumes that there is a criterion Y, on which all persons belonging in category A have scores less than Y' and all those belonging in category B have scores greater than Y'. Then if a true A (score Y less than Y') is classified as an A the loss is zero; if he is classified as a B the loss is proportional to $|Y-Y'|$. There is a similar rule for true B's, with a possibly different constant of proportionality. The seriousness of errors is thus taken into account, but all correct classifications are considered equally beneficial.

Classification

Interest in single-stage classification decisions, vigorous in the ten years just after the war, subsided about the time our first edition was published. Most subsequent work has been concerned with finding the best decision rule, not with designing the test battery on which classification will be based. Whereas at one time cut-and-try methods were necessary for allocating men to treatments (given scores capable of predicting outcome), the development of computers and of the mathematics of linear programming quickly produced a routine method of making allocations. The reader is referred to Arnoff and Sengupta (1961) for a valuable review of this theory and to the bibliography of Riley and Gass, 1958.

The work started from the so-called transportation problem where one determines how to minimize the cost of delivering goods from several similar factories to several markets. This problem, of rather general interest in economics, was solved by Koopmans, Dantzig, and others. The personnel-assignment problem, stated mathematically, proves to be a special case of the transportation problem. Arnoff and Sengupta recommend the "Hungarian" method of Kuhn (1955) as the best computational procedure for arriving at the assignments that maximize utility (see also Flood, 1956), and draw attention to an illustrative application by Friedman and Yaspen (1957). There has been some work on computational approximations to the linear programming solution (e.g., Horst, 1960). A computerized assignment procedure based on the work of Brogden and Dwyer is now reported to be in use in U.S. Army classification.

Ward (1958) suggests a way in which counselors working with one person at a time can make assignments that are reasonably near the optimum. Votaw (1958) deals with the "quota problem," a classification problem where it is known whether each man is qualified for each job and the task is to allocate the sample of men to fill the several job quotas, without being required to maximize payoff. Votaw offers a data-processing algorithm for attaining such a solution.

Brogden (1959) extends his earlier studies of the utility of classification (pp. 111-113, above). He assumes, as before, that there are n treatments (plus "reject"), that the payoffs for these treatments are normally distributed with equal variances and are predicted with validity R, and that the estimates of the payoffs have uniform intercorrelations r. The quotas for the several treatments are uniform. He confirms that utility is linearly related to R, other things being held constant. For fixed R, utility is proportional to $\sqrt{1-r}$. "The possibility of an efficient differential classification battery is not lost until the intercorrelations of the estimates of job performance are quite high (for example, with intercorrelations of .8, efficiency of classification could still be 45% as high as with zero intercorrelations)." The relation of utility to number of jobs n, and selection ratio (percentage of total group used in some job) is indicated in Table S2, assuming that $R = 1.00$ and $r = 0$. Similar trends would be found for other R and r, but the values would be lower. As the number of jobs increases, classification becomes much more profitable. A low selection ratio is most advantageous where the number of treatments is small. These results are consistent with those in Figure 35, p. 112, making allowance for the fact that there R is taken to be .50 and ϕ is variable, equal to $.2n$.

Solutions of the classification problem have generally required a

TABLE S2. EXPECTED UTILITY PER MAN ASSIGNED, AS A FUNCTION OF PERCENTAGE
OF APPLICANT POOL UTILIZED AND THE NUMBER OF JOBS*
(after Brogden, 1959, p. 189)

NUMBER OF JOBS (n)	PER CENT OF MEN UTILIZED									
	100	90	80	70	60	50	40	30	20	10
1	.00	.20	.35	.50	.64	.80	.97	1.16	1.40	1.75
2	.56	.73	.85	.97	1.09	1.22	1.37	1.54	1.75	2.07
3	.85	.99	1.10	1.21	1.32	1.44	1.57	1.73	1.93	2.23
4	1.03	1.17	1.27	1.37	1.48	1.59	1.71	1.86	2.05	2.35
5	1.16	1.29	1.39	1.49	1.59	1.70	1.82	1.95	2.14	2.43
6	1.27	1.38	1.48	1.58	1.68	1.78	1.90	2.04	2.22	2.51
7	1.35	1.46	1.56	1.65	1.75	1.86	1.97	2.10	2.28	2.55
8	1.42	1.53	1.63	1.72	1.81	1.91	2.03	2.16	2.33	2.60
9	1.49	1.59	1.68	1.77	1.86	1.96	2.07	2.20	2.38	2.64
10	1.54	1.65	1.73	1.82	1.91	2.01	2.11	2.24	2.41	2.68

* R is taken to be 1.00 and r to be 0.00. To calculate expected utility for other specified values of R and r, multiply the tabled entry by $R\sqrt{1-r}$.

payoff matrix or function stating what value the institution attributes to each level of criterion performance on each treatment. Ward and Davis (1963; see pp. 268-272) propose instead to employ judgments about the predictor information. In one approach, individuals are randomly allocated (on paper) among the several treatments, and a decision maker is asked to evaluate each assignment by comparing the scores describing the person with the presumed requirements of the job. The analysis converges on a set of weights and a decision rule for handling new groups of subjects so as to produce assignments that will receive a high evaluation from the decision maker. This procedure, which bypasses validity studies, obviously is vulnerable to any misconception the evaluator has regarding the relevance of any aptitude to job performance.

An alternative mentioned by Ward and Davis but not specifically applied to classification is to feed the computer the data describing persons, together with the assignments actually made by the institutional decision maker. The computer develops regression weights for predicting the decision that would be made regarding any subsequent case. This "predicted decision" for a new person then becomes his assignment. Such a method substitutes "machine judgment" for human judgment by reproducing the human's implicit strategy within the computer. Computer judgments will be more consistent and therefore somewhat more valid than human judgments from the same information; in effect, the validity is raised by correcting for "attenuation" arising from fluctuations in the judge's standards and attentiveness, and, if several judges are used in establishing weights, for attenuation due to idiosyncracies of the judges. But if the judges have common misconceptions about the validity of any of the information and so weight it improperly, the simulation method will also use a less-than-optimal strategy. Ideas very similar to those of Ward and Davis are found in J. W. Smith's determination (1956) of the policies accounting for industrial procurement decisions. He requires the decision makers to deal with specially designed artificial problems and from the decisions made identifies the policies apparently in use. His method is elaborated in a detailed and realistic model of the Navy's procurement operation for electronic equipment by Aumann and Kruskal (1959).

There have been several applications of operations research methodology to the planning of personnel systems, none of which has yet been described in the general literature. One broad study deals with activities of the Navy personnel system, including recruitment, assignment, training, utilization in the field, and eventual separation (Knetz, 1963). A mathematical model was designed to simulate the many processes of the system so that the effects of possible policy changes could be traced. The fidelity of the simulation was tested by comparing the computer output with actual experience over several years with personnel flow in the Electronics Technician rating. These studies are concerned more with policy than with test data *per se,* but a decision, for example, about the washout rate acceptable in a certain school inevitably affects the demands placed on the test battery used to make school assignments. The contribution of the test can here be traced far beyond the immediate criterion of school survival, using various transition probabilities calculated from the histories of men classified in previous years. Kossack and Beckwith (1959) conclude that a personnel processing system can be simulated mathematically as a Markov process. They give more attention to the mathematical structure than does Knetz's report, but deal only with a few artificial illustrations whereas Knetz deals with an extended attempt at simulating a real system. Briefer accounts of the Air Force studies appear in Finch (1960, pp. 32-49).

There has been considerable interest in the possibility of programming computers to diagnose medical patients. Overall and Williams (1961) suggest a sequential classification procedure in which one decision rule is used to assign persons to gross disease categories and a further rule, different for each category and perhaps using different information, is used to make a finer classification. Papers on diagnosis have generally considered only the conditional probabilities relating diseases to indicators, and the probabilities (base rates) for the several diseases, not the losses associated with various errors. Birnbaum and Maxwell (1960; see below pp. 234-253) study psychiatric categorization of patients. They consider various alternative decision rules that might be applied to test data, and derive a matrix of error rates showing how often that rule places a person of true diagnosis i in category j. They search, not for an optimal rule, but for a set of "admissible" rules. For each set of data—and a particular set of base rates—an admissible rule is one that cannot be altered without raising the rate of at least one kind of error. Decision makers with differing views as to the relative seriousness of the errors will prefer different ones among the admissible decision rules. Error rates can be weighted by payoffs and combined into a composite utility index, but Birnbaum and Maxwell consider that more is to be gained from an intuitive examination of the entire matrix of error rates. Essentially, what they have done is to process formally the "validity matrix," leaving values for separate consideration. This partitioning of the decision problem is necessary where many different sets of values may be applied to the same data (as is notably the case in individual decisions). But until values are introduced explicitly, there is no possibility of dealing with questions about test design, since one's choice of data to be collected depends on what errors one wants most to guard against.

SEQUENTIAL DECISION MAKING

Selection Decisions

Sequential testing for selection purposes has flourished in fields remote from personnel testing. In the pharmaceutical industry a large number of drugs may be synthesized, all of which are conceivably potent against a certain condition or organism; the problem is to select, through brief trial, the ones worthy of a thorough clinical investigation (Davies, 1958; Dunnett, 1961). Likewise, a great number of hybrids are produced in an agricultural experiment, and only a few can be given an extensive field trial (Finney, 1960). The number of "applicants" is greater than can be accepted for thorough investigation. Federer (1964) assembled a bibliography of several hundred titles covering selection and allocation processes, single-stage and multi-stage, as treated in basic statistics and in applied fields such as these.

Finney (1962c), drawing on his experience with biological trials, recognized the process of selection for British universities as involving at least two stages of data collection. His treatment (reprinted below, pp. 182-212) seeks an optimal first-stage decision rule. What proportion (P_1) of pupils, he asks, would it be wise to admit to the grammar school track that leads to the university, on the assumption that only a fraction (P_2) of these will pass the screening at university entrance? In most respects his analysis resembles our thinking about pre-reject decisions, though he includes the possibility of allocating the fraction ($1-P_1$) of the group to an inferior track and salvaging the fraction P_2* for the university to fill the quota π. Finney's tables F1 through F4 show how the expected utility (university success) varies with π, P_1, P_2, and P_2*, assuming certain correlations among the early and later tests and the criterion. His summary table F14 considers both the ideal cutting point on the first screen and the relation of utility to test validity. Finney's discussion, and that of the educators and statisticians in his British audience (see pp. 212 ff.), touches on some of the practical and philosophical problems in university selection.

Finney's problem is not truly one of selection, by our definition, since no student is rejected and taken out of the social balance sheet at either the first or second stage. Rather, there are four treatments representing the combinations of grammar school or secondary modern school with university or no university education. There is some expected payoff to British society for each person under each combination of treatments. Cronbach's comments on Finney's paper (below, pp. 229-233) suggest changes in the model to take the payoff from the non-university groups into account. A particularly interesting feature of Finney's problem is that there are two stages of treatment as well as two stages of decision making, so that the score used as predictor in the second stage is in part a payoff from the treatment initially selected. Our Figure 3 (p. 18) suggests that the individual is static during the decision making, and it thereby does less than justice to a problem such as Finney's.

Another selection situation extended in time is treated by Kao and Rowan (1959). They are concerned with selection where a fixed number of positions must be filled with *satisfactory* employees, that is, employees who, after training, meet a specified criterion of performance. At first glance this appears to be a reanalysis of the single-stage selection problem; formally, however, theirs is a two-stage decision process. A test is used to select persons for training; they seek the cutting score that will produce optimal results, considering both the loss from training a man who proves to be unsatisfactory and the cost of recruiting additional applicants if too few survive training. This is a two-stage decision in which the second investigatory stage (training and post-test) is very costly. Second-stage decisions are based entirely on the post-test, which is treated as the final criterion. Theirs is a Pre-reject strategy in which the first test has no weight in the second stage. The "recruiting cost" they add to the model can be treated as a cost of the first test. When they examine the effect of varying selection ratio, they treat two-stage decisions much as we treat the single-stage decision on page 40, locating the cutting score that maximizes utility per man finally accepted. In two-stage Pre-reject decisions the aim at the end of the first stage may be to reject persons below a certain ability level, with little risk of rejecting a good man. This might be the appropriate policy, for example, in a doctoral preliminary examination where a written examination must be passed before admission to the more costly oral examination.

Gupta and Sobel (1958) consider the first-stage decision rule required to hold down the risk of discarding qualified men. We have already discussed van Naerssen's study of two-stage processes.

Mathematics of Multi-Stage Experiments

The mathematics of sequential testing has been much extended in recent years; see N. L. Johnson's review paper (1961) and Jackson's bibliography (1960). Greatest attention has centered on multi-stage processes, in particular, on processes in systems that are changing between stages. Optimum decisions are made by a technique referred to as "dynamic programming." The chief source in the field is Bellman (1957), but the novice should begin with two companion papers by Simpson (1961) and Lindley (1961) that survey the field. A more technical review is that of Dreyfus (1961). Riley and Gass (1958) offer an exhaustive bibliography of work to that date on linear and dynamic programming.

Lindley's paper is memorable for discussing the delightful problem of choosing a marriage partner from an inexhaustible supply of ladies under the rules that (i) you may inspect one lady at a time; (ii) you must propose to her, or she goes out of your life forever; (iii) your first proposal will be accepted. Under these circumstances, how many ladies do you inspect before proposing? The analysis does more to display the logic of sequential experimentation than to advise the bachelor, but perhaps the result—briefly, and without its full qualifications, when the last lady is the best you've seen, propose—contains a moral for those who have to select a university president.

Sobel and Wald (1949) set forth a sequential procedure for allocating a person to one of three categories. Paulsen (1963) has now extended this line of work to the more general placement procedure with n treatments.

Mathematical work on sequential-ranking problems may prove to have direct applicability to personnel decisions. In our first edition (pp. 91 ff.) we considered multi-stage decision rules and the resulting utilities where a certain proportion of a normal population is to be accepted. While this is useful enough for surveying relationships among parameters, in making actual decisions it is often necessary to fill a fixed quota by hiring, say, the best 5 men out of 15 candidates. The sample of candidates may have an ability distribution quite unlike that in the population, and the level of ability that marks the lower limit of acceptability cannot be determined from population parameters. The decision maker is to select the best N' of N candidates, that is, those whose true ability is highest. At each stage of testing he may accept some men and reject others, continuing until the quota is filled. Mathematical statisticians are examining the appropriate decision rule, the expected cost of experimenting, and the expected distribution of ability in the group selected, under various assumptions about the distribution of observed scores for the person and various ways of assessing or limiting the cost of erroneous decisions. It is generally assumed that the tests used at the several stages are identical in statistical properties. The most directly useful paper is that of Bechhofer (1958), which deals with selecting the best individual; the generalization to $N' > 1$ is not yet published (Bechhofer *et al.*, in preparation).

In guidance testing and some forms of diagnosis one is interested in obtaining a description of the person's salient abilities, interests, or limitations. This can be seen as a problem of selecting a certain number of dimensions from a set of potentially significant dimensions. Somerville's two-stage procedure (p. 95, above) was a step in this direction. It seems likely that the sequential-ranking procedures mentioned earlier can provide a more complete mathematical model for this type of descriptive investigation. We might assume, for instance, that the counselor wishes to identify the person's three highest interests, out of a dozen, as a basis for conversations about courses and careers. This is formally the problem of selecting the three components in a 12-variate distribution that have the highest means. Work on this problem is also in progress (Bechhofer *et al.*).

The problem shifts from one of choosing a sequential decision rule to one of sequential design of experiments when the investigator can choose among tests at stage k, on the basis of results at stages 1 to $k-1$. This is a problem studied by Chernoff (1959; 1960a, 1960b, 1961) and his students; the 1960b paper, while mathematical in content, is an unusually lucid account. Suppose there are two ability-level categories, each corresponding to an indicated treatment, and two repeatable tests having different operating-characteristic curves (regressions of observed score on ability). Then, after collecting information about a person with one of the tests, the investigator should be able confidently to assign him to one of the treatments or, if not, to decide which of the two tests to use next for greatest efficiency in preceding toward a final allocation. The chief difficulty from a mathematical point of view is that if the two ability categories are contiguous—as is usual in personnel decisions—the testing is long extended for a person close to the borderline. Second, the investigator is directed to act, at each stage, as if convinced that the maximum likelihood estimate of ability level based on the data so far collected is very nearly accurate. But this is tenable and the procedure is highly efficient only where it costs little to obtain data of considerable accuracy. The former difficulty can evidently be overcome (Chernoff, 1960a). No substantial theory exists, however, for the case where it is costly to obtain precise information, as in personnel testing.

Raiffa (1961) considers the design of a procedure for assigning the person to one of two categories on the basis of multivariate information. He summarizes the work as follows (pp. 188-189):

> . . . it is helpful to keep in mind two hypothetical problem areas for application: (1) medical diagnostics and (2) prediction of ultimate performance in pilot training. In the case of medical diagnostics we are often confronted with relatively few potential item predictors, and these predictors vary in cost or even in the risk of administration (e.g., an X-ray, a guinea-pig test, an exploratory operation). The formal treatment recognizes that in practice sequential plans are often used, and therefore we have to depart from the classical notion of an optimal selection of k items from N to allow for the case where the choice of the next item to be selected at a given stage can depend on the responses to the items previously chosen. That is, not all individuals will be given the same items, and, generalizing, we can even allow the number of item predictors to vary from individual to individual. Formally, this problem reduces to a problem in the sequential design of experiments and, as is the case in sequential designs, optimal stopping rules will naturally involve an analysis of the marginal cost of adding a specific item versus the marginal decrease in risk of making wrong terminal predictions attributable to the addition of this item. For the case where the number N of potential item predictors is small (less than 7, say) we shall give an algorithm for the solution of this problem, which is optimal in senses to be prescribed below.
>
> For the case where the number N of potential predictors is large—as is the case in predicting pilot performance by pretraining indices—but the number of predictors to be chosen is small, we can at least conceptually provide an algorithm for an "optimal" solution that is identical to the case where N is small. Computationally, however, the suggested optimal procedures may be impractical—perhaps, even for large-scale machines—and "reasonable" procedures, which are recognized to be non-optimal, are suggested. In particular, we shall define "forward Bayes sequential procedure of order s" ($s = 1, 2, 3, \ldots$), which essentially looks ahead s steps and chooses at each stage the next best s items, or, more generally, $r < s$ best items, conditional upon the information available at that stage.
> More formally, this problem can be viewed as a dynamic programming

problem with a horizon of s steps. As selections of items are made, the analysis is repeated, keeping a floating fixed horizon ahead of us. . . .

A penalty e_s is introduced that gives the cost of the effort of analyzing an order s procedure; this "effort penalty" can be roughly approximated prior to any detailed analysis. Naturally, $e_1 < e_2 < e_3 < \ldots$. Reasonable over-all procedures must take into account (1) losses due to wrong terminal decisions, (2) costs of observing items, and (3) effort of analyzing a procedure. The quantity e_s is (among other things) a function of the total number of potential item predictors; hence preliminary reductions in the number of item predictors enable us to utilize higher-order analyses for the remaining contenders. To cope with the case in which sequential selection of items is not practical, we define, in an analogous manner, a "forward Bayes non-sequential procedure of order s." In the completely sequential case we suggest making a preliminary reduction in the number of item predictors by means of a first-order non-sequential procedure prior to the sequential analysis.

The rest of the book in which the Raiffa paper appears is also likely to be of interest to specialists in psychometrics. Papers by Sitgreaves and Solomon, in particular, deal with the use of statistical properties of test items to design efficient tests. In its present stage the work has implications more for psychometric theory than for test application. (Birnbaum's work with the logistic as a model for operating characteristics of items [1957] is also in this category.) The reader interested in this book will wish to examine also an illuminating review by Lord (1962) which closes with these blunt comments: "Any appreciable progress in test design in the future must surely be based on the application of decision theory and related techniques to appropriate mathematical models for the test responses. The present book shows clearly how this is done. . . . The serious student who is interested in the content of the book but finds himself unable to follow the mathematics will have to consider whether he is receiving the mathematical training necessary for creative professional work in the field of his interests."

Sequential Measurement in Psychology

It seems likely that the next decade will see the development, at least on a pilot basis, of multi-stage psychological and educational tests. Studies reported to date, however, are wholly theoretical projections regarding possible measurement designs.

Paterson (1962) simulated a sequential test with homogeneous items in a computer. His interest centered on the distribution of item difficulties, as it affects accuracy of measurement (estimation of true ability score). The computer simulated the behavior of a population of persons whose ability scores are normally distributed. Conventional and sequential measurement strategies were compared. The former was a single-stage procedure in which each subject responded to six items of uniform difficulty ($p = .50$). In the sequential procedure, the first stage was an item of that same difficulty, but the subject who passed moved on to a slightly harder. item, and the subject who failed to an easier item. After five such branches (six items), the subject was assigned a score representing a best estimate of his ability. (A number-right score is of course meaningless where the subject may take any of 26 item sequences, but one can infer the posterior distribution of ability scores for persons passing each particular sequence.) Paterson was limited by his computer program to exactly six items per subject, and neither his sequential nor his single-stage procedure is necessarily the most efficient possible procedure of that structure. The reason for expecting a sequential program to be somewhat advantageous in this measurement problem, as it is in Chernoff's two-category placement, is that dichotomous items of unequal difficulty have different operating characteristics; an able person is measured more efficiently by a hard item and a weak person by an easy one.

Paterson's sequential method gave more precise estimates of ability than the single-stage method. The data are difficult to summarize, but one of his calculations may be described. From each test, the student gets an estimated ability score; these scores are normalized with s.d. 10. Consider, now, the subjects with true ability in the top 1.8% of the true ability distribution. The variance of scores derived from the conventional test for these persons is 6.8; this is a sort of error variance, inflated because it includes the true variance remaining in the curtailed distribution. Using data from the sequential test, the comparable variance for the same persons is 3.9. This accuracy is equal to that of a conventional test of ten or more items. There is another comparison for subjects of average true ability; the six-item sequential test is as good as a seven- or eight-item conventional test.

All these results are for a normal distribution of ability and an assumed biserial correlation between item and ability of .75. This implies a much higher level of item intercorrelation (or precision of measurement) than is normally found; indeed, the variances within ability groups indicate that the six-item conventional test had a reliability well above .80. While Paterson also experimented sequentially with items whose precision is more like items in actual use, he did not compare these sequential tests with a comparable single-stage procedure. Sequential testing would probably have little advantage where precision is at more reasonable levels, so long as items are homogeneous in content and a fixed number of items is used for all persons.

Keith Smith (1961) discusses sequential collection of psychophysical data. Here the stimuli are arranged on a continuum, in much the same way as items in any ability test may be ordered according to difficulty. If one wants to know the stimulus level at which the person responds correctly on some proportion (say, .70) of the trials, he can more efficiently determine this by selecting stimulus strength for each trial on the basis of the subject's previous responses. It is not clear from Keith Smith's report whether these proposals have been tried in actual experiments and how great a gain in efficiency is to be expected.

The concept of sequential testing is being realized crudely, but on a fairly large scale, in "branched" programmed instruction where a wrong answer dictates the explanation to which the student will next be exposed and the questions he must then answer. The "computer-based" instruction now undergoing laboratory trial is demonstrating the almost unlimited possibilities for assembling an idiosyncratic sequence of learning experiences for each learner, adapting the series of questions on the basis of his successive responses. Since the person is changing from trial to trial, drawing inferences is more complicated than in sequential testing where the person is, by hypothesis, fixed. It therefore seems quite feasible to design computer-based testing for such purposes as educational diagnosis, interest measurement, and even psychiatric diagnosis. In such a system, there would be a library containing thousands of items testing different aspects of behavior, knowledge, attitude, or mental functioning; the predetermined program would administer, say, ten items and then select items 11-15 on the basis of the first ten responses, according to predetermined rules. The potentialities of such a system cannot be realized by merely plotting a few specific intersecting pathways through a field of questions. The number of conceivable permutations of items and responses being astronomical, it will be necessary to program a general strategy of item selection. For a given objective this might require classification of the items within a multidimensional space or system, and mathematical determination of a criterion for stopping testing along one or another dimension. Unlike conventional testing that scores all persons on the same task, a sequential test will be poorly suited to making comparisons; but it will be very well suited to making absolute decisions about one person after another.

Though computer-based testing has apparently not yet been attempted, relevant ideas may be borrowed from theoretical studies of instructional programming. Smallwood (1962) describes a strategy for determining what block of instructional material to present next. From past responses, he estimates the student's probable performance (test score) on each one of the blocks under consideration as alternatives, and his probable time for that work. The person's score at the end of a block is u; the decision rule is based on an "acceptable" score u_{min}. If one or more blocks are expected to make $u \geqslant u_{min}$, the block within that set that will require the least time is chosen. If no block has an expected u for the student greater than or equal to u_{min}, the block expected to yield the best score is chosen, regardless of time. For sequential testing one could use some of Smallwood's mathematical machinery, but a new decision rule would be needed. In another mathematical study of branching, Dear and Atkinson (1962) set out a strategy to teach two simple concept identifications, one of which helps in learning the second. As this strategy is derived from a stimulus-sampling learning model, it does not appear to be as directly related to sequential testing as does Smallwood's. A paper by Restle (1964) demonstrates how mathematical models may be used to formalize decisions. He shows, for example, that under certain assumptions optimum class size depends on the ratio of the value of the teacher's time to the value of the learner's time. A programmatic discussion by Arnold Roe (1963) considers much the grandest use of utility theory yet. He envisions, as a logical possibility, a system that sequentially designs training for each individual and at the same time collects information about the learning process so as to sequentially revise its instructional strategies, all this being aimed to maximize the value of the lifetime productive output of some series of learners. An illustrative analysis of alternative strategies is given.

The possibilities of sequential analysis of training data were explored in a generally neglected paper by Lawrence (1954). He formulated mathematically the problem of training design, where one stage of training is intended to facilitate the next stage. The cost of training must be offset by one or both of two benefits: an improved initial performance level on the transfer test and an improved rate of learning. The analysis suggests that the second gain has much greater utility, though transfer research ordinarily emphasizes the former. He points out that the first training serves both a selection and a placement function; final training is more efficient if persons are grouped according to initial training results, and given final training fitted to their characteristics. Furthermore, the initial training can in principle be adapted sequentially, as the early trials provide information on parameters that predict the individual's learning *and transfer*. Whenever the estimate of asymptotic performance on the final task falls below some predetermined value, the individual is summarily eliminated. This analysis was perhaps no more than a provocative exercise when it was published; today, with computer control of training a realistic possibility, it becomes a source of highly experimentable questions.

Computer-based instruction is, at least in principle, a completely adaptive, completely sequential decision making capable of supplanting "placement decisions." One can imagine, for example, a computer system for teaching college mathematics that deals simultaneously with 50 students of highly diverse backgrounds and aptitudes. Each successive instructional block is a new placement decision; one student can be "sent back" to a review of elementary coordinate geometry while another is started into differential calculus. But unlike semester long assignments made from a Freshman Week test, these decisions have only a temporary effect. With each hour of instruction a new placement decision is made on the basis of the newly acquired data. In those types of instruction for which computers are economical, they may render obsolete the sectioning or streaming of students on the basis of pretests.

Sequential Design in Configural Prediction

Configural prediction based on "moderator variables" may call for a type of two-stage testing quite unlike that envisioned in Chapter 6. If variable a predicts criterion c for subjects with low scores on variable b, but not for subjects with high scores on b, the regression surface is a complex function involving product terms of the form ab; b is said to be a moderator variable (Saunders, 1956). Frederiksen and Melville (1954) found that the importance of interests as a predictor of grades depended on whether a student was compulsive or not. For non-compulsive students, interests might profitably be used as a predictor; for compulsives, only aptitude measures seem useful. This finding, though cross-validated, it not so well established that it is ready for practical application. If such findings are ever to be used, the efficient procedure is a two-stage battery in which the first stage measures variable b, and thus indicates which individuals should subsequently be measured on a.

Ghiselli's work on "the prediction of predictability" (1960) is logically similar to the search for moderator variables, and leads to a two-stage selection process. His procedure is to develop a "differential predictability" measure that indicates, in a particular selection situation, which of two predictor tests will best predict the criterion for each individual in turn. This measure is then used as a first screen to determine which of the two tests should constitute the second screen. Whether this is superior to the administration of both predictors, to be combined into a battery score, depends on the costs of the three tests and the interrelations of the scores with each other and the criterion. The theory of the procedure requires considerable elaboration, though C. D. Johnson (1960) has taken some steps in this direction. Ghiselli's work (1960) is well illustrated by the following account of one study:

The subjects in this investigation were taxicab drivers, 170 of whom were used as the experimental group and 87 as the cross-validation group. Among several tests given to these men at the time of hiring was a motor test (paper-and-pencil tapping and dotting) and a spatial test (discrimination of distance). These two tests were taken as predictor variables and production, dollar volume of fares collected during the first eight weeks of employment, was used as the criterion.

The subjects in the experimental group were subdivided into those for whom the standard scores on the motor test were more similar to [their] standard criterion scores and those for whom the standard scores on the spatial test were more similar to [their] standard criterion scores. Available on these men were scores on four interest inventories (occupational

TABLE S3. VALIDITY COEFFICIENTS FOR PRODUCTIVITY USING FOR VARIOUS PROPORTIONS OF SUBJECTS THEIR SCORES ON THE MOTOR AND SPATIAL TESTS
(after Ghiselli, 1960, p. 682)

CUTOFF SCORE ON THE DIFFERENTIAL PREDICTABILITY VARIABLE	PER CENT OF CASES WHOSE SCORES WERE USED ON THE:		VALIDITY COEFFICIENT
	MOTOR TEST	SPATIAL TEST	
...	100	0	.20
−1.0	94	6	.21
−0.7	68	32	.33
−0.4	55	45	.31
−0.1	41	59	.28
+0.2	29	71	.25
+0.5	21	79	.16
+0.8	10	90	.04
...	0	100	.02

level, jobs done out-of-doors, active occupations, and occupations involving dealing with people) together with age and years of education. None of the four interest inventory scores distinguished between the two subgroups, but significant differences were found for age and education. [In other studies, inventory scores had been useful.] Those individuals for whom the spatial test gave better predictions were older and had less education. . . . As a [differential predictability] variable, standard scores were computed for age and education and they were averaged, with the former carrying twice the weight of the latter [whose scale was reversed].

The results obtained for the application of this differential predictability variable to the cross-validation group are shown in Table [S3]. The validity coefficient of the motor test alone was .20 and of the spatial test alone .02. However, taking an optimal cutoff point on the differential predictability variable such that for 68 per cent of the cases their motor test scores were used and for the remaining 32 per cent their spatial test scores, the validity coefficient was .33.

This increase in validity represents a 60% gain in utility, as a result of using a test that over *all* subjects has a validity of zero! Some further gains might conceivably be obtained by some combination of the first- and second-screen scores in the hiring decision. Whereas, for research purposes, motor and spatial tests were given to all men, Ghiselli would propose to administer only the motor or spatial test in subsequent hiring (unless convenience and cost factors suggested giving both tests and ignoring one score for each man).

APTITUDE-TREATMENT INTERACTIONS

One of the most striking concepts emerging in the first edition is that placement decisions call for tests that have differential validity (pp. 67, 126). A test that predicts payoff within a treatment may not predict which treatment is best for an individual. The first edition argument that psychologists should search for aptitude dimensions and treatment dimensions that interact to determine outcome was presented to a wider audience by Cronbach (1957). This theme has now been echoed by a considerable number of methodological or theoretical essays (e.g., Stanley, 1960; Carroll, 1962). Lubin (1961) concludes a discussion of experiments on treatment effects with these remarks:

Disordinal interaction [crossing of regression lines within the range of the independent variable] has certain philosophical implications. If we conduct an experiment to answer questions like "Is Method A better than Method B?" "What is the best treatment?" etc. and we find disordinal interaction, then in my opinion we have asked the wrong question. Remember Murphy's Maxim: "For good answers, good questions can always be found, but some good questions have no answers."

Much of the history of medicine can be thought of as a search for disordinal interaction. The Hippocratic physician of the fourth and fifth century B.C. had a clear concept of diagnosis, but the idea that differential diagnosis implies differential treatment was alien to him. There was only one treatment: to increase the healing force of nature. Since then, the notion of diagnosis as an indicator for differential treatment has grown so strong and has had such great success that physicians like Paul Ehrlich have willingly spent most of their professional lives looking for a specific cure for one disease. Yet, there are still psychiatric studies in which drugs are applied to many types of mental patients, and no attempt is made to ascertain whether there is an interaction between treatments and diagnosis. Experiments of this kind may be good fun; they cannot be said to be good medicine.

The acceptance of interactions as important has not been followed by an outpouring of new data on aptitude-treatment interactions. There have been, however, many scattered reports of interactions, and much research now underway is designed so as to reveal interactions if they are present.

A representative study is that of Osburn and Melton (1963) who correlated various aptitude tests with several criterion tests in a novel and a traditional high school algebra course. There were three classes in each treatment group (82 and 73 cases, respectively). The published results are most simply summarized in terms of a rough classification of the correlations of each predictor with the several post-tests:

Tests showing higher *r*'s in experimental group: PMA Space, Word Fluency; DAT Numerical, Abstract, Mechanical, Sentences.

Tests showing similar *r*'s in both groups: Iowa Algebra Aptitude; PMA Verbal, Reasoning; DAT Verbal, Space.

Tests showing higher *r*'s in traditional group: PMA Number; DAT Clerical, Spelling.

The significance of these results is obscure, as is true of most interactions reported to date. The small numbers of classes, instructors, and pupils make us hesitate to take the differences seriously, and any explanation of the results is speculative. Both of these difficulties can best be dealt with by carrying out further experiments.

Studies of interactions too often—as in the Osburn-Melton paper —report correlations rather than regression equations or data from which the equations might be constructed. Such complete information tells whether differences in correlation reflect differences in variability only. Also, it indicates whether the regressions cross within the range of talent. If they do not, one treatment is better for all cases and placement would have no advantage.

Osburn and Melton have supplied unpublished data that permit a better understanding both of the events they investigated and the methodology of interaction research. The data (Table S4) are for a common final examination that was given to both groups; this is only one of several outcome variables whose correlations entered into the summary above. On this criterion, the mean difference of about 0.2 s.d. is not significant and—since the experimental group tended to be about equally superior on the predictors —can be disregarded. The difference in s.d.'s is significant at the .05 level, and is not accounted for by pretreatment differences. The experimental procedure leads to more striking successes and more severe failures than the traditional method, which poses a nice policy question for the school administrator!

The correlations in Table S4 suggest that PMA Space, DAT Abstract, DAT Space, and DAT Spelling all interact with treatment in determining final common performance. But the greater s.d. in the experimental group offsets the higher correlation for spelling

TABLE S4. COMPARISON OF WITHIN-TREATMENT REGRESSIONS
(data from Osburn and Melton)

TEST	GROUP	MEAN	S.D.	CORRELATION WITH FINAL COMMON EXAMINATION	REGRESSION SLOPE, FINAL ON PREDICTOR	CROSSOVER POINT RAW	CROSSOVER POINT S.D.-UNITS
PMA	Exp.	21.30	10.83	.37	.125	11.0	−1.0
Space	Trad.	19.94	10.80	.23	.062	11.0	−0.8
PMA	Exp.	23.39	8.03	.50	.228	<0	<−5
Verbal	Trad.	23.75	6.92	.54	.226	<0	<−5
DAT	Exp.	29.69	8.73	.57	.239	24.0	−0.6
Abstract	Trad.	29.67	7.90	.29	.106	24.0	−0.7
DAT	Exp.	43.59	22.74	.49	.079	27.9	−0.7
Space	Trad.	42.47	23.13	.26	.032	27.9	−0.6
DAT	Exp.	44.53	25.41	.47	.068	253.8	>5
Spelling	Trad.	37.74	23.99	.57	.069	253.8	>5
Final	Exp.	14.56	3.66				
common	Trad.	13.81	2.90				
exam.							

in the traditional group, so that there is no interaction; the regression slopes are nearly the same. The interaction for the abstract and space tests is such that the regression lines cross in the neighborhood of $-.5$ to -1.0 s.d.; this implies that the fraction of the group lowest in non-verbal reasoning would learn more from the traditional than the experimental course. The gain from such placement is not expected to be large, as the regression slopes do not differ greatly. Assuming that, in the population, DAT Abstract is distributed normally with mean 30 and σ 8 and that the group is divided at 24.5 (-0.69, ca. 25th percentile), we estimate the following expected means:

Experimental course		Traditional course		Diff.
Upper three-fourths	15.43	Upper three-fourths	14.19	1.24
Lower one-fourth	12.23	Lower one-fourth	12.78	$-.55$
All cases	14.63	All cases	13.84	.79

With placement:

$$\tfrac{1}{4}[3(15.43) + 12.78] = 14.77.$$

The gain from placement turns out to be only .55 points per case for the low group assigned to traditional mathematics (.14 points for the average over all cases). It would be necessary to accentuate the interaction, probably by deliberate design of the experimental course to capitalize much more on non-verbal abilities, before placement would have practical value. There seems to be little doubt that, for the next decade at least, the study of aptitude-treatment interactions will be more important for what it tells us about the psychology of instruction than for immediate use in placement.

Studies such as that of Osburn and Melton obviously invite comparison of multiple-regression functions for the two treatments, though they did not take this step (wisely, considering their sample size and large number of predictions). It seems worthwhile to sound a warning against constructing regression equations in the usual way and comparing the beta weights for each variable from one treatment to another. If predictors x and y are highly correlated, the equations $5x + y$ and $x + 5y$ represent almost identical vectors in the underlying factor space and lead to very similar multiple correlations (Ward, 1962b). To compare regression weights under different treatments, it is necessary to orthogonalize the variate set, preferably by a method of factor analysis that produces maximally interpretable transformations (Heermann, 1963). The same transformed variables can then be used in both groups. Even with this procedure, no meaningful interpretation is possible if the original correlations among predictors vary substantially from one treatment group to another.

The payoff function relating outcome to aptitude and treatment is a "response surface," in the terminology of Box and his associates. Maxwell (1957) and Meyer (1963) have discussed experimental designs for the exploration of such surfaces with psychological and educational variables.

When and if interactions are clearly established, decision makers will want to adjust treatments and assignments to capitalize on these facts. But adaptation can be realized in only a very loose way. Even if instructional procedures were carefully engineered to adjust the chief parameters to their optimum values for a certain type of subject, those adjustments will in time be rendered obsolete by changes in the society or the institutional setting. To obtain a perspective on what it means to adjust treatments for true efficiency, Box's description (1957) of "evolutionary operation" should be studied. He draws on experience with industrial processes, such as attempts to adjust temperature and the concentrations of reagents to maximize the yield of a chemical process. Instead of determining the best combination, and setting all production lines to that pattern, he finds it worthwhile to continually vary the parameter values, trying various departures from the erstwhile ideal. This permits him to discover new relevant variables and to discover when the established formula no longer holds good. The same philosophy of continued experimentation during normal operations could well apply in education and in psychiatric treatment.

THE STATISTICAL EVALUATION OF EDUCATIONAL ALLOCATION AND SELECTION

By D. J. FINNEY*
*Department of Statistics and A.R.C. Unit of Statistics,
University of Aberdeen*

SUMMARY

This paper is an attempt to formulate some of the problems of educational allocation in statistical terms, and to indicate how optimal solutions can be sought. An oversimplified model of the process that selects university entrants is presented and examined in detail. Attention is concentrated on the two stages of selection at 11+ and at the age of leaving school, and the effects of varying proportions at these stages on the operating characteristics of the whole process are discussed. It seems clear that such a process must fail to discover a high proportion of those who are above the minimum standard for suitability for a university, even though it makes provision for correction of gross errors of judgement at 11 + , but these failures will consist largely of marginal cases.

In later sections, the model used is criticized and various modifications proposed. A more realistic model for the existing situation, taking account of additional factors and stages of selection, might have a better operating characteristic. The consequences of increasing the proportion of the population admitted to universities are briefly mentioned, but this step is in the main a change of standards rather than an improvement in detection of the most suitable entrants. A model appropriate to comprehensive secondary schools, with their opportunities for frequent sifting and regrading, might give much better results, but at present the mathematical complexity prevents its further discussion. Comments are made on the adjustment of the model to take account of the effect of type of secondary school on the subsequent abilities of the children, and on the recognition that the dichotomy "university-or-not" is an inadequate summary of the purpose and success of education. The statistical techniques used in the paper could be adapted to some of the more general and

* Reprinted from *J. Roy. Stat. Soc.*, 1962, ser. A, 125, 525-564.

more realistic problems; clearer definitions of aims and criteria are first needed, and very heavy computations could then be undertaken.

Finally, I must emphasize that I neither assert nor believe that educational policy on allocation or selection can be reduced to problems of pure mathematical and statistical analysis. I fully recognize that the fundamental questions are for experts on education to discuss and to answer. The sole virtues of the present approach are objective examination of how to implement most efficiently an agreed general policy and a consequent focusing of attention on the questions that need to be answered before a determinate policy can be stated. My intention throughout has not been to produce new educational dogma, or even to subscribe to old dogma, but to show the kind of help that the statistician ought to be able to give to the quantitative evaluation of educational policy.

1. JUSTIFICATION

This paper is not an attempt by a statistician to usurp the functions of educational experts or to suggest that educational planning can be reduced to problems of statistical theory; it does advance the claim that some aspects of educational policy are largely statistical in character and that there is no excuse for not making the statistical treatment as efficient as possible.

A few months ago, in his contribution to a series of articles on "The gifted child," Sir Cyril Burt (1961) remarked that "On the dull, the defective and the mentally subnormal, the literature is nearly 10 times as voluminous as the literature dealing with the gifted." He later wisely commented: "The nation's pool of ability is strictly limited; and we still allow much of it to run idly to waste." Few today would question the need for providing adequately for the education of the subnormal, even though here the concern may be largely with the effect on the child and less with his individual contribution to the community. If we neglect the other end of the scale, at our peril we leave to haphazard development that most valuable of natural resources, the mental abilities of our ablest citizens. Moreover, any consideration of educating the gifted child must take into account not only the effect on him but also his potential value for the enrichment of the life of the community.

I hope no one will quarrel with these statements, but their relation to statistics may not be clear. However, if we are to develop to best advantage the mental abilities of all, emphasis on the manner in which children are guided into different channels of education must grow. Under authoritarian rule, guidance may be submerged in some more rigid control. Surely the principle needs equal recognition even under a democracy that leaves much to personal choice, at least to the extent that those responsible for the provision of educational facilities from public funds must be concerned to design them and encourage their use for the maximum benefit of the community. Some system of allocation to different types of school, or to different streams within a school, is then seen to be inevitable; the aims of that system deserve careful study and definition, and the manner in which those aims are to be achieved must then be examined. Of course, "allocation" might imply only recommendation rather than compulsion. (In most democracies, parents are permitted to bypass the "system" by way of fee-paying schools; discussion of the educational merits and of the ethics of this is of undoubted importance, but forms no part of the present subject, and my paper does not relate to children from these schools.) The specification of the ideal pattern of allocation is a task for, and doubtless a source of great argument among, educational experts. Once the ideals have been agreed, however, there can be no excuse for not attempting to approach as closely to them as the available instruments for measuring ability will permit. Even if those who determine policy were to be unsure of their aims, so that, either on account of differences of opinion (in effect the present position in respect of different Local Education Authorities) or for an experimental period, different policies were allowed to coexist, implementation of each with maximal efficiency would be desirable.

This paper is an attempt to discuss some of the problems of achieving optimal allocation. It is open to criticism as being too strongly oriented to the success with which those of highest ability are allocated. As in other contexts, no evaluation of an optimal is possible until a criterion for deciding between alternatives has been agreed. The criteria used below may indeed be prejudiced in favour of the more able; the method, however, can be adapted to other criteria, and the only barrier is the necessity of first reaching agreement on the ideal criterion, which is not really a statistician's responsibility.

2. THE ROLE OF THE STATISTICIAN

When a criterion has been decided, the statistician can begin to make his contribution. The measuring instruments available as a basis for allocation—tests, examinations, school records, interviews —are notoriously imperfect predictors of future performance, but there is no escape from using them. The best way of using them, "best" in the sense of maximizing agreement between the actual and the ideal allocation, is open to investigation. In particular, any simplified but tolerably realistic model of the system to be operated will recognize that there must be more than one point in the career of a child at which he is exposed to the process of allocation, and the statistician should be able to offer advice on the optimal balance between proportions at these different *stages*. The purely statistical problems involved are not easy, and any progress seems likely to require very extensive computations. This paper attempts a beginning by consideration of one very simple model, discussion of which will illustrate some of the difficulties, statistical and non-statistical, that are involved.

A complete separation between formulation of policy and statistical study of its optimal implementation is undesirable, for each will benefit from a proper understanding of the other. Moreover, examination of the results of the statistical analysis may sometimes be a pointer to the inadequacy of the information on which the policy was based or to oversimplifications in the statement of that policy. The analysis will be entirely objective, and, provided that mathematical and numerical errors have been eliminated, any foolish appearance of its results can derive only from some folly implicit in the model to which it was applied.

Sections 3 to 8 of this paper, then, present and discuss a very simple model and its far from simple analysis. I am well aware of some of the grave imperfections in this; however, I suggest that a broad general consideration of some of the flaws in the model, as in Sections 9 and 10, may indicate qualitatively the changes in conclusions that are desirable. And, perhaps far more important, critical study of these flaws may aid the fuller understanding of the problems and the subsequent formulation of a more realistic model, may indeed help to concentrate research on the gap between educational intention and educational practice.

3. THE POPULATION MODEL

I propose to discuss a model that involves allocation or selection at two stages only, perhaps the simplest non-trivial case. Although I am concerned more with method than with particular numerical values, I think it important to see examples of the numerical behaviour of the model; I shall therefore present the method as applied to two stages in the life of each cohort of children, grammar school admission (i.e., "11+") and university admission, for which certain statistical parameters will later be guessed (Section 7). Moreover, I propose to concentrate attention on the question of whether or not the right persons receive a university education, admittedly a grave narrowing of the objectives of secondary schooling.

For simplicity, suppose that at each of the two stages individual decisions are based on scores compounded from all test and examination results and other information then thought relevant; the optimal manner of combining many different measurements available at one stage into a single index or score is not under discussion here, but is supposed already to have been decided, perhaps by techniques of multiple regression. The grammar school admission score will be termed y_1 and the university admission score y_2. As an ideal criterion, suppose that there exists a quantity x for each individual, representing his suitability for university education. One would like to think that, for those who *are* admitted to a university, x was closely related to performance in the final degree examination, but that would imply a validity for university examinations greater than their more objective critics dare claim. Thus x cannot be determined for any individual, but perhaps some guess as to its distributional properties will prove reasonable.

Without any loss of essential generality, x, y_1, and y_2 may be taken as normally distributed for the whole population in an age group, with means zero and variances σ^2, ω_1^2, ω_2^2 respectively; any other distributions can be rescaled to these. (The further simplification of scaling so that all variances are unity would have the disadvantage of destroying numerous simple checks on the "dimensions" of formulae.) In addition, however, x, y_1, y_2 will be assumed to have jointly a trivariate normal distribution in this population, with correlation coefficients ρ_1, ρ_2 between x and y_1, y_2 and ρ_y between y_1 and y_2.

Suppose now that at the first stage the population is divided into two parts on the basis of the known values of y_1; a fraction P_1 of the whole with the highest values of y_1 forms one part and the remaining fraction Q_1 $(= 1 - P_1)$ forms the other. In general, the two subpopulations thus created will no longer be normally distributed in respect of any of x, y_1, y_2. However, unless P_1 or Q_1 is very small or ρ_1 and ρ_y are very large, the distortion of the form of the distributions of x and y_2 will not be great. Moreover, as is well known, correlation coefficients will usually be reduced in absolute magnitude within the subpopulations.

Properties of the distributions in these subpopulations are easily obtained.° They are expressible in terms of functions of the standardized normal distribution. If $T(P)$ and $Z(P)$ are functions of a proportion P, $O \leqslant P \leqslant 1$, defined by

$$P = \int_{T(P)}^{\infty} \frac{1}{\sqrt{2\pi}} \; e^{-\frac{1}{2}t^2} \, dt \tag{F1}$$

and

$$Z(P) = \frac{1}{\sqrt{2\pi}} \; e^{-\frac{1}{2}[T(P)]^2} \tag{F2}$$

then the function $\nu(P)$ is defined as

$$\nu(P) = Z(P)/P, \tag{F3}$$

and differential coefficients of ν *with respect to* T are denoted by ν', ν'' . . . etc. Pearson (1931) has tabulated T and ν for $P = .001 \; (.001).999$. Elsewhere (1956), I have tabulated T, ν, and its first four derivatives for a few values of P, and an unpublished table by Lipton covers the range up to $P = .5$ fairly thoroughly.

In the subpopulation with the fraction P_1 of highest values of y_1, the mean values are

$$E(x) = \sigma \rho_1 \; \nu(P_1), \tag{F4}$$

$$E(y_1) = \omega_1 \; \nu(P_1), \tag{F5}$$

$$E(y_2) = \omega_2 \; \rho_y \; \nu(P_1). \tag{F6}$$

The corresponding variances are

$$V(x) = \sigma^2[1 - \rho_1^2 \; \nu'(P_1)], \tag{F7}$$

$$V(y_1) = \omega_1^2[1 - \nu'(P_1)], \tag{F8}$$

$$V(y_2) = \omega_2^2[1 - \rho_y^2 \; \nu'(P_1)]. \tag{F9}$$

The correlation coefficients in this subpopulation are

$$\rho(x, y_1) = \rho_1 \left[\frac{1 - \nu'(P_1)}{1 - \rho_1^2 \; \nu'(P_1)} \right]^{\frac{1}{2}}, \tag{F10}$$

$$\rho(x, y_2) = \frac{\rho_2 - \rho_1 \rho_y \nu'(P_1)}{[1 - \rho_1^2 \nu'(P_1)]^{\frac{1}{2}} \; [1 - \rho_y^2 \nu'(P_1)]^{\frac{1}{2}}}, \tag{F11}$$

° This symbol indicates omission of a reference given as documentation in the original paper.

$$\rho(y_1, y_2) = \rho_y \left[\frac{1 - \nu'(P_1)}{1 - \rho_y^2 \nu'(P_1)} \right]^{\frac{1}{2}}. \tag{F12}$$

Hence as a first approximation, the distribution may be taken as trivariate normal with the nine parameters just specified. Similarly the distribution in the Q_1 fraction will have for its parameters these expressions with $\nu(P_1)$ replaced by $-\nu(Q_1)$ and $\nu'(P_1)$ replaced by $\nu'(Q_1)$.

When attention turns to the second stage, only the joint distribution of x and y_2 is of interest. The bivariate normal approximation will often be adequate, since the greatest distortion of normality will be that affecting y_1; both this approximation and an improvement on it are employed in Section 8. As Finney (1956, 1962a) and Tallis (1961) have shown, the general moments or cumulants of this distribution are easily obtainable. If κ_{ij} is written for the bivariate cumulant of order i in x and j in y_2, then for $i + j > 2$

$$\kappa_{ij} = (\sigma \rho_1)^i (\omega_2 \rho_y)^j \left(-\frac{\partial}{\partial T_1} \right)^{i+j-1} \nu(P_1) \tag{F13}$$

for the P_1 fraction and

$$\kappa_{ij} = - (\sigma \rho_1)^i (\omega_2 \rho_y)^j \left(\frac{\partial}{\partial T_1} \right)^{i+j-1} \nu(Q_1) \tag{F14}$$

for the Q_1 fraction.

4. SELECTION AND ALLOCATION

I have elsewhere (1958) contrasted educational selection with the type of selection used by the plant breeder. There is superficial resemblance, in that the plant breeder has annually a new cohort of new varieties out of which, on the evidence of performance in one or more annual trials, he tries to select the best. One obvious difference is that each variety is, or should be, an entity of constant character not permanently affected by the environment to which it is exposed for a single season of growth, whereas one may expect the educational environment of a child at one period to modify permanently his capacity to respond to future environments. On this, more will be said in Section 10. A second difference of immediate importance is that new varieties of a crop of economic value will be discarded completely as soon as the evidence that they are outclassed by alternative varieties is adequate. The education of a child whose performance in a test at age 11 is markedly inferior to that of some of his contemporaries may on that account be modified in pattern but will rightly be continued. The fate of a discarded variety is of no interest to the plant breeder, and his plan for an optimal selection programme will take no account of it; to use an epithet such as "discarded" as applicable to a child of indifferent or poor intellectual capacity would be a gross distortion of human values, and nothing is further from the intention of this paper.

This vital difference lies at the root of the distinction that many are careful to draw between *selection* of children for a more academic type of education and *allocation* of each child to that form of education best suited to his abilities and needs. The 1944 Education Act requires Local Education Authorities to secure that the schools available for an area are "sufficient in number, character, and equipment to afford for all pupils opportunities for education offering such variety of instruction and training as may be desirable in view of their different ages, abilities and aptitudes." The recent tendency has therefore been to emphasize allocation rather than selection. In so far as the distinction serves to ensure that lesser intellectual capacity is not used as an excuse for giving a child an intrinsically inferior education, it is valuable. Once the ideal of having several streams of education, each excellent of its kind, is conceded, and children are placed in one or another according to estimates of their capacities, the purely verbal distinction becomes unimportant except for the images that the two words evoke in the public. Selection of the more academic minds for one educational stream or allocation of the less academically proficient to an educational pattern thought especially suitable will be much the same in practice. The one essential proviso, as safeguard against the extreme selectionist outlook, is that decisions shall not be irrevocable. First must come recognition that any allocation based upon imperfect information carries a certainty that errors of judgement will occur; then follows insistence that when mistakes at one stage subsequently become apparent they shall be corrected as soon as possible.

5. A SIMPLE SELECTION MODEL

About the simplest mathematical model that covers the two stages of grammar school and university admission for a cohort is one that begins as in Section 3. At the first stage, the fraction P_1 having the highest values of y_1 is admitted to grammar schools. At the second stage, a fraction P_2 is selected as having the highest values of y_2 within the P_1 subpopulation, these constituting the grammar school entry to the university. In addition, provision is made for correcting erroneous judgements at the first stage by also selecting a fraction P_2^* as having the highest values of y_2 within the Q_1 subpopulation. The total proportion of the age group admitted to universities is therefore π, where

$$\pi = P_1 P_2 + (1 - P_1) P_2^*. \tag{F15}$$

In practice, one would expect P_2^* to be much smaller than P_2, but the existence of a non-zero P_2^* is the assurance that a decision at the first stage is not irrevocable.

It is implied here that y_2 represents the same system of scoring within each subpopulation, as would be true if it were based on G.C.E. results. This is mentioned again in Section 9.

This paper is chiefly concerned with the optimal choice of the allocation parameters P_1, P_2, P_2^*, subject to a fixed value of π and the constraint (eq. F15). The proportion of the cohort entering universities is supposed determined by external factors, but the allocation fractions at the two stages can be varied in order to meet other requirements.

6. OPTIMAL SELECTION

Vastly oversimplified though the model in Section 5 is, it includes a wide range of possibilities. One extreme is $P_1 = 1$, $P_2 = \pi$ (P_2^* is indeterminate), which implies accepting every child for grammar school education and in effect deferring all selection until the stage of university entrance. Another is $P_2^* = 0$, or "the irrevocable 11 +," and even more particularly $P_1 = \pi$, $P_2 = 1$, $P_2^* = 0$, implying that the eventual university entrants are chosen at 11. Still more absurd, but serving to illustrate the range of possibilities covered, is any system with $P_2 = 0$: all university entrants are to be chosen from those who had the lower scores at 11!

From among all these, a choice of the best is to be made. In practice, the availability of suitable teachers and the necessity of dividing children between existing school buildings will impose some constraints, but these should be regarded primarily as inhibitors of sudden large changes. The aim of the present analysis is to seek the optimal steady state; if values of P_1, P_2, P_2^* very different from those now existing were proved desirable, they could be achieved by slow changes.

How then is "best" to be defined? One reasonable definition would be implicit in a decision to maximize the mean value of the "university suitability" for the university entrants, or rather to maximize its statistical expectation under repeated trial: the difference is small because of the large number of individuals concerned. The inevitable concomitant of this is that the mean value of x for those not securing admission to a university is minimized.

A proposal to judge the merits of an educational system primarily by the success with which it enables the universities to receive the intellectual cream might be criticized as paying too little attention to the needs of the great majority of the less gifted. An alternative, perhaps less open to misrepresentation, would be to state the ideal situation as that in which the division between those who enter a university and those who do not is made exactly correctly for the proportion π. In other words, a perfect allocation is that in which every child for whom $x \geqslant \sigma T(\pi)$ is admitted to a university and others are not; within the limitations of the simple model and a predetermined value of π, each child eventually receives the education for which he is best suited. Errors of allocation are then of two types: a child with $x \geqslant \sigma T(\pi)$ may fail to secure admission and a child with $x < \sigma T(\pi)$ may be admitted. However, if the proportion actually admitted is maintained at π, the two types of error must be equally frequent. "Best" is now taken to mean maximizing the expected proportion of correct allocations. As Dunnett (1960) has pointed out in a similar context, the two definitions are not as different as they may seem: the second maximizes the expected frequency with which x in the final selection exceeds $\sigma T(\pi)$, whereas the first can be regarded as maximizing the average amount by which individuals exceed $\sigma T(\pi)$. The one procedure simply counts correct allocations, whereas the other uses a weighted mean in which the weight is the deviation of x from $\sigma T(\pi)$; evidence presented in Section 8 suggests that the two may lead to very similar conclusions.

The problem is now completely specified. For any ρ_1, ρ_2, ρ_y, and π, mathematical and numerical analysis can be directed at finding the allocation parameters, P_1, P_2, and P_2^*, that unconditionally maximize either the mean value of x or the proportion of correct allocations. No account has been taken of costs or any other factors that may affect the relative numbers who are to experience different kinds of secondary education. Perhaps this is right; some would object strongly to any suggestion that the allocation of an individual to one of two alternative educational streams should be influenced by their relative costs. If the aim of maintaining alternatives of equal esteem is achieved, the contention that, irrespective of costs, each child should be allocated to the stream best suited to him has great force. If grammar schools both have higher prestige and cost appreciably more per child, any proposal to increase P_1 would inevitably raise questions about the justification for generosity to marginal cases. Again, it could happen that the unrestricted optimal involved a value of P_1 very much greater than π, so that inevitably a high proportion of grammar school entrants were later disappointed of their university hopes, which might be regarded as psychologically bad for the unsuccessful. This aspect of the general problem perhaps becomes more prominent if a third stage is introduced into the system, the possibility of dismissal from the university if performance during the first year is unsatisfactory. A university would probably find obvious attractions, and equally obvious disadvantages, in having a large number of admissions from whom a selection could be made at the end of the first year, so that those who eventually graduate have been selected largely on internal evidence of ability instead of on school examinations and records. An independent objection to such a policy might be the ill effects of discouraging large numbers of young men and women, who would secure university admission and then be classed as failures after only one year. Which is the better on balance, to admit say 5% of any age group and ensure that all but a very few graduate, or to admit 10%, half of whom will be asked to leave after a year but the other half who continue including some individuals who were not placed in the top 5% at admission? Attention is drawn to such difficult questions of educational policy here only in order that the possibility of modifying the statistical investigation by taking into account additional constraints may be mentioned. For example, in a model such as that implicit in equation F28, the value of $[P_1 P_2 + (1 - P_1) P_2^*]$ might have an upper limit; this would require replacement of the unconditional by an appropriate conditional maximization.

7. THE CORRELATION COEFFICIENTS

This paper is a study in methodology, and not primarily a presentation of numerical answers. To discover reasonable values for the three population correlation coefficients ρ_1, ρ_2, ρ_y has proved surprisingly difficult. However, in order to illustrate the method, calculations have been made to specifications that are intended to be not too unrealistic.

The only estimates that could be found from the literature are based upon the work of Nisbet and Buchan (1959); for 102 students who entered the University of Aberdeen in 1953, they presented information on correlations between scores on which grammar school and university admissions were based with results of degree examinations. To identify x with a measure of performance in final degree examinations is far from satisfactory, but no alternative is at present available and, for the sake of the present discussion, x is assumed at any rate to have about the same correlation structure with y_1, y_2 as do these examination marks. Rough averages from Nisbet and Buchan then seem to be

$$\left.\begin{array}{l} \rho(x, y_1) = .25, \\ \rho(x, y_2) = .30, \\ \rho(y_1, y_2) = .25, \end{array}\right\} \tag{F16}$$

within a university population derived by two-stage selection under conditions that are perhaps approximately described by $P_1 = .2$, $P_2 = .2$, and P_2^* very small.

Equations F10 to F12 can be applied to the two stages successively, so as to relate these correlation coefficients within the university to ρ_1, ρ_2, ρ_y for a whole age group. Solution of the equations leads to

$$\left.\begin{array}{l} \rho_1 = .70, \\ \rho_2 = .75, \\ \rho_y = .70, \end{array}\right\} \tag{F17}$$

as round figures. It is only fair to Nisbet and Buchan to mention that they explicitly declined to quote estimates for the population, in view of the small numbers in their university study and the consequent imprecision of their correlation coefficients within the university. Without imputing to them the responsibility, however, if any progress with this problem is to be made, extrapolation must be risked and used until such time as further studies provide more precise values. Such extrapolation may be in gross error if the various regressions involved are not linear, as would be the case, for example, if above a certain value of x the scores y_1 and y_2 are insensitive to differences in x because good performance in school examinations by children of this ability is nearly certain; heterogeneity of variances might also have serious effects.

The numerical values just obtained have the property of implying a partial correlation coefficient between y_1 and y_2, with x held constant, of magnitude

$$\frac{.70 - .70 \times .75}{(.51 \times .4375)^{\frac{1}{2}}} = .37. \tag{F18}$$

Thus the two scores have characteristics in common independently of their correlation with x. This is not surprising, but an alternative situation in which this partial correlation coefficient is zero also deserves consideration. By approximate calculations based upon equations F10 to F12, but constraining the partial correlation coefficient to be zero, conditions not seriously at variance with Nisbet and Buchan's results, the values

$$\left.\begin{array}{l} \rho_1 = .55, \\ \rho_2 = .60, \\ \rho_y = .33, \end{array}\right\} \qquad \text{(F19)}$$

were obtained. At first glance, these are unrealistic in meaning that scores at $11+$ are more highly correlated with suitability for a university than they are with the scores on which university admission is based. Although this is perhaps an unlikely state of affairs, equations F19 do represent a lower extreme in which the scores at two ages relate to very different aspects of individual ability and their consequences merit comparison with those from equations F17.

8. THE ALGEBRA OF SELECTION

If it be assumed that the distribution of x, y_2 within each of the two subpopulations created by the dichotomy at the first stage can be approximated by the bivariate normal, as will be true when neither P_1 nor Q_1 is very small and ρ_2, ρ_y are not very large, the formulae in Section 3 can be applied a second time in order to study properties of x in the subpopulations created at the second stage. There are now four distinguishable subpopulations, hereafter labeled f, f^*, g, g^*. A fraction $P_1 P_2$ of the age group, known as f, is selected from the grammar schools as having the highest values of y_2. Its expectation for x is

$$E_f \equiv E(x) = \sigma\left[\rho_1\nu(P_1) + \frac{\rho_2 - \rho_1\rho_y\nu'(P_1)}{[1 - \rho_y^2\nu'(P_1)]^{\frac{1}{2}}} \nu(P_2) \right], \quad \text{(F20)}$$

and the variance of individuals within it is

$$V_f \equiv V(x) = \sigma^2\left[1 - \rho_1^2\nu'(P_1) - \frac{[\rho_2 - \rho_1\rho_y\nu'(P_1)]^2}{1 - \rho_y^2\nu'(P_1)} \nu'(P_2) \right]. \text{(F21)}$$

Similarly, the fraction $(1 - P_1)P_2^*$, known as f^*, selected for university admissions from those who had the lower y_1 scores at the first stage, has

$$E_{f^*} = \sigma\left[-\rho_1 v(Q_1) + \frac{\rho_2 - \rho_1 \rho_y v'(Q_1)}{[1 - \rho_y^2 v'(Q_1)]^{\frac{1}{2}}} v(P_2^*)\right], \quad (F22)$$

and

$$V_{f^*} = \sigma^2\left[1 - \rho_1^2 v'(Q_1) - \frac{[\rho_2 - \rho_1 \rho_y v'(Q_1)]^2}{1 - \rho_y^2 v'(Q_1)} v'(P_2^*)\right]. \quad (F23)$$

Analogous expressions are easily written for g, the fraction $P_1(1 - P_2)$, consisting of the grammar school pupils who do not secure university admission, and for g^*, the fraction $(1 - P_1)$ $(1 - P_2^*)$, constituting the remainder of the age group.

For the whole university intake, the mean and variance will therefore be

$$E_\pi = [P_1 P_2 E_f + (1 - P_1)P_2^* E_{f^*}] \div \pi, \quad (F24)$$

$$V_\pi = \left[\frac{P_1 P_2(1 - P_1)P_2^*}{\pi} (E_f - E_{f^*})^2 \right. $$
$$\left. + P_1 P_2 V_f + (1 - P_1)P_2^* V_{f^*} \right] \div \pi. \quad (F25)$$

Tables F1 to F4 show E_π for $\pi = .1$ and $\pi = .04$, and for the sets of correlation coefficients given as equations F17 and F19. The second value of π is of the order of magnitude of current British practice, the first is a proportion of university admissions at which Britain may aim; both have been chosen here because of convenience for existing tables of v and its derivatives. For these tables, particular pairs of P_1, P_2^* have been taken and the corresponding P_2 (not shown in the tables) calculated from equation F15. Higher values of P_2^* could have been included without violating the mathematical form of the model, but discussion of any situation in which P_2^* exceeds P_2 would scarcely be realistic and could only lead to

TABLE F1. VALUES OF E_π/σ FROM EQUATION F24, FOR $\pi = .1$ AND THE CORRELATION COEFFICIENTS IN EQUATIONS F17

P_1 P_2^*	.08	.1	.125	.2	.25	.4	.5	.8	1.0
.00	.....	1.228	1.311	1.353	1.351	1.321	1.298	1.252	1.316
.01	.....	1.336	1.374	1.383	1.370	1.320	1.290	1.239	1.316
.02	.....	1.386	1.402	1.386	1.365	1.302	1.268	1.220	1.316
.05	1.412	1.400	1.381	1.320	1.284	1.202	1.167	1.154	1.316
.10	1.142	1.116	1.088	1.023	.991	.937	.927	1.023	1.316

TABLE F2. VALUES OF E_π/σ FROM EQUATION F24, FOR $\pi = .1$ AND THE CORRELATION
COEFFICIENTS IN EQUATIONS F19

P_1 / P_2^*	.08	.1	.125	.2	.25	.4	.5	.8	1.0
.00	.....	.965	1.071	1.152	1.165	1.159	1.142	1.076	1.053
.01	.....	1.079	1.139	1.188	1.191	1.167	1.143	1.070	1.053
.02	.....	1.138	1.175	1.198	1.194	1.159	1.131	1.059	1.053
.05	1.179	1.186	1.184	1.161	1.142	1.091	1.064	1.015	1.053
.10	.973	.962	.949	.922	.908	.885	.881	.922	1.053

TABLE F3. VALUES OF E_π/σ FROM EQUATION F24, FOR $\pi = .04$ AND THE CORRELATION
COEFFICIENTS IN EQUATIONS F17

P_1 / P_2^*	.025	.032	.04	.05	.1	.125	.2	.25	.4	.5	.8	1.0
.000	....	....	1.508	1.595	1.659	1.657	1.634	1.616	1.566	1.540	1.507	1.616
.002	....	....	1.582	1.642	1.685	1.679	1.647	1.624	1.565	1.535	1.499	1.616
.004	....	....	1.628	1.674	1.699	1.689	1.648	1.622	1.557	1.525	1.490	1.616
.010	....	1.669	1.710	1.726	1.708	1.688	1.630	1.595	1.517	1.481	1.457	1.616
.020	1.728	1.738	1.735	1.726	1.660	1.628	1.550	1.508	1.419	1.385	1.395	1.616
.040	1.518	1.500	1.480	1.458	1.370	1.335	1.256	1.217	1.150	1.138	1.256	1.616

TABLE F4. VALUES OF E_π/σ FROM EQUATION F24, FOR $\pi = .04$ AND THE CORRELATION
COEFFICIENTS IN EQUATIONS F19

P_1 / P_2^*	.025	.032	.04	.05	.1	.125	.2	.25	.4	.5	.08	1.0
.000	....	....	1.185	1.298	1.420	1.435	1.440	1.433	1.398	1.372	1.299	1.293
.002	....	....	1.260	1.344	1.445	1.456	1.454	1.443	1.401	1.372	1.296	1.293
.004	....	....	1.309	1.377	1.459	1.466	1.457	1.444	1.397	1.367	1.291	1.293
.010	....	1.338	1.401	1.436	1.473	1.470	1.446	1.427	1.372	1.339	1.271	1.293
.020	1.405	1.433	1.446	1.452	1.438	1.424	1.384	1.359	1.300	1.271	1.230	1.293
.040	1.247	1.239	1.230	1.220	1.181	1.166	1.131	1.115	1.087	1.082	1.131	1.293

TABLE F5. APPROXIMATE PERCENTAGES OF UNIVERSITY ENTRANTS HAVING $x > 1.282\sigma$, FOR
$\pi = .1$ AND THE CORRELATION COEFFICIENTS IN EQUATIONS F17

P_1 / P_2^*	.08	.1	.125	.2	.25	.4	.5	.8	1.0
.00	....	45.3	49.2	51.4	51.4	50.1	49.1	47.6	49.2
.01	....	50.4	52.3	52.8	52.1	49.8	48.5	47.1	49.2
.02	....	52.9	53.6	52.6	51.6	48.7	47.4	46.6	49.2
.05	53.9	53.1	52.0	48.7	47.0	43.9	43.1	44.7	49.2
.10	38.1	36.8	35.3	32.8	31.9	32.2	33.7	41.5	49.2

values of E_π smaller than those tabulated. In Tables F1 to F9 and F16, the highest value of P_2^* tabulated is equal to π, which corresponds to $P_2^* = P_2$ and an indeterminate value for P_1.

Inspection of the tables shows surprisingly little variation over wide ranges of values of the three allocation parameters. In any one table, the function E_π is evidently flat near the maximum. Nevertheless, the position of the maximum can be roughly located for each table, although that for Table F1 is perhaps just outside the range of values tabulated.

In order to examine also the alternative criterion suggested in Section 6, rough estimates of the expected percentages of incorrect allocations have been formed for each of f, f^*, g, g^*. For this purpose the distribution of x in f has been taken as normal with mean E_f and variance V_f, and the proportion of such a distribution falling below $\sigma T(\pi)$ obtained from standard tables, with similar calculations for f^*, g, g^*. This involves a more serious approximation, since departures from normality will be greater after two stages of selection, and not surprisingly the figures obtained for frequencies of errors of the two types are less close to equality than was hoped. There seems to be little point in discussing this discrepancy in any detail when the normal distributions used are obviously crude approximations. Perhaps the broad sense can be conveyed by saying that the proportion of the whole population wrongly placed in g or g^* (i.e., wrongly denied university admission) appeared consistently greater than the proportion wrongly placed in f or f^* (i.e., wrongly granted admission), the ratio of the two proportions being of the order of 1.1 for conditions used in forming Tables F1 and F3, of the order of 1.05 for Tables F2 and F4. However, the pairs have been averaged and, in Tables F5 to F8, expressed as the percentages of university entrants whose true values of x lie above the ideal point of division, $\sigma T(\pi)$. For example, for Table F6, with $P_1 = .2$,

TABLE F6. APPROXIMATE PERCENTAGES OF UNIVERSITY ENTRANTS HAVING $x > 1.282\sigma$, FOR $\pi = .1$ AND THE CORRELATION COEFFICIENTS IN EQUATIONS F19

$\dfrac{P_1}{P_2^*}$	.08	.1	.125	.2	.25	.4	.5	.8	1.0
.00	....	35.0	38.8	42.4	43.0	42.8	42.1	39.4	38.2
.01	....	39.3	41.8	43.9	44.1	43.0	42.0	39.2	38.2
.02	....	41.7	43.3	44.3	44.1	42.6	41.4	38.8	38.2
.05	43.5	43.8	43.7	42.6	41.8	39.7	38.7	37.4	38.2
.10	34.0	33.5	33.0	32.0	31.7	31.6	32.0	34.8	38.2

$P_2 = .42$, $P_2^* = .02$, it was estimated that a proportion .1113 of the whole population is wrongly allocated, this being totaled from .0542 wrongly in f and f^* and .0571 wrongly in g and g^*; hence the fraction .1 admitted to universities includes .0575 for whom $x < 1.282\sigma$, and therefore the proportion *of the university entrants* with $x \geqslant 1.282\sigma$ is $(.1 - .0557)/.1$, or 44.3%.*

At first sight, these tables are very disturbing, for they appear to indicate that scarcely more than 40 to 50% of those who are most suitable for university education will be admitted under the systems here described! Of course, the trouble lies largely in the marginal cases. If 10% of the population is to be taken into universities, $x = 1.282\sigma$ represents the ideal point of division, so that admission of one person with $x = 1.290\sigma$ will be classed as correct and admission of another with $x = 1.280\sigma$ will be classed as an error; the difference between these two persons is really unimportant, and the two will have almost equal probabilities of success in the two-stage selection. For any set of allocation parameters, a curve could be constructed to show the probability of admission as a function of x, the operating characteristic of the system, and although this will approach unity for large x, zero for small x, it is bound to show poor discrimination in the neighborhood of $x = \sigma T(\pi)$. Although further study of operating characteristics is desirable, it seems sufficient to note here the near coincidence of the positions of the maxima in corresponding tables from Tables F1 to F4 and Tables F5 to F8. Since maximization of E_π is the easier to examine computationally, concentration of effort on it could still be justified even if it were to be regarded only as an approximation to a preferred maximization of the proportion of correct allocations.

Even those admitted to universities after the second stage of selection will vary widely in their values of x. To the order of approximation used in Tables F1 to F4, the variance of x in the subpopulation formed by f and f^* is easily computed from equation F25. Table F9 shows this variance for the systems summarized in Table F1, and indicates that at best only about half the variance in the whole population has been eliminated by the selection process. Even though Table F3 corresponds to much more intensive selection, the variance of those finally selected remains large, never less than $.44\sigma^2$; under the conditions of Tables F2 and F4, the situation is

---

* Of course, these figures can be presented in ways that put the emphasis very differently. "Only 44.3% of those worthy of university education are admitted" but "Of the whole age-group, 88.9% are correctly allocated in respect of university admission."

even more disappointing, the minimal variances being about $.60\sigma^2$ and $.58\sigma^2$ respectively. Only Table F9 is presented here, and the approximation may not be good, but it is worth noting that the system of P_1, P_2, P_2^* that maximizes E_π seems always to have V_π appreciably above its minimum.

The assumption that normality will not be seriously disturbed by the first stage of selection generally leads to exaggeration of the value of $E(x)$ in the university population, $(f + f^*)$. By insertion of the general cumulants stated in Section 3 into the series obtained elsewhere (Finney, 1961), improved approximations have been obtained. The result for E_f is

TABLE F7. APPROXIMATE PERCENTAGES OF UNIVERSITY ENTRANTS HAVING $x > 1.751\sigma$, FOR $\pi = .04$ AND THE CORRELATION COEFFICIENTS IN EQUATIONS F17

P_1 / P_2^*	.025	.032	.04	.05	.1	.125	.2	.25	.4	.5	.8	1.0
.000	....	....	33.6	36.9	39.7	39.8	39.2	38.7	37.6	37.3	37.2	37.5
.002	....	....	36.5	38.9	40.7	40.5	39.4	38.8	37.4	36.9	37.1	37.5
.004	....	....	38.3	40.2	41.1	40.8	39.3	38.5	37.0	36.5	36.9	37.5
.010	....	40.0	41.7	42.2	41.0	40.1	38.0	36.9	35.3	35.0	36.2	37.5
.020	42.3	42.5	42.2	41.6	38.0	36.6	34.0	32.9	31.8	32.1	35.1	37.5
.040	29.8	28.5	27.4	26.1	22.5	21.5	20.5	20.6	22.9	25.2	32.9	37.5

TABLE F8. APPROXIMATE PERCENTAGES OF UNIVERSITY ENTRANTS HAVING $x > 1.751\sigma$, FOR $\pi = .04$ AND THE CORRELATION COEFFICIENTS IN EQUATIONS F19

P_1 / P_2^*	.025	.032	.04	.05	.1	.125	.2	.25	.4	.5	.8	1.0
.000	....	....	23.9	26.8	31.3	32.0	32.3	32.1	31.1	30.4	28.6	26.8
.002	....	....	26.0	28.5	32.1	32.6	32.6	32.3	31.1	30.3	28.4	26.8
.004	....	....	27.4	29.6	32.6	32.9	32.7	32.3	31.0	30.1	28.3	26.8
.010	....	28.4	30.4	31.7	33.1	33.0	32.1	31.5	29.9	29.1	27.8	26.8
.020	30.6	31.6	32.1	32.2	31.6	31.1	29.7	29.0	27.6	27.1	26.9	26.8
.040	23.8	23.4	23.0	22.6	21.3	20.8	20.5	20.5	21.2	21.9	25.1	26.8

TABLE F9. VALUES OF V_π/σ^2 FROM EQUATION F25, FOR $\pi = .1$ AND THE CORRELATION COEFFICIENTS IN EQUATIONS F17

P_1 / P_2^*	.08	.1	.125	.2	.25	.4	.5	.8	1.0
.00	....	.593	.514	.478	.472	.468	.470	.490	.533
.01	....	.541	.501	.472	.468	.470	.477	.507	.533
.02	....	.508	.487	.472	.473	.486	.498	.534	.533
.05	.506	.506	.509	.524	.536	.572	.595	.634	.533
.10	.574	.582	.592	.626	.649	.722	.768	.825	.533

$$E_f = \sigma\rho_1\nu(P_1) + \sigma\nu(P_2)\Bigg[\frac{\rho_2 - \rho_1\rho_y\nu'(P_1)}{[1 - \rho_y^2\nu'(P_1)]^{\frac{1}{2}}}$$

$$+ \frac{\rho_y^2\nu''(P_1)\,T_2}{6\,[1 - \rho_y^2\nu'(P_1)]^2}\,[3\rho_1 - 2\rho_2\rho_y - \rho_1\rho_y^2\nu'(P_1)]$$

$$- \frac{\rho_y^3\nu'''(P_1)\,(T_2^2 - 1)}{24\,[1 - \rho_y^2\nu'(P_1)]^{\frac{5}{2}}}\,[4\rho_1 - 3\rho_2\rho_y - \rho_1\rho_y^2\nu'(P_1)]$$

$$- \frac{\rho_y^5\,[\nu''(P_1)]^2\,(2T_2^2 - 1)}{36\,[1 - \rho_y^2\nu'(P_1)]^{\frac{7}{2}}}\,[6\rho_1 - 5\rho_2\rho_y - \rho_1\rho_y^2\nu'(P_1)]\Bigg], \qquad \text{(F26)}$$

where T_2 is written for $T(P_2)$. The first additional term multiplying $\sigma\nu(P_2)$ is a first-order improvement, the second and third additional terms together are a second-order improvement. From the general series (Finney, 1961), the terms for two further orders of approximation can be formed easily, but numerical computation with them would be very laborious; for this paper, only the first additional

TABLE F10. VALUES OF E_π/σ WITH FIRST-ORDER ADJUSTMENT FOR $\pi = .1$ AND THE CORRELATION COEFFICIENTS IN EQUATIONS F17

P_1 / P_2^*	.08	.1	.125	.16	.2
.012	......	......	......	1.3692	1.3680
.016	......	1.3422	1.3655	1.3714	1.3663
.020	......	1.3548	1.3706	1.3711	1.3624
.024	......	1.3638	1.3729	1.3686	1.3566
.028	1.3457	1.3696	1.3728	1.3642	1.3491
.032	1.3582	1.3724	1.3705	1.3578	1.3400
.036	1.3660	1.3725	......	......	......
.040	1.3700	1.3700	......	......	......

TABLE F11. VALUES OF E_π/σ WITH FIRST-ORDER ADJUSTMENT, FOR $\pi = .1$ AND THE CORRELATION COEFFICIENTS IN EQUATIONS F19

P_1 / P_2^*	.125	.16	.2	.25
.012	......	......	......	1.1899
.016	1.1570	1.1822	1.1913	1.1908
.020	1.1680	1.1875	1.1931	1.1898
.024	1.1761	1.1906	1.1929	1.1871
.028	1.1817	1.1916	1.1909	1.1828
.032	1.1850	1.1907	1.1872	1.1770
.036	1.1860	......	......	......

term has been used. If more extreme selection were under examination, further terms would be needed, and indeed the approximation may be barely good enough for $\pi = .04$. The corresponding series for E_{f*} must of course have Q_1, P_2^* in place of P_1, P_2 respectively, and also the signs of $v(Q_1)$, $v''(Q_1)$ must be reversed (those of $v'(Q_1)$, $v'''(Q_1)$ being left to correspond with those of the functions of (P_1), in accordance with equations F13 and F14). Equation F24 then gives the revised values of E_π, and for the interesting combinations of the allocation parameters these are shown in Tables F10 to F13.

Comparison of corresponding entries in Tables F1 to F4 and F10 to F13 shows the relatively small extent to which the crude approximation overestimates E_π. Nevertheless, this overestimation usually increases as P_1 decreases and P_2^* increases, so that the

TABLE F12. VALUES OF E_π/σ WITH FIRST-ORDER ADJUSTMENTS, FOR $\pi = .04$ AND THE CORRELATION COEFFICIENTS IN EQUATIONS F17

$\dfrac{P_1}{P_2^*}$	.032	.04	.05	.08	.1
.002	......	......	......	......	1.6779
.004	......	......	......	......	1.6831
.006	......	......	......	1.6875	1.6835
.008	......	......	1.6816	1.6882	1.6801
.010	......	......	1.6890	1.6853	1.6736
.012	......	......	1.6923	......	......
.014	......	1.6905	1.6919	......	......
.016	1.6854	1.6918	......	......	......
.018	1.6892	1.6891	......	......	......
.020	1.6882	1.6826	......	......	......

TABLE F13. VALUES OF E_π/σ WITH FIRST-ORDER ADJUSTMENTS, FOR $\pi = .04$ AND THE CORRELATION COEFFICIENTS IN EQUATIONS F17

$\dfrac{P_1}{P_2^*}$	.05	.08	.1	.125	.2
.002	......	......	1.4434	1.4543	1.4550
.004	......	......	1.4553	1.4624	1.4568
.006	......	......	1.4620	1.4658	......
.008	......	1.4577	1.4650	1.4657	......
.010	......	1.4608	1.4647	1.4625	......
.012	......	1.4608	1.4615	......	......
.014	1.4424	1.4578	......	......	......
.016	1.4445	1.4521	......	......	......
.018	1.4432	1.4438	......	......	......
.020	1.4385	......	......	......	......

position of the maximum is shifted by the revision although the magnitude of E_π at its maximum differs little from what it was before. The change is more marked for the first set of correlations, equations F17, than for equations F19. Table F14 summarizes the comparisons but only very roughly; the function E_π is always so flat in the neighbourhood of the optimal that any careful interpolation seems a waste of effort.

Tables F10 to F13 may be better appreciated if they are compared with what would be achieved if direct selection on x were possible. Selection of the top fraction $\pi = .1$ of the x distribution would take all values of x exceeding 1.2816σ and their mean would be 1.7550σ. Similarly, with $\pi = .04$, all values of x would exceed 1.7507σ and their mean would be 2.1543σ. Evidently even the optimal selection systems are not very satisfactory, those in Tables F11 and F13 giving values for E_π below the lower boundary of the best fraction π of the distribution of x. Although at first sight this may seem paradoxical, it is unfortunately to be expected when the scores are not very highly correlated with the criterion, x; in the extreme case of zero correlations, the distribution of x would be unaltered by selection, and E_π would be zero whatever the values of π and the allocation parameters. One way of summarizing the present numerical findings is to specify the fraction of the x distribution which would have E_π as its mean; for Tables F10 to F13, the optimals correspond with the means of fractions .210, .284, .114 and .177 from the top of the x distribution. Put differently, the expected means for x in those selected for the universities are what would be achieved in a simple one-stage selection based on a score whose correlation coefficient with x is .783, .680, .786 and .680 respectively.

An interesting feature of E_f, E_{f*}, and therefore of E_π, is that

TABLE F14. OPTIMAL VALUES (VERY APPROXIMATE) OF ALLOCATION PARAMETERS AND OF E_π/σ FOR TABLES F1 TO F4 AND F10 TO F13

Table	P_1	P_2	P_2^*	E_π/σ
F1	.08	.675	.05	1.412
F10	.125	.618	.026	1.374
F2	.2	.420	.02	1.198
F11	.2	.412	.022	1.194
F3	.032	.645	.020	1.738
F12	.05	.553	.013	1.693
F4	.1	.310	.010	1.473
F13	.125	.271	.007	1.466

they are linear functions of ρ_1 and ρ_2, though not of course linear in ρ_y. This is a general result, which will extend to many forms of multi-stage selection. It follows because of the assumption that x, y_1, y_2 are jointly normal in distribution, so that x can be regarded as having a normal linear regression on y_1, y_2; E_x is therefore a linear function of the means of y_1, y_2 in the final selection. For example, choosing $P_1 = .16$, $P_2 = .499$, $P_2^* = .024$ as allocation parameters close to the optimals in Tables F10 and F11, and taking $\rho_y = .7$, use of all the terms in equation F26 and those of next higher order gives

$$E_x = .4425\rho_1 + 1.4043\rho_2;$$

with $\rho_1 = .7$, $\rho_2 = .75$, the value of E_x is 1.363, instead of 1.369 as in Table F10. Equation F26, indeed, makes clear that a score for grammar school allocation not itself correlated with x (i.e., $\rho_1 = 0$) may still be useful as long as it is correlated with y_2; first-stage allocation based upon such a score then reduces the variance of y_2 in the two parts of the population by removing some of the variation not associated with x, and so eventually improves the quality of discrimination at the second stage.

From the last paragraph, it is apparent that the whole scheme of calculations could be approached differently, by first finding $E(y_1)$ and $E(y_2)$ in f and f^*, this involving bivariate truncation of the distribution of y_1, y_2 at points determined by P_1, P_2 and by $(1-P_1)$, P_2^* respectively. Appropriate formulae have been given by Young and Weiler (1960) and by Tallis (1961). Then the corresponding expectations of x are obtainable from the regression on y_1, y_2. Although exact formulae instead of approximations by series would be used, the computational labour might be increased by the necessity for interpolation in tables of the normal integral, especially as probabilities for the bivariate normal have been tabulated only at wide intervals.

As is apparent from equation F26, E_x is not linear in ρ_y, and some interest attaches to the nature of the dependence on ρ_y. Of course, the value of ρ_y sets limitations on the possible values of ρ_1, ρ_2; for example, if $\rho_1 = \theta\rho_2$ where $0 \leqslant \theta \leqslant 1$, then ρ_2 must lie between the limits

$$[\theta\rho_y \pm (1 + \theta^2 - \rho_y^2)^{\frac{1}{2}}]/(1 + \theta^2);$$

these take the values $\pm (1 + \theta^2)^{-\frac{1}{2}}$ at $\rho_y = 0$, increase steadily to $-(1 - \theta^2)/(1 + \theta^2)$, 1 at $\rho_y = \theta$, and the range contracts to $0, 2\theta/(1 + \theta^2)$ at $\rho_y = 1$. A small study of the extent to which the magnitude of the correlation between the two scores influences E_π has been made on four sets of allocation parameters, all corresponding to $\pi = .1$. These are

$$
\begin{array}{cccc}
& P_1 & P_2 & P_2^* \\
\text{(i)} & .080 & .675 & .050 \\
\text{(ii)} & .125 & .660 & .020 \\
\text{(iii)} & .160 & .499 & .024 \\
\text{(iv)} & .200 & .500 & .000
\end{array} \quad \left. \right\} \quad \text{(F27)}
$$

all of which are close to the optimal in Table F10. From equation F26 with only the first additional term included, it appears that if $\rho_1 = \rho_2$ the value of E_π declines steadily as ρ_y increases from 0 to 1; on the other hand, if $\rho_1 = .5\rho_2$, as ρ_y increases E_π first decreases to a minimum at about $\rho_y = .5$ and then increases again until $\rho_y = 1$. The implications of this behaviour are far from clear, but it certainly illustrates the complexity of the dependence of E_π upon the various parameters of the relatively simple model whose main features are expressed by equation F15. Table F15 summarizes a selection from the calculations, in order to illustrate the trends for values of ρ_1, ρ_2 that are always possible. There can be no assurance that the sets of allocation parameters (i)–(iv) remain near to the optimal for different sets of correlations, and far more extensive calculations would be needed in order to examine the situation thoroughly; higher order terms in equation F26 are likely to assume great importance at extreme values of ρ_y, but will perhaps scarcely affect the qualitative indications of Table F15.

From the calculations on which Table F15 is based, it is possible

TABLE F15. VALUES OF E_π/σ WITH FIRST-ORDER ADJUSTMENTS, FOR $\pi = .1$ AND THE SETS OF ALLOCATION PARAMETERS SPECIFIED AS F28

ρ_y	$\rho_1 = \rho_2 = .6$				$\rho_1 = \frac{1}{2}\rho_2 = .4$			
	(i)	(ii)	(iii)	(iv)	(i)	(ii)	(iii)	(iv)
.0	1.300	1.319	1.361	1.319	1.361	1.232	1.352	1.198
.1	1.271	1.289	1.321	1.283	1.343	1.213	1.327	1.176
.2	1.242	1.260	1.283	1.250	1.327	1.197	1.306	1.158
.3	1.214	1.232	1.246	1.220	1.315	1.185	1.290	1.144
.4	1.186	1.205	1.211	1.192	1.306	1.177	1.279	1.136
.5	1.159	1.179	1.178	1.165	1.303	1.174	1.275	1.133
.6	1.133	1.153	1.145	1.140	1.307	1.178	1.280	1.136
.7	1.108	1.128	1.114	1.116	1.322	1.192	1.299	1.150
.8	1.085	1.103	1.084	1.094	1.353	1.225	1.338	1.181
.9	1.065	1.081	1.059	1.074	1.417	1.297	1.419	1.243
1.0	1.053	1.068	1.046	1.064	1.596	1.502	1.601	1.392

to evaluate reasonable upper limits to the consequences of selection. Since a first draft of this paper was prepared, Mr. W. D. Furneaux has suggested to me that in some circumstances ρ_1 and ρ_2 might rise to .8 and .9 respectively, and they can scarcely reasonably be expected to be much higher. For such close correlations, ρ_y must lie between .46 and .98, and a value about .9 is suggested. With set (iii) of the allocation parameters in equation F27, E_π/σ takes the values 1.693 at $\rho_y = .5$, 1.624 at $\rho_y = .7$, and 1.591 at $\rho_y = .9$. Thus, under favourable conditions, a two-stage system of the kind under discussion, with $\pi = .1$, might achieve $E_\pi/\sigma = 1.60$, corresponding to the mean of the best fraction .137 of the population, but only if the correlation between scores could be kept low would it approach $E_\pi/\sigma = 1.70$, corresponding to the mean of the best fraction .112. Other good sets of allocation parameters can scarcely be very different in result, and evidently even two stages of selection could approach closely to the ideal of $E_\pi/\sigma = 1.75$.

9. GENERAL COMMENTS

Earlier sections of this paper have elaborated a statistical approach to two-stage educational selection (or allocation!), and have illustrated this numerically by reference to the two stages of grammar school admission and university admission. I must again emphasize that what is being presented is an outline of a methodology for comparing alternative combinations of selective intensities, not a dogmatic assertion of the superiority of certain numerical values. Consideration of the theory and the numerical illustrations should help the reader to realize the need for clearer definition of the aims of selection in education, without which the search for an optimal selection programme cannot be begun, and the need for much greater knowledge of the magnitudes of intercorrelations between tests and other assessments at different ages. When these two needs have been met, the method described can be applied or adapted to the appropriate model.

Statistical analysis of this kind cannot tell how methods of education within schools or universities can be improved, nor is it concerned with either the need for such improvement or criteria for measuring improvement. The questions discussed presuppose that types of school and their effects on their pupils, diverse though both may be, remain unaltered under different systems of allocation.

Nothing I have said implies acceptance of any particular scheme of testing or examining pupils at either stage. The method can be applied by using any combination of marks and assessments at one stage as the score; evidently the quality of selection will benefit from defining the score so that it correlates as highly as possible with the ultimate criterion, but the problem of how to do this is not at present under discussion. Nor is there any implication that the first stage must fall at age 11, for the method would still apply were some other age chosen. The formulae shown and used in Section 8 do assume that two stages are needed and are sufficient for a good system, although the analysis could controvert the need for the first stage by showing the optimal to occur with $P_1 = 1$.

For the qualitative discussion of the problems that this paper presents, fairly rough approximations have seemed adequate, but modern techniques of high-speed computing would readily permit greater refinement if this were desired and if the population parameters were known with sufficient accuracy to make it worthwhile. Only large sample theory has been employed, leading to expectations of means after selection; in view of the large numbers of individuals involved, this is surely good enough, but of course within any relatively small sample of a few hundred the results of selection might differ appreciably from the expectations.

An evident need is for refinement in the concept of suitability for a university and in the definition of the criterion x. Put baldly, one cannot adequately discuss which members of a population ought to receive university education without definition of what ideally constitutes suitability, and one cannot define suitability without first agreeing on the purpose of universities; of course, no exclusion of multiplicity of purpose is implied. Certainly reliance upon performance in university examinations must denote both a failure to appreciate the statistical unreliability of examination marks and a complacency about purpose. What alternatives can be offered by those who have for long discussed the aims and ideals of universities?

Although Tables F5 to F8 are only approximate, they clearly show a disappointing performance of the two-stage selection: of those individuals who fall within the top fraction .1 or .04 in respect of the criterion x, more than half fail to secure university admission. As stated in Section 8, marginal cases will account for much of this trouble, but an immediate intuitive reaction to these tables is bound to be: "Increase π and take more of the population into the university, for it is better to ensure that more of the good students are admitted even at the cost of increasing the proportion of those who are unsuitable." This argument is in part fallacious, although it is related to a point mentioned at the end of Section 6 and again in Section 10. The logical approach seems to be first to define what level of the criterion separates the suitable from the unsuitable; the distribution of x is unlikely to have an antimode there, and consequently many members of the population will lie close on either side. Unless π, the proportion of the population admitted, is equated with the proportion having x greater than the ideal point of division, the total errors of allocation will be greater than they need be. However, if errors on marginal candidates (in either direction) are regarded as less serious than errors on those whose x is very large or very small, some form of weighting will be appropriate. The linear weighting involved in E_r seems a fair allowance to make, but an alternative could be tried; the chief difficulty would lie in securing agreement on the alternative!

Burt (1962) has written, "In a country like the United Kingdom, with a population of about 50 million, there must be at least 12,000 geniuses, in the sense defined by Galton. I estimate that the talents of more than half of them are virtually wasted—largely owing to the inadequacy of our methods of selection and training." This statement would be comparable with an analysis on the present lines with $\pi = .00025$; probably tables analogous to Tables F5 to F9 at this extreme would be even more discouraging, but ability of a very high order is perhaps more likely to be detected than would be predicted from correlations such as those of Section 7. Even for the more modest selection intensities envisaged as appropriate to universities, improvement in methods of selection and training should be sought as strongly as an increase in π. Though the latter will reduce the errors of wrong rejection, it must also dilute the quality within the university and will possibly affect adversely the conditions experienced by the best.

In Section 8 and elsewhere, a fixed value of π has been implicit in the argument, optimal values of P_1, P_2, P_2^* being sought subject to the constraint of a fixed π in equation F15. Any consideration of an optimal value for π must introduce entirely new factors, not least of which must be assessments of economic value to the community. An analogous but intrinsically easier problem in the context of plant breeding has been attacked elsewhere (Finney, 1960).

The propriety of assuming the second-stage score to have the same nature in the two subpopulations created at the first stage of selection is open to question. To apply exactly the same tests for assessing the standards of would-be university students whether or not they come from the grammar school stream is not essential and may not be desirable. In the absence of any information about appropriate scores, their distributions, and their correlations, however, a provisional assumption that y_2 for the two streams will have the same basic statistical parameters, without necessarily being identical in origin, seems reasonable.

10. CRITICISMS AND MODIFIED MODELS

The careful reader will have noticed neglect of one possibility of improving the two-stage selection in Section 8. At the first stage, only the first score (y_1) is available, and selection *must* be based upon it. At the second stage, not only is the second score (y_2) known for each individual but also y_1 is still known from past records; why should it not be used, so that the child is judged on the combination of the two? A statistical technique involving this could be devised, but perhaps the model would thereby lose in educational realism: the possibility of permitting a child to gain admission to a university because his excellent results at 11 + compensated for only indifferent success in G.C.E. will not appeal to many!

This leads naturally to another important criticism of the methodology of my paper. I have implicitly assumed that inherent qualities of the individual determine his university suitability and success without his being affected by schooling; the method does not require schools to be any more than convenient boxes for separating the bright students from the less bright and maintaining a provisional classification made at 11 until the child is old enough for universities to operate the second stage of selection. This could be true, but would indeed be a severe indictment of the effects of education! In reality one would hope that exposure of a child to the educational experience of a grammar school will tend to increase his suitability for a university. A simple modification to the model would be to suppose that each member of the fraction P_1 selected at the first stage has his x increased to $(x + u)$ because of his subsequent enjoyment of a grammar school environment. Possibilities here are: (i) u is constant; (ii) u is a function of x, perhaps $u = a + bx$; (iii) u has a frequency distribution. Doubtless the aim should be to have P_1 sufficiently large to keep negligibly small the danger that a child fails to enter a university because he was earlier denied the possibility of gaining u.

The optimal allocation parameters, P_1, P_2, P_2^*, and the optimal division of university entrants between the grammar school and non-grammar school stream are very sensitive to u. The consequences of the simplest case, a constant u, are easily seen. Evidently

E_f will be increased by u and E_{f*} unaltered, so that E_π is increased by uP_1P_2/π. Table F16 shows the behaviour of this function for $\pi = .1$, and thus for Tables F1, F2, F10, F11. Whatever the value of u, the addition to E_π will tend to move the maximum towards higher values of P_1 and lower values of P_2^*. For example, if $u = .2\sigma$, the maximum of Table F1 moves from $P_1 = .08$, $P_2 = .675$, $P_2^* = .05$ to approximately $P_1 = .125$, $P_2 = .660$, $P_2^* = .02$; $u = .5\sigma$ would take the maximum to $P_2^* = 0$ and approximately $P_1 = .2$, $P_2 = .5$. Qualitatively this is what would be intuitively expected for any reasonable form of u: if the child benefits from the grammar school by improvement in university suitability, then to increase the proportion of children exposed to the grammar school and to reduce or even to eliminate P_2^* will be advantageous. Quantitatively, it makes clear that, once the existence of an influence of type of secondary school on individual suitability for university education is conceded, information on the magnitude of this influence is essential to any objective study of optimal selection. Although the desirability of giving prospective university students a more academic pattern of secondary schooling than their less able contemporaries receive has long been asserted, what quantitative knowledge is there of the benefit from this? By how much are the bright child's chances reduced if ill luck in a test takes him to the wrong type of school?

Of course, y_2 is also likely to be affected by the type of secondary school experienced. Simple addition of a constant to y_2 would not modify the present argument, since exactly the same individuals would be in the best fraction P_2, but any more complicated increment in y_2 might have a greater differential effect. If the increment in y_2 is stochastic rather than deterministic, the whole problem will become much more difficult because of the different possible patterns of correlation between y_2, x, and u. This complex of questions seems fundamental to any real understanding of the relative merits of different systems of secondary education, yet I doubt whether it is

TABLE F16. VALUES OF P_1P_2/π WHEN $\pi = .1$

P_1 / P_2^*	.08	.1	.125	.2	.25	.4	.5	.8	1.0
.00	.....	1.000	1.000	1.000	1.000	1.000	1.000	1.000	1.000
.01	.....	.910	.912	.920	.925	.940	.950	.980	1.000
.02	.....	.820	.825	.840	.850	.880	.900	.960	1.000
.05	.540	.550	.562	.600	.625	.700	.750	.900	1.000
.10	.080	.100	.125	.200	.250	.400	.500	.800	1.000

adequately recognized by those who determine policy or whether real attempts have been made to provide quantitative answers for even the simpler cases.

This paper has been written around a model using two stages of selection. Such a model may indeed be inadequate to describe either what happens today or what ought to happen, but it can easily be extended to include more stages. For example, a three-stage model could easily be formed in an obvious manner with

$$\pi = [P_1 P_2 + (1 - P_1) P_2^*] P_3 + P_1 (1 - P_2) P_3^* \qquad \text{(F28)}$$

as its basis. Examination of this would involve the same kind of calculations, though they would be vastly more laborious, especially as the consequences of non-normality might be more serious. For a fixed π, the value of $E(x)$ in the final upper selection will increase as the number of stages is increased, though the gain by going beyond three stages is likely to be small.

Perhaps of even greater interest would be a model appropriate to a system of large comprehensive secondary schools, into which all children go without first-stage selection. This is quite distinct from the simple one-stage system obtained by putting $P_1 = 1$ in equation F15. The essential feature is that, within a school, streams of different ability are maintained, so that the upper streams either make more rapid progress or follow an enriched curriculum. Annually, or even more often, the position of each child is reviewed in terms of some score representing his current performance, and he may then be moved up or down to the next stream. A "simple" model would be one with only two streams, for proportions π and $(1 - \pi)$; at each review time, a small fraction, p, of the whole population would be moved up from the lower stream and an equal fraction moved down from the upper stream. Generalizations to values of π and p that change during the school life of a cohort and to several streams are easily stated, but even the simple case is probably too complicated for mathematical analysis. To examine such models may become important, for comparison of their operating characteristics with those of the two-stage process in Section 5 might begin to bring some objectivity into discussion of the merits of comprehensive schools, and perhaps recourse must be had to computer simulations. One may guess that a nearly continuous sifting process of this kind could give values of $E(x)$ for the final upper selection appreciably higher than obtainable by simple two- or three-stage systems, but of course many non-statistical and purely educational factors would also have to be considered.

Some readers may be reluctant to accept the assumption that selection or allocation at any stage is based upon a single score for the individual, instead of simultaneously employing measurements of several qualities. However, the oversimplified model discussed provides only two alternative decisions at each stage; for this situation, even though many different measurements may be available (Section 3), any reasonable rule of allocation must be equivalent to the formation of a function of these as a composite score followed by a dichotomy in the right proportions so that high values go to one alternative and low to the other. Only when individuals are to be allocated between three or more categories can methods for achieving a division optimal in respect of scores for two or more dimensions of ability be distinguished from purely hierarchical selection—that is to say, selection that divides the population between categories solely on the basis of the interval within which a composite score falls. For example, even if the proportionate allocation between grammar, technical, and modern schools were exactly specified by external factors, the ideal manner in which these proportions would be taken from the population would still need definition; merely to propose placing the ablest 20% (judged on a single score) in the grammar schools, the next ablest 25% in the technical, and the remaining 55% in the modern would not suffice. Some combinations of abilities will obviously indicate the desirability of one type of school in preference to either of the others, but inevitably others will be marginal in respect of two or of all three.

A simple illustration will show how difficulties increase when such generalizations are discussed; both aims and criteria are difficult to define and the mathematical and computational complexities are much greater. Suppose that in a one-stage system children are to be allocated between three categories, and the suitability of any one child is represented by quantities x_1, x_2 (instead of simply x). Then a plane in which (x_1, x_2) are two coordinates needs to be divided into regions so that each region contains combinations of (x_1, x_2) regarded as ideal for allocations to one of the available alternatives. This division needs to put assigned proportions π_1, π_2, π_3 ($\Sigma\pi = 1$) in the three categories, and the method of drawing the boundaries ought to be based upon a rule that specifies the ideal allocations whatever arbitrary values are assigned to the π_i. Only then is the specification advanced as far as in Sections 3 and 4. Next must come agreement on what criterion of good allocation is to be adopted; is this to lead to maximization of the total proportion of correct allocations, or is some weight to be attached to each

(x_1, x_2) after which a weighted total is maximized (Section 6)? Presumably at least two scores will be available for the one stage of allocation, and all intercorrelations of these and x_1, x_2 are needed (Section 7). Computations analogous to those of Section 8 can then begin. Obviously similar problems arise in any attempt to separate educational provisions into subcategories, for example by recognizing that different university subjects have different requirements and success in them may be differently related to school scores. The analysis of Sections 3 to 8 is only a superficial, though I believe a necessary, first step to the whole question of guiding each child into his ideal educational channel.

Although this geometrical and mathematical representation might seem an unreal abstraction to the educationalist, I suggest that any policy of allocating children between three or more types of school (or between universities, technical colleges, and no higher education), in such a way that each child is intended to receive the treatment best suited to him, must involve something of this kind. The essential problems are the same whether the answers given are based on the intuition of the wise educationalist or on the type of numerical analysis outlined here, and both approaches to solving them have their part to play. Certainly I have no intention of belittling the first, but I suggest that more intensive study of the second could bring objectivity into arguments that today are often left largely to the emotions. Recognition of the logical relations between aims, criteria, and operational success of an allocation scheme and discussion of their inherent statistical complexity does not mean rigid adherence to a policy that neglects the human values of particular cases; however imperfect the statistical analysis, it should at least be corrective of loose thinking about aims and the possibilities of their fulfillment.

DISCUSSION ON DR. FINNEY'S PAPER*

Mr. T. LEWIS (in proposing the vote of thanks): The importance of the topic of Dr. Finney's paper needs no underlining. Thinking only of academic education—the context in which Dr. Finney places his argument—we have, for example, the Ministry of Education's recent estimate° that by the end of the next decade there will be three times as many children staying on at school until 17

---

* Following its presentation to the Royal Statistical Society in May, 1962. Parts of the discussion are omitted here; omission is indicated by a row of dots. Again, the symbol ° indicates omission of an incidental reference.

or 18 as there are at present. But the implications of the paper are much wider—including the best choice of people for the various professions, for work at many different levels in industry, for Parliament, and so on.

Dr. Finney refers to his paper as a study in methodology, and says in Section 9 that his statistical analysis is not concerned with the need for improvements in methods of education or with criteria for measuring improvement, and that the problem of defining scores is not under discussion. I suggest, however, that . . . the non-statistical issues are the vital ones for discussion here, and they are in any case implied by Dr. Finney's mathematics. Whatever the approximations involved in the calculations, these show unmistakably that, for efficient allocation, the criteria used for prediction must be very highly correlated with the characteristic for which one is selecting. The 70% and 75% correlations of the numerical examples, high as they appear, are not good enough. In other words, much of the effort spent on examining may be misdirected. This is perhaps a platitude, but one whose implications we are not on the whole very keen to face. The question *What are examinations examining?* urgently needs to be examined.

What, for example, is the relation between the examination results of medical students and their subsequent effectiveness as doctors? I am told that, perhaps not surprisingly, there has been no follow-up study of this question.

. . . . .

I am sure Dr. Finney is right to stress the importance of a study of the operating characteristics of his models, and we shall eagerly await the detailed results on operating characteristics when he gets his computer. In the meantime it might be worth pointing out that the operating characteristic (O.C.) can be calculated quite easily in one at least of the cases Dr. Finney has considered, viz. when $\rho_y = \rho_1 \rho_2$ (cf. his eq. F19 and Tables F2, F4, F6, F8). To do this one works in terms, not of P_1, P_2, P_2^*, but (as suggested by Dr. Finney in Section 8) of the equivalent parameters a, b, c, a being the truncation value of y_1/ω_1 at the first selection stage, and b, c those of y_2/ω_2 for $y_1/\omega_1 > a$, $y_1/\omega_1 < a$ respectively at the second stage. Thus, if G, L are the upper univariate and bivariate normal probability integrals,

$$G(a) = P_1, \quad L(a, b, \rho_y) = P_1 P_2, \quad L(-a, c, -\rho_y) = Q_1 P_2^*.$$

The O.C. comes out in terms of G only, as

$$\text{O.C.} = G\left(\frac{b - \rho_2\, x/\sigma}{\sqrt{1 - \rho_2^2}}\right) G\left(\frac{a - \rho_1\, x/\sigma}{\sqrt{1 - \rho_1^2}}\right)$$

$$+ G\left(\frac{c - \rho_2\, x/\sigma}{\sqrt{1 - \rho_2^2}}\right) G\left(\frac{-a + \rho_1\, x/\sigma}{\sqrt{1 - \rho_1^2}}\right). \tag{A}$$

For instance, taking ρ_1, ρ_2, ρ_y as in equation F19, and choosing tabular values° of a, b, c so as to reproduce as nearly as possible the set of values

$$P_1 = .2,\ P_2 = .42,\ P_2^* = .02,\ \pi = .1 \tag{B}$$

discussed as an example by Dr. Finney in Section 8, we have:

$$a = .8,\ b = .6,\ c = 1.9;$$
$$P_1 = .212,\ P_2 = .430,\ P_2^* = .0194,\ \pi = .106;$$

and the operating characteristic of the scheme comes out from equation (A) as follows:

x/σ	-1.2	$-.4$	$+.4$	$+1.2$	$+2.0$	$+2.8$	$+3.6$	$+4.4$
Proportion selected	.002	.020	.094	.282	.564	.818	.947	.990

There is 5% chance of selection when $x/\sigma = 0$, and 95% chance when $x/\sigma = 3.6$. When $x/\sigma = 3.481$, the value which corresponds to the least brilliant of Burt's 12,000 geniuses, the chance is 93.4%, the integrated loss amounting to some 550 geniuses. It is also worth noting that $T(\pi) = 1.25$ and that the O.C. ordinate has, as one would expect when one comes to think about it, a low value—30%— for this value of x/σ.

While one is about it, one can multiply the O.C. function by $(1/\pi)$ times the standardized normal density function, to get the distribution of x/σ in the selected subpopulation $(f + f^*)$ and see how near to normal it is. The result is very satisfactory; the skewness and flatness coefficients γ_1 and γ_2 turn out to be $+.07$, $+.02$ respectively, and one could hardly want anything more normal than that.

Something more can be done to sketch in without much computing effort the outline of the O.C. pattern, since the O.C. again comes out quite simply at the further boundary of the parameter space where

$$\begin{vmatrix} 1 & \rho_y & \rho_1 \\ \rho_y & 1 & \rho_2 \\ \rho_1 & \rho_2 & 1 \end{vmatrix} = 0,$$

that is, in the degenerate case when x is an exact linear function of y_1 and y_2:

$$x/\sigma = [(\rho_1 - \rho_y\rho_2)(y_1/\omega_1) + (\rho_2 - \rho_y\rho_1)(y_2/\omega_2)]/(1 - \rho_y^2)$$

$$\equiv \xi(y_1/\omega_1, y_2/\omega_2), \text{ say.}$$

In this case the O.C. function

$$= G\left(\frac{b - \rho_2 \, x/\sigma}{\sqrt{1 - \rho_2^2}}\right) \text{ for } x/\sigma > \xi(a, c),$$

$$= G\left(\frac{b - \rho_2 \, x/\sigma}{\sqrt{1 - \rho_2^2}}\right) - G\left(\frac{-a + \rho_1 \, x/\sigma}{\sqrt{1 - \rho_1^2}}\right)$$

$$+ G\left(\frac{c - \rho_2 \, x/\sigma}{\sqrt{1 - \rho_2^2}}\right) \text{ for } \xi(a, c) > x/\sigma > \xi(a, b),$$

and $$= G\left(\frac{c - \rho_2 \, x/\sigma}{\sqrt{1 - \rho_2^2}}\right) \text{ for } \xi(a, b) > x/\sigma.$$

For example, suppose (cf. eq. F17) that

$$\rho_1 = .9, \; \rho_2 = .941, \; \rho_y = .7; \tag{C}$$

taking $a = .8$, $b = 1.1$, $c = 1.5$ we get P_1, P_2, P_2^*, $\pi = .212$, .422, .0198, .105 respectively, reproducing fairly closely the values (B); then there is 5% chance of selection when $x/\sigma = 1$ and 95% chance when $x/\sigma = 1.76$. If we interchange the values of ρ_1, ρ_2 in (C), the corresponding values of x/σ are .87 and 2.02.

While I do not think that there is much to worry about in regard to the assumptions of approximate normality of scores in the various curtailed subpopulations, granted that the underlying joint distribution of x, y_1, y_2 is trivariate normal, this latter assumption does call for comment. As Dr. Finney explains, his criteria, E_π/σ and the proportion of incorrect allocations, do not tell the whole story; it is not the marginal cases that really matter, but the incidence of severe misallocation—the unsuitable individuals who get selected, and the first-rate ones who fail to. In other words, the lower tail of the distribution of selected scores and the upper tail of the complementary distribution are what matter. Although one might expect a location measure such as E_π/σ to be fairly insensitive to the form of the underlying multivariate distribution of scores, the same is unlikely to be true for the tails, and if this underlying distribution were not in fact multinormal then the validity of some of the conclusions in the paper might be affected.

If I am not mistaken, Dr. Finney does not anywhere in his paper adduce any evidence in support of his assumption of a jointly normal distribution of x, y_1 and y_2. However, I am sure it is a reasonable one. In this connection I would mention the investigation (Petch, 1961) carried out by Mr. J. A. Petch on the G.C.E. A-level results and subsequent degree examination results for 2,228 candidates who sat the Northern Universities Joint Matriculation Board's A-level examination in a particular year, 1956. There was, in effect, a sample of size 2,228 from a conditional bivariate distribution of x and y_2 in $(f + f^*)$. This large sample proved to be well fitted by a normal bivariate model, with a correlation—$\rho(x, y_2)$ in Dr. Finney's notation—of about 40%. One may, I think, regard this as supporting evidence for the joint normality of y_1, y_2 and x, as it is reasonable to suppose that y_1 has a marginal distribution of the same form as those for y_2 and x. It often happens that in trying to settle one problem you raise others, and in this instance I came to realize, on taking a hand with the data at one stage, that the score y_2 had quite a heterogeneous structure. The 2,200-odd candidates could be split into some 1,300 who were attempting the A-level examination for the first time in the year of observation, and about 900 who were sitting it for the second or third time; the pattern of the distributions was markedly different for the two groups. The "second-shotters" included, without doubt, some who had done badly at their first attempt but improved through experience at their second, and again others who had done well the first time, had sat again without any particular need to do so and had then performed indifferently through lack of interest. This is just one of the many complexities which need to be considered in the extensive further work which will, I am sure, be set going by Dr. Finney's paper.

Indeed, if sufficient effort is put into following up the lines of advance and opportunities for basic rethinking which this important paper opens up, there is a real chance of a significantly better future for the coming generation of schoolchildren and students. So perhaps I may be permitted to speak, hopefully, in their name as well as on behalf of us here today when I propose, as I do now, a vote of very appreciative thanks to Dr. Finney for his paper.

Dr. W. D. WALL: I feel rather like an interior decorator in a meeting of expert cooks. I am not competent to criticize the meal so I am going to talk about the decorations. May I point out that any interest shown by anybody in education is welcomed, particularly when it comes from somebody who has something of value to say from the standpoint of his own science. Most pundits work on the assumption that, having been educated themselves, they are therefore fully competent to talk about education, even about that part of education which they themselves have fortunately escaped; indeed, the greater the area of education they have escaped, the more likely they are to pontificate about it.

May I join Mr. Lewis in saying that, in a sense, the non-statistical issues raised by this paper are the vital ones; I welcome the paper because it draws attention in a rather vigorous way to these non-statistical issues and I would hope that more Fellows of the Society will give their attention to the problems raised by this model and perhaps give us professional help with some of the problems about which it has led me to think.

My first point is, that while the model is applicable to any type of two-stage selection, in the reality of the schools, although selection may take place only at two stages openly, it is in fact taking place all the time. This continuous selection affects the individual and any prophecies we make about him, because, in selecting him for a particular kind of environment, and in acting on our prophecy, we deeply influence him by the very environment into which we put him. In fact, we tend to make our prophecy come true. Therefore, the two-stage model proposed enables us to define a criticism of an overt two-stage process of selection—particularly by exposing the bases of our selection processes in education.

As Dr. Finney himself points out, a major problem is presented by the factor of the effects of the "treatment" decided upon as a result of selection. Now if you are attempting to do anything in school, it is to change people; if you are not changing them, then you are wasting your time. The purpose of education is to maximize certain aspects of the individual and perhaps to create others. What, then, psychologically is this x and what does education do to it? What are the differential effects of different decisions about allocation? This x is likely to have a normal distribution, I would suggest, because it is a bit of a hotch-potch of all sorts of things combined in more or less random but different ways in different people. For example, there is likely to be in it something of an innate intellectual endowment, there is likely to be in it the accumulated effects of education, there will probably be the attitudes which the child has acquired from his teachers, there will be modifications of his value systems; in fact, all manner of things about which we just do not know much.

The problem here then is that, if we assume that the quality or ability with which we are concerned is more or less unitary and can therefore be measured by fairly simple examinations or tests, we may induce it to behave in the way which we expect. We confirm our convictions by acting upon them. This seems to me to be what happens in a good deal of grammar school selection. Pupils are allocated as suitable to a grammar school and, because the school does its job, the child becomes suitable. Within certain limits the borderline of suitability for an academic type of education can be moved up or down in terms of how far a particular grammar school is effective in educating the children it receives.

This vitally affects the second stage, that of university selection. Universities in general behave as though they have no broad educational responsibility and as though the onus were entirely on the student. Present means of selection of students could be improved so that more perhaps would be selected who could survive and even profit from what they have to offer. If, however, universities were to change their policy and to accept the fully educational role that some would have them assume then predictions based on present circumstances would probably go astray. In terms of current preoccupations, the "pool of ability" depends upon how far academic schools and universities can and do change their students by the education they give. The danger of our current methods of selection or allocation—which are essentially based upon the prediction of future performance in a more or less unchanging situation—is that (a) they are self-justifying and therefore to some extent circular and (b) they tend to an increasingly inflexible set of attitudes and behaviours in the receiving institutions.

If, on the other hand, it becomes accepted that the purpose of education is to change and if necessary to change radically, then equally the defeating of at least adverse predictions is a goal. If, for example, a child is mentally subnormal we tend to put him into a school for the mentally subnormal; the purpose of the school is to make him better than he would be if he were left out. If the school is very highly successful, the child will operate perhaps even above the level of subnormality and all the school's efforts are directed to that purpose—one wonders whether sometimes university efforts are not directed to the reverse!

Some of the difficulty over allocation and selection arises because of misunderstanding and deliberately aroused political passion. We have been concerned with the simple single problem of selecting children suitable for a limited supply of a scarce commodity, not with finding all those who might profit from a particular kind of schooling or higher education. Basically, however, the educationist is not concerned with selection. He is concerned with guidance. He is concerned with finding out about a child or adolescent in detail as a step towards maximizing any strengths and remedying any deficiencies—in knowledge or what you will.

If, then, Dr. Finney's model, or anything like it, can be pushed this much farther, if it can be constructed to deal, on the one hand, with a probably complex series of measurements which describe an individual as at present and, on the other, with a complex series of criteria towards the attainment of which you aim to lead him, then we should all rejoice. Such a model would make the educationist define his aims in terms of measures of a much wider variety and a more precise kind than at present. It might also direct our attention to the fact that a variety of different combinations of qualities in the individual may in fact produce the same result. For example, a not very bright child who is highly motivated may do much better than a much brighter child who is not well motivated. If we look at our problem in this way we concentrate our attention on guidance; and the psychometrist and statistician are challenged, not only to select those whose chances of success are high, but to provide the grammar or any other kind of school with a description of the present status of the pupils they are receiving with a clear indication of what they should do, and with an estimate of the probability of success in their efforts.

Finally, there are one or two small points. I do not think we should confine ourselves to predictions from one set of scores obtained at one time. We should, in fact, attempt to use dynamic patterns. There is evidence that the rates and directions of growth in children differ and that if we take measures at more than one point in time, we find different patterns for different children who might at any one point seem to have the same problem. Some children may be going up, some down. And the direction of growth is possibly as important in prediction as is status at any given time. Hence the differences within scores for a child from one time to another may ultimately be as important in allocation, treatment or guidance as anything else.

The other point I want to stress, and am coming back to, is that we should beware of the convention of normality in our distributions and what it tends to force us to do. Most of our tests are based on the assumption that what we are measuring is more or less normally distributed and most of our statistical predictions assume the same thing. However, many of the psychological factors we are concerned with may not be really normally distributed. I am therefore wondering how far—and I ask for guidance from any statistical colleagues —our tests should continue to be constructed and used on the assumption of a basically normal distribution of scores.

I should like to close by strongly seconding the vote of thanks to Dr. Finney.

The vote of thanks was put to the meeting and carried unanimously.

Dr. [A.] YATES: The first point I want to make is that there is a real difference between the mean x and the percentage correctly allocated. Dr. Finney, it struck me, rather leaned over backwards to say that there was little to choose between the two measures. I feel strongly that statisticians should give a clear lead in indicating which of the many measures that are available is, in their opinion, the right one to use.

It is frequently necessary in statistical analysis to group quantitative data into classes, the dividing lines of which are largely arbitrary. One must beware, however, of subsequently attaching an importance to these subdivisions which they do not really possess. If a child has an x which is very close to the dividing value then it is of little consequence in which of the two classes he is placed. What is important, as Dr. Finney has indicated, is that we should get the people who are likely to benefit greatly from university education to the universities and that we should avoid committing to the universities those who are definitely unsuitable.

Dr. Finney expressed doubt, or repeated the doubts of the university authorities, that the x value should be identified with the examination result. The examination result is certainly an imperfect measure of what we are really looking for. If a person does badly in his final university examination he is handicapped at the start of his career but he can frequently rectify this in the first few years of his work. It is clear that much further research is needed into methods of testing of all kinds, including the use of interviews. The main difficulty here is to find out and assess the performance of an individual in his future life after he has left the university.

My general impression from Dr. Finney's tables, Table F1 and Table F4 in particular, is that it does not very much matter what proportions of selection are used at different levels. If this is so then it gives us a much freer hand to vary the proportion selected according to other needs. It is clear that in any reasonable educational policy more educational effort will be devoted to the brighter individuals, and the determination of the optimal proportions of selection at each stage will in part be governed by the amount of extra educational effort which is considered appropriate for the brighter individuals.

.   .   .   .

Mrs. J. FLOUD: I should like to comment on the status and distributional properties of Dr. Finney's postulated quantity x. For each individual, x represents his innate suitability for a university education, and x is taken to be normally distributed in the whole population of an age group.

Of course, x is an inaccessible quantity; for all practical purposes it must be equated with performance in university examinations, or at any rate with some comparable though possibly more relevant or perfect criterion, if and when one is devised.

This fact, that x cannot be expressed otherwise than operationally as a prediction about an individual's performance in some test or examination, seems to me to oblige us to scrutinize the status of x in our discussion. Is it indispensable for the formulation and solution of our problem? If it is not directly accessible—if one cannot select directly on x—has it any compensating explanatory value which might deter us from abandoning it on grounds of intellectual economy? If we retain it, as in one of Dr. Finney's models, are we making the best guess as to its distributional properties?

The status of x, and our guess as to its distributional properties, depend on the notion we have of educational selection. A serious difficulty with Dr. Finney's methodology is his underlying assumption that the inherent qualities of the individual determine his university suitability. This criticism he acknowledges, in Section 10 of his paper, and he introduces the quantity μ to represent the increment of improvement in an individual's suitability for a university education brought about by selective secondary (grammar) schooling. He enumerates the possible ways in which the increment might relate to x; in fact we know a little (from studies of "early leaving" from grammar schools) about the differential distribution of the μ increment by social class—it accrues more readily to the children of parents in non-manual occupations. But this is not the important point here.

The important point is that the value of x is in a state of continual modification, at least from the moment a child sets foot in the infant school; and I do not see that we can afford to ignore this fact in devising allocation models.

All schools are selective institutions. The allocation at 11+ merely institutionalizes, consolidates, and reinforces a continuous long-term process of social-cum-academic selection (for which Dr. Finney's simple model of a two-stream comprehensive school will serve only as the crudest illustration). Many factors enter into the process, of course: random accidents of individual life history; the organizational characteristics of schools (e.g., whether or not pupils are "streamed"), and their characteristics as social systems— as well as systematic and cumulative social influences on the individual's life-chances, such as those of geographical region, ethnic origin, religious affiliation, and social class.

But the upshot is that it can virtually never be reasonable at any point in the educational process to take x to be normally distributed —and certainly not in an age group of 11-year-olds facing selection for secondary schooling.

This enormously complicates the problem of calculating allocation parameters, for, as Dr. Finney points out, these are very sensitive to modifications of x. If selection is continuous, the calculation of allocation parameters at 11+ and 18+ must allow for the cumulative impact upon x of a whole hypothetical series of anterior, more or less informal, selection stages, as well as of the special reinforcing effect of the formal procedure at 11+. And since the mathematical complexities of even a three-stage process are very great, it seems essential to explore, as Dr. Finney suggests, the possibilities of computer simulations. It would be a fascinating task to translate existing research findings into population parameters for this purpose.

This, however, is still to retain x; and I find this difficult to justify. Without x, as I see it, the formulation of the problem gains enormously in economy and clarity. We see immediately the tasks confronting us, and the kinds of sociological investigation and statistical exercise which are needed to cope with them. I have in mind close definitions of the multiple purposes of higher education and the related search for criteria and predictors; the forecasting of effective demand for higher education (here again a case for computer simulations); and the calculation of the optimal provision of university places on various social, educational, political, and economic assumptions.

Dr. R. N. CURNOW: I am rather surprised that Dr. Finney has

made no mention of the selection of pupils to receive sixth-form education. Selection at this stage is probably not as intense as at 11+ and university admission, but it does make university selection three-stage rather than two-stage.

Dr. Finney dismisses the possibility of using 11 + scores to improve the accuracy of the second-stage selection based on university admission scores. On p. 202, the optimal two-stage schemes are shown to be equivalent to one-stage schemes in which the correlation coefficients between university performance and test score are about .78 and .68 for correlation sets F17 and F19 respectively. The corresponding correlation coefficients for a scheme in which no selection is applied at 11+, but in which optimal use is made of the 11+ scores at the time of university admission, are the multiple correlation coefficients of x with y_1 and y_2, $R = .79$ and $R = .71$. These values are slightly higher than those obtained by Dr. Finney for his optimal schemes even though they refer to schemes in which there is no selection at 11+. These strange results are due partly to the inadequacy of the model and, perhaps more importantly, to the rather high partial correlation coefficients between the 11+ score and university performance for students having the same university admission score, $\rho = .37$ and $\rho = .47$ for correlation sets F17 and F19 respectively. Both the sets of correlation coefficients considered by Dr. Finney do have some rather strange implications and I should like to suggest that other sets may give results differing substantially from those obtained in this paper.

. . . .

The reasons given for maximizing the proportion of students correctly allocated depend on a rather severe dichotomy of ability. The arguments for maximizing the average ability of selected students seem much stronger.

One further small point. On p. 210 Dr. Finney says that the value of $E(x)$ will increase as the number of stages is increased. This is obviously true if optimal schemes are used but the gains from a non-optimal three-stage scheme may well be much less than those from an optimal two-stage scheme.

Dr. P. M. Levy: Many educationists will welcome the interest shown by Dr. Finney in this sort of problem and will encourage other contributions by statisticians. But I do not wish to comment on the educational aspects of this paper: Dr. Finney has, I believe, countered many possible criticisms on these grounds in his statement of aims and in the more qualitative sections of his paper.

The point at which my comments begin has already been referred to briefly by previous speakers. In the first paragraph of Section 10 a criticism is dismissed which I believe indicates a most serious omission in the model presented. Dr. Finney says, of using y_1 and y_2 jointly to predict university suitability, that: "the possibility of permitting a child to gain admission to a university because his excellent results at $11+$ compensated for only indifferent success in G.C.E. will not appeal to many!"

Surely a correlation does not disappear because we find it distasteful. Even if we do reject the use of score y_1 seven or eight years later we can surely measure the underlying abilities again with advantage.

More generally though, and stemming from this criticism, I regret that Dr. Finney's advisers do not appear to have referred him to an important text: Cronbach and Gleser°. In their chapter on two-stage sequential selection they compare a number of selection strategies, among which are the following: (a) a non-sequential battery, that is, y_1 and y_2 used jointly to predict x; (b) a fully sequential strategy, that is, on the basis of y_1 the group is divided into three subgroups—those rejected, those accepted and those awaiting decision until both scores are known; (c) a pre-reject strategy, in which some are rejected on the basis of y_1 and the remainder (P_1) sorted out on the basis of both scores; (d) a pre-accept strategy, which means accept some on the basis of y_1 and then select some of the remainder (Q_1) on the basis of both scores.

Dr. Finney's model corresponds to none of these; he has used what psychologists call a "multiple cutoff" method which is most suited to the situation where y_1 does *not* have a linear relationship with the criterion x and generally where there is some hindrance to using y_1 and y_2 jointly. It should also be noted that the $100\pi\%$ of people selected for university are to some extent different people from one strategy to the next, depending upon the relationships of equation F17 and P_1.

Secondly, of all these strategies, the non-sequential battery—or simple joint use of y_1 and y_2—is always optimal under Dr. Finney's assumptions of linearity of relationships and for his criterion of maximizing the expected mean university suitability score for a fixed π. Using these same assumptions Cronbach and Gleser have to impose an additional restraint, concerning the cost of obtaining y_2, before they can discuss any other strategy as optimal.

Thirdly, and this is the crux of my criticism, if Dr. Finney took account of the joint prediction of y_1 and y_2 at the second stage, the optimal value for P_1 is always unity for all values of π. With this strategy, $\pi = .1$, .04 and a multiple correlation of .789 obtained from the data in equation F17, the values of $E(x)_\pi$ would be 1.384 and 1.700 respectively. These values may be compared with lines 2 and 6 of Table F14. Certainly the differences are small as far as the university population is concerned, but there is a world of difference educationally between Dr. Finney's optimal values of P_1 (Table F14), all of which are less than 13%, and the true optimal value I have demonstrated of 100%.

Thus the existence of other optimal values of P_1 in the paper before us does depend upon the non-optimal strategy of ignoring y_1 at the second stage, and I suggest that the present model is not adequate to decide what is the optimal value of P_1. Only if additional restraints were imposed, such as the extra cost per child of grammar school education, could optimal values be discovered which are other than the statistically trivial but educationally important one of $P_1 = 1$.

· · · · ·

REPLY BY D. J. FINNEY

Dr. Finney commented briefly on some of the points raised in the discussion. He subsequently replied in writing as follows: I must begin with a word on Mr. Lewis' comment regarding the limited scope of the paper. I restricted my investigation to certain aspects of educational allocation to which I felt able to make a new quantitative approach; an already long paper would have become unbearably tedious if I had tried to discuss other aspects on which I had nothing new to contribute. Of course, I recognize that the definition of scores is very much a question for the statistician, that his advice is also often relevant in the devising of criteria, and that if he is to work in the field of education he needs a good understanding of any proposals for improvement in educational methods.

Mr. Lewis has made an important step in the evaluation of operating characteristics, and I look forward to examining this more carefully. I suspect that $\rho_y = \rho_1 \rho_2$ is an unlikely state of affairs, but it perhaps has interest as a lower limit for ρ_y; to have some information on O.C. curves without excessive computation may prove very valuable. It is, of course, just because of the desirability of assessing the frequency of really bad allocations that I have stressed the need to examine O.C. curves. Taken in conjunction with the approximate normality that Mr. Lewis finds remaining even after two stages of selection, there is perhaps reason to hope that his approach may lead to a first-order approximation to the O.C. even for a more general correlation structure. However, before undertaking much more computation, I would want to look further at the allowance to be made for the effect of school on subsequent performance and ability; my remarks on u are very crude, but comparison of O.C. curves will not tell us much until the model takes account of this in a not too unrealistic way. Can it be true that no empirical quantitative evidence exists?

I also find interesting Mr. Lewis' information on normality of distribution and on the heterogeneity of the population. Without in any way decrying the importance of this heterogeneity, I would guess that in our understanding of the whole problem a more urgent need is to take account of heterogeneity of aims. How shall we amend my attempt to skim the cream and replace it by a search for a system of allocation that recognizes the need to achieve a balanced community in which the different professions and trades are filled optimally? The question is perhaps largely non-statistical, but statisticians ought to be concerned in giving numerical expression to the criterion; this criterion must involve constraints on numbers or proportions in different categories, representation on a single scale of the losses from imperfect allocation to these categories, and recognition of a non-linear situation in that the value that the community loses by a particular imperfect allocation may not be simply related to the sum of the losses by individuals.

Dr. Wall made some remarks very pertinent to the nature of x; his insistence that education is concerned with remedying deficiencies as well as with recognizing innate talent is a timely reminder. Without disagreeing with his outlook, I want to emphasize my belief that we must be able to talk about x however much we may modify its definition. My simplification to a univariate model here is doubtless extreme, and perhaps we must develop the theory in relation to a multivariate x that represents different aspects of ability vectorially. Perhaps x for any child must correspond to the highest of which he will be capable under ideal educational conditions, leaving the statistical model to associate with various categories not only scores but measures of failure to bring x up to its full value. I do not see how this can be done without many parameters, but that is no excuse for evading the problem. Both educationists and statisticians, however, must insist that far more effort be put into the analysis of all records that may help us to estimate the parameters of the existing educational system: these are the only guide we have to the quantitative effect of changes.

I assure Dr. Yates that I did not intend to give the impression that I saw no difference between use of the mean x and of the percentage correctly allocated. I believe that the interests of the community are better served by the former, but individual parents and perhaps some teachers may be more attracted by the percentage criterion. I therefore think it useful to investigate the alternative: if optimal conditions for it are similar to optimal conditions for x, both points of view can be accommodated without sacrifice of the statisticians' preference. Only by study of the operating characteristics can we see the consequences of different systems of weighting values of x to give a single index of the quality of the selection. Dr. Yates stressed the importance of having in the universities those who are most likely to benefit greatly, but a form of loss function is essential in order to evaluate on one scale all the possible wrong allocations.

With much of what Mrs. Floud said, I agree completely. She has rightly emphasized many weaknesses in my model and indicated other very important factors. I share her wish both to construct from past research reasonable numerical values of population parameters and to extend my type of calculation to more realistic and necessarily more complicated models. However, I cannot understand her wish to remove x from the discussion: with all its modifications, x remains simply the characteristic of an individual at any instant on which ideally selection would be based. I have in Section 3 answered Mrs. Floud's objection to taking x to be normally distributed: her worry may arise from confusion of the statistical and colloquial uses of the word *normal*.

I suspect that Dr. Curnow's tongue was in his cheek when he commented on selection for sixth forms. I am well aware that my model ought to be at least three-stage, and commend to his attention this formidable computational problem. I am not surprised that closer correlations are obtainable if all selection is deferred until university admission, but rather am pleased that my two-stage scheme approaches so closely to this. Implicit in my argument is the assumption that selection at $11+$ is at present an administrative necessity (on whose educational merits and demerits I express no opinion), and I am comforted to find that E_x is not too adversely affected thereby. I think that Dr. Curnow is wrong in suggesting that still higher correlation coefficients could be obtained by some selection at $11+$; Dr. Levy pointed out the optimality of the multiple correlation.

I am very grateful to Dr. Levy for his valuable comments, which give me much to think about. I can assure him that I had no wish to imply that a distasteful correlation can be put equal to zero! I had thought it unlikely that, even if appreciable statistical advantages appeared to come from using y_1 as well as y_2 at the second stage of selection, this would be acceptable even for serious discussion at the present time; bearing in mind the oversimplification of my model and the fact that both x and y_2 are likely to be modified for the grammar school pupils, I therefore did not explore this line further. He is of course quite right in stating that "simple joint use of y_1 and y_2 is always optimal," but I was concerned to look for an optimal within the present framework of ignoring y_1 at the second stage. To do as Dr. Levy proposes would involve occasionally telling a boy that, despite good performance in an examination at age 18, he could not be admitted to a university because of his poor test record seven years earlier. I do not deny that this *may be* the right policy, but my first reaction on being faced with such a situation would be to suspect a flaw in the model rather than the existence of a small proportion of inherently awkward and unfortunate individuals. Dr. Wall's remarks about the need to use dynamic patterns strike me as relevant here. The small numerical difference between using y_2 alone and using $y_1 + y_2$ at the second stage is comforting, and the considerations summarized in what I termed u will reduce it further; I remain convinced that to use y_2 alone is the more realistic but am very well aware that the real need is to take account of rates and directions of change as well as instantaneous scores.

Before this meeting, I had not heard of Cronbach and Gleser's work, and one personally satisfying outcome of my paper is that subsequently I have not only seen their book but have also talked with Dr. Cronbach. There is evidently much in common between their approach and mine, and their classification of selection strategies is important. Nevertheless, I think that they have been largely concerned with a different class of problems, those in which two or more stages of selection are to be applied in quick succession. To hold some individuals in a marginal class pending further tests may then be practicable. If several years and an educational programme that modifies abilities come between one stage and the next, some allocation must take place after each stage. For example, the fully sequential strategy might be very appropriate if the $11+$ selection

itself were broken down into two stages; its application to the
system I discussed would mean a threefold classification at 11 into
those who were assured of eventual admission to a university whatever happened during the remainder of their school days, those who
were thereafter denied all hope of university admission, and the
intermediate class of those for whom no decision could be made
until 18. I question whether tests yet available have sufficiently
high validity for any substantial numbers to be put (at age 11) into
the first class. In fact a simple multiple cutoff method can be highly
efficient, as is well known to animal breeders who use it under the
name of "independent culling" (Young, 1961; Finney, 1962b). My
equation F15 is more complex on account of its second term, and,
under the modified conditions that I suggest in Section 10, I would
expect it to be little inferior to a complete joint use of y_1 and y_2.
I must agree with Dr. Levy that the various Cronbach and Gleser
strategies need closer examination from my point of view, remembering that a balance must be maintained between realism of model,
practicability of strategy, and statistical efficiency. Some of the
difficulties would disappear for a system based upon comprehensive
secondary schools; although this is scarcely in itself sufficient reason
for advocating such a system, small-scale empirical sampling investigations that I have recently begun make it seem increasingly
desirable because of the magnitude of individual discrepancies that
occur between values of x actually selected and the highest values in
the population.

COMMENTS BY LEE J. CRONBACH*

It is a pleasure to thank Professor Finney for his paper and to
voice hearty agreement with its philosophy. Educational decisions
allocate resources and arrange treatments; the best decision is that
which maximizes some composite social outcome. Casting the practical problem in the formal mold of decision theory is indeed of
value; it brings attention to aspects of the decision previously overlooked, and sometimes it shows that the educator has seriously
misconceived what he is doing. Institutional decision making has
three equally vital elements: there must be a clear statement of
desired outcomes, provided by spokesmen for society; there must

---

* Presented as invited discussion of the above paper when it was given by
Dr. Finney as an invited address, American Statistical Association, September,
1962. This discussion was based on the paper only, the British discussion not
yet having appeared.

be a clear statement of empirical predictor-treatment-outcome relations, provided by research in the field; and there must be a rational combination of these two into an optimal decision rule. The statistician shows how the third problem is to be solved, and by doing so clarifies the tasks left to the educational statesman and the educational researcher.

It is perfectly true that a model such as we have before us radically simplifies a complex social process, but this is a fundamental objection only if the findings are naïvely applied. The model can always be complicated to come closer to the real situation, though such a model demands estimates of far more parameters and so puts a greater burden on empirical research. But this is only a sign that the statistical analysis is showing what facts are needed in order to make rationally the decisions that are already being made. I do have some criticism of the model offered here, but this is not because I disagree with Professor Finney. Rather, I am choosing to emphasize and expand certain points in his own qualifying and critical remarks.

I may say at the outset that the differences between British and American education have little bearing on the value of this paper. Our decision-making processes at the college and graduate school level are very much like those bracketing British secondary education, and our decisions at the secondary level have much in common with those emerging in the British comprehensive school. The statistical parameters certainly differ. We take many more young people into college. Our correlations resemble Finney's set F17, though they are probably appreciably higher. If it is true that the correlation between early and late tests is very high, then little is gained by two-stage selection. It is probably unsound, however, to assume that $\rho_{y_1 y_2}$ is independent of the secondary school to which the person is assigned; this matter—which we shall see is vital—is one on which no factual evidence presently exists, so far as I am aware.

The Finney Decision Rule

While Professor Finney has plausible extrastatistical reasons for proposing to select university students entirely on the basis of y_2, ignoring y_1, I think that we will learn more if we do not accept this constraint. Both y_1 and y_2 predict university success; I suggest that we examine the consequences of using all the information available at the second stage. In Figure F1, y is the composite of y_1 and y_2

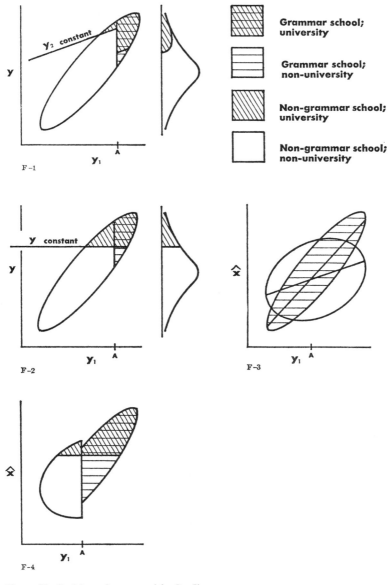

Figure F1. Decision rule proposed by Dr. Finney
Figure F2. Optimum decision rule, if secondary allocation has no effect
Figure F3. Joint distributions of expected outcome for two treatments
Figure F4. Optimum decision rule considering effect of secondary allocation on outcome

that best predicts university success. Persons to the right of cutting point A go to grammar school. The second-stage cutoff lines, where y_2 is constant, are set to maximize the average y. Figure F2 is a similar diagram in which the second-stage decision is based on y. Using the information in y_1 to the full extent of its validity (as in F1) increases the expected value of x, for any given π; but the effect is quite negligible unless $\rho_{y_1 y_2}$ is low.

It is most important to note in Figure F2 that the location of A and therefore the size of P_1 has no effect on the results. The ultimate average outcome is the same whether we send everyone or no one to grammar school. This is unreasonable; it implies that something is radically wrong with the model.

Conditions for Allocation

Success in the university surely depends on secondary school experience, hence the function linking x to y_1 ought to differ for each type of school.

There is a general theorem regarding allocation which may be stated (elliptically) as follows: Consider the regression line relating outcome to the composite predictor, within treatments; allocation is profitable only when the lines for different treatments cross within the range of predictor scores. Like Professor Finney, I assume that there is no ultimate limit on the number of grammar school places. If grammar school is beneficial at every value of y_1, then in the "steady state" that Professor Finney contemplates every pupil should be sent to grammar school. Allocation is warranted only if the state of affairs is like that in Figure F3. This figure shows what might be found if every pupil went to grammar school (shaded), and if every pupil went to, say, a secondary modern school. The ordinate $\hat{x}$ is an estimate of university success. It is based on a separate regression equation for each treatment relating outcome x to all predictor data available at the second stage. I allow not only that the correlations of Professor Finney's model may vary with treatment, but that at the second-stage different tests may be given to the two groups. The best first-stage strategy is to cut at A, where the regression lines cross. Then as Figure F4 shows, we cut at some level of $\hat{x}$ to select the university entrants.

I consider it essential to change the model in one other respect. To consider the success of only the university entrants distorts the problem. We are trying to maximize social benefits and to this end recommend a treatment for each person. The essential difference between selection and allocation is that in allocation we are concerned with the outcome for *every* person. We must express on some common payoff scale the social benefit accruing from the career of each university entrant and the benefit from each person in the grammar school–non-university and non-grammar–non-university categories. The statistical problem is then to maximize total payoff, subject to whatever costs and constraints we acknowledge. These remarks have sketched a model for studying sequential placement decisions where different treatments are given after the first stage of testing. Such decision problems have not been analyzed formally, but I believe that neither the mathematics nor the computations will prove to be unconquerable.

Our great impediment is inadequate empirical knowledge. The long familiar selection model led aptitude testers to learn a great deal about what tasks predict success *within* an academic program. But they were not led to inquire about what predicts *differential* success under various educational methods or about how different types of schooling modify aptitude. For allocation we need to predict which treatment among all the possibilities will make the most of the talents of the individual. We should not assume that standard university training is best for everyone.

This leads us to consider the range of educational options. The models discussed have assumed that one must choose between two fixed types of secondary school. This is a conservative and short-sighted statement of the problem. If we have it within our power to build and staff new schools, we also have it within our power to create new educational designs. Our real task is to find that combination of aptitude indicators and treatments, within the whole range of conceivable treatments, that will produce the greatest payoff from a school generation. This is a psychological, more than a statistical, problem. But the statistician contributes by stating the problem correctly: the problem is not one of maximizing predictive validity or payoff within one fixed treatment; it is one of discovering those aptitudes and treatments that have the greatest interaction, so that each child will truly "receive the treatment best suited to him."

Professor Finney has broken new and important ground; my criticisms suggest only the form subsequent work might take. We are united in our belief that the restatement of educational problems in decision-theoretic terms will add greatly to the soundness and clarity of policy, both directly and by inspiring new types of empirical research.

CLASSIFICATION PROCEDURES BASED ON BAYES'S FORMULA

By ALLAN BIRNBAUM
Institute of Mathematical Sciences, New York University

and A. E. MAXWELL*
Institute of Psychiatry, University of London

In this article Dr. Birnbaum and Dr. Maxwell describe some methods of classification based on the classical probability formula of Bayes, and on some of its applications suggested by the theory of statistical decision functions. The classification problems considered are general, utilizing no restrictive assumptions about possible distribution forms, but assuming that distributions can be estimated from large samples of data. The method is illustrated by an exploratory application to preliminary diagnostic classification, using data on 772 patients of a psychiatric hospital.

INTRODUCTION: CLASSIFICATION PROBLEMS

We are concerned here with statistical problems of a kind usually designated by the term "classification," but sometimes designated by broad usages of the terms "estimation," "prediction," or "correlation." These problems have the following form: we consider some number k of categories from each of which random observations may be obtained; thus each category is a statistical population. For example, each category may consist of individual persons, from whom a sample of persons may be selected randomly; for these individuals, the observations obtained consist of some specified characteristics or measurements or "scores"—we shall use the term "measurement" in its broadest sense to designate whatever specified qualitative or quantitative information constitutes the complete "observation" obtained for one individual.

The central problem is to infer, on the basis of the measurement on an individual, the category to which the individual belongs. Thus it is the category which is to be "predicted" or "estimated" from the observation; in some contexts the category is referred to as the "criterion" which is to be predicted. The categories may be strata

* Reprinted from *Appl. Stat.*, 1960, 9, 152-169.

or subpopulations of some specified population. Any procedure or rule for inferring, on the basis of the measurement on an individual, the category to which he belongs, may be represented formally by an *inference function* (which in some contexts will be called a predictor, or estimator, or a decision function). If we introduce u as a generic symbol for any one of the values which may be obtained by making a measurement of a given kind, any inference function may be represented by $d(u)$: for each possible measurement u, the given inference function designates a certain category, namely category number $i = d(u)$; thus the values assumed by $d(u)$, for various u's, are the numbers (or names, other designating labels) of the various categories. It is sometimes convenient to represent an inference function simply by listing the u's in some convenient order, with each u followed by its corresponding i.

An important aspect of this problem is the *evaluation of* various alternative *inference functions* $d(u)$ defined for a given kind of measurement u, to provide a basis for selecting the inference function to be used in a given situation. A more inclusive problem is the *evaluation of* the usefulness of various possible *kinds of measurement* for a given classification problem, to provide a basis for selecting one of them for use.

In the problem discussed in detail on pp. 247 ff., the combined categories constitute the patients admitted to a mental hospital during a certain period; the individual categories are defined by alternative diagnoses of the patients, namely, (1) neurosis, (2) schizophrenia, (3) affective disorder, or (4) abnormality of personality. The diagnoses of admitted patients are not generally made until some time after admission, but upon admission certain more specific observations are available; in the example quoted these are represented by nine different traits, whose presence or absence is noted for each patient at the time of admission. The resulting "measurement" places each patient in one of the $2^9 = 512$ logically possible patterns of traits. It is of interest to consider the problem of predicting the future diagnosis of the patient from such a measurement: that is, the problem of devising a rule for making preliminary diagnoses on the basis of such measurements alone. The reader who prefers to begin with a detailed discussion of an example, rather than general discussion of methods, may proceed from this point directly to p. 247, possibly referring back to earlier sections for supplementary discussion of the method applied there.

Methods of classification may be discussed generally in the following terms: let k denote the number of categories, and let i and j

be generic labels for the categories, $i, j = 1, 2, \ldots, k$ (i is the main label; the reason for the alternative label j will be clear from the next paragraph); let m denote the number of distinct values which are logically possible for the kind of measurement under consideration, and let u be a generic label for one of these possible values, $u = 1, 2, \ldots, m$. (The restrictive assumption that the measurements are of a kind which can take only a finite number of different values can be relaxed, but to avoid technical complication the present discussion is restricted to the finite case. The infinite case becomes appreciably different only in connection with the problems of sampling discussed on pp. 246-247.) Let $p(u|i)$ denote the probability that an individual will have measurement u if he is randomly selected from category number i; if each population consists of a finite number of individuals, then $p(u|i)$ is also the proportion of individuals in category i who have measurement u, for each value of i and u. Each possible inference function $d(u)$ takes one of the k values i for each of the m values of its argument u.

When a given kind of measurement has been adopted, the merits of any particular inference function $d(u)$ are described exhaustively (for the purposes considered in this paper) by the probabilities of errors of the various possible sorts which its use entails. When a specified $d(u)$ is used, let $r(j|i)$, for each pair i, j, denote the probability that, for an individual randomly selected from category i, $d(u)$ will take the value j (i.e., will lead to the inference that the individual is from category j). An ideal solution of a classification problem would be an inference function $d(u)$ having all error-probabilities $r(j|i) = 0$, $j \neq i$; but in the problems which are of serious interest, such ideal solutions do not exist. Questions of interest are of two types: (1) With a specified kind of measurement, and any of the possible inference functions $d(u)$, what are the attainable sets of error-probabilities $r(j|i)$, $i \neq j$? What considerations and techniques may lead to the selection of an appropriate one of the inference function for use in a given application? (2) Among the various kinds of measurement which might be used, what considerations and techniques may lead to the selection of an appropriate one for use in a given application? There are many considerations relevant to such choices other than the error-probabilities attainable by the use of each kind of measurement. These include convenience, costs, purposes, and perhaps the relative frequencies with which individuals from the various categories may be expected to be encountered in a given situation of application. These other considerations will not be discussed here (these aspects of classification problems have been stressed in an interesting recent study [Cronbach and Gleser, 1957]); but it is important to note that all such considerations must be taken into account, jointly with the error-probabilities attainable, in any practical appraisal of alternative kinds of measurement in classification problems.

The preceding notions may be further developed and illustrated as follows; for simplicity, the discussion at this point (but not in what follows) will be formulated in terms of the special case of two categories. If $k = 2$, just two sorts of errors are possible: $r(1|2)$ is the probability that an individual randomly selected from category 2 will, when a specified $d(u)$ is used, be inferred to be from category 1; and $r(2|1)$ is the probability that an individual from category 1 will be inferred to be from category 2. If we consider one kind of measurement, and all possible inference functions $d(u)$, we obtain for each $d(u)$ a pair of error-probabilities $r(1|2)$ and $r(2|1)$. As in the schematic Figure B1, the latter probabilities may be used as the coordinates of a point which represents a given $d(u)$; the set of points representing the various possible inference functions typically fills out some convex region within the unit square. The points along the lower-left boundary of the shaded region represent inference functions none of which can be strictly improved upon: in comparison with any such point, each possible alternative point in the shaded region represents an inference function which is worse in at least one of its error-probabilities. On the other hand, as between any two points on this lower-left boundary, there is no simple and categorical basis for choosing the "better" one, since each of

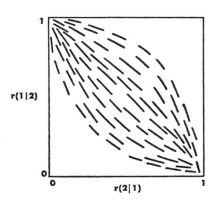

Figure B1. Error-probability patterns with two categories and various possible inference functions (schematic diagram)

the two points is better with respect to one of its error-probabilities. Each of the latter boundary points, and their corresponding inference functions, may be called *admissible* for reasonable further consideration for possible use; whereas other points, and their corresponding inference functions, may be called *inadmissible* for further reasonable consideration, since each of these can be strictly improved upon (i.e., one error-probability can be decreased without an increase in the other) by choosing instead a point below and/or to the left on the boundary of the shaded region.

The questions (1) above reduce formally to the problem of determining those sets of attainable error-probabilities (and corresponding inference functions) which are admissible, and to the problem of making a reasonable choice among these.

The question (2) above may be approached as follows: suppose that three alternative kinds of measurement, A, B, and C, are available for use in a given classification problem. Each of these may be represented by a graph representing the admissible inference functions based on it, as in the schematic Figure B2; each such graph corresponds to the lower-left boundary of the shaded region in a figure analogous to Figure B1. Such graphs would be expected to arise, for example, if C denotes a measurement consisting of the response-pattern on a test consisting of six dichotomous items (e.g., a measurement like that used in the example on p. 247, but based on six rather than nine traits); if A denotes a measurement like that of this example consisting of the response-pattern based on nine such items, including the six items underlying C; and if B de-

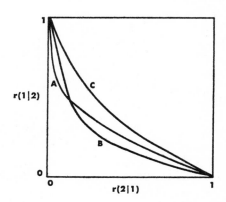

Figure B2. Error-probability patterns for admissible inference functions based on three different kinds of measurement A, B, and C, with two categories (schematic diagram)

notes a similar measurement based on nine items, those underlying C and another three items not included in A.

In this comparison, the measurement C appears inadmissible for further consideration provided that A or B can be adopted without incurring relative disadvantages (such as costs or inconvenience) which would outweigh the advantages over C with respect to error-probabilities; if A and B are much more expensive to use than C, then of course C might reasonably be preferred. No such simple comparison is possible between A and B; in fact, if other considerations such as costs leave A and B equally attractive, then it is clear that one might prefer either A or B, depending on which particular point on the A or B curves in Figure B2 one chose to attain.

If in a given classification problem we find that a specified kind of measurement gives no inference function whose various error-probabilities are suitably small, we are led to conclude that the *kind* of measurement being used is not sufficiently informative, and we are led to seek an alternative kind of measurement which may prove more satisfactory. On the other hand, if one kind of measurement leads to inference functions whose error-probabilities are considerably smaller than is necessary in some application, we may wish to consider another kind of measurement, less expensive or easier to use, which would not increase the error-probabilities intolerably.

Finally, on the basis of one or more kinds of measurement, there may be several inference functions available, each of which has error-probabilities sufficiently small to be tolerated in a given application.

Considerations like those described above have helped us up to this point in simplifying the problems of choice among inference functions and kinds of measurement, but they leave unresolved the problem of making a final choice from the many admissible inference functions remaining under consideration. Since the various sorts of possible errors are generally of qualitatively different kinds, there appears to be no requirement of reasonableness which compellingly leads us to seek some formal rule by which to make such selections. It could perhaps be postulated that each of the possible sorts of errors has a "cost," and that these costs could be expressed on some single numerical scale of utility. This may be the case in some applications, but in many others, such as the later example, the possibility of measuring these costs in terms of some single unit of utility seems quite hypothetical (except for limited administrative purposes). Any attempt to apply such a formulation even as a formal step toward choosing an inference function would seem to risk distorting or obscuring some of the practical judgements and value-judgements appropriate to the specified situation of application. Such judgements can well be brought to bear informally in direct consideration of the merits of various rules as represented simply by their error-probabilities.

There is an extensive literature and body of theory devoted to problems of inference or decision making formulated in terms of costs and utilities associated with the various possible errors (see, e.g., Luce and Raiffa [1957] and references therein). In the statistical theory of decision functions initiated by Wald (1950), inference problems are formulated by the introduction of loss functions which represent, in terms of some common unit of utility, the costs of the various possible sorts of errors. It seems unfortunate that much writing in the field of statistical decision theory fails to mention the fact that, even when such loss functions are quite hypothetical from the standpoint of the situation of application, nevertheless the inference function (or decision functions) determined by their formal use are typically admissible when they are appraised more directly and simply in terms of the probabilities of errors of various sorts to which their use leads. A notable exception is the paper by Lindley (1953); parts of the present paper may be regarded as informal exposition of parts of Lindley's paper.

CONSTRUCTION OF ADMISSIBLE INFERENCE FUNCTIONS

A general method for constructing various admissible inference functions is based on the introduction, in a *hypothetical formal* way, of possible *a priori* probabilities for the k categories of interest. Let us *imagine* that there exists a population which consists of our k categories as subpopulations or strata, combined in the proportions g_i, for $i = 1, 2, \ldots, k$; in other words, let us imagine that there is a composite population such that if we randomly select an individual from it, the probability is g_i that the selected individual belongs to category i, $i = 1, 2, \ldots, k$. Among all individuals within a given category i, we have, as before, that the measurements u of some specified kind have the probability distribution function $p(u|i)$. It then follows formally from the formula of Bayes in the elementary theory of probability that, if an individual is randomly selected from this hypothetical composite population and if only his measurement u is observed, then the probability that he belongs to category number i is given by $p(i|u) = g_i p(u|i)/p(u)$. Here

$p(u)$ is the probability that any individual randomly selected from the hypothetical composite population has measurement u, that is, $p(u) = \sum_{i=1}^{k} g_i p(u|i)$. An important simplification, which is useful in many applications, is obtained by noting that the *relative* magnitudes of the $p(i|u)$'s, for a given measurement u, are available without computation of $p(u)$, since $p(i|u)$ is simply proportional to $g_i p(u|i)$. In this hypothetical context, Bayes's formula suggests the inference that, if an individual is observed to have measurement u, then he is most likely to belong to that category i for which the quantity $g_i p(u|i)$ is largest. This Bayesian rule of inference may be represented by an inference function $d(u)$ defined as follows:

For each u, let

$d(u) =$ that number i which maximizes $g_i p(u|i)$.

(If two or more i's give the same maximum value, the arbitrary choice of one of them, or the definition of a random method for selecting one of them each time such a u is observed, leads to a definition of a particular Bayesian rule.) It is important to note that the definition of each Bayesian inference function $d(u)$ makes use of constants g_i which may be *completely arbitrary (and hypothetical, as probabilities)*. Once such a $d(u)$ is defined, however, we can immediately compute and consider the various error-probabilities $r(j|i)$ which will result from the use of $d(u)$. *Each such Bayesian $d(u)$ is recommended for serious consideration by its fundamental property of admissibility, namely that there is no alternative $d(u)$ which gives smaller values to any of the error-probabilities $r(j|i)$ except at the price of increasing some other error-probabilities. This property is not at all affected by the arbitrary or hypothetical nature of the constants g_i used.*

This fundamental property of Bayesian inference rules has taken a central place in the development of the theory and techniques of mathematical statistics, beginning with its use by Wald in his theory of statistical decision functions. However, it seems not yet widely appreciated that the method of demonstration of this property is essentially an elementary one: in the hypothetical composite population having probabilities g_i for the various categories, the problem of classifying a randomly selected individual on the basis of a measurement u, so as to maximize the probability of correct classifications, is a simple problem of classical probability theory. Its solution is given by the Bayesian rule represented by the $d(u)$

defined above, and the resulting minimized probability of misclassifications is given by

$$\sum_{i=1}^{m} g_i \sum_{j \neq i} r(j|i)$$

where the second summation symbol $\sum_{j \neq i}$ denotes taking a sum of all the error-probabilities $r(j|i)$ for a given i, $j \neq i$. If such a $d(u)$ were not admissible, there would exist another inference rule having none of its error-probabilities larger, and one or more of them smaller, than the $r(j|i)$'s of $d(u)$ in the above expression. But this would give a smaller value to the above expression for probability of misclassifications, contradicting the fact that $d(u)$ minimizes this probability. This contradiction proves that $d(u)$ is admissible — a property not compromised by the fact that the g_i's are arbitrary or hypothetical. (This proof tacitly assumed that each g_i was positive, not zero, as will usually be the case in applications of interest. Even if some g_i's are taken equal to zero, an equally simple proof is possible provided that tied maximized values of the expression $g_i p(u|i)$ (for various i's), which is used in the definition of $d(u)$, occur with negligible probabilities: if there are no such ties, then the Bayesian $d(u)$ is determined uniquely for each u in the above definition. Hence every different inference function gives a larger probability of misclassifications, and hence every inference function different from $d(u)$ has at least one of its error-probabilities larger than the corresponding $r(j|i)$ of $d(u)$.)

The working methods which are suggested by these considerations are the following. In any classification problem, as soon as the respective distributions $p(u|i)$, of some given kind of measurement u within each category i, are known, we can immediately write the definitions of a number of admissible Bayesian inference functions $d(u)$ defined as above in terms of the relative magnitudes of the quantities $g_i p(u|i)$; each arbitrary choice of the hypothetical probabilities g_i defines one such function. In a given classification problem it will often be of interest to consider for possible use at least several different such functions $d(u)$ and to appraise and compare them (and the kind of measurement u on which they are based) on the basis of their respective sets of error-probabilities $r(j|i)$. In order to calculate the error-probabilities of any given inference function $d(u)$, we have merely to apply the formula.

$$r(j|i) = \sum_{u \text{ in } A_j} p(u|i)$$

where A_j denotes the set of values of u for which $d(u) = j$. Calculations which are generally easier to carry out, and which may suffice for some purposes (especially for preliminary consideration of a given decision function) are those of the respective probabilities of correct classifications:

$$r(i|i) = \sum_{u \text{ in } A_i} p(u|i).$$

As soon as the error-probabilities of several Bayesian inference functions have been obtained, the problem of evaluating, comparing, and possibly adopting one of them can be considered further in the ways discussed and illustrated in the introductory section. If the number of categories k is larger than two, then diagrams like Figures B1 and B2 cannot be used to represent the sets of $r(j|i)$'s of the various inference functions. But inspection of the numerical values of these $r(j|i)$'s and/or of the $r(i|i)$'s can be the basis for judgements of the sort illustrated by use of these figures. (It may sometimes be useful to sketch such figures for a given pair of categories, temporarily omitting from consideration all but two categories; in this way, for example, if k exceeds two, a figure like Figure B1 above would result from plotting points with coordinates $r(2|1)$ and $r(1|2)$ computed for several Bayesian $d(u)$'s; other figures might be sketched to represent the $r(i|j)$ and $r(j|i)$ values attainable for other pairs i and j of categories.)

An important practical question which must be met in any application of these methods is the choice of one or several sets of hypothetical probabilities g_i to use in defining the first Bayesian inference rules to be examined; and then at each stage of consideration of inference rules, the choice of successive new sets of g_i's to be tried when additional exploration of the class of Bayesian inference rules seems worthwhile. Unfortunately, there are no general rules available which give very useful quantitative information to guide these choices, and an element of trial-and-error seems inevitable in the selection of trial values of g_i's, except for the initial choice in the case where *a priori* estimates are available. However, much qualitative information becomes available as to the directions in which the g_i's should be varied to obtain desired modifications of successive inference rules considered. The basic consideration here is the property of admissibility of each of the inference rules obtained (illustrated by Figures B1 and B2, and by similar figures or analogous tables of $r(j|i)$ values, which may be filled in progressively in a given application as successive inference rules are considered). The knowledge that the set of points (whose coordinates are $r(j|i)$'s, $j \neq i$) which one is exploring is a convex curve or surface is of great help. Also useful is the fact that, if a given set of g_i's gives error-probabilities which include too small a probability of correct classification for individuals from a certain category i, then by increasing only the corresponding g_i, and decreasing some or all of the other g_i's, one will generate a new inference function with smaller probabilities of errors of each kind possible for individuals from the given category. To increase probabilities of correct classifications for individuals from a specified pair of categories, one should try some increase in only the corresponding two g_i's, adjusting some or all of the others downward, and so forth. The information obtained by inspection of the error-probabilities $r(j|i)$ (and/or the probabilities $r(i|i)$ of correct classifications) for each inference rule examined will provide, along with such general qualitative considerations, more useful guidance in an application of these methods than it seems possible to provide in any more formal suggestions.

If $k > 2$, the "simple Bayesian rules" discussed up to this point, which can be generated by varying the g_i's, do not include all admissible rules, but for many applications it will be simpler and sufficient to restrict attention to them. The additional admissible rules, which may be called "generalized Bayesian inference rules," are distinguished from the "simple" rules so far considered by two features: (1) on consideration of their probabilities $r(i|i)$ of correct classifications alone, they can each be strictly improved upon by some simple Bayesian rule; (2) they are not on that account inadmissible, since each of them has a pattern of probabilities $r(j|i)$, $j \neq i$, of incorrect classifications which cannot be matched or improved upon by any other (simple or generalized) Bayesian rule. In exploring the class of admissible rules for a given application, it will be simplest to restrict initial consideration to simple Bayesian rules; and to consider some generalized Bayesian rules only if the particular *patterns* of $r(j|i)$'s, $j \neq i$, found among simple Bayesian rules are unsatisfactory. It may then be worth trying to modify them, even at the cost of some worsening of a set of $r(i|i)$'s attainable by a simple Bayesian rule.

The basic method of constructing generalized Bayesian rules is the following generalization of the above method. Let (h_{ji}) be a k by k array of arbitrary positive numbers, except that $h_{ii} = 0$ for each i. For every inference rule $d(u)$, the weighted sum of its error-probabilities

$$R = \sum_{i=1}^{k} \sum_{j=1}^{k} h_{ji} \mathrm{r}(j|i)$$

can, in principle, be computed. A generalized Bayesian inference rule is one which minimizes R, for any given array (h_{ji}). It follows, by an argument similar to that above, that such a rule is admissible. Since $\mathrm{r}(j|i) = \sum_{u \text{ in } A_j} \mathrm{p}(u|i)$, it is easily seen that R is minimized by the inference function which takes, for each u, the value j for which

$$\mathrm{R}_j(u) = \sum_{i=1}^{k} h_{ji} \mathrm{p}(u|i)$$

is minimized. Thus to construct a generalized Bayesian rule, given the distributions $\mathrm{p}(u|i)$ and an array (h_{ji}), requires the computation and comparison, for each u, of the k quantities $\mathrm{R}_j(u)$, as contrasted with the k quantities $g_i \mathrm{p}(u|i)$ required for a simple Bayesian rule.

In exploring the class of such rules for a given application, it is useful to note that increasing one h_{ji}, $j \neq i$, while leaving the others unchanged, tends to reduce the corresponding $\mathrm{r}(j|i)$ and of course to increase one or more other error-probabilities.

(The h_{ji}'s can be taken as non-negative, rather than *positive*, subject to qualifications; cf. Lindley, 1953, for a precise theoretical discussion.)

INTERPRETATION OF ADMISSIBLE INFERENCE FUNCTIONS IN RESEARCH

The preceding discussion has centred on the problems of finding kinds of measurement, and inference functions, which minimize error-probabilities $\mathrm{r}(j|i)$. In some contexts of application, the principal interest in the quantities $\mathrm{r}(j|i)$ will be in their direct practical interpretations as probabilities of error. In other contexts, however, they may also serve a research purpose. For example, relations between a given set of symptom-patterns (u) and a given set of diagnostic categories or diseases (i) are represented, in the form of an admissible inference function and its $\mathrm{r}(j|i)$'s, in ways which may prove interesting and possibly suggestive for purposes of theoretical investigation; of course the choice of categories, methods of measurement, and interpretation of such results all lie in the area of responsibility of the empirical research scientist.

RELATIONSHIPS TO OTHER METHODS; SAMPLING ERRORS

Although the method presented here is a simple and logical one for problems of classification, it seems to have received relatively little consideration in comparison with other methods. One reason for this, no doubt, is that this method requires relatively extensive data for its application since the distribution functions $p(u|i)$, for each category i, must be known. If the method of measurement is such that the number of values which may possibly be assumed by u for a given i is large, then the precise estimation of $p(u|i)$ will require a very large sample from each category i. For this reason the method might be called an actuarial method; it will be applicable generally only where large masses of data are easily available or are accumulated from large samples of individuals in a routine way. In cases where the number of possible values of u is small, the required sample sizes will be relatively small, but they must still be large enough to give precise estimates of all $p(u|i)$'s.

The principal advantage of this method, as compared with others, is that no restrictive theoretical assumptions are imposed on the forms which the distributions $p(u|i)$ may take. To the extent that special known forms may be assumed to hold for the $p(u|i)$'s (on empirical or theoretical grounds), derivations like those above lead to admissible (Bayesian) inference functions having special forms related to those of the $p(u|i)$'s. If the $p(u|i)$'s can be assumed known except for the values of several parameters (e.g., to have multivariate normal distributions, with common unknown covariances matrices°), then considerably smaller random samples from each category will suffice to give the required precise estimates of the $p(u|i)$'s; the refinements required to take precise account of the errors of estimation with moderate sample sizes in such cases have been investigated to a considerable extent but have not yet been completely solved. The corresponding refinements required to take precise account of errors of estimation of the $p(u|i)$'s in the present method from samples which are not very large (relative to the number of possible values of u) have not yet been developed, although some relevant research has been carried out.° It seems clear that such developments would require the solution of some quite difficult problems of theoretical statistics, and that the results of such investigation would not obviate the need for quite large sample sizes in typical applications of the method.

If the $p(u|i)$'s are estimated from samples which are not very large, then the formal application of the methods described above to such estimates of the $p(u|i)$'s will lead to inference functions and error-probabilities which are estimates of the unknown desired inference functions and their error-probabilities. These estimates will typically be subject to fairly large sampling errors, and to appreciable biases in the direction of underestimating both (a) the error-probabilities which actually hold for the obtained inference function, and (b) the error-probabilities which are attainable when the $p(u|i)$'s are known or precisely estimated. There seems to be no general method now available which is useful in determining the magnitudes of such biases. Analogous questions have been investigated in a special classification problem by Stoller (1954).

ILLUSTRATIVE EXAMPLE

The methods outlined above were applied to a sample of 772 males, aged 16-59, who had been inpatients at the Bethlem Royal and Maudsley Hospitals, London. Information concerning the *presence* or *absence* of numerous psychiatric characteristics was readily available for these patients on Hollerith punched cards, and on the basis of this and other information the patients had been allotted to one or another of the customary psychiatric classification categories.

For our purpose nine traits were chosen which appeared to give a reasonable cross-section of patient traits and which themselves overlapped only to a small degree (the tetrachoric correlations between the traits were known from an earlier study [Trouton and Maxwell, 1956]). The nine traits were:

1. Hysterical symptoms, lifelong or episodic
2. Anxiety
3. Schizophrenic type of thought disorder
4. Depression
5. Compulsive acts and/or obsessional thoughts
6. Lack of confidence when in society
7. Definite mood variations before present illness
8. Impulsiveness and/or aggressiveness
9. Hypochondriacal attitude toward illness.

Current psychiatric diagnostic categories are numerous, but for this study it was possible to group the 772 patients into four broad categories. An estimate of the *a priori* probability that a patient entering the hospitals in question would fall into a given one of these categories was obtained from hospital records for a larger group of patients than the sample of 772. The actual sample sizes N_i and the estimated *a priori* probabilities g_i' of each category are given below:

CATEGORY	N_i	g_i'
Neurotics	341	.461
Schizophrenics	174	.237
Affective disorders	148	.157
Abnormal personality	109	.145
	772	1.000

The methods described here might equally well have been applied with one or more of these broad categories subdivided into more refined categories. For example, the neurotic group of 341 patients is composed of

Anxiety reactives	104
Hysterics	35
Obsessionals	31
Neurotic depressives	123
Psychoneurotics and others	48
	341

However, had groups as small as these been employed the number of traits used—for reasons of sampling discussed above—should probably have been reduced considerably.

If we use nine dichotomously scored symptoms, the number m of distinct answer patterns possible is 2^9, or 512. By means of a Hollerith sorter, the 772 cards, one for each patient, were divided into two groups, depending on whether the response to the first symptom was affirmative or negative. These two groups of cards were subdivided further depending on the responses to the second symptom, and so on until all nine symptoms had been considered. This task proved much less onerous than had been expected, for of the 512 possible answer patterns only 178 occurred.

The number of patients from each diagnostic category giving each of the 178 observed answer patterns was then recorded. These numbers were expressed as proportions of the total number in the category to which they belonged, giving the required (estimated) values $p(u|i)$. These proportions were each multiplied by the corresponding g_i'. Each answer pattern u was then allotted to the category i for which the weighted proportion, $g_i' p(u|i)$, was largest. For example, the answer pattern

$$- \quad - \quad - \quad + \quad - \quad + \quad - \quad - \quad -$$

occurred 28 times, 13 times among neurotics, 8 times among affective disorders, 5 times among schizophrenics, and twice among abnormal personalities. Since the numbers in these categories are 341, 148, 174, and 109 respectively, the proportions of patients in the respective categories having this answer pattern are

$$.0381, \quad .0541, \quad .0287, \quad .0183.$$

When these proportions are multiplied by the *a priori* probabilities g'_i of the categories we obtain .017573, .008513, .006807, .002655, respectively; these numbers are proportional to the *a posteriori* probabilities that a patient with the given answer pattern will belong to the respective categories. Since the first of these weighted proportions is the largest, the answer pattern in question is allotted to the neurotic group.

Of the 178 different answer patterns observed, 81 were allotted in this manner to neurotics (eight of them accounting for 34% of the cases), 12 to affective disorders, 57 to schizophrenics (eight of them accounting for 36% of the cases), and 28 to abnormal personalities.

This completed the determination of a Bayesian rule for making preliminary diagnoses on the bases of the specified nine traits, and illustrates the general procedure for determining Bayesian inference rules $d(u)$. Such a rule can be conveniently represented simply by a listing of the answer patterns u in some convenient order, each followed by the number i of the category to which it is allotted.

It must be stressed that although in this example estimated *a priori* probabilities g'_i have been used as a starting point in developing a rule, there is no necessity for this. Any self-consistent set of g_i values may be used to develop a rule. But where, as in this case, estimates of *a priori* probabilities are available, it is logical to use them first and to examine the consequences of the rule to which they lead.

On the assumption that the proportions $p(u|i)$ used are correct (or estimated with sufficiently high precision), then regardless of the source of the g_i's used one can say that the inference rule obtained is admissible, that is, that any other rule having some error-probabilities smaller will necessarily have others larger. To evaluate the rule obtained, its probabilities $r(i|i)$ of correct classifications and $r(j|i)$ of incorrect classifications were computed as indicated on pp. 242–243, and are given in Table B1.

The diagonal entries, in parentheses, are probabilities of correct

classifications: for example, the (estimated) probability that a
"neurotic" will be correctly classified is .856. The (estimated)
probability that a "neurotic" will be classified as a "schizophrenic"
is .038; the (estimated) probability that a "schizophrenic" will be
classified as a "neurotic" is .241; etc.

On this basis, the evaluation and revision of such a classification
rule might proceed as follows: if the probabilities of correct classifications for individuals in categories 3 and 4 (.338 and .450 respectively) are judged intolerably low, these can be raised by constructing a new classification rule based on appropriately modified
g_i values, but only at the cost of lowering one or both of the probabilities of correct classification for individuals in categories 1 and
2 (.856 and .706 respectively).

If any lowering of the latter probabilities would also be intol-
erable, then the kind of measurement (set of nine traits) being used
must be judged inherently too uninformative for the purpose intended; consideration might be given to alternative and/or more
extensive sets of traits which might prove more informative. On
the other hand, if some lowering of the last mentioned probabilities
of correct classification might be tolerated, consideration could be
given to another classification rule, developed just as that described
above except for the use of larger values of g_3 and g_4. To this end,
taking each $g_i = .25$, a new classification rule was determined on
the basis of the same data; its probabilities of correct and incorrect
classifications are given in Table B2.

It might be thought illogical to use g_i values which differ markedly from the prior probabilities estimated with a fair degree of
precision, as assessed by sampling error. However, it must again be
stressed that the g_i values are hypothetical quantities introduced
for the purpose of developing objective rules; they are a means to

TABLE B1. $r(j|i)$ = THE (CONDITIONAL) PROBABILITY THAT A PATIENT FROM CATEGORY i WILL BE CLASSIFIED AS BELONGING TO CATEGORY j; THE CLASSIFICATION RULE IS BASED ON THE ESTIMATED PROBABILITIES g'_i

		\multicolumn{4}{c}{i}			
		1	2	3	4
		NEUROTICS	SCHIZO-PHRENICS	AFFECTIVE DISORDERS	ABNORMAL PERSONALITY
	1	(.856)	.241	.595	.422
j	2	.038	(.706)	.034	.073
	3	.073	.034	(.338)	.055
	4	.032	.017	.034	(.450)

an end and may be adjusted to give various patterns of error-probabilities. The use of a g_i different from the estimate of the prior probability does not necessarily imply that the estimate is considered to be incorrect.

The probabilities of correct classifications have been raised as intended for category 3 (from .338 to .772) and category 4 (from .450 to .800), at the cost of decreasing those for category 1 (from .856 to .388) and category 2 (from .706 to .577).

Evaluation of this second classification rule can now be made on the basis of Table B2; this might proceed as follows. If the probabilities of correct classification for categories 1 and 2 are now judged too low, and if no lower values for probabilities of correct classification for categories 3 and 4 could be tolerated, then the kind of measurement being used must be judged too uninformative, and alternative kinds of measurement considered. If the pattern of probabilities in Table B2 is judged satisfactory for the purpose at hand, this classification may be adopted, with the assurance that it is admissible (cannot be strictly improved upon using the present kind of measurement) as well as satisfactory. Finally, still other sets of values g_i could be used to generate alternative admissible classification rules; consideration of each such additional rule on the basis of its $r(j|i)$ values contributes to a more complete picture of the possibilities inherent in the given kind of measurement (generalizing the considerations of the simple case represented in Figure B1 above).

The validity of the quantities $r(j|i)$ given for the above classification rules, in application to new incoming patients, would depend crucially on the assumption that distributions $p(u|i)$ of response patterns within each category i are the same for new patients as for the previous patients represented by the data used in deriving

TABLE B2. $r(j|i)$ = THE (CONDITIONAL) PROBABILITY THAT A PATIENT FROM CATEGORY i WILL BE CLASSIFIED AS BELONGING TO CATEGORY j; THE CLASSIFICATION RULE IS BASED ON THE SECOND SET OF g_i VALUES (EACH g_i = .25)

		i			
		1 NEUROTICS	2 SCHIZO- PHRENICS	3 AFFECTIVE DISORDERS	4 ABNORMAL PERSONALITY
	1	(.388)	.057	.140	.072
j	2	.000	(.577)	.008	.000
	3	.384	.229	(.772)	.128
	4	.228	.137	.080	(.800)

the rules. If these probabilities change, then the computed values of
$r(j|i)$'s would generally no longer be correct; the actual probabilities
of incorrect classifications of various kinds could then become
higher, or lower, than the computed values. This validity also
depends on the assumption that errors in estimation of the $p(u|i)$'s
are negligible. Validity of the (conditional) probabilities $r(j|i)$ does
not depend on the actual proportions of patients in the categories
(i), nor on whether these proportions remain constant.

Another quantity of possible interest for the appraisal of a
classification rule is the total probability of correct classifications.
However the interpretation and use of this quantity requires
additional careful qualifications. If we write g'_i to denote an *assumed true proportion* of incoming patients in category i, in contrast
to g_i which has above denoted merely a convenient algebraic vari-
able, and apply a classification rule with known $r(j|i)$'s, then the
proportion of incoming patients correctly classified will be (in ex-
pected value) $C = \sum_{i=1}^{4} g'_i r(i|i)$. For example, for the first rule above
(Table B1), if we now assume each $g'_i = .25$, we obtain

$$C = \tfrac{1}{4} (.856) + \tfrac{1}{4} (.706) + \tfrac{1}{4} (.338) + \tfrac{1}{4} (.450) = .587.$$

But taking the g'_i values actually estimated from the data above
and used as g_i values in deriving this classification rule, we obtain
similarly $C = (.461) \ (.856) + \ldots = .680$. Finally, if the second
classification rule (Table B2) is used, and we assume the true g_i
values each to be .25, we obtain $C = \tfrac{1}{4} (.388) + \ldots = .634$. (It is
an algebraic fact, which was used in derivations in previous sections,
that for any given values g'_i, C is maximized by use of the classification rule derived as above with the variables g_i taken equal to the
given values g'_i.)

The validity of such a computed value C depends, in addition to
the above mentioned requirements for validity of $r(j|i)$'s of a given
rule, on the correctness of the values g'_i for the population of
patients to whom the rule is currently being applied. The significance
of a numerical value for C, or equivalently for the total probability
of incorrect classifications with a given rule:

$$1 - C = \sum_{i=1}^{4} g'_i \sum_{j \neq i} r(j|i)$$

is limited, since the last expression is a weighted average of probabilities of quite different kinds of errors; for different purposes, the

different sorts of errors will be of quite different seriousness and significance. For special purposes it might be desired to assign a numerical measure of cost to each type of error: if $W(j|i)$ denotes the cost of the type of error whose probability is $r(j|i)$, then the expected cost of classification errors, per patient, is

$$W = \sum_{i=1}^{4} g'_i \sum_{j \neq i} W(j|i)\, r(j|i).$$

If such purposes were of primary importance, and if it were desired to adopt a classification rule which minimized W when certain values g'_i were assumed, the desired rule could be found as indicated earlier, by identifying the h_{ji}'s there with the $g'_i W(j|i)$'s here.

When values of the quantity C are considered, another way of appraising over-all the kind of measurement used is available. If it is assumed that the true proportion g'_i of neurotics is .461, and that the other g'_i values are smaller, without use of response patterns it is possible to achieve the probability of correct classifications $C = .461$ by use of the simple rule which classifies all patients as neurotic, and this probability will be the maximum obtainable with this simple type of rule. The usefulness of the kind of measurement used is reflected in the increase from this number to the value $C = .680$, an increase in correct classifications of 21.9%.

ACKNOWLEDGMENT

We are grateful to Miss N. Hemsley for carrying out the Hollerith work. This research was supported by School of Aviation Medicine, USAF.

A DOLLAR CRITERION IN FIXED-TREATMENT EMPLOYEE SELECTION

By WILLIAM J. ROCHE, JR.
Medical Department, Caterpillar Tractor Co.

INTRODUCTION

Personnel testing in industry is aimed primarily at offering an objective means of selecting from among untried applicants those who have the greatest likelihood of job success. Recently Cronbach and Gleser (1957) have dealt with the use of psychological tests in making personnel decisions in the context of decision theory, advocating the approach that provides a more meaningful criterion for evaluating the worth of a psychological test used in selecting and placing personnel. "The value of a test," they contend, "can be stated only in terms of the specific type of decision problem, the strategy employed, the evaluation attached to the outcome, and the cost of testing."

Their utility model for the selection process calls for finding the strategy that maximizes the average gain (or minimizes the average loss) over many similar decisions. To define a gain and maximize it, it is assumed that the value of various outcomes or payoffs can be expressed in "equal units of satisfaction" which are additive over many decisions. The expected payoff from an individual in a particular category can be determined by weighting the value of each outcome that might result for him by its probability, and then summing over all outcomes. The cost of the procedure for gathering the information on which the decision is made must be expressed in utility units and then deducted from the expected payoff.

Cronbach and Gleser express the net gain in utility per person accepted in a fixed-treatment selection problem by the following equation:

$$\Delta U = \sigma_e r_{ye} \frac{\xi(y')}{\phi(y')} - \frac{C_y}{\phi(y')}$$

where ΔU is the net gain in utility, σ_e is the standard deviation of the payoff, r_{ye} is the correlation of the predictor with the evaluated payoff, $\xi(y')$ is the ordinate of the normal curve at the cutting score on the test, $\phi(y')$ is the area (upper tail) corresponding to the cutting score, and C_y is the cost of testing.

A method for empirically determining an expected payoff in utility units has been proposed by Brogden (1949a) and Brogden and Taylor (1950). In order to cope with some of the problems in the development of an adequate criterion against which to validate a test or test battery, they proposed to use a "dollar criterion." To develop a dollar criterion for an industrial employee, one must convert his production units, errors, time of other personnel consumed, etc. into dollar units. By using this approach Brogden and Taylor claim to be able to give direct face validity to the weighting of individual components of the criterion measure.

In order to develop an adequate criterion they suggest the use of cost accounting procedures, and point out two approaches. The first grew out of the need for developing a common metric by which it would be possible to combine various criterion measures into one index representative of the overall efficiency or contribution of the individual. The second approach grew out of the question of what a criterion should measure. Brogden and Taylor stress that the only functions of the criterion are: (1) to establish the basis for choosing the best predictor, and (2) to provide an estimate of the validity of the predictor. Their argument led them to the conclusion that "the criterion should measure the contribution of the individual to the overall efficiency of the organization."

They next dealt with the objectives of a business enterprise. In the simplest terms, the objective of a business is to make money. Consequently, monetary gain is the appropriate measure of the degree to which on-the-job activity of the individual contributes to or detracts from this overall objective. Brogden and Taylor (1950) summarize this notion as follows:

Only after we have succeeded in evaluating on-the-job performance in these terms can we be sure that our criterion measures conform to the objectives of the organization. The variables that are used to measure the job performance of the individual must be converted into dollar units, for unless criterion elements are of such a nature that they can be expressed in dollar units, their use as criterion measures cannot be justified and do not satisfy the requirement of logical face validity.

In using cost accounting to develop a dollar criterion a number of elements must be considered. Brogden and Taylor list the following as examples:

1. Average value of production or service units.

2. Quality of objects produced or service accomplished.
3. Overhead—including rent, light, heat, cost depreciation, rental of machines and equipment, etc.
4. Errors, accidents, spoilage, wastage, damage to machines or equipment due to unusual wear and tear, etc.
5. Such factors as appearance, friendliness, poise, and general social effectiveness where public relations are involved.
6. The cost of time of other personnel consumed. This would include not only the time of the supervisory personnel but also that of other workers.

DESIGN OF THE STUDY

Probably the most important problem facing the personnel psychologist interested in test validation is the development of a meaningful criterion of an employee's performance. Traditionally the approach has followed a line of least resistance, and global measures such as supervisors' ratings have been used to represent a complex behavior. The validity of a selection device is then described by the coefficient of forecasting efficiency, coefficient of determination, or some other similar index. These measures have obvious limitations when the personnel psychologist is pressed to show the value of a test to inquiring business executives. The interdisciplinary approach to criterion development advocated by Brogden and Taylor permits a closer investigation of the inner workings of criterion measures as well as the dollar value of a selection program. Cronbach and Gleser's utility model provides a means for observing the applicability of a dollar criterion. This study reports on the applicability of the utility function for a fixed-treatment selection problem, and the actual dollar payoff resulting from an employee's work is observed. The study was conducted in a large midwestern industrial plant which employs approximately 25,000 persons. The company is engaged in the manufacture of heavy equipment.

In designing the study it was necessary to insure a sufficiently large group of subjects, all of whom perform essentially the same kind of work. Data supplied by the Job Analysis Division of the company suggested use of the job classification, Radial Drill Operator. At the time the study was undertaken 291 persons were working in this classification. Experienced factory management personnel state that the duties of employees within this classification are much the same.

The company's job description for a radial drill operator

(RDO-1) is as follows: "Sets up and operates a radial drill, performing drill, ream, line ream, tap (stud, pipe and standard), countersink, chamfer, bore, counterbore, spotface, backface, and hollow mill operations. Involves various types of parts such as castings, forgings, bar stock, structural steel and welded fabrications. Grinds drills when necessary." There are three subclassifications of radial drill operation; only employees at the beginning level are included in this study. Specifically this job involves the following duties: "Performs less complex combinations of the work described in the general definition except boring where the operator sets the tools. Accuracy is largely dependent upon crib ground tools; jigs and fixtures are provided for the job. Tool sequences are limited. May perform common drilling machine operations involving liberal tolerances either from layout or with the use of improved jigs and fixtures." Men move into the RDO classification from unskilled or other semiskilled jobs, training being provided on the job by the employee's foreman. Advancement from this classification is usually to the two higher level radial drill classifications, RDO-2 and RDO-3 or to other jobs requiring comparable skill. Work assignments to the RDO-1's are made by the Planning Department according to machine number, and not to specific operators. Consequently, the RDO-1's have no control over the type of parts on which they perform machining operations. Typically, any single worker will work on a variety of parts, the mix differing from man to man.

It was assumed that the dollar profit which accrues to the company as a result of an individual's work provides the best estimate of his worth to the company. The following procedures were used to develop this dollar criterion.

Cost Accounting

To arrive at a reasonable estimate of the profit which accrues to the company as a result of an employee's work, the cost accounting methods developed by the company were used. Essentially, the method is one of "standard costing" which is an effective tool for volume production accounting. It also permits the application of the "principle of exception" whereby attention is directed chiefly to variations from standard cost that disclose trends in volume output. Standard cost for the company's products is determined by procuring cost data on three basic factors: material used to produce products; direct labor hours used to alter the size, shape, quality, or consistency of material; and facility usage required to perform direct labor. Standard cost must remain stable or fixed for a specific period in order to attain its objective. Usually all standards remain frozen for a period of five years, or until a general cost revision is officially authorized.

The company uses "Lifo" (last in—first out) inventory accounting, so that latest costs are used first to allocate costs in a manner closely related to price levels prevailing at the time of sale. The seven major cost elements in the accounting are: material—unformed steel; material—grey iron castings; material—forgings, stampings, etc.; material—purchased finished; direct labor; general burden; and machine burden.

Prime product costs are built up from costs of piece-parts or units into costs for assemblies, then costs for groups, arrangements, and finally for the general arrangement or complete model. The total cost figure has four basic components: variable, fixed, office, and parts warehousing. Variable or out-of-pocket cost includes only those costs that fluctuate with production output; it includes actual cost of material f.o.b. manufacturing plant, plus material-handling burden; direct labor cost plus an allocation to cover indirect labor, supplies, etc.; and facility usage, which generally reflects normal maintenance, power consumption, perishable tool usage, and facility supplies. These variable costs are most useful in determining costs where facility usage is not affected; however, fixed costs are used where facility usage is affected. Fixed costs are based on a given percentage of the production capacity of the plant. In determining them allocations are made to cover portions of material-handling burden, plant labor and burden (overtime premium, special indirect labor and management salaries, etc.), and plant facility usage (building and machinery depreciation, repairs and maintenance, tool design, etc.). Office and parts warehousing costs are figured as a percentage allocation.

The income from the RDO's work is readily determined, since the parts manufactured are sold to dealers, and a price for each part has been established. Subtracting the cost at standard production from the price provides a profit figure. This method appears to take into account most of the factors which Brogden and Taylor consider necessary in the development of a dollar criterion.

Determination of Individual Performance

The payoff for each individual depends on a productivity measure called the performance ratio. For each machining operation that is performed on a piece-part, the Time Study Division of the company has established a time standard. The length of time it takes a competent operator to complete the machining operation on a particular piece-part has been established by standard time study procedures, hence the number of piece-parts per hour that an operator should be able to process is known. His performance ratio for any period of work is then computed by dividing his *actual* production per hour by the standard hourly production for the piece-part on which he is then working. For example, if the standard production for a piece-part is ten pieces per hour and an operator produces seven pieces in a hour, his performance ratio for that one hour's work is .70. This index makes it possible to determine the operator's performance ratio over a month or more during which he has worked on a number of different piece-parts, each of which has a different production standard. Only rarely does an operator turn out more than standard production over an extended period of time. Operators have had varying lengths of time of company service, ranging from a few months to over ten years. The number of months of experience as RDO-1 is also quite variable. A rigid attempt to control the experience factor would seriously reduce the size of the group. Management personnel state that most individuals with no previous machine operator experience reach their typical level of RDO-1 performance within a few weeks. Ideally, performance data would be available on each operator from the time he started on the job; records containing performance data, however, are not retained beyond 30 days. In this study, performance ratios for each operator were obtained monthly for a six-month period, the mean being taken as the operator's typical performance.

Burden Adjustment for Below Standard Performance

If an operator produces at less than standard, the actual burden per hour for this inefficiency is greater than the standard burden per hour determined for his operation. An operator producing at 80% of standard actually takes one and one-quarter hours to produce an hour's work. In order to take into account this additional burden each below standard performance ratio was "corrected." It was assumed that the amount of burden in excess of the standard burden reduced in a proportional amount an operator's contribution. The formula used for such corrections was

$2 - 1/PR$. Thus, where a person is working at 80% of standard, the burden is 1.25 hours instead of 1.00 hours, and the "corrected" performance ratio is .75.

Determination of Payoff (e)

The procedures for determining each operator's payoff are as follows:

1. Computation of each operator's typical performance ratio. This figure was his mean performance ratio for the six-month period of the study.
2. Adjustment of the typical performance ratio for below standard production.
3. Computation of the average profit at standard production, attributable to the radial drill operation: (a) Tabulation of the standard production rate for each type of piece-part machined by radial drill operators. These data were provided by the Time Study Division. (b) Profit for each type of piece-part attributable to the radial drill operation. These data were provided by the Cost Analysis Division. (c) Profit per hour for each piece-part attributable to the radial drill operation at standard production. These figures were determined by multiplying the profit per piece by the standard production rate for the piece. (d) Average hourly profit attributable to the radial drill operation at standard production. This was determined by weighting the profit per hour for each piece-part (step 3c) by the number of such parts in the work flow.
4. Determination of e, the profit for each radial drill operator at his "corrected" performance ratio and the standard hourly profit.
5. Computation of σ_e. This is merely the standard deviation of the e-values computed in step 4.

Determination of r_{ye}

Values of r_{ye} were determined by computing the Pearson product-moment correlations between e-values and scores on the following predictors: The Personnel Test (Wonderlic, Form F), the Test of Mechanical Comprehension (Bennett, Form AA), the Cornell Word Form, and the Cornell Selectee Index. These tests constitute the basic battery used in the selection of factory personnel by the company.

Determination of ξ (y')

In order to maximize the gain in utility that results from using tests in selecting personnel it is necessary to establish a cutting point at and above which selection is made. Over the ten years preceding the study the company's average selection ratio for factory personnel had been .33. In applying the utility function, the y' value was set at the point corresponding to this selection ratio. In other words, it was assumed that RDO-1's are taken at random from the highest third of the test-score distribution of applicants. Assuming a normal distribution, $\xi(y')$ is therefore .366.

Cost of Testing

In the summary or the cost accounting procedures, it was indicated that the burden factors include some elements that can be attributed to the cost of testing an applicant. Management personnel salaries, rental of office space, heat, light, and taxes, for example, are all included in the burden factor. Because of this, only the actual cost of the tests used in the employment battery was considered in the determination of C_y. The cost of each test was taken from the most recent publisher's catalogue. Since the element σ_e is expressed in dollars per hour it was necessary to express the cost of testing in comparable units. Cost of testing must be distributed over the period of time that an employee can be expected to work as a radial drill operator. For present purposes it was assumed that an employee will work in this classification for one year, or 2,080 hours. In determining C_y, the cost of those not selected must also be included in the cost of those selected. The cost of testing per employee selected, in dollars per hour, is arrived at by multiplying the cost of one battery of tests by three (three persons are tested for each one hired), and dividing by 2,080 (hours per year). This cost is probably a high estimate for Employment Division data indicate that most employees assigned to the RDO-1 classification remain there for more than one year.

Computation of ΔU

For each significant predictor, ΔU was computed by substituting into the following equation,

$$\Delta U = \sigma_e r_{ye} \frac{\xi(y')}{\phi(y')} - \frac{C_y}{\phi(y')}.$$

RESULTS

Stability of Performance Ratio

To examine the stability of the level of job performance for the radial drill operators, monthly job performance data were used. The means and standard deviations are presented in Table R1.

TABLE R1. MONTHLY PERFORMANCE RATIOS

MONTH	MEAN	S.D.
First	79.92	17.84
Second	81.21	17.88
Third	79.70	16.71
Fourth	83.16	16.87
Fifth	79.23	20.25
Sixth	80.69	17.72

The stability of the group's performance over the six-month period was tested by an analysis of variance, and the resulting F-ratio was not found to be significant. It was concluded that the group's performance was stable over the period of the study, and the mean performance for each of the operators was used as his typical performance.

Payoff Values

Several steps were involved in the determination of e, the payoff for each operator. The 291 radial drill operators worked on approximately 2,500 different piece-parts. Because an enormous amount of clerical work would be involved in determining the profit attributable to the radial drill operation for every piece-part, a random sample of 275 parts (about 10% of the total) was drawn and the necessary computations were performed for these. Averaged over the sample of parts, the profit per hour attributable to the radial drill operation was $5.512; the standard deviation was $3.947. This so-called "profit" figure, while appropriate for purposes of this study, is not directly a part of company earnings. Out of this line in the balance sheet must come various costs of doing business, such as interest on loans and bonds, taxes, etc.

The e-value for each operator was the hourly profit at standard production attributable to RDO-1 multiplied by his "corrected" performance ratio. The standard deviation of this distribution (σ_e) was $0.585.

Validity and Cost of Testing

Among the test-payoff correlations, only that for the Test of Mechanical Comprehension was significant ($r = .313$). Only for this variable was the utility function examined.

For the Personnel Test, the Test of Mechanical Comprehension, and the two Cornell emotional health questionnaires, the most recent publishers' catalogue prices were $0.070, $0.032, $0.009, and $0.007 respectively, for a total of $0.117. Distributing this over the entire number of applicants tested and over the working hours in a year, the cost of testing per employee selected is $0.0002 per hour.

Computation of ΔU for the Significant Predictor

The gain in utility per man selected on the basis of the *Mechanical Comprehension Test* is:

$$\Delta U = (\$0.585) \ (.313) \ \frac{(.366)}{(.326)} - \frac{(\$0.0002)}{(.326)} = \$0.203$$

where ξ (y') was read from the normal table at the sixty-seventh percentile. Therefore, when the company selects a radial drill operator on the basis of the test score rather than by a random process, the company can expect an average gain of 20 cents *per hour* for the duration of his employment. This represents a potential gain in profit per hour of 3.7% at standard production.

DISCUSSION

The results of the study clearly demonstrate that a dollar criterion, such as suggested by Brogden and Taylor, can be developed and then applied in the Cronbach and Gleser utility function equation for a fixed-treatment employee selection procedure. There may well be errors, however, in the payoff figures obtained. The profit which accrues to the company as a result of a radial drill operator's work was determined almost entirely by the company's cost accounting procedures. Although the methods are relatively straightforward, many estimates and arbitrary allocations enter into the cost accounting.

The objectivity of performance ratio figures can also be questioned. Gaylord *et al.* (1951) have pointed out some of the difficulties encountered in obtaining objective job performance measures. Our study depended on the accuracy with which the individual operator reported his daily production and the accuracy of the timekeeper's computation of the performance ratio.

Determining cost of testing also required difficult judgments. The analysis took into account only the cost of the tests themselves. Factors classified by the cost accountants as overhead, such as management personnel salaries, cost of utilities, and rent, were included in the determination of e rather than C_y. The Employment Division of the company offered the figure of \$105.00 as a conservative estimate of the cost of placing a factory employee on the job. This figure includes the cost of recruiting, interviewing, physical examination, etc. It can be argued that a C_y that includes only the cost of tests is sufficient, as most other employment procedure costs would be constant values if tests were not used. These other costs need not be added to the determination of C_y. There are other factors recognized as important in the determination of C_y, such as the salary paid the Placement Testing Assistant who administers and scores the tests, the cost of utilities for the operation of the Placement Testing Office, and a portion of the supervising psychologist's salary. It would be impossible to extract these costs from σ_e and then add them to C_y. The chief reason for wishing to transfer these costs to C_y is that they are now treated as a charge against profits that would arise even if there were no selection testing. Cost analysts could offer no solution to this problem, and therefore these costs were left within the burden factor used in the determination of σ_e.

Although many questions have been raised by the results of the study, it is apparent that through the joint efforts of cost accountants and personnel psychologists, that it is possible to develop a criterion measure which embodies many of the elements suggested by Brogden and Taylor. Such elements as the cost of material used in producing the company's products, the cost of direct labor hours consumed in the manufacture of a product, and the cost of capital investment, jigs, fixtures, power, perishable tools, and floor space were all expressed by a dollar metric. It is apparent that the procedures used did not take into account all of the subcriterion elements that comprise the ultimate criterion. It was necessary to make estimates of specific costs, but this was a function of the company's cost accounting method. Cost accountants are not in universal agreement as to what factors should be included in performing a cost analysis. As other studies derive dollar criteria it will be possible to learn more about the effect of various cost accounting procedures on such a criterion.

The results also demonstrate that a test of relatively low validity has appreciable practical value, as Cronbach and Gleser argued on theoretical grounds. In this case, selection with the aid of a test having a validity of .313 appears to make possible an increase in earnings (before taxes and fixed charges) of 3 or 4% on the operation in question. Benefits of this magnitude are by no means unimportant to management.

In the present day when employment procedures are becoming more highly regulated by governmental legislation and labor union contracts, the importance of improving personnel selection and placement decisions is becoming more apparent. Personnel psychologists, in planning testing programs to be used in selection and placement of employees, must decide which tests to use, and how many. This requires balancing costs against estimated benefits. Thus the evaluation of a testing program will require a study of the benefits associated with any level of test validity.

SUMMARY

Psychological tests in industry offer an objective means of personnel selection. Personnel psychologists have had to rely heavily on statistical bases for describing the value of tests in achieving these aims. The statistician has used expectancy charts, correlation coefficients, and other indices for the presentation of test validity information. Recently Cronbach and Gleser have developed models which propose to evaluate tests in terms of utility, elaborating on the Brogden-Taylor proposal of a dollars-and-cents criterion. This study developed a dollar criterion using the cost accounting approach advocated by Brogden and Taylor, and applying it to ascertain utility in a fixed-treatment employee selection problem. The purpose of the study was more to examine the feasibility of such an analysis than to investigate a particular job and a particular selection test battery.

In a large midwestern industrial plant engaged in the manufacture of heavy equipment, the job classification, Radial Drill Operator, was chosen for study. Job performance data were gathered monthly over six months and used to compute a performance ratio for each operator. Profit accruing to the company as a result of a radial drill operator's work at standard production rate was estimated by the company's cost accounting procedures. A percentage of the total profit on a given piece-part was attributed to the machining operations performed by radial drill operators. As an operator had no control over the types of piece-parts he machined, and since some operators worked on high profit items and others on low profit items, an average hourly profit figure was used to cancel any "profit inequities." This profit figure was then multiplied by the performance ratio of each operator in order to arrive at his payoff value. For purposes of utility appraisal, only the cost of purchasing tests was treated as "cost of testing," other costs having been considered in determining payoff figures.

Among the four tests used in the pre-employment evaluation of factory applicants the Test of Mechanical Comprehension (Bennett, Form AA) showed apparent validity as a predictor. Using a selection ratio of .33 based on company experience the benefit from testing was computed to be $0.203 per hour per man selected.

COMMENTS BY LEE J. CRONBACH

I have had the opportunity to read Dr. Roche's complete thesis, and to discuss it with him. His reports on the employment situation in his company and on his efforts to extract the needed information from the accountants make it clear that the dollar payoff from an employee is an elusive concept, and that our theory is monstrously oversimplified. The facts that, for example, workers can voluntarily shift out of radial drill operation to another job if they have sufficient seniority, and are shifted downward by the company in times when business is poor (again on a seniority basis) are quite incompatible with the neat model in which $x\%$ of applicants are hired for and assigned to a certain job.

This study relies heavily on the discipline—or art—of accounting, and Roche, a psychologist, was necessarily dependent on the advice of the accountants. It is not entirely certain that the accountants perceived the problem clearly, and it may well be that in future studies a more thoroughly interdisciplinary attack will produce better solutions to the accounting problems. There are numerous costs evidently not charged off in figuring profit per hour of RDO work; one wonders if the cost of company indebtedness, for example, should not be allocated just as is capital outlay. The correction introduced into the production ratio is difficult to rationalize, the problem it attempts to cope with being a treacherous one. The hourly profit for a man at standard production on part 1 is a price A_1 less a fixed cost F_1 (burden, wages) and a variable cost V_1 (materials). If his production is slower (or faster) by a factor $P.R.$, the profit for an hour's work is $P.R. \times (A_1 - V_1) - F_1$. To estimate from production records such a profit for each piece-part a man works on would be prohibitively difficult, yet the fact that *A*, *V*, and *F* have different relative magnitudes on different parts makes any overall correction suspect. It seems likely that the applied psychologist who wants to make a thorough study of the benefits from personnel selection will have to train himself to the journeyman level in accounting so as to work out better compromises between the requirements of the problem and the traditions of accounting.

Where Roche bases his report on an assumed joint normal distribution of test and payoff, it would be preferable to use the actual joint distribution. If data are available for the *a priori* population, complete information on skewness and curvature is taken into account. Roche's payoffs have a marked skew, since few workers performed far above standard. If the available data come only from workers screened by a test or by on-the-job observations, extrapolation to the *a priori* population is required; even so, it might be better to compare the actual mean payoff in the selected population with that estimated for the unselected population. This estimate would depend on the regression line but would not entail an assumption of normality.

Despite the various puzzles left by Roche's study, it presses the study of payoffs forward in several ways. Perhaps most important, he shows that the dollar criterion can be determined even where men in a job classification are working on different tasks, where the tasks assigned a particular man vary from week to week, and where the tasks vary in profitability. His basic benefit-from-testing figure of more than 20 cents per hour is also of great interest.

TEACHING A DIGITAL COMPUTER TO ASSIST IN MAKING DECISIONS

By JOE H. WARD, JR., and KATHLEEN DAVIS*

In our complex, highly organized society, machines are relieving the human operators of more and more data-processing drudgery: tallying, analyzing, indexing, forecasting. Decision making remains an important function of management. Human beings determine an organization's objectives, establish policies that conform with those objectives, and then make operational decisions that seem in line with the policies.

There is a practical technique for combining machine and human capabilities in the decision-making process. This technique is not an abstract, theoretical model where relationships are often logical inferences, unverified experimentally. It is based on an experimental approach in which the computer learns by trial and error to make decisions that are satisfying to management.

The machine services are not limited to processing information. If the digital computer has the same information as the human decision maker, it can capture the essentials of human information processing in reaching decisions. Given this information and a sample of several decisions satisfying to management, the machine learns the policy and applies it in similar situations.

The basic technique is simple. The computer treats the sample of decisions as a dependent variable to be predicted; the information on which these decisions were based is used in the form of predictor variables. There is no problem of asking people how to combine the variables or what weights they should have. The regression equations developed to predict the dependent variable constitute a quantitative statement of policy that is often more accurate than most humans can give us.

The utility of this technique has been demonstrated in a number of different situations in which we have been interested in simulating human decision making. Among the policies that we have been able to describe mathematically in terms of regression equations have been those governing Air Force pay and grade (Madden,

---

* Reprinted from *Tech. Doc. Rep.*, Lackland Air Force Base, 1963.

1963), and judgments of cross-training time from one job to another (Ward, 1962a). The technique is readily adapted to a wide range of other applications involving human judgments (Christal, 1963).

ESTIMATING CROSS-TRAINING TIMES

Suppose management needs to know how long to allow for cross-training 500 people, who now occupy 500 existing jobs, to 500 new, possibly different, jobs. Given sufficient time, an expert who had the necessary information about both the jobs and the people might estimate the 250,000 cross-training times. This task is so large, however, that even several experts would find it hard to maintain a consistent policy over the period of time required to make all the estimates. Hence we turn to a computer and have the experts teach it how to use the job and personnel information. To learn the experts' policy, the computer needs the information they used and their actual estimates of the cross-training times for only a small sample of the jobs. Once the machine has learned to account for their decisions, it can estimate all the cross-training times rapidly and consistently according to the experts' policy. This procedure has been tested experimentally with a small sample of Air Force jobs.

ASSIGNING PERSONNEL TO JOBS

In another application, which has been demonstrated to Air Force managers, a computer is used to assist in assigning personnel to jobs so as to maximize the payoff of the assignments. When the elements of the payoff matrix are not known, management itself can supply the information needed to determine the values. In this case, the computer learns a system of evaluating assignments from a small sample of assignments which management has evaluated. The machine uses this system to predict management's evaluation of all the elements of the payoff matrix. It can then assign the personnel so as to maximize the sum of these payoff values. The procedure for developing the prediction system has been described by Greenberger and Ward (1956), the assignment procedure by Ward (1959). A sample of the computer's new assignments can be given to management for review. Any predicted values in the payoff matrix that are not satisfactory to management are then revised so as to provide the machine with additional information that will improve its learning of management's evaluation system. This process can be repeated and, if management's policy can be adequately simulated, the procedure will stabilize at a level where the machine's assignments are completely satisfactory to management.

To demonstrate this approach for personnel assignment we have used an IBM 650 Tape-Disk System, setting up the problem so that communication between the human and the computer is through an IBM 838 Inquiry Station. At the beginning of the machine's learning session, the human decision maker is provided with a random assignment of 22 people to 22 jobs. After studying the characteristics of the 22 people and the requirements of the 22 jobs, the decision maker evaluates each assignment, using a scale that runs from zero through ten. The computer takes these 22 decisions together with the person-job characteristics and develops a prediction system to obtain estimates for all 484 elements of the payoff matrix. A Decision Index procedure (Ward, 1959) is then used in an attempt to reassign the 22 men in a way that will maximize the sum of the corresponding payoff values. This procedure is quite fast and frequently yields a maximum sum—which could be obtained, of course, by an assignment algorithm. The computer proposes these 22 new assignments to the decision maker, and the evaluation procedure continues. The assignments soon stabilize, and the machine's assignments are usually satisfactory to the human decision maker. This assignment policy is now in a form appropriate for application to a larger set of data.

SIMULATING EFFECTS OF A POLICY CHANGE

In debating adoption of a new policy, management must make some estimate of the effects. If the computer-learning procedure is used to simulate the new policy, the effects can be more accurately assessed.

In the problem shown in Table W1, we consider two situations in which personnel assignments are made. In Case I, decision-policy A is repeatedly communicated to the computer until the machine's assignments stabilize at a satisfactory level. Then, *without erasing* the computer's memory for policy A, policy B is communicated to the computer until its assignments according to this new policy become stabilized. The performance of the computer in this situation can be compared now with Case II in which the computer has learned only decision-policy B and has no residual memory of policy A. The data in the table indicate the evaluation of actual machine assignments in these two situations. At the end, equivalent assignments representing policy B are made. In Case I, however,

TABLE W1. COMPUTER-DETERMINED JOB ASSIGNMENTS THAT MAXIMIZE PAYOFF

| | Case I | | | | | | | | | | Case II | | | | | |
| | Policy A | | | Policy B | | | | | | | Policy B | | | | | |
Trial	1	2	3	4	5	6	7	8	9	10	1	2	3	4	5	6
Person																
1	1	1	1	5	10	5	11	10	3	3	1	3	3	3	3	3
2	2	6	6	2	6	2	12	3	22	22	2	22	22	22	22	22
3	3	7	7	3	1	3	15	15	15	15	3	15	15	15	15	15
4	4	9	9	4	2	4	16	11	17	17	4	17	17	17	17	17
5	5	12	12	1	5	1	1	9	21	21	5	21	21	21	21	21
6	6	13	13	21	18	21	18	16	16	16	6	16	16	16	16	16
7	7	15	15	17	11	17	17	21	14	14	7	7	7	7	14	14
8	8	18	18	16	13	16	20	12	9	9	8	9	9	9	9	9
9	9	19	19	13	19	13	19	5	18	18	9	18	18	18	18	18
10	10	22	22	14	7	14	14	6	11	11	10	11	11	11	11	11
11	11	5	5	15	15	15	13	4	13	13	11	13	13	13	13	13
12	12	17	17	12	14	12	21	19	19	19	12	19	19	2	19	19
13	13	11	11	11	3	11	22	20	10	10	13	10	10	10	10	10
14	14	8	8	18	21	18	9	14	12	12	14	14	14	12	12	12
15	15	3	3	10	17	10	10	1	1	1	15	1	1	1	1	1
16	16	14	14	6	4	6	7	7	20	20	16	20	20	20	20	20
17	17	2	2	8	16	8	8	8	8	8	17	8	8	8	8	8
18	18	10	10	7	22	7	6	13	4	4	18	12	12	14	4	4
19	19	4	4	22	12	22	5	2	2	2	19	2	2	6	2	2
20	20	20	20	20	20	20	4	18	5	5	20	4	4	4	5	5
21	21	21	21	19	8	19	3	17	6	6	21	6	6	19	6	6
22	22	16	16	9	9	9	2	22	7	7	22	5	5	5	7	7
Payoff Sum	153	201	41	84	72	84	94	130	140	140	89	140	140	140	140	140
No. of Changes	..	19	0	20	19	19	17	19	16	0	..	20	0	5	7	0

the number of trials required to reach a satisfactory application of
policy B reflects the amount of reinforcement with policy A before
policy B was implemented.

As a rather trivial variant of this problem, we set the machine
the frustrating exercise of making decisions when it was alternately
instructed with opposing policies. Policy A was taught first in an
amount k, followed by an opposing policy B in the same amount,
and the alternation of the two policies continued for a period of
time. In the early stages, the computer tends to accept policy A
because the amount of instruction with policy A is greater than or
equal to that with policy B. In the later stages, however, as the
alternations continue, the ratio of the amount of policy A to policy B gets smaller and, as a result, the machine becomes increasingly
uncertain about the acceptance of policy A. The only time the ratio
is greater than 1 is at the completion of an application of policy A.
It might prove useful to specify an uncertainty threshold at which
point the machine would respond, "No decision possible."

CAPABILITY OF DECISION SIMULATION

1. If the computer can adequately simulate the decision maker, it
   can tirelessly make many routine decisions, perhaps more reli-
   ably than a human.
2. A mathematical representation of the policy provides indications of the accuracy of the prediction system so that the
   expected utility of the system can be evaluated prior to its use.
3. The representation of judgments by a general regression model
   permits study of both inter- and intra-individual policy differences.
4. Such a mathematical representation permits an investigation of
   those pieces of information that contribute to prediction of the
   judgments as well as the determination of those variables that
   contribute to both inter- and intra-individual differences in
   policy. The implication of this last feature is useful in helping
   to resolve problems of disagreement among conflicting points of
   view.

The machine cannot provide a satisfactory simulation of management's decisions unless (a) the sample of such decisions accords
with a consistent policy; and (b) the machine receives all the
pertinent information management uses to reach the decisions.

APPLICATION OF THE DECISION-THEORETICAL APPROACH TO THE SELECTION OF DRIVERS

By R. F. VAN NAERSSEN*
University of Amsterdam

INTRODUCTION

This is a translation of a large part of two chapters of a book *Selectie van chauffeurs* (Selection of drivers), published in Dutch (van Naerssen, 1963). In the last part of the book where these chapters appear the author explains how a few of the simplest decision-theoretic methods of Cronbach and Gleser, and some variants of these, can be applied to the selection of drivers in the Royal Army.

For the sake of brevity here, a number of paragraphs—and two whole chapters—have been omitted from this translation. These concern either summaries of results of Cronbach and Gleser or topics of secondary importance. The omitted Chapter 12 deals with selection from two populations (e.g., one group of candidates with, and another without, driving experience); Section 8 of Chapter 14, also omitted here, again treats of selection from two populations with examples from driver selection. The omitted Chapter 13 deals with the theory of two-stage selection. Also omitted, for example, are Section 3 and Section 4 of Chapter 11, in which a quick but rough method is shown for determining the optimum battery length. On the other hand, a number of paragraphs that repeat formulas of Cronbach and Gleser have been included in the translation, because otherwise confusion could be caused when these are referred to later.

The numbering of the book has been retained in the English translation, in order that the communication between readers of the book and those reading the translation will not be made more difficult. After this explanation the reader will not be amazed when he sees that this presentation starts at Chapter 11, Section 2.

* Translation prepared by Mrs. J. Wassing, working with the author.

11. UTILITY AND THE OPTIMUM NUMBER OF APPLICANTS

2. The Basic Formula

One assumes a cardinal utility, and a bivariate normal distribution between utility and score of the test or battery. Use this notation:

ϕ = the proportion of the persons tested who are accepted on the basis of the test (the selection ratio)

ξ = the ordinate of the normal curve corresponding to ϕ

M = the mean utility per person of an unselected group

M' = the mean utility per person of the group selected by means of the test

σ = the standard deviation of utility in an unselected group

r = the product-moment correlation between utility and test for an unselected group (validity)

Then, according to a well-known formula for the biserial correlation coefficient,

$$r = \frac{(M' - M)\,\phi}{\sigma\xi}. \tag{N2.1}$$

From this it follows (ignoring costs of testing) that through selection a gain in utility per accepted person of

$$M' - M = \frac{r\sigma\xi}{\phi} \tag{N2.2}$$

is obtained, on the average. This formula was deduced by Jarrett (1948).

Offset against the gain in utility is the test cost of, say, C utility units per tested man, or C/ϕ units per accepted man, so that the net utility per accepted man (called ΔU) becomes

$$\Delta U = \frac{r\sigma\xi - C}{\phi}. \tag{N2.3; CG1.10*}$$

For the net utility to be positive $r\sigma\xi$ must be greater than C, as Cronbach and Gleser indicate. If this is not the case, when validity is low, selection ratio is extreme, test cost is high, and/or the range of utility is small, then it is better to let candidates be chosen by chance than to test them.

6. Optimum Selection Ratio

Finding the optimum number of persons to be tested means cal-

---

* Code used for: Cronbach and Gleser (1957), Appendix 1, formula 10.

culating the selection ratio ϕ (in eq. N2.3) that gives the maximum utility ΔU. It is assumed, for the moment, that a fixed-test battery is available, with cost per man C and validity r against the utility criterion. It is assumed also that the group of persons tested forms an unbiased sample of the population (so that r does not change with ϕ). The optimum is found by differentiating U with respect to ϕ and putting this derivative at zero. Consider further that $d\xi/d\phi = y$, y being the deviation from the center of the normal curve that corresponds to ϕ and ξ, that is, the cutting score expressed in standard-score units. One then finds that

$$\xi^* - \phi^* y^* = C/r\sigma = K. \qquad \text{(N6.1; CG1.13)}$$

Here the asterisk denotes an optimum.

Using this formula of Cronbach and Gleser and with the assistance of the normal curve tables, the optimum selection ratio ϕ^* can be iteratively calculated from the relative cost $C/r\sigma$, which will be indicated by the letter K. One can also use Table N1, in which the relative cost K and the corresponding optimum ϕ are given for a number of values of y.

If ξ^* from equation N6.1 is substituted in formula 2.3, one finds the gain in utility corresponding to the optimum selection ratio:

$$\Delta U^* = r\sigma y^*. \qquad \text{(N6.2)}$$

We shall later examine further $y^* (= \Delta U^*/r\sigma)$. It is a multiple of the optimum utility that, by analogy to the "relative cost" $K (= C/r\sigma)$ we shall call relative utility.

Now if it is possible to alter test length and hence test validity, it is possible to calculate the optimum combination of test length

TABLE N1. RELATION BETWEEN RELATIVE COST K, OPTIMAL SELECTION RATIO ϕ^* AND RELATIVE UTILITY y

$K = C/r\sigma$	ϕ^*	$y = \Delta U/r\sigma$	$K = C/r\sigma$	ϕ^*	$y = \Delta U/r\sigma$
0.399	0.500	0.00			
.351	.460	.10	.069	.136	1.10
.307	.421	.20	.056	.115	1.20
.267	.382	.30	.046	.097	1.30
.230	.345	.40	.037	.081	1.40
.198	.309	.50	.029	.067	1.50
.169	.274	.60	.023	.055	1.60
.143	.242	.70	.018	.045	1.70
.120	.212	.80	.014	.036	1.80
.100	.184	.90	.011	.029	1.90
.083	.159	1.00	.008	.023	2.00

and selection ratio. One way to begin is to judge what is the maximum number of candidates likely to be available, and to convert this into a minimum selection ratio. Then one can calculate the test length that would be most profitable at this selection ratio. After determining the expected validity at this length, one then determines the optimum selection ratio for this validity. By iterative adjustments of ϕ and r in turn, one may locate the optimal pair of values as accurately as is required.

7. The Rectangular Model

In the work discussed to this point we have assumed a bivariate normal distribution of utility and test score. We propose now to examine the implications of treating one or the other distribution as rectangular. We shall assume a linear regression of the second variable on the one whose distribution is fixed, but shall not necessarily specify the joint distribution or the distribution of the second variable.

Actual test scores, we may note, are never distributed normally. Very often the distribution is platykurtic, somewhere between normal and rectangular. Some authors even aim at making the distribution completely rectangular (Ferguson, 1949), because the test then allows the greatest number of discriminations. Whereas the test distribution is to some degree under the control of the test developer, the distribution of payoffs is not. It often departs greatly from normality, as in the skew distribution for number of hours needed to complete driver training. Indeed, the payoff distribution may be unspecifiable if the utility is only given on an ordinal scale; in this event it is probably safest to assume a rectangular distribution.

By exploring a model with a rectangular distribution—"rectangular model" for short—one can gain an idea of the influence of the distribution shape on the results. This is not to dismiss the normal model as without value. One advantage of the rectangular model is that it leads to much simpler formulas than the normal model. This is of little importance in the present problem, but it does make a great deal of difference in the "sequential testing" dealt with in Chapter 13 (not translated). In addition it appears (as Cronbach and Gleser remark) that moderate changes in the parameters, test length, and selection ratio in the neighborhood of the optimum only cause small alterations in the utility. In other words, the unknowns of the decision problem need be estimated only roughly. Keeping this in mind, one will sometimes prefer the rectangular model when the distribution of test score and of utility is normal.

8. Optimum Selection Ratio with a Rectangular Model

One assumes a rectangular distribution of the test scores and a linear regression of utility upon test score. Let the mean utility of the unselected group be put at zero, and let the mean utility of the persons with the highest test score be b. Considering selection ratios of .50 and .00,

$$\bar{u} \, (\phi = .50) = 0 \qquad (\text{N8.1})$$
$$\bar{u} \, (\phi = 0) = b.$$

Then if $\bar{u}_\phi$ is the mean utility of the persons at that "critical score" that separates the accepted from the rejected,

$$\bar{u}_\phi = (1 - 2\phi) \, b. \qquad (\text{N8.2})$$

The mean utility U of the accepted group (ignoring cost) is now equal to the average utility of the persons with a critical score corresponding to the selection ratio $.5\phi$. The test cost is C/ϕ per accepted person, just as with the normal model. Thus we have the basic formula (cf. eq. N2.3):

$$U = (1 - \phi) \, b - \frac{C}{\phi}. \qquad (\text{N8.3})$$

In order to find the optimum selection ratio one once again puts the derivative of U to ϕ equal to zero. This gives

$$\phi^{*^2} = \frac{C}{b}. \qquad (\text{N8.4; cf.N6.1})$$

Substitution in equation N8.3 gives the utility corresponding to this optimum selection ratio:

$$\Delta U^* = b - 2\sqrt{bC}. \qquad (\text{N8.5; cf.N6.2})$$

Testing can pay only if ΔU is positive, which requires C less than $b/4$. That is to say, the cost of testing per man must be less than a quarter of the difference in payoff between average men and top-scoring men. As appears from equation N8.3, when ϕ is not optimum C/b must be even smaller than $\phi(1 - \phi)$.

The curve relating utility ΔU to selection ratio ϕ (eq. N8.3) is a hyperbola. When $\phi = 0$, ΔU has an indefinitely large negative value. ΔU is positive when

$$\tfrac{1}{2} - \left(\tfrac{1}{4} - \frac{C}{b}\right)^{\tfrac{1}{2}} < \phi < \tfrac{1}{2} + \left(\tfrac{1}{4} - \frac{C}{b}\right)^{\tfrac{1}{2}} \tag{N8.6}$$

and has a maximum $[= b - 2(bc)^{\tfrac{1}{2}}]$ when $\phi = (C/b)^{\tfrac{1}{2}}$. Finally, when $\phi = 1$, $\Delta U = -C$. With the normal model also the values of ϕ that make ΔU equal to zero are symmetrical about .50, as Brogden (1949b) showed.

In a platykurtic distribution of test scores, the population range of the scores cannot be determined accurately. When applying the above formulas it is therefore best to define b as the difference between the mean utility of the persons at the seventy-fifth percentile and those at the twenty-fifth percentile.

9. The Connection with the Coefficient of Long

In the preceding discussion no assumption has been made as to the distribution of utility. In general it will be platykurtic (more or less trapezoidal) if the distribution of the test scores is rectangular and the regression linear. It would be equally possible, however, to take a rectangular distribution of the utility variable as a starting point, for the moment without an assumption concerning the form of the regression line and the distribution of the test scores. Instead of using the formula for the biserial correlation coefficient as we did with the normal model, one can now begin with Loevinger's homogeneity coefficient H (1947), which, if the influence of ties is ignored, is equal to the coefficient of Long (1934). If the N tested individuals, of whom n are accepted, are arranged according to a rising criterion score, for every member of the rejected group one counts the number of persons of the accepted group with a lower criterion score. If one calls the sum of all these numbers—as Long does—"passes below fails," then

$$H = 1 - \frac{2 \text{ "passes below fails"}}{n(N - n)}. \tag{N9.1}$$

H is, as is already known, the same as Kendall's tau, except for the denominator.

If one assigns the individual with the lowest criterion score rank 1, etc., so that the highest is assigned rank N, and if ΣR equals the sum of the ranks R of the individuals in the accepted group, one can deduce from equation N9.1 that

$$H = \frac{2\Sigma R - n(N + 1)}{n(N - n)}. \tag{N9.2}$$

To change from an ordinal scale to an interval scale in which the individuals are placed at equal (utility) distances, the ranks can be replaced by "proportion scores" equal to $(R-\frac{1}{2})/N$. One once more defines M (cf. Section 2) as the mean utility of the unselected group and M' as that of the group selected by the test, and finally one introduces S to represent half the range of the utility variable.*

Then we have

$$\frac{\bar{R} - \frac{1}{2}}{N} = \frac{M' - M + S}{2S} \qquad (\text{N9.3})$$

in which $\bar{R}$ is the mean rank of the accepted group $(= \Sigma R/n)$.

Equation N9.3 can be solved for $\bar{R}$; this value $(\Sigma R/n)$ is substituted into equation N9.2. It is found that

$$H = \frac{M' - M}{S(1 - \phi)}. \qquad (\text{N9.4; cf. N2.1})$$

Here $M'-M$ is again the gain in utility per accepted man. Taking into account the cost of testing, one finds that the total gain in utility per man is

$$\Delta U = (1 - \phi)HS - \frac{C}{\phi}. \qquad (\text{N9.5; cf. N8.3, N2.3})$$

In the normal model the biserial correlation coefficient is independent of ϕ. This is not necessarily so with H, so that equation N9.5 is not of much use without further assumptions, unless one thinks it easier to calculate H from equation N9.1 than from equation N9.4. It is not unlikely that the coefficient H can be nearly independent of ϕ, with certain bivariate distributions (and possibly between certain limits of ϕ), but this is probably most easily checked by finding out whether gain in utility (excluding cost of testing) is proportional to $(1-\phi)$. If one assumes that this gain is proportional to $(1-\phi)$, then the utility is given by equation N9.5; in this equation, H—now of course independent of ϕ—is equal to the coefficient of Long when the distribution of the utility is rectangular.

Comparison of equations N8.3 and N9.5 shows that HS has taken the place of b. Thus, with the above mentioned assumption the formulas N8.4, N8.5, and N8.6 can also be used, substituting the product HS in every case for b.

---

* In concrete cases to be measured as the $Q25$-$Q75$ distance of the utility variable (cf. Section 8).

10. Rectangular Distributions and Linear Regression

With a rectangular distribution of both utility and test score the regression will generally be, not linear, but S-shaped. Distributions are conceivable where rectangular distribution of both variables goes hand in hand with linear regression (e.g., a rectangular distribution along the diagonal superposed on an even distribution over the whole field, making both regressions linear). These do not actually occur, however. But one can, of course, assume the combination of rectangular marginal distributions and linear regression with an eye to utilizing the formulas obtained from this assumption for *estimating* the reality, a not unusual procedure when using models.

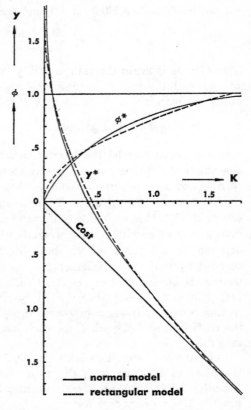

Figure N1. Optimal selection ratio ϕ^* and relative utility y^* as functions of relative cost K. Benefit, disregarding cost, is represented by the vertical distance from the cost line. Net gain, taking cost into account, is the distance above or below the K axis.

With this combination of assumptions, one can transform both variables to change the distribution field from rectangular to square. The slope of the regression line then becomes equal to the product-moment correlation between utility and test score, but at the same time equal to b/S. Since, in a rectangular distribution, the standard deviation is $1/\sqrt{12}$ times the range,

$$b = rS = r\sigma\sqrt{3}. \qquad (\text{N10.1})$$

In this model, b in the formulas N8.3 through N8.6 can be replaced by $r\sigma\sqrt{3}$, making them comparable to the corresponding formulas N2.3, N6.1 and N6.2 of the normal model.

Figure N1 plots the optimum selection ratio ϕ^* and the optimum relative utility y^* as functions of the relative cost K, both for the normal model and the rectangular one. The curves are very similar.[*] Thus it can be concluded that within certain limits the relationship between the parameters is not very sensitive to the distribution of the variables. It can be expected, in general, that for platykurtic distributions the true optimum selection ratio and utility fall between those given by the formulas of the rectangular and of the normal model.

For rectangular marginal distributions and linear regression, finally, b is equal to HS, so that $H = r$ and consequently is independent of the selection ratio. Wherever the model of this section is used instead of the normal model, ξ is replaced by $\phi(1-\phi)\sqrt{3}$. This last function of ϕ allows a rough estimate of ξ. When $\phi = 0$ and when $\phi = 1$ both this function and ξ are equal to zero; the maximum of ξ and the function are both reached when $\phi = .5$. Other values are:

$\phi = .1, .9$	.2, .8	.3, .7	.4, .6	.5
function $= .89\xi$	$.99\xi$	1.05ξ	1.08ξ	1.09ξ

The function is equal to ξ when $\phi = .214$ or $.786$. For all ϕ between .12 and .88 the function departs by less than 9% from ξ.

14. APPLICATION OF THE UTILITY FORMULAS

1. General

In order to make decisions concerning choice and length of test,

---

[*] For comparison: the value of K at which the optimum utility drops to zero, when $\phi = \frac{1}{2}$, is $\frac{1}{4}\sqrt{3} = .433$ in the rectangular model as against .399 in the normal one.

selection procedure, etc. using decision-theoretic formulas, the utilities must first be estimated. In the Army, even in peacetime, it is extremely difficult to calculate accurately the cost of, for example, drivers' training or accident damage. It is easier to use the "operations research" methods in companies, which have detailed calculations available, than in an institution such as the Armed Forces. This is also possible with the latter, however, and in fact such affairs are already being examined in a more economic manner both in the Dutch Armed Forces and elsewhere.

Although no accurate calculations are possible at this moment, a rough estimate of a number of relevant costs can be made. The use of these approximations is always to be preferred to neglecting utilities completely. With the assistance of rough estimates, one can at least to a certain extent verify whether it is useful to test, under which conditions testing should be carried out, which criteria can be used, and what effect can be expected.

The calculations worked out in this chapter could also serve a more or less didactic purpose. The way in which a problem can be tackled decision-theoretically will be clearer from these examples than if only theoretical chapters are available. For this reason a number of arithmetical examples will be included that are not based on fact. In general we have tried to keep as near to reality as possible, for example, by using correlation coefficients found in the empirical part of *Selectie van chauffeurs*.

2. The Cost of Testing

An important item both in the cost of testing and in cost of instruction is the time of the soldier himself. Earlier estimates arrived at a sum of 6,000 guilders per serviceman per annum.* The cost of meals, clothing, housing, pay, medical care, supervision, etc. are included. The costs per man during basic training and while in the troops come under the heading of "State of preparedness of the Army," but costs during driving lessons should be charged to the driving training, and during testing they naturally should be charged to the testing procedure. Roughly estimated, the cost is fl. 24 per working day or fl. 3 per working hour, per man.

In the case of group tests, the cost of scoring the tests must be included. If one calculates that the scorer (e.g., a corporal at fl. 4 per hour) can score four tests in the time that the soldier fills one in,

---

* The guilder (abbreviated *fl.* for *florin*) is worth about 25 U.S. cents. Its purchasing power is closer to 50 U.S. cents — Ed.

the cost of scoring is one guilder per man per test hour. At five guilders per hour, supervision for a group of 20 costs 25 cents per man per hour. Finally, if we figure various costs such as paper, integration of test data, etc. at 25 cents we reach a sum of four and one-half guilders per man per hour for group tests. This amount must be considered a minimum. What strikes one in these estimates is that it does not make much difference how large the group is, as long as the number is not less than 20. Groups of 20 are easily managed; very little is to be saved by having larger groups per supervisor, and any saving would be at the expense of the reliability of the test results.

For individual (apparatus) tests there is a basic cost of fl. 3 for the man himself and fl. 5 for the administrator (per hour). As well as these, depreciation and repair costs of the apparatus (which, even in the case of the most expensive equipment, are only a small fraction of the cost of the salary of the tester) and the cost of the scoring must also be included. One can therefore reckon upon a minimum of fl. 8.50 per man per hour, for individual tests. This minimum obtains in the case of an ideal (unattainable) organization where no time is lost, especially for the man himself. For every hour extra that one detains the man (that is to say, where the test procedure prevents lessons being taken) another fl. 3 will have to be charged. Waiting time is unavoidable, particularly in the case of individual tests.

Therefore, the attainable minimum cost of individual apparatus tests when organization is almost perfect can be fixed at a round figure of fl. 10 per man per hour, and the cost of group tests at about fl. 5 per man per hour. The minimum cost, for example, of the 15-item driving experience questionnaire, which takes about 12 minutes and which can be taken directly during or after a lesson, is thus fl. 1 per man, and that of the three-minute steering apparatus test, 50 cents per man. But when a further half hour of the soldier's time has been wasted, this last amount has increased to fl. 2 per man, that is to say, the cost of testing has quadrupled. The great importance of good organization in administering individual tests can be seen from this. Time wasted can be kept to a minimum when several individual tests are carried out in rotation within one session.

Overhead costs, such as those of test research, have not been taken into account. If, for example, fl. 30,000 is spent on development of three tests that remain in use for ten years, and 20,000 recruits are tested with these each year, the research cost averages only fl. .05 per test per man. But research costs can be burdensome for tests applied to only a small number of men.

3. Cost of Drivers' Instruction

These can be divided into the cost of general military training and the like (these are allocated as a cost of keeping the Army in a state of readiness), the cost of theory lessons, and that of driving lessons. The number of theory lessons is the same for all candidates. This number can be smaller when the class is intelligent or has had a great deal of driving experience, but there are no data on this. Because decision-theoretic calculations are concerned not with the total cost of training but with the standard deviation of this cost, the theory lessons can be ignored.

Rough estimates of the cost of driving lessons can be made. Earlier estimates of the cost of depreciation of the truck, petrol, oil, and repairs led to an amount of fl. 8 per hour of lesson. To this must be added fl. 5 for the instructor and fl. 3 for the soldier. For organizational reasons, three or four men per truck are usually sent out together; these men take turns in driving. Some time is also lost in driving to the exercise ground, etc. Hence the minimum total cost of driving lessons can be put at the round figure of fl. 20 per man per hour of lesson.

The variation of the number of driving lessons is not the same in different driving schools. The standard deviation at the Transport Troops Training Depot (TTD) is 12.9 hours. Figuring fl. 20 per hour, this gives for the standard deviation s of the utility a round figure of fl. 250 in the TTD.

Finally, considering the pass-fail criterion, the number of failures in driver training is small (6-7% in one sample from four bimonthly drafts). A great deal is invested in each man, however. With the TTD the failures were calculated to have had an average of 31 hours of driving lessons. Without taking into account "own time," this is an investment of fl. 528. If the cost of the man himself (at fl. 24 per work day) and that of the theory lessons is added, there is an investment of about fl. 800 per failure, at least in this army unit.

4. Accident Damage

Only a *very* rough estimate can be made of economic loss from accidents. The accident survey of the Transport Troops for 1961 shows that 228 accidents happened that year. Considering four categories—no damage, light damage (up to fl. 100), medium-heavy damage (from fl. 100 to fl. 1000), and heavy damage (more than fl. 1000)—the division of damage to military vehicles over the four categories was 67, 128, 27, and 6, respectively in 1961. Damage to second vehicles involved in the accidents was distributed over the four categories with the frequencies 66, 129, 24, and 9, respectively. If one puts the mean damage for the first group at zero, the second at fl. 50, the third at fl. 550 and the fourth at fl. 2000, one then reaches a rough estimate of fl. 70,000 for damage to vehicles.

Of the 228 accidents, in 193 cases (85%) there was no personal injury. One civilian died. This loss, which is difficult to estimate, will be left out of consideration. Further, there were recorded: 8 cases of concussions, 3 back injuries, 3 shoulder injuries, 4 bruises, 2 broken bones, and 16 grazes and cuts. The economic damage of these 36 injuries (hospital nursing, treatment, out of service) could easily be fl. 20,000. If one takes into consideration the unremunerative condition of the vehicles, the lost time of all concerned (also including military police, tribunal, etc.) one then reaches a total economic damage of around fl. 100,000 per annum for the Transport Troops. In 72% of these accidents the soldier was indicated to be at fault. If one uses this figure, then more than fl. 70,000 can be charged to accidents caused.

The human suffering will also be ignored in the next section. Any attempt to take into account the human suffering and death of accident victims would give very unreliable results. The number of victims in any other year may be none or ten; on the other hand, the amount of money to be reckoned per person is very high. One could start from the amounts spent annually on traffic safety. One could also bear in mind the amount for which civil servants are insured during an air journey (fl. 100,000). In fact, van Dantzig and Kriens (1960), in their decision-theoretic consideration of the Delta plan [regarding the appropriate height of dikes to surround reclaimed land]—where the possibility of evaluating human lives is scrutinized—point out that the amounts calculated in several ways vary a great deal. It appears in the case of the Delta plan. that such costs can be neglected. Even if one takes into account a sum of fl. 100,000 for each human life, then the optimum height of the dikes would be increased by only three centimeters, because one has already taken into account the enormous economic damage that would result if the dikes were breached. With driver selection the situation is completely different. It would make a very great difference in the total whether the "value of a human life for the government" is put at, say, fl. 50,000 or fl. 100,000. Thus it is completely useless here to take into account human lives or suffering. One can only work from the economic damage and endeavor to discover which selection battery is indicated by this. Afterwards, recognizing the added cost of suffering and lives lost, this battery can be considered as a minimum that on rational grounds must be used for the selection.

5. Using Häkkinen's Test Battery

We shall now examine the utility by an accident criterion and the best test battery to be found in literature, that of Häkkinen (1958). This battery of individual apparatus tests, which, at an estimate, needs an hour's test time, had a validity of .50-.60 against a criterion of accidents over a period of eight years (criterion reliability = .81).

The "exposure" of Häkkinen's bus drivers, who were continuously in busy traffic, was much greater than that of the TT-drivers, who work mainly outside city centers and are on the road fewer hours per month. Both with Häkkinen and with the TT even the smallest accidents were recorded; let us assume that the criteria for recording are the same. In a sample of 22 months 475 accidents were reported by the Transport Troops, 43.2 per two-month period; that is to say, one bimonthly draft of 170 men, in their whole period of service, caused a mean of 43.2 accidents. A group of 101 of Häkkinen's drivers, on the other hand, caused not less than 687 accidents in six years. Let us assume that the reliability of the accident variable is only dependent upon the number of accidents per driver, in order to be able to compare the groups with different exposures. The TT-man has an average of $\frac{43.2}{170} = .254$ accidents in his period of service; Häkkinen's drivers $\frac{687}{6 \times 101} = 1.134$ accidents per year. The entire period of service of the TT-man, as far as exposure to accidents is concerned, is the same as $\frac{.254}{1.134} = .224$ years driving a bus in Helsinki. Recognizing that this much shorter experience produces a much less reliable criterion, it can be calculated, using the Spearman-Brown formula as a starting point, that in the military situation the battery has an estimated validity of .20 rather than .55. This means that when using Häkkinen's battery in selecting for the TTD one must reckon with a validity of .20 against the accident criterion during the whole period of service.

Because it is seldom that more than one accident is registered for one driver, one cannot calculate the utility using the method of Brogden and Cronbach and Gleser, and so must use the Taylor-Russell tables (1939). The 170 drivers can be selected from a group of about 225 men, so that the selection ratio is 75%. The percentage of drivers who have no accidents is also 75%. With a validity of .20 this gives, according to the tables, a gain through selection of 3% (of the 170), thus roughly a gain of five fewer accidents.

Using Häkkinen's battery for selection, then, it can be expected that the number of accidents caused by one bimonthly draft during its period of service will decrease by five. Balanced against this is the cost of testing of fl. 2,250 per draft (fl. 10 per man). It is thus economically justifiable to use Häkkinen's battery for testing in the TTD if the mean cost per accident is more than 2,250/5 or fl. 450, that is to say, if in the TTD annual accident damage costs $450 \times \frac{475}{22} \times 12$ or more than fl. 100,000. This is a very rough estimate, but it does give *some* information. With a more favorable selection ratio of 50% one reaches the lower figure of fl. 400 per accident, but if the ratio is less than 50% this figure increases again. Not much is gained in this case by having a more favorable selection ratio.

As the annual economic loss from accidents in the Transport Troops was estimated in Section 4 at fl. 70,000 to 100,000 per annum, it is unlikely that using Häkkinen's battery in the TTD would have much economic effect through reduction in the number of accidents. More favorable results are obtainable by homogeneous shortening of the battery. If, for example, it were to last 12 minutes, the validity would only decrease from .20 to .15. It can be calculated that the accidents have only to cost a rough average of fl. 120 to make the test worthwhile (so long as annual damage is at least fl. 30,000). But it may not be possible to shorten Häkkinen's battery homogeneously. This calls for shortening each part proportionally; it is not enough to leave out some of the tests.

The validity against an accident criterion of the variables tested in *Selectie van chauffeurs* is unknown, but from the correlation with intermediate criteria it appears to be lower than the expected .15 of the shortened battery of Häkkinen. In Part II it was demonstrated that accidents in the Army form a criterion too unreliable for selection tests. From the calculations above it appears that even with the best-known test little economic effect can be expected through reducing the number of accidents. The most important factor—which, from the point of view of selection, is negative—is exposure. This is exceptionally low for drivers in the services, compared, for example, with that of bus drivers in the city. About 75% of the TT drivers leave the service without having a single recorded accident. This percentage is so high that selection is rather ineffective economically.

This does not mean that accidents do not carry much weight in determining the selection. Human life and suffering certainly ought to be an argument toward good selection, but decision-theoretic calculations of these factors cannot yet be carried out. The only thing that can be said is that the economic loss itself is too slight to justify the use of Häkkinen's extended selection procedure. In Section 7 a possibility of assimilating the damage in a subjective criterion will be considered. The cost of the driver training is a different matter; selection can reduce this in an acceptable way.

6. Reduction of the Cost of Training

Selection using the driving experience questionnaire reduces (in the TTD) both the number of failures and the necessary number of driving lessons.

If one starts with 7% failures (as in the TTD), a validity against the pass-fail criterion of .67 and a selection ratio of 75%, it is then found, using the Taylor-Russell tables, that the fail percentage can be reduced from 7 to 2.5 (profit 4.5%). (Because the tables are not very fine, graphic interpolation was used.) If one calculates, as in the previous sections, with a group of 170 drivers turned out per draft (183 accepted persons), the gain in utility per draft is .045 × 183 × 800, or more than fl. 6,500. On the other hand the cost of testing is less than fl. 250 $\left(\dfrac{183}{.75} \right)$.

The utility reached by decreasing the number of driving lessons can be calculated with equation N2.3 of Chapter 11 (normal model) and with equation N8.3 of Chapter 11 (rectangular model). In this case: $C = 1$; $\sigma = 250$ (see Section 3), $\phi = .75$ (from which $\xi = .318$), $r = .66$ (data given in Part II, not translated), and $b = 286$ (at least when calculated as $r\sigma\sqrt{3}$). With these figures, the normal model gives a utility of 68.2 and the rectangular a utility of fl. 70.2 per driver trained. For a bimonthly draft (170 men) we can expect a gain of more than fl. 11,500 or, if the number of failures is taken into account, more than fl. 18,000. This amount is "only theoretical," in that it would be difficult to locate in the defense budget. It is mainly the value of "being earlier in a state of readiness," as expressed in money.

Although the gain in other Army units will be smaller (because the supply of persons with driving experience is smaller), even so it is clear that the driving experience questionnaire pays amply for itself. What is the situation as regards the other tests and their effect on the cost of training? The paper-and-pencil test that correlates most highly with speed of training—excepting the driving experience questionnaire—is the motor-technical test ($r = .211$). Adding this test, the validity of the battery is increased from .662 to .669, which means a gain of less than fl. .60 per man tested ($.007 \times 250 \times .318$). Adding in the estimated profit from reducing failures, this might become fl. .90, whereas the cost of testing is estimated to be fl. 1.25. Hence, in the TTD, adding another paper-and-pencil test gives no increase in utility. This could very well be the case in other Army units, though no figures on this are available. In the group of TTD drivers without civilian driving experience a standard deviation of 8.5 hours of training was found, hence σ in utility units is fl. 170. If one accepts this value, it appears that a test battery with $C = 5$ (this is an hour written or a half-hour individual test) in a population without any driving experience, with a selection ratio of 75%, only needs a correlation of $\dfrac{5}{170 \times .318} = .093$ with speed of training to be economically justifiable. But, on the other hand, where many professional drivers are included (as with the recruits of the TTD) tests additional to the driving experience questionnaire are not necessary.

7. Evaluation in the Troop

Nothing is known about the utilities connected with the evaluation (rating) in the troop. This important criterion cannot yet be used. But we can outline a route for using this criterion in the future.

One driver is preferred to another not only because he causes fewer accidents (which is difficult to predict in the Army where one is less exposed to dangerous traffic situations) and because it takes less time to train him, but mainly because he also "drives better," which is more pleasant for passengers or other users of the road, causes less wear to vehicles, uses less gasoline, etc. These gains cannot be calculated, but they can be evaluated subjectively.

During the TTD research the drivers already with the troop were divided by supervisors into five categories, according to certain criteria. This rating includes a number of factors that can be grouped under the heading "good driving." The questions were specially developed in the U.S. Army in order to obtain a high correlation with accidents. The accident factor—which is itself very difficult to predict in an economic way—is thus also part of this criterion. Now one can ask the employer—here, the government—what it is worth to him to replace a driver chosen at random from, for example, category C by one from category B; or, if this evaluation is too difficult, what he would give (either expressed in money, or, for example, in the number of N.C.O.'s provided for testing) to have the mean standard of drivers raised one category. When this (more or less "political") evaluation has been carried out, the selection technician can then put together the battery that gives the optimum increase.

Example: Let it be decided that it is worth fl. 100 to replace a driver by one rated a full category higher. For convenience, let the distribution over the five categories be rectangular, in such a way that the total range of the criterion is fl. 500 ($S = 250$). Further, let there be a choice from four paper-and-pencil batteries, so that one can test for a quarter of an hour ($C = 1.25$) with a validity of .20, half an hour with $r = .25$, three-quarters of an hour with $r = .27$ or an hour with $r = .28$. These are reasonable inferences from the real test validities and intercorrelations. If one assumes that $b = Sr$, the utility per trained driver can be fixed using equation N8.3 of Chapter 11. When $\phi = .75$ one finds utilities of 10.8, 12.3, 11.9, and 10.8 for the respective tests. Consequently, one chooses the 30-minute battery, for which the net gain per driver is fl. 12.30. The mean rating of the drivers increases in this way by $(1 - \phi)b$ or more than 16% of the difference between categories.

The more the difference between categories is valued, the more tests come into the battery. If this difference is put, for example, at fl. 1,000 (only a fraction of the total cost of a serviceman), then a 15-minute test need only increase the multiple correlation with the judgmental criterion by .0027 in order to be accepted.

For convenience the utilities in the above mentioned examples were expressed in units of money. This is by no means essential. The main point of the calculations is not the money value of the cost of testing or of the man's utility, but simply the proportion C/σ. This ratio can be evaluated without even thinking about money. The assessor—the employer—can be allowed to choose between situations in which C and σ are implicitly represented.

INTERPRETATION OF RELIABILITY AND VALIDITY COEFFICIENTS: REMARKS ON A PAPER BY LORD

By LEE J. CRONBACH and GOLDINE C. GLESER*

It was formerly held that only test scores with high reliability and validity were practically useful. Taylor and Russell (1939) were the first of many writers to modify this viewpoint by pointing out conditions under which a test can make a substantial contribution even though its validity or reliability is low.

Lord (1958) has recently contributed a valuable paper on the usefulness of unreliable difference scores. Two comments are to be made about this paper: (a) Lord's method of analysis is general and applies to *all* reliability and validity coefficients; his paper therefore has implications far beyond the interpretation of difference scores, (b) modifying Lord's evaluation procedure in one particular leads to an important change in the conclusions. For many decision makers Lord's formulation is less suitable than the alternative analysis, and his interpretation regarding the value of tests is *insufficiently conservative.*

Most statements describing the usefulness of tests as judged from their reliability or validity coefficients assume that a decision is made about every person tested. The Cooperative Test Division of ETS (1955), in making recommendations to interpreters of certain aptitude and achievement batteries, adopts the contrary position that decisions might better be made only about persons for whom the test provides dependable information. Bloom (1942) noted that even an unreliable test permits one to divide a group into a few broad categories with considerable confidence. In applying this concept to differences between subtests of the SCAT and STEP batteries, the CTD suggests that, where there is a large difference, a test permits an accurate inference that one true score is higher than another, even though the difference score has quite modest reliability. For persons with small observed differences, on the other hand, the CTD suggests that the best course of action is to make no differential interpretation. Specifically, the following rule is

* Reprinted from *J. educ. Psychol.*, 1959, 50, 230-237.

proposed: if a difference score is larger in absolute value than k, interpret it as a true difference; if it is less than k, act as if there is no difference, at least until further information about the person is taken into account. Considering the V and Q scores for SCAT, for example, this strategy calls for assigning the person to one of three groups: $V > Q$, $V < Q$, and no difference established.

STRATEGY WITH FIXED α RISK

The value of k may be determined in many ways. The CTD proposal makes k proportional to the standard error of measurement of the difference score; specifically, k is set equal to $\sqrt{2}$ S.E.$_d$. A paper by Mendenhall (1959) adopts a similar approach, setting k equal to 1.96 S.E.$_d$. We shall refer to a strategy which makes the cutting score a multiple of S.E. as a "fixed α" strategy, for reasons which will be made clear shortly.

The most obvious virtue of the CTD rule is the convenience with which it may be applied. It is recommended for such batteries as SCAT and STEP that each score be plotted on the profile sheet not as a point, but as a band extending 1 S.E. above and below the observed score. A difference larger than $\sqrt{2}$ S.E.$_d$ will be present only when the bands plotted do not overlap. The counselor is instructed to interpret only differences where the pupil's V-score and Q-score bands show no overlap (i.e., if V is plotted as a band 40—50 and Q as a band 48—58, no interpretation is made).

Lord's paper is devoted to an evaluation of this strategy. He takes into account two consequences of the rule, as applied to a difference score with a specified reliability: the proportion of persons about whom differential interpretations are made (p), and the average risk (q_c) of making a differential interpretation when the true difference is in the opposite direction. For example, when $r_{dd} = .42$, and difference scores are converted to a scale with unit standard deviation, S.E.$_d = .76$ and $k = 1.07$. Then 28% of the subjects have differences greater than 1.07, and *in 90% of those cases* the observed difference is in the same direction as the true difference. Hence, the average risk of an incorrect differential interpretation is 10% when the CTD rule is applied to this test.

This argument (like Bloom's) sets aside the conclusion of Bennett and Doppelt (1948) that the minimum acceptable reliability for a difference score is about .75. Their position was based on Kelley's (1923b) calculation of "the proportion of differences in excess of chance." Since this proportion does not relate in any direct way to the goodness of decisions based on the difference score, as a basis for evaluating a test it is much inferior to Lord's which has a clear relation to the utility of decisions.

Lord concludes that the CTD rule is an acceptable one, as the average risk is low even when the score has a reliability as low as .40. Indeed, he points out that if $r_{dd} > .90$, the average risk is extremely low, so that the counselor ignores differences which could very safely be interpreted. He implies that a better strategy would be to adjust k so as to maintain a fixed average risk, no matter what the score reliability. This may be referred to as a "fixed q_c" strategy, and the difference between fixed α and fixed q_c strategies may be explained with reference to Figure C1.

In this sketch, x is any score which is to be interpreted, and y is the score with respect to which persons would ideally be classified (criterion score, true score, or true difference score). Persons are to be identified who may confidently be classified as having $y > y'$ or $y < y'$. In the problem of identifying non-zero differences, $y' = 0$. Persons for whom $x > k$ are classified as having $y > y'$. Under the fixed α strategy, k is placed on the x scale at a distance from zero determined by S.E.$_x$. The standard error is the standard deviation of any horizontal array. The line $x = k$ cuts off a certain proportion of persons in the array where $y = 0$, that is, where the null hypothesis is true. We may refer to this proportion as $\alpha/2$, recognizing that there are an equal number of cases where $y = 0$ and $x < -k$. Then α is the risk of incorrectly making a differential interpretation when the null hypothesis holds. Setting k equal to a fixed multiple of S.E.

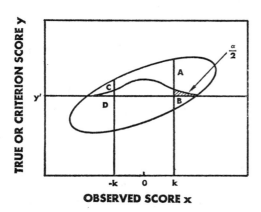

Figure C1. Sketch to illustrate α risk and average risk q_c

has the effect of holding α constant as r_{xy} varies. Specifically, when $k = \sqrt{2}$ S.E., α is fixed at .16.

The average risk q_c, which Lord uses to evaluate the fixed α strategy, takes into account all cases for whom a decision is reached, that is, all cases where $x > k$ or $x < -k$. Those in areas B and C of Figure C1 are erroneously interpreted. The proportion of decisions p reached is the sum of the volumes under the normal bivariate distribution, $p_A + p_B + p_C + p_D$. The proportion of correct decisions $p_c = (p_A + p_D)/p$ and the average risk $q_c = (p_B + p_C)/p$.

Lord suggests that the value of k might be adjusted, as r_{xy} changes, to keep q_c constant. This would require that k be a smaller multiple of S.E. as r increases. Though Lord appears to regard this fixed q_c strategy as superior to the fixed α strategy, he does not discuss it in detail, and we shall give it no further direct attention.

Our paper differs from Lord's in placing emphasis upon the maximum risk of erroneous interpretation, rather than upon the average risk. It is obvious that the risk of a wrong decision is greater for the person whose observed score is near the cutting point k than for the person with an extreme score. Looking at only the average risk, as Lord does, one may conclude that a procedure is conservative even when appreciable risks are taken in making decisions about persons near the borderline. The CTD rule proposes to interpret differences which, considered individually, are quite likely to be due to chance. Specifically, in the example considered above where $r_{dd} = .42$, Lord reports an average error rate of 10%, but we find that for persons with differences near k the expected error rate is 18%. Some users who would be quite prepared to accept one erroneous interpretation in ten would not consider an error rate close to one in five are adequately conservative.

Though average risk is sometimes an appropriate loss function to use in evaluating a strategy, maximum risk is more appropriate in other situations. Arbous and Sichel (1952) and Arbous (1952) have compared the two in discussing industrial selection. They point out that a test of low validity may profitably be used as the first stage in a sequential procedure for selecting employees, where unpromising applicants are ruled out and the remainder are given a further test. The benefit of this procedure to the institution (employer) may properly be judged in terms of the average quality of the men finally selected and the cost of testing per man hired. Such emphasis on average risk is not, however, appropriate from the individual's viewpoint. Arbous and Sichel protect the interests of the individual by fixing a cutting score x' on the pretest such that the *maximum* risk ϕ of a false decision (rejection of a man who would pass the second test) is .001 or some other suitable value. Scores near the cutting point x' can then be interpreted at a predetermined level of confidence, and more extreme scores can be interpreted with even greater confidence. This is preferable to a strategy yielding a specified average risk whenever individual rather than institutional decisions are being made, since the risk for any single individual is limited. An institutional decision is one of a series of decisions all of which contribute to the benefit of the same institution. An individual decision is one intended to serve the interests of an individual; it recurs rarely or never, and consequently the individual cannot average his risks over many decisions. Decisions reached in counseling and guidance are individual decisions.

Introducing the concept of maximum risk raises two questions: How great is the maximum risk under the fixed α strategy, and what light does this shed on the conclusions of Lord and Mendenhall? What procedure would guarantee that the maximum risk does not exceed a specified value, and how satisfactory is such a "maximum ϕ" strategy? We begin with the former question.

For convenience, we shall express x in units such that $\bar{x} = 0$, $s_x = 1$, and $r_{xy} \geqslant 0$. The scale for y will be given by the data if y is a criterion score, but if y is a true score $\bar{y} = \bar{x} = 0$ and $s_y = s_x \sqrt{r_{xx}} = \sqrt{r_{xx}}$. Figure C1 shows the scatter diagram relating x and y, however these may be defined.

Then within any vertical array (x fixed) y is normally distrib-

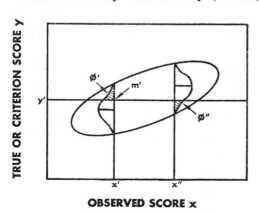

Figure C2. Sketch to illustrate maximum ϕ risk

uted with $\bar{y}_x = \bar{y} + r_{xy}s_yx$ and $s_{y.x} = s_y\sqrt{1 - r^2_{xy}}$. The line $y = y'$ cuts this distribution at a point whose location, expressed as a normal deviate within the distribution, is m. By the usual transformation,

$$m = \frac{y' - (\bar{y} + r_{xy}s_yx)}{s_y\sqrt{1 - r^2_{xy}}}. \tag{C1}$$

Now ϕ_x is the proportion of the cases falling above or below m. The strategy under consideration will employ two cutoffs, as shown in Figure C2: if $x \leqslant x'$, the person will be classified as having $y < y'$; if $x \geqslant x''$, as having $y > y'$. (Introducing x' and x'', which need not be symmetric about zero, formulates the problem more generally than does the use of $\pm k$ as cutting scores.) Since we are concerned with the risk of misclassification, the proportion above m is taken as the risk ϕ when $x \leqslant x'$, and the proportion below m is used when $x \geqslant x''$. Among those arrays where $x \leqslant x'$, the risk ϕ is greatest when $x = x'$; similarly, among the arrays where $x \geqslant x''$, the risk is greatest when $x = x''$. Call these maximum risks ϕ' and ϕ'', respectively; the associated values of m may be referred to as m' and m''.

For any specified y', x', and x'', the maximum risks may be determined by substituting in equation C1 to obtain m' and m'', and using the tabled normal distribution to find the area above m' (call this ϕ') and the area below m'' (ϕ''). In the CTD interpretation of difference scores, persons are to be classified as above or below $y' = 0$. The fixed α procedure sets $x' = -\sqrt{2(1 - r_{xx})}$. Noting that $r_{xx} = r^2_{xy}$ and $\bar{y} = 0$, and substituting in equation C1, we find that $m' = \sqrt{2r_{xx}}$. Likewise $m'' = -\sqrt{2r_{xx}}$. Over the range of values of r_{dd}, the CTD proposal fixing α at .16 and y' at 0 leads to the following consequences:

r_{dd}	PROPORTION OF PERSONS FOR WHOM DECISIONS ARE MADE (p)	AVERAGE RISK (q_c)	MAXIMUM RISK ($\phi' = \phi''$)
.95	.78	<.01	.08
.80	.53	.02	.10
.60	.37	.06	.14
.40	.27	.11	.19
.20	.21	.19	.26
.00	.16	.50	.50

(The first three columns are similar to Lord's.)

When $r_{dd} \to 1$, $m' \to \sqrt{2}$ and $m'' \to -\sqrt{2}$, so that under the CTD procedure, the maximum risk is never less than .078. The maximum risk is of course greater than the average risk (save where $r_{dd} = 0$), and becomes several times as large as q_c when r_{dd} is large.

The acceptable risk depends on the type of decision being made. In individual decisions (particularly counseling), it is generally desirable to be conservative, seeking additional information rather than accepting a hazardous conclusion. When a terminal decision is under consideration, it appears reasonable to set the maximum risk at .10 or .05. An even lower level might be desired for an important decision that could not be reversed should it prove to be wrong in the light of later experience. On the other hand, some counseling interpretations are easily and cheaply reversed as more information comes to light (e.g., performance in verbal and mathematical courses may reverse an impression of difference given by test scores). A risk of .20 seems none too high for a tentative decision where reversal costs little.

The problems considered to this point are also pertinent to Mendenhall's (1959) paper. His discussion is in many ways like that of Lord, representing an attempt by a test-publishing organization to state how useful is differential information from one of its tests. Following conventional statistical logic, Mendenhall calls an observed difference "significant at the .05 level" if it exceeds 1.96 S.E.$_d$. He then judges the utility of the test by calculating the proportion of cases expected to have "significant" differences. When $r_{dd} = .81$, for example, he finds that 39% of the persons have significant difference scores. He thus implies that a cutoff at ± 1.96 S.E. would permit decisions to be made about 39% of the cases, with 5% risk of misclassification.

This is a fixed α strategy, differing from the CTD proposal in that 1.96 replaces 1.41 as a multiplier, so that α is .05 instead of .16. Mendenhall calculates, as does Lord, the proportion p of cases for whom a decision is reached. He fails, however, to consider that the α risk is not an indication of the dependability of the decisions made, a matter with which the decision maker is normally concerned. The table above shows that both the average risk p_c and the maximum risk ϕ may exceed α. Moreover, we find that when $r_{dd} = .81$, we can make decisions about only 26% of the cases with a guaranteed ϕ risk no greater than .05 (cf. Mendenhall's 39% above). The risk of interpreting a null difference (α) is not the same as the risk ϕ of misinterpreting (reversing) a difference. The α risk answers the question: given a person for whom the true difference is zero, how likely are we to interpret an observed difference for him? The ϕ risk answers the question: given a person with a borderline observed difference, how likely are we to be incorrect in interpreting that difference? Mendenhall's analysis, though technically accurate, by implication gives an unduly favorable impression of the value of the difference scores in question.

STRATEGY WITH FIXED MAXIMUM ϕ RISK

We turn now to the consideration of a strategy designed to fix the maximum risk ϕ' and ϕ'' at some stated level ϕ_m. It is desired to use x scores to identify individuals who are above and below some level y', with a maximum risk ϕ_m of an incorrect identification. Two cutting scores on the x scale are determined: a lower score x' such that when $x = x'$, $P(y > y') = \phi_m$, and an upper score x'' such that when $x = x''$, $P(y < y') = \phi_m$ (see Figure C2). From the given ϕ_m, m is determined from the normal table. For the lower cutting score x', ϕ_m is the proportion of cases in the upper tail, hence, the sign of m is positive. For the upper cutting score x'', ϕ_m is the proportion of cases in the lower tail, hence the sign of m is negative. Solving equation C1 for x gives

$$x = \frac{y' - \bar{y} - m s_y \sqrt{1 - r^2_{xy}}}{s_y r_{xy}}.$$ (C2)

TABLE C1. UTILITY OF TEST FOR CLASSIFYING PERSONS AS ABOVE AND BELOW AVERAGE WITH MAXIMUM RISK $\phi = .10$

VALID-ITY	RELIA-BILITY	x''	PERCENTAGE OF PERSONS FOR WHOM DECISION IS REACHED		PRO-PORTION CORRECT	AVERAGE RISK	α RISK
			ANY DECI-SION	COR-RECT DECI-SION			
			p	$p_A + p_C$	p_c	q_c	
1.00	1.00	.00	100.0	100.0	1.000	.000	1.00
.95	.90	.42	67.4	66.4	.985	.015	.18
.90	.81	.62	53.5	52.2	.976	.024	.15
.80	.64	.96	33.7	32.4	.961	.039	.11
.70	.49	1.30	19.4	18.4	.948	.052	.07
.60	.36	1.70	8.9	8.4	.936	.064	.03
.50	.25	2.22	2.6	2.5	.932	.068	.01
.30	.09	4.07	....	....	....		

Tables C1 and C2 indicate the consequences of applying such a maximum ϕ strategy at various levels of reliability or validity.

In Table C1, persons are to be judged as above or below average. Though this table covers the problem Lord considered, of detecting positive and negative differences within a profile, it also applies to interpreting any other decision about standing relative to the group mean. For high reliability (or validity) the results under this strategy are very similar to the results reported by Lord for the fixed α strategy, with regard to both number of decisions made and average risk. For low reliabilities, however, we find that the number of decisions that can be made with confidence is much lower than Lord's report suggests. Even when $r_{dd} = 0$, the CTD strategy allows decisions regarding 16% of the subjects, but our strategy allows none. The maximum ϕ strategy, on the other hand, runs a greater risk of overlooking a true difference than does the fixed α strategy.

It is of interest that average risk q_c remains much more constant over the possible range of reliabilities than it does under the fixed α strategy. The maximum ϕ strategy to some degree overcomes the difficulty which led Lord to suggest a fixed q_c strategy in place of the fixed α procedure. Fixed q_c and maximum ϕ strategies are by no means identical, however. While an average risk q_c of .01-.07 corresponds to a maximum risk ϕ of .10, further calculations indicate that q_c must be set near .002 to guarantee that ϕ is no larger than .05.

Table C2 deals with the situation where it is desired to discriminate persons with $y > + 1s_y$ from those below that point. The upper cutoff is used in identifying persons with a marked superiority. The lower cutoff is used to identify persons for whom y is thought to be less than y'. (The same values, with a change in sign of x' and x'', apply when the test is used to identify persons with a marked weakness.)

Our tables provide a corrective to the optimism of Lord's table. According to Table C1, a score with validity .80 or reliability .64 permits classifying one-third of the subjects as above or below average on the criterion (or true score) with a maximum risk of .10. Likewise, a difference score of reliability .64 permits us to report one-third of the subjects as having definite positive or negative differences with, at most, 1 chance in 10 of being incorrect. If we set the tolerable risk ϕ_m at 1 in 20, reliability must be about .85 to permit an equal number of decisions. According to Table C2, the test of low reliability or validity permits a somewhat greater num-

TABLE C2. UTILITY OF TEST FOR CLASSIFYING PERSONS AS HAVING $|y| > s_y$ WITH MAXIMUM RISK .10

Validity, Index of Reliability, r	Identification of Superior Cases				Identification of Non-Superior Cases				Total Decisions		
	Upper Cutoff	Decisions Reached		Proportion Correct	Lower Cutoff	Decisions Reached		Proportion Correct	Number Reached	Number Correct	Proportion Correct
	x''	Any Decision p_A+p_B	Correct Decision p_A	p_{q_1}	x'	Any Decision p_C+p_D	Correct Decision p_D	p_{q_2}	p	p_A+p_D	p_c
1.00	1.00	15.9	15.9	1.00	1.00	84.1	84.1	1.00	100.0	100.0	1.00
.95	1.47	7.1	6.9	.972	.63	73.6	73.0	.992	80.7	79.9	.990
.90	1.73	4.2	4.0	.952	.49	68.8	67.9	.987	73.0	71.9	.985
.80	2.21	1.4	1.3	.928	.29	61.4	60.0	.977	62.8	61.3	.976
.70	2.73	.3	.25	.833	.13	55.2	53.3	.965	55.5	53.6	.965
.60	3.37			...	−.03	48.8	46.8	.959	48.8	46.8	.959
.50					−.22	41.3	39.1	.947	41.3	39.1	.947
.40					−.43	33.4	31.4	.940	33.4	31.4	.940
.30					−.73	23.3	21.5	.923	23.3	21.5	.923
.20					−1.25	10.6	9.6	.906	10.6	9.6	.906
.10					−2.74	.3			.3		

ber of decisions as y' moves away from the mean, but this gain is mostly in singling out non-deviates, that is, persons for whom y is *not* more extreme than y'. A test with reliability .64 identifies, at the desired level of confidence, *less than one-tenth* of the superior persons for whom $y > + 1s_y$.

It somewhat oversimplifies the problem to treat all errors of classification as equally serious. In a specific situation, the most satisfactory analysis of the usefulness of a test and decision-making strategy would usually be obtained by specifying for each y the exact benefit or loss from each possible decision. A much simpler formulation, however, will often be appropriate. Suppose that in evaluating certain difference scores for counseling purposes, it is recognized that large differences are much more important to detect than small ones. The level y' may be specified so as to distinguish between *true* differences regarded as important and those regarded as trivial. Using equation C2, cutting scores may be determined so as to permit the judgment $y > y'$ or $y < -y'$ with an acceptable risk of error. Two symmetric cutting scores are determined: a lower score x' such that for $x \leqslant x'$, $P(y > -y') \leqslant \phi_m$, and an upper score, x'', such that for $x \geqslant x''$, $P(y < y') \leqslant \phi_m$. Interpretations or decisions are made for persons for whom $x \leqslant x'$ and $x \geqslant x''$. If $x' < x < x''$, no decision is made. The operation of this strategy may be illustrated by reference to Table C2, if we suppose that true differences less than s_y in absolute value are considered negligible. Then the number of persons confidently ($\phi_m \leqslant .10$) identified as having a large difference in one direction or the other is obtained by *doubling* the entries in the $p_A + p_B$ column, and the average accuracy is given by p_{c1} (without doubling). Obviously, a test will identify very few persons as having differences greater than s_y if its reliability is below .80 (index of reliability below .90).

DISCUSSION

We have identified three risks which may be taken into account in fixing strategies for test interpretation and for evaluating the usefulness of a test interpreted by a particular strategy. It is assumed that the persons are to be divided into three classes: those whose true scores (or true differences between scores) are believed to be greater than a specified criterion score y'; those believed to have true scores less than y'; and persons for whom neither interpretation may safely be made.

The risk α is the risk of interpreting a score as indicating $y > y'$ or $y < y'$ when y actually equals y'. The risk q_c is the average risk, over all decisions made, of concluding that $y > y'$ when y actually is less than y', and vice versa. The risk ϕ' or ϕ'' is this same risk of misinterpretation for persons at the score where the risk of misinterpretation is greatest. The CTD and Mendenhall suggest a strategy which fixes the α risk at a predetermined value. Fixing the α risk is a logically defensible method of establishing a strategy. It is not appropriate, however, to describe the utility of decisions actually made in terms of the α risk, as Mendenhall does. The answer to this question is contained in the q_c and ϕ risks. The former is more important in institutional decisions (e.g., selection, placement) and the latter in individual decisions (e.g., counseling). A strategy designed to fix either q_c or ϕ_m, depending on the type of decision, is logically to be preferred over a fixed α strategy. The fixed α strategy, as Lord shows, is unduly conservative when applied to highly reliable scores. In addition, it results in a high rate of error for scores of very low reliability and validity.

We agree with Lord and Bloom that there is no arbitrary level of validity or of reliability which makes a score useful. The suitability of a test depends upon these coefficients, but it also depends upon the importance of the decisions to be made and on the rules by which scores are to be converted into interpretations. Where a test is used, for example, to identify those persons who are clearly above or below the mean, a test of reliability .49 permits confident decisions ($\phi_m = .10$, $q_c = .05$, $\alpha = .07$) regarding 19% of those tested. This may or may not be a profitable information yield, depending on the situation, cost of testing, etc. Where the primary aim is to select superior individuals (more than s_y above the mean), the test reliability must reach .86 before as many as one-third of the superior individuals are identified with $\phi_m = .10$, $q_c = .035$. On the other hand, a test of reliability .36 is capable of identifying more than half of those who are definitely *not* superior; as the first stage in a sequential screening process, this test can rule out persons who need be given no further consideration.

The test designer and selector of tests must abandon his quest for a rule of thumb, and instead interpret Tables C1 and C2 (and similar tables for other decision problems and risk levels) in the light of his particular situation. For the typical counseling decision, it is our opinion that the maximum individual risk ϕ_m is the most important consideration in determining the interpretability of scores. From this point of view, the difference scores for certain published batteries discussed by Lord and Mendenhall are somewhat less useful than their papers imply.

This study was aided by USPHS Grant M-1839. The comments of F. M. Lord on a draft of this paper are gratefully acknowledged.

APPENDICES TO *PSYCHOLOGICAL TESTS AND PERSONNEL DECISIONS*

UTILITY IN FIXED-TREATMENT SELECTION AND PLACEMENT

DEFINITION OF THE SELECTION PROBLEM

The following development formally defines the selection problem where information is univariate and the treatment to be given accepted men is specified independently of the test. The argument indicating the relation of utility to test validity is a restatement of that presented by Brogden (1946, 1949b) and Cochran (1951). We make the following assumptions:

1. Decisions are made regarding an indefinitely large population of persons. This "*a priori* population" consists of all applicants after screening by any procedure which is presently in use and will continue to be used.
2. Regarding any person i, there are two possible alternative decisions: accept (t_A) and reject (t_B).
3. Each person has a test score y_i, which has zero mean and unit standard deviation.
4. For every person there is a payoff e_{it_A} which results when the person is accepted. This payoff has a linear regression on test score. The test will be scored so that r_{ye} is positive.
5. When a person is rejected, the payoff e_{it_B} results. This payoff is unrelated to test score, and may be set equal to zero.
6. The average cost of testing a person on test y is C_y, where $C_y > 0$.
7. The strategy will be to accept high scoring men in preference to others. A cutoff y' will be located on the y continuum so that any desired proportion $\phi(y')$ of the group falls above y'. Above that point probability of acceptance is 1.00; below it, 0.00. Cochran shows that such a strategy is optimal for selection with fixed quota.

From assumption 4, the expected payoff from accepting a man is

$$e_{yt_A} = \sigma_e r_{ye} y + e_{ot_A}. \tag{1.1}$$

Here, σ_e and r_{ye} are computed on the *a priori* population, and e_{ot_A} is the payoff expected when an average man in that population is assigned to treatment t_A.

UTILITY AS A FUNCTION OF VALIDITY IN SELECTION

The expected utility of a set of decisions is obtained by summing e_{yt}, the expected payoff, over all persons and subtracting cost of testing. Let U represent the total utility resulting from decisions about N persons, cost of testing being taken into account.

$$U = \sum_{i=1}^{N} (p_{t_A/y_i}e_{y_it_A} + p_{t_B/y_i}e_{y_it_B} - C_y). \tag{1.2}$$

Using assumption 5 and equation 1.1,

$$U = \sum_{i=1}^{N} p_{t_A/y_i}(\sigma_e r_{ye}y_i + e_{ot_A}) - NC_y. \tag{1.3}$$

If individuals in any y array are accepted, their total utility is

$$U_y = Np_y p_{t_A/y_i}(\sigma_e r_{ye}y + e_{ot_A}) - NC_y. \tag{1.4}$$

From assumption 7, $\int_{y'}^{\infty} p_y dy = N\phi(y')$. Therefore, summing over all values of y,

$$U = N\sigma_e r_{ye}\int_{y'}^{\infty} p_y y \, dy + N\phi(y')e_{ot_A} - NC_y. \tag{1.5}$$

The *a priori* utility U_o is the utility resulting when $N\phi(y')$ men are selected from the population by chance:

$$U_o = N\phi(y') \, e_{ot_A}. \tag{1.6}$$

The gain in utility from test y is

$$\Delta U = U - U_o = N\sigma_e r_{ye}\int_{y'}^{\infty} p_y y \, dy - NC_y. \tag{1.7}$$

It will be noted that, for any *a priori* distribution, gain in utility is a linear function of r_{ye}. We shall be chiefly concerned with the case where we can assume a normal distribution of y. We shall let $\xi(y)$ and $\phi(y)$ represent the ordinate and area (upper tail) corresponding to any value of y under this assumption. Then equation 1.7 becomes

$$\Delta U = N\sigma_e r_{ye}\xi(y') - NC_y, \tag{1.8}$$

which is the net gain from testing N men. Hereafter, we shall divide equation 1.8 by N and let ΔU represent the gain in utility *per man tested*.

As we proceed to study a variety of types of decision, we shall employ B_{yd} as a general symbol for the contribution of a particular test y to a specified decision d, apart from cost of testing. In fixed-treatment selection, $B_{yd} = \sigma_e r_{ye} \xi(y')$, so that the gain in utility per man tested

$$\Delta U = B_{yd} - C_y. \tag{1.9}$$

Rewriting equation 1.8 in this form will simplify several later mathematical developments.

The gain in utility *per man accepted* is

$$\sigma_e r_{ye} \frac{\xi(y')}{\phi(y')} - \frac{C_y}{\phi(y')} \quad \text{or} \quad \sigma_e r_{ye} \bar{y} - \frac{C_y}{\phi(y')}, \tag{1.10}$$

since the average test score $\bar{y}$ for accepted men equals $\xi(y')/\phi(y')$.

Region Where Test Is Admissible

From equation 1.8 it is evident that $\Delta U > 0$ for any y' such that

$$\xi(y') > \frac{C_y}{\sigma_e r_{ye}}. \tag{1.11}$$

For any positive value of $C/\sigma_e r$ there are two values of y', symmetrically located about $y = 0$, beyond which selection with the test is less beneficial than random selection. Outside these limiting values, use of the test is an inadmissible strategy, in Wald's sense.

Optimum Strategy

The maximum utility per person accepted is obtained by differentiating equation 1.10 with respect to $\phi(y')$:

$$\sigma_e r_{ye} \frac{y'\phi(y') - \xi(y')}{\phi^2(y')} + \frac{C_y}{\phi^2(y')} = 0 \tag{1.12}$$

$$\xi(y') - y'\phi(y') = \frac{C_y}{\sigma_e r_{ye}}. \tag{1.13}$$

Only one value of y' satisfies this equation. Equation 1.13 is meaningful only when $\xi(y') > C/\sigma_e r$, since testing is otherwise not profitable. Therefore $y'\phi(y')$ must be positive, and y' must be greater than zero.

When there is a fixed numerical quota $N\phi(y')$, setting the optimum y' according to equation 1.13 determines the optimum number of persons to be tested. For maximum utility with a fixed quota, enough men should be tested so that the cutting point is above the mean.

UTILITY IN PLACEMENT WITH FIXED QUOTAS

The above relationship may be generalized to consider placement decisions where any number of fixed treatments are to be used.

For each of the n treatments there is a linear payoff function, whose parameters will vary from treatment to treatment. The y continuum is to be divided into n segments, each containing some predetermined proportion of the cases. Each segment is bounded by two cutting scores, y_t' and y_t'', the latter being the upper boundary. y_t'' is also, of course, the lower boundary for the next treatment, $t+1$. $\phi(y_t') - \phi(y_t'')$ is the quota for treatment t.

If all men above y_t' were assigned to treatment t the utility per man tested would be (from eq. 1.5, invoking the normal assumption),

$$\sigma_{e_t} r_{ye_t} \xi(y_t') + \phi(y_t') e_{ot} - C_y. \tag{1.14}$$

A similar expression may be written in terms of y_t''. The utility when men between y_t' and y_t'' are so assigned is, by subtraction,

$$U_t = \sigma_{e_t} r_{ye_t} [\xi(y_t') - \xi(y_t'')] + e_{ot} [\phi(y_t') - \phi(y_t'')] - C_y. \tag{1.15}$$

We may write $\Delta\xi_t$ and $\Delta\phi_t$ for the bracketed terms, so that

$$U_t = \sigma_{e_t} r_{ye_t} \Delta\xi_t + e_{ot}\Delta\phi_t - C_y. \tag{1.16}$$

Over all treatments,

$$U = \sum_t \sigma_{e_t} r_{ye_t} \Delta\xi_t + \sum_t e_{ot}\Delta\phi_t - C_y. \tag{1.17}$$

The *a priori* strategy with fixed treatment is to assign randomly selected men to each treatment to fill the quota. From equation 1.6, for each treatment

$$U_{ot} = e_{ot}\Delta\phi_t. \tag{1.18}$$

Subtracting,

$$\Delta U = \sum_t \sigma_{e_t} r_{ye_t} \Delta\xi_t - C_y. \tag{1.19}$$

This again may be written as $B_{yd} - C_y$, B_{yd} thus being defined in fixed-treatment placement by the first term of equation 1.19.

UTILITY IN PLACEMENT WITH ADAPTIVE QUOTAS

If treatments are fixed and arranged according to the slopes of their payoff functions, but quotas are not specified, it is possible to increase utility by altering the quotas. Maximizing equation

1.17 with respect to y_t', and using $t-1$ and t to indicate two adjacent treatments such that $y_{t-1}'' = y_t'$,

$$\frac{\partial U}{\partial y_t'} = \sigma_{e_{t-1}} r_{ye_{t-1}} y_t' \xi(y_t') + e_{o(t-1)} \xi(y_t')$$
$$- \sigma_{e_t} r_{ye_t} y_t' \xi(y_t') - e_{ot} \xi(y_t') = 0. \qquad (1.20)$$

Simplifying,

$$\sigma_{e_{t-1}} r_{ye_{t-1}} y_t' + e_{o(t-1)} = \sigma_{e_t} r_{ye_t} y_t' + e_{ot} \qquad (1.21)$$

or

$$y' = \frac{e_{o(t-1)} - e_{ot}}{\sigma_{e_t} r_{ye_t} - \sigma_{e_{t-1}} r_{ye_{t-1}}}. \qquad (1.22)$$

Equation 1.22 specifies the best dividing point between the two treatments. Similar boundaries may be set between any other adjacent pair of treatments. Each value of y' locates a point at which the payoff functions for two treatments intersect. If such computations for any treatment yield a value of $y_t'' < y_t'$, that treatment drops out of the series of treatments used. Its quota is zero.

When the decision maker is allowed to alter quotas, his best *a priori* strategy is to assign *all* men to whichever of the allowed treatments gives greatest utility when $y = 0$. We will designate it t_o. Considering all treatments, if adaptive quotas are used,

$$\Delta U = \sum_t \sigma_{e_t} r_{ye_t} \Delta \xi_t + \sum_t (e_{ot} - e_{ot_o}) \Delta \phi_t - C_y. \qquad (1.23)$$

A PAYOFF SURFACE DEPENDING ON A UNIVARIATE APTITUDE

To consider problems involving choice among many treatments, we develop a general function relating payoff to a univariate aptitude. Parameters are employed such that this surface will fit a variety of actual data.

It was pointed out in Chapter 3 that when many scores are available it is possible to perform a factor analysis, deriving the orthogonal factors $s_i = s_1, s_2 \ldots$. Of these factors, the ones which determine payoff under any of the treatments are referred to as *aptitude* factors. In this appendix we restrict ourselves to the case where all tests under consideration measure only one aptitude dimension s (although they may also measure common factors not related to payoff). We assume that s has zero mean, unit standard deviation, and normal distribution.

We assume that the expected payoff under any treatment is a linear function of s:

$$e_{st} = \sigma_{e_t} r_{se_t} s + e_{ot}. \tag{2.1}$$

Our problem is to examine the possible changes in payoff when treatments are allowed to vary. As discussed in Chapter 3, treatments may vary along many dimensions. As the treatment varies, either σ_{e_t} or r_{se_t} or both may vary, and e_{ot} may vary. Change in either of the first two parameters affects the slope of the payoff function, and we therefore introduce a slope parameter $m_{st} = \sigma_{e_t} r_{se_t}$. If two treatments have the same slope, it will always be preferable to assign men to the treatment for which e_{ot} is greater. For each slope m_{st}, then, only one of the set of treatments need be considered.

We desire to postulate a relatively simple form for the payoff surface and therefore assume that the intercepts e_{ot} vary in the following manner:

$$e_{ot} = c + bm_{st} - am_{st}^2, \text{ where } a > 0. \tag{2.2}$$

This assumption is adopted because it is the simplest function which defines a non-trivial case. While b is likely to be greater than zero, this is not required. Substituting in equation 2.1, we have the equation for the surface relating expected payoff to aptitude s:

$$e_{st} = m_{st}s + c + bm_{st} - am_{st}^2. \tag{2.3}$$

The parameters a, b, and c would change if a different aptitude were measured, or if a different set of treatments were under consideration. Empirical values for the parameters can only be obtained by administering several of the treatments in the series to persons for whom an estimate of s_i is available.

At any level of aptitude s, there is a treatment t_s which yields the greatest payoff. Maximizing e with respect to m_{st},

$$\frac{\partial e}{\partial m_{st}} = s + b - 2am_{st} = 0 \tag{2.4}$$

$$m_{st_s} = \frac{s + b}{2a}. \tag{2.5}$$

Substituting this in equation 2.3 gives the maximum payoff obtainable for a person having aptitude s:

$$e_{st_s} = \frac{(s + b)^2}{4a} + c. \tag{2.6}$$

When a *group* with average ability s is assigned to the treatment best for the average man in the group, the utility per man assigned is expressed by equation 2.6.

appendix **3**

UTILITY WITH ADAPTIVE TREATMENT

It will be advantageous to determine the utility from placement with adaptive treatment before considering adaptive selection. The opposite order is employed in describing the findings in the text.

PLACEMENT WITH FIXED QUOTAS

It is assumed that a large number of treatments are available, and that a particular test is under consideration. The aptitude s is common to test and treatments, and the payoff function is described by equation 2.3. The decision maker is to divide persons into a certain number of groups, the proportion to be placed in each group being specified. Each group will receive a different treatment, the decision maker being allowed to select the treatment best fitted to the estimated aptitude of each group. Throughout this discussion, utility will refer to utility per man tested; that is to say, N is dropped from all equations.

If the test is not given, the best *a priori* strategy under these conditions is to divide men at random into groups, and to assign all groups to the treatment best when $s = 0$. From equation 2.5, this treatment t_0 is such that

$$m_{t_o} = b/2a. \tag{3.1}$$

This is not the same t_0 as appeared in equation 1.23. If $\phi(y')$ persons, randomly selected, are assigned to t_0, it follows from equation 2.6 that the *a priori* utility per man tested is

$$U_{oto} = \phi(y') \ (c + b^2/4a). \tag{3.2}$$

When the test y is used as a basis for dividing the group, utility is increased. As in Appendix 1, we assume that the cutting scores

y' and y'' are fixed so that $\Delta\phi_t = \phi(y'_t) - \phi(y''_t)$ is the quota for treatment t.

The average test score of men between y' and y'' is $\dfrac{\xi(y'_t) - \xi(y''_t)}{\Delta\phi_t}$ or $\dfrac{\Delta\xi_t}{\Delta\phi_t}$. Assuming a linear regression of s on y, the average value of s in this group is $r_{ys}\dfrac{\Delta\xi_t}{\Delta\phi_t}$. From equation 2.6, the payoff when these individuals are given the treatment optimum for them is,

$$e_{st_t} = \frac{\Delta\phi_t}{4a}\left(r_{ys}\frac{\Delta\xi_t}{\Delta\phi_t} + b\right)^2 + c\Delta\phi_t. \tag{3.3}$$

The utility is

$$U_t = \frac{1}{4a}\left(r_{ys}^2\frac{\Delta^2\xi_t}{\Delta\phi_t} + 2br_{ys}\Delta\xi_t + b^2\Delta\phi_t\right) + c\Delta\phi_t - \Delta\phi_t C_y. \tag{3.4}$$

Over all treatments, $\sum_t \Delta\xi_t = 0$ and $\sum_t \Delta\phi_t = 1$. Therefore

$$\left.\begin{array}{l} U = \dfrac{r_{ys}^2}{4a}\displaystyle\sum_t \frac{\Delta^2\xi_t}{\Delta\phi_t} + \dfrac{b^2}{4a} + c - C_y \\[2ex] U_{ot_o} = \dfrac{b^2}{4a} + c. \end{array}\right\} \tag{3.5}$$

and

The gain in utility is

$$\Delta U = \frac{r_{ys}^2}{4a}\sum_t \frac{\Delta^2\xi_t}{\Delta\phi_t} - C_y. \tag{3.6}$$

In adaptive placement where quotas are specified, therefore, ΔU is a function of r_{ys}^2 — regardless of quotas or number of treatments. B_{yd} is here equivalent to $\dfrac{r_{ys}^2}{4a}\displaystyle\sum_t \frac{\Delta^2\xi_t}{\Delta\phi_t}$.

For men assigned to any one treatment, the gain in utility is found by subtracting equation 3.2 from equation 3.4:

$$\Delta U_t = \frac{r_{ys}^2}{4a}\frac{\Delta^2\xi_t}{\Delta\phi_t} + \frac{r_{ys}b\Delta\xi_t}{2a} - \Delta\phi_t C_y. \tag{3.7}$$

ADAPTIVE SELECTION

The expression for utility in adaptive selection now follows readily from equation 3.7. In adaptive selection a quota to be accepted, $\phi(y')$, is specified, and all accepted men are assigned to the one most suitable treatment. The remainder are rejected, and their payoff is zero.

A priori, a randomly selected group of size $1 - \phi(y')$ would be rejected, and payoff is zero. After testing, the utility is zero less the cost of testing the rejected persons. Therefore the gain in utility from testing depends entirely on the increase in utility for accepted men, less the cost of testing the rejectees. Modifying equation 3.7 to take into account the fact that $y_i'' = \infty$, and subtracting $(1 - \phi(y'))C_y$, the gain in utility is

$$\Delta U = \frac{r_{ys}^2}{4a} \frac{\xi^2(y')}{\phi(y')} + \frac{r_{ys}b\xi(y')}{2a} - C_y. \tag{3.8}$$

The first two terms of equation 3.8 define B_{yd} for adaptive selection.

To clarify certain points discussed in the text, expressions are required for utilities which might result under several different conditions. Consider three treatments: t_A, some treatment which happens to be in use a $priori$; t_O, which is best suited to randomly selected men; and t_s, suited to men with test scores above y'. U_{ot} is the utility from assigning $\phi(y')$ randomly selected men to treatment t. From equation 2.2:

$$U_{ot_A} = \phi(y') \ (c + bm_{t_A} - am_{t_A}^2). \tag{3.9}$$

U_{oto} has already been given in equation 3.2. Substituting equation 2.5 in equation 2.2 with $s = r_{ys} \dfrac{\xi(y')}{\phi(y')}$, we have

$$U_{ot_s} = \phi(y') \left[c + \frac{b^2}{4a} - \frac{1}{4a} \left(r_{ys} \frac{\xi(y')}{\phi(y')} \right)^2 \right]. \tag{3.10}$$

The a $posteriori$ utilities for men selected on the basis of test y may be denoted U_{yt}. The average ability for these men is $r_{ys} \dfrac{\xi(y')}{\phi(y')}$, hence

$$U_{yt_A} = \phi(y') \left[m_{t_A}r_{ys} \frac{\xi(y')}{\phi(y')} + c + bm_{t_A} - am_{t_A}^2 \right] - C_y. \tag{3.11}$$

$$U_{yt_O} = \phi(y') \left[\frac{br_{ys}\xi(y')}{2a\phi(y')} + \frac{b^2}{4a} + c \right] - C_y. \tag{3.12}$$

$$U_{yt_s} = \phi(y') \left[\frac{1}{4a} (r_{ys} \frac{\xi(y')}{\phi(y')} + b)^2 + c \right] - C_y. \tag{3.13}$$

PLACEMENT WITH ADJUSTED QUOTAS

We shall next consider the case where the maximum number of treatments is fixed, but the decision maker may alter the quotas as well as the treatments. The optimum cutting score y_i' between any two treatments $t-1$ and t may be located by differentiating equation 3.6 with respect to y'_t.

$$\frac{\partial \Delta U}{\partial y'_t} = \frac{r_{ys}^2}{4a} \left[\frac{2\Delta\phi_{t-1}\Delta\xi_{t-1}y'_t\xi(y'_t) - \Delta^2\xi_{t-1}\xi(y'_t)}{\Delta^2\phi_{t-1}} \right.$$

$$\left. - \frac{2\Delta\phi_t\Delta\xi_t y'_t\xi(y'_t) - \Delta^2\xi_t\xi(y'_t)}{\Delta^2\phi_t} \right] = 0. \qquad (3.14)$$

Simplifying this expression,

$$y'_t = \tfrac{1}{2} \left[\frac{\Delta\xi_t}{\Delta\phi_t} + \frac{\Delta\xi_{t-1}}{\Delta\phi_{t-1}} \right]. \qquad (3.15)$$

This equation applies to any cutting point. With n_t treatments, there are $n-1$ boundaries, and equation 3.15 provides $n-1$ simultaneous equations. No general solution for this set of equations has been found.

TWO-STAGE SEQUENTIAL STRATEGY

Two tests, y_a and y_b, are available. One of these, designated y_1, will be given to all persons. Persons scoring above a certain value y_1'' will be accepted at once, and persons scoring below some other value y_1' will be rejected. The remaining persons will be given the second test and will be finally accepted or rejected on the basis of the combined information from both tests. The appropriate cutting scores y_1' and y_1'' to provide the desired proportion ϕ_A of accepted men are to be determined.

Men are to be accepted for a fixed treatment t_A. The assumptions of Appendix 1 will be retained, save for the introduction of a second test. Since the two tests y_a and y_b may be correlated, y_2 is used to designate the standardized component of the designated second test which is independent of the first. The validities of the two independent scores are r_{y_1e} and r_{y_2e}. These two scores may be combined into a battery score Y, using weights that maximize the battery validity r_{Ye}.

$$r_{Ye}^2 = r_{y_1e}^2 + r_{y_2e}^2 \tag{4.1}$$

$$Y = \frac{r_{y_1e}y_1 + r_{y_2e}y_2}{r_{Ye}}. \tag{4.2}$$

Since all persons for whom Y is constant contribute equal expected payoff (from equation 1.1), the optimum cutoff for selecting among the men given the second test is a value $Y = Y'$ (shown as line MN in Figure 15). We now seek the values of Y', y_1', and y_1'' which give the greatest utility per man tested, with any selection ratio.

Men in Region II of Figure 15 are accepted on the basis of the first test. The gain in utility for these men, over the utility from men chosen by chance, using equation 1.8 and momentarily disregarding cost, is

$$\Delta U_{\text{II}} = \sigma_e r_{y_1e}\xi(y_1''). \tag{4.3}$$

In Region III, the analogous gain is

$$\Delta U_{III} = \int_{v_1 - v_1'}^{v_1''} \int_{Y-Y'}^{\infty} \sigma_e r_{Ye} Y \xi(y_1, y_2) \, dy_1 dy_2. \tag{4.4}$$

Men in regions I and IV are rejected, and thus their utility is zero. Let $y_{2.1}$ be the cutting score on y_2 for a specified y_1, and also let y_2' and y_2'' represent the values of $y_{2.1}$ corresponding to y_1' and y_1''. From equation 4.2,

$$y_{2.1} = \frac{r_{Ye} Y' - r_{y_1 e} y_1}{r_{y_2 e}}. \tag{4.5}$$

Noting that $\xi(y_1, y_2) = \xi(y_1) \xi(y_2)$, equation 4.4 becomes

$$\Delta U = \sigma_e \int_{v_1 - v_1'}^{v_1''} \int_{v_{2.1}}^{\infty} (r_{y_1 e} y_1 + r_{y_2 e} y_2) \xi(y_1) \xi(y_2) dy_1 dy_2$$

$$= \sigma_e \int_{v_1'}^{v_1''} [r_{y_1 e} y_1 \phi(y_{2.1}) + r_{y_2 e} \xi(y_{2.1})] \, \xi(y_1) dy_1. \tag{4.6}$$

We may designate the costs of the two tests as C_{y_1} and C_{y_2}. Since all persons are given the first test, while those between y_1' and y_1'' are given the second, the average cost per man tested is

$$C_{y_1} + C_{y_2} [\phi(y_1') - \phi(y_1'')]. \tag{4.7}$$

The net gain in utility as a result of testing,

$$\Delta U = \sigma_e \xi(y_1'') r_{y_1 e} + \sigma_e \int_{v_1'}^{v_1''} [r_{y_1 e} y_1 \phi(y_{2.1}) + r_{y_2 e} \xi(y_{2.1})] \, \xi(y_1) dy_1$$

$$- C_{y_1} - C_{y_2} [\phi(y_1') - \phi(y_1'')]. \tag{4.8}$$

The selection ratio is the combined proportion in II and III:

$$\phi_A = \int_{v_1''}^{\infty} \xi(y_1) dy_1 + \int_{v_1'}^{v_1''} \xi(y_1) \phi(y_{2.1}) dy_1. \tag{4.9}$$

Since $\phi(y_{2.1})$ is a function of Y and y_1, equation 4.9 establishes a relationship between y_1', y_1'', and Y'. Therefore only two of these can be independent variables. To maximize ΔU we follow the method of Lagrange for a restrained maximum, introducing an undetermined multiplier λ. Three simultaneous equations define the conditions for the maximum:

$$\left.\begin{array}{c} \dfrac{\partial \Delta U}{\partial y_1'} + \lambda\, \dfrac{\partial \phi}{\partial y_1'} = 0 \\[2mm] \dfrac{\partial \Delta U}{\partial y_1''} + \lambda\, \dfrac{\partial \phi}{\partial y_1''} = 0 \\[2mm] \dfrac{\partial \Delta U}{\partial Y'} + \lambda\, \dfrac{\partial \phi}{\partial Y'} = 0. \end{array}\right\} \quad (4.10)$$

Substituting the appropriate values in equation 4.10 and transposing,

$$\left.\begin{array}{c} \sigma_e r_{y_1 e} y_1' + \dfrac{\sigma_e r_{y_2 e}\xi(y_2') - C_{y_2}}{\phi(y_2')} = -\lambda \\[3mm] \sigma_e r_{y_1 e} y_1'' - \dfrac{\sigma_e r_{y_2 e}\xi(y_2'') - C_{y_2}}{1 - \phi(y_2'')} = -\lambda \\[3mm] \sigma_e r_{Y e} Y' = -\lambda. \end{array}\right\} \quad (4.11)$$

Eliminating λ from equations 4.11 and noting that $1 - \phi(x) = \phi(-x)$ and that $\xi(x) = \xi(-x)$ gives

$$\left.\begin{array}{c} r_{y_1 e} y_1' + r_{y_2 e} \dfrac{\xi(y_2')}{\phi(y_2')} - \dfrac{C_{y_2}}{\sigma_e \phi(y_2')} = r_{Y e} Y' \\[3mm] r_{y_1 e} y_1'' - r_{y_2 e} \dfrac{\xi(-y_2'')}{\phi(-y_2'')} + \dfrac{C_{y_2}}{\sigma_e \phi(-y_2'')} = r_{Y e} Y'. \end{array}\right\} \quad (4.12)$$

These equations define y_1' and y_1'' respectively in terms of $r_{y_1 e}$, $r_{y_2 e}$, C_{y_2}/σ_e, and Y'.

For computational purposes it is advantageous to determine the y_2 coordinates of points M and N, that is, y_2' and y_2''. We use equation 4.5 to eliminate Y' from equations 4.12,

$$\left.\begin{array}{c} r_{y_1 e} y_1' + r_{y_2 e} \dfrac{\xi(y_2')}{\phi(y_2')} - \dfrac{C_{y_2}}{\sigma_e \phi(y_2')} = r_{y_1 e} y_1' + r_{y_2 e} y_2' \\[3mm] r_{y_1 e} y_1'' - r_{y_2 e} \dfrac{\xi(-y_2'')}{\phi(-y_2'')} + \dfrac{C_{y_2}}{\sigma_e \phi(-y_2'')} = r_{y_1 e} y_1'' + r_{y_2 e} y_2''. \end{array}\right\} \quad (4.13)$$

Hence

$$y_2' = \frac{\xi(y_2')}{\phi(y_2')} - \frac{C_{y_2}}{\sigma_e r_{y_2 e}\phi(y_2')} = -y_2''. \quad (4.14)$$

Thus y_2' and y_2'' are equal in absolute value and depend only on $C_{y_2}/\sigma_e r_{y_2 e}$.

The optimum Pre-reject or Pre-accept strategy could be derived separately. However, the fact that the partial derivative with respect to y_1' is independent of y_1'' in equations 4.11 shows that the values of y_1' and y_1'' so obtained would be identical to those for the complete sequential strategy.

In order to simplify comparison of the various testing strategies it is advantageous to express equations 4.12 and 4.14 in terms of the correlation of each test with the total battery rather than in terms of their validity coefficients. The validity of either stage of testing can be written thus:

$$r_{y_1e} = r_{y_1Y}r_{Ye} \quad \text{and} \quad r_{y_2e} = r_{y_2Y}r_{Ye}. \tag{4.15}$$

The terms r_{y_1Y} and r_{y_2Y} are not independent since

$$r_{y_1Y}^2 + r_{y_2Y}^2 = 1. \tag{4.16}$$

Then equations 4.12 become

$$\left. \begin{array}{l} r_{y_1Y}y_1' + r_{y_2Y}\dfrac{\xi(y_2')}{\phi(y_2')} - \dfrac{C_{y_2}}{\sigma_e r_{Ye}\phi(y_2')} = Y' \\[3mm] r_{y_1Y}y_1'' - r_{y_2Y}\dfrac{\xi(-y_2'')}{\phi(-y_2'')} + \dfrac{C_{y_2}}{\sigma_e r_{Ye}\phi(-y_2'')} = Y' \end{array} \right\} \tag{4.17}$$

and for equation 4.14 we have

$$y_2' = \frac{\xi(y_2')}{\phi(y_2')} - \frac{C_{y_2}}{\sigma_e r_{Ye} r_{y_2Y}\phi(y_2')} = -y_2''. \tag{4.18}$$

Using this formulation it is possible to treat $C_{y_2}/\sigma_e r_{Ye}$ as a single constant C_2 which is given (or can be specified hypothetically). Figure A1 based on equation 4.18 permits ready determination of y_2'.

To solve a particular problem one begins with r_{y_1Y} and C_2, and some trial value of Y' such that $\phi(Y')$ is near the desired selection ratio. Then y_2' and y_2'' are obtained from Figure A1, and y_1' and y_1'' are found from equation 4.5.

Any Y' yields one pair of first-screen cutoffs. The selection ratio obtained for the trial Y' is found from equation 4.9. The gain in utility is given by equation 4.8, but it is convenient to rewrite that equation in this form:

$$\frac{\Delta U}{\sigma_e r_{Ye}} = r_{y_1Y}\xi(y_1'') + \int_{y_1'}^{y_1''} \left[r_{y_1Y}y_1\phi(y_{2.1}) + r_{y_2Y}\xi(y_{2.1}) \right] \xi(y_1)dy_1$$

$$- \frac{C_{y_1}}{\sigma_e r_{Ye}} - \frac{C_{y_2}}{\sigma_e r_{Ye}} \left[\phi(y_1') - \phi(y_1'') \right]. \tag{4.19}$$

There is no simple procedure for solving directly for ϕ_A. Successive trials with interpolation will determine the values of y_1', y_1'', and Y' that yield a desired ϕ_A.

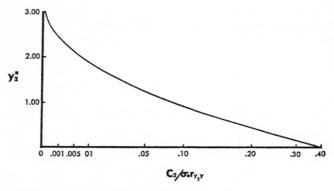

Figure A1. Chart for determining optimal cutting scores on second test

appendix 5

OPTIMUM LENGTH OF A TEST

A test is said to be lengthened homogeneously when we combine unit tests having the same cost, equal intercorrelations $r_{y_1y_1}$, and the same relation to criteria (i.e., the same r_{y_1e}). The relation of the unit test to the criterion is assumed to be the same regardless of the unit's position in the series. Correlation increases with length k according to this well-known equation:

$$r_{y_ke_t} = r_{y_1e_t} \sqrt{\frac{r_{y_ky_k}}{r_{y_1y_1}}} = r_{y_1e_t} \sqrt{\frac{k}{1 + (k-1)r_{y_1y_1}}} . \qquad (5.1)$$

A similar equation may be written for r_{ys}.

The cost, formerly denoted by C_y, may be divided into two components, C_0 and C_1. C_0 consists of the basic cost of setting up the test, giving directions, etc.; C_0 is constant as k changes. C_1 represents the costs associated with taking a test of unit length (supplies, time of examiner and subjects if paid, etc.). This cost increases proportionally to length. Hence for a test k times as long as the unit test, the total cost

$$C_{y_k} = C_0 + kC_1. \qquad (5.2)$$

FIXED TREATMENT, FIXED QUOTAS

From equation 1.19, gain in utility per man tested in either selection or placement is

$$\Delta U_k = \sum_t \sigma_{e_t} r_{y_ke_t} \Delta\xi_t - C_y = B_{y_kd} - C_{y_k}. \qquad (5.3)$$

Substituting from equations 5.1 and 5.2,

$$\Delta U_k = B_{y_1d} \sqrt{\frac{r_{y_ky_k}}{r_{y_1y_1}}} - (C_0 + kC_1). \qquad (5.4)$$

B_{y_1d} is defined for fixed treatment by the value of the first term of equation 5.3 when k is 1. The function has a maximum, provided $\Delta U > 0$ for some value of k. The maximum occurs where

$$\frac{\partial \Delta U}{\partial k} = \frac{B_{y_1d}(1 - r_{y_1y_1})}{2\sqrt{k}\,[1 + (k-1)r_{y_1y_1}]^{\frac{3}{2}}} - C_1 = 0. \qquad (5.5)$$

This condition may be rewritten thus:

$$\left[(1 - r_{y_1y_1})\frac{B_{y_1d}}{2C_1}\right]^2 = k\left[1 + (k-1)r_{y_1y_1}\right]^3. \qquad (5.6)$$

One root of this equation gives the desired optimum length.

In selection or placement a single-stage battery of v tests may be used. If $R_{Y_\bullet e_t}$ is the correlation of the battery score with payoff,

$$\Delta U = \sum_t \sigma_{e_t} R_{Y_\bullet e_t} \Delta \xi_t - C_y. \qquad (5.7)$$

Since utility of the battery with the vth test removed is expressed by the same formula with $v-1$ substituted for v, the gain from adding the vth test is the increment

$$\Delta U_v = \sum_t \sigma_{e_t} \Delta \xi_t (R_{Y_\bullet e_t} - R_{Y_{v-1}e_t}) - C_v. \qquad (5.8)$$

$R_{Y_\bullet e} - R_{Y_{v-1}e}$ is unlikely to be the same for all treatments.

If the problem is one of selection for a single treatment, equation 5.8 becomes

$$\Delta U = (R_{Y_\bullet e_t} - R_{Y_{v-1}e_t})\,\sigma_e \xi_t - C_v = \Delta R_v \sigma_e \xi_t - C_v. \qquad (5.9)$$

We may now consider the advisability of adding a unit test of such length that its variable cost is C_1. The battery may be augmented profitably by adding a unit of any test already in the battery if for that unit

$$\Delta R_v > \frac{C_1}{\sigma_e \xi_t}. \qquad (5.10)$$

or a unit of any test y not yet in the battery if for that unit

$$\Delta R_v > \frac{C_{0y} + C_1}{\sigma_e \xi_t}. \qquad (5.11)$$

Among all units available, that one should be added first which provides the greatest increment in utility. Horst (1949) has developed general procedures for adjusting the length of the tests in a battery so as to maximize R_{Ye}, under the assumption that C_0 is negligible.

ADAPTIVE PLACEMENT, FIXED QUOTAS

When treatments may be adjusted to fit the aptitude s of selected men, from equation 3.6

$$\Delta U_k = \frac{r_{y_{ks}}^2}{4a} \sum_t \frac{\Delta^2 \xi_t}{\Delta \phi_t} - C_{y_k}. \qquad (5.12)$$

Substituting from equations 5.1 and 5.2,

$$\Delta U_k = B_{y_1d} \frac{r_{y_k y_k}}{r_{y_1 y_1}} - (C_0 + kC_1). \qquad (5.13)$$

Here B_{y_1d} is the benefit under adaptive treatment, defined by the first term of equation 5.12 when $k=1$. This function has a maximum (provided $\Delta U > 0$ for any k) where

$$\frac{\partial \Delta U}{\partial k} = B_{y_1d} \frac{(1 - r_{y_1 y_1})}{[1 + (k-1)r_{y_1 y_1}]^2} - C_1 = 0. \qquad (5.14)$$

This condition may be rewritten:

$$(1 - r_{y_1 y_1}) \frac{B_{y_1d}}{C_1} = [1 + (k-1)r_{y_1 y_1}]^2. \qquad (5.15)$$

The positive root is the desired optimum length k. Notation being simplified,

$$k = 1 - \frac{1}{r} + \frac{1}{r} \sqrt{\frac{B(1-r)}{C}}. \qquad (5.16)$$

ADAPTIVE SELECTION, FIXED QUOTAS

In selection, from equation 3.8

$$\Delta U_k = \frac{1}{4a} \frac{\xi^2(y')}{\phi(y')} r_{y_{ks}}^2 + \frac{b}{2a} \xi(y') r_{y_{ks}} - C_{y_k}. \qquad (5.17)$$

Hence

$$\Delta U_k = \frac{1}{4a} \frac{\xi^2(y')}{\phi(y')} r_{y_{1s}}^2 \left[\frac{r_{y_k y_k}}{r_{y_1 y_1}} \right]$$
$$+ \frac{b}{2a} \xi(y') r_{y_{1s}} \sqrt{\frac{r_{y_k y_k}}{r_{y_1 y_1}}} - (C_0 + kC_1) \qquad (5.18)$$

$$\frac{\partial \Delta U_k}{\partial k} = \frac{1}{4a} \frac{\xi^2(y')}{\phi(y')} r_{y_{1s}}^2 \frac{(1 - r_{y_1 y_1})}{[1 + (k-1)r_{y_1 y_1}]^2} \qquad (5.19)$$
$$+ \frac{b}{2a} \xi(y') r_{y_{1s}} \frac{(1 - r_{y_1 y_1})}{2\sqrt{k}\,[1 + (k-1)r_{y_1 y_1}]^{\frac{3}{2}}} - C_1.$$

Setting this equal to zero gives an expression in k one of whose roots is the optimum length of test for adaptive selection.

appendix 6

STRATEGY FOR MULTI-STAGE SELECTION

The following appendix describes the procedures developed by the Statistical Research Group (SRG) (1945) and Freeman *et al.* (1948) for dividing persons into two groups so as to minimize risks associated with misclassification. We have paraphrased their argument to fit the personnel problem.

A unit test y_1 is to be used at each stage of testing. The person has a "true score" y_∞ which is his average score after an infinite number of stages of testing. Since y_∞ is a predictor of criterion performance, it is desired to select persons whose true quality is above a certain level y'_∞, either rejecting the remainder or assigning them to a second treatment. The reliability $r_{y_1y_1} = r^2_{y_1y_\infty}$ is known; assuming the variance of true scores to be 1.00, the standard deviation σ of y_1 for persons having the same y_∞ can be computed.

While no serious loss attaches to a decision to accept a person slightly below y'_∞, or to reject a person slightly above this value, losses become more serious when erroneous decisions are made about persons farther from the cutting line. In the usual manner for Neyman-Pearson risks, two values $y'_\infty - w_1$ and $y'_\infty + w_2$ are located. A judgment is then made as to the tolerable risk α of accepting a person whose true ability is $y'_\infty - w_1$, and the tolerable risk β of rejecting a person whose true ability is $y'_\infty + w_2$. These risks constitute the specifications for a desirable strategy.

Strategy

Three functions are now calculated:

$$h_1 = b\sigma^2/(w_2 - w_1) \tag{6.1}$$

$$h_2 = a\sigma^2/(w_2 - w_1) \tag{6.2}$$

$$S = (w_1 + w_2)/2. \tag{6.3}$$

The parameters a and b are functions of α and β which have been tabled by SRG:

$$a = ln(1 - \beta)/\alpha \qquad b = ln(1 - \alpha)/\beta. \qquad (6.4)$$

The person's score is totaled at the end of every stage of testing. If, at the kth stage, the score is greater than $h_2 + kS$, the person is accepted; if less than $h_1 - kS$, the person is rejected. If it is between these values, testing is continued. A simple graphical procedure for making these decisions is available.

Operating Characteristic and Selection Ratio

The strategy has an operating characteristic function, which describes $p_{A/y\infty}$, that is, the probability of accepting a person at each true quality level. This function is approximately ogival in shape and passes through the points (w_1, α) and $(w_2, 1-\beta)$, and is described by

$$p_{A/y\infty} = (e^{g_1} - 1)/(e^{g_2} - 1). \qquad (6.5)$$

Here, e is the base of the natural logarithms and the parameters g_1 and g_2 are defined by

$$g_1 = 2h_1(S - y_\infty)/\sigma^2 \qquad g_2 = 2(h_1 + h_2)(S - y_\infty)/\sigma^2 \qquad (6.6)$$

If, as in our work, the distribution of y_∞ is assumed to be known, $\Sigma p_{y\infty} p_{A/y\infty}$ indicates the proportion of applicants who will be accepted, or the selection ratio.

Average Sample Number and Cost of Testing

The number of tests to be given each person will depend on his scores. For a large number of persons having the same true score, we can predict the average number of stages of testing k which will be required.

$$k_{y\infty} = (h_2 + h_1)p_{A/y\infty} + \frac{h_1}{S - y_\infty}. \qquad (6.7)$$

Multiplying by the probability of each y_∞, and summing, gives the total number of tests. Introducing the cost of the unit test then permits an estimate of the total cost of all tests.

Calculating Operations

A computer program has been prepared that permits calculation of the relation between selection ratio, average quality of persons accepted, and cost of testing. The program assumes that $\alpha = \beta$, which is not a very restrictive assumption, and that ability is normally distributed and error of measurement uniform for all values of y_∞. The parameters for any given calculation are α, $r_{y_1 y_1}$, and C_1, the cost per unit test. A working parameter y'_∞ is also introduced, but drops out of the functions obtained. This program was employed to obtain the results given in the text.

The program also permits a person seeking a good strategy for a particular decision to start with a known selection ratio and cost of testing. Assuming a value for $w_1 = w_2$ and using nomograms not reproduced here, one can determine appropriate values of α and y'_∞ for these conditions, and then derive the strategy from equations 6.1 and 6.2. This strategy will probably be different from the true optimum obtained by Wald's recursion formula, but it is expected to be a good approximation.

DISTRIBUTION OF EFFORT IN COMPOUND DECISIONS

When several decisions are to be made, and a test is available relevant to each, a decision must be made regarding the optimum length of each test. That is to say, the composition of the testing battery is to be adjusted so as to maximize utility. Assume that there are w independent decisions, each dependent on a different aptitude so that payoffs are uncorrelated. There is a test y_d bearing on decision d and irrelevant to the others. The unit of length for each test is such that its cost is C_1. The remaining parameters for each test are $B_{y_i d}$, $r_{y_1 y_1 d}$, and C_{0d}. We shall assume that C_{0d} depends only on the time necessary to distribute the test, give instructions, etc., and thus is fixed for each test regardless of its length but can vary from test to test.

For any test, as in equation 5.2, the cost at length k is

$$C_{y_k d} = C_{0d} + k C_1. \tag{7.1}$$

We shall fix the total allowable cost C_T for the battery. Since we assume that costs depend only on time, this is equivalent to assuming a fixed total testing time.

FIXED TREATMENT

As in equation 5.4, if treatments and quotas are fixed, when test y_d is used at length k_d, the gain in utility per man for that decision is

$$\Delta U_d = B_{y_i d} \sqrt{\frac{r_{y_k y_k d}}{r_{y_1 y_1 d}}} - (C_{0d} + k_d C_1). \tag{7.2}$$

For the w decisions, there are w tests, but we shall consider the utility of any battery of v tests where $v \leq w$. Then summing with respect to d,

$$\sum_{1}^{v} C_{y_k d} = \Sigma C_{0d} + C_1 \Sigma k_d = C_T \tag{7.3}$$

$$\sum_{1}^{v} \Delta U_d = \Sigma B_{y_1 d} \sqrt{\frac{r_{y_k y_1 d}}{r_{y_1 y_1 d}}} - C_T. \tag{7.4}$$

It may be noted from equation 7.3 that the total number of items $(\Sigma k_d = K)$ which can be used for any battery is a constant determined by $(C_T - \Sigma C_{0d})/C_1$. In order to maximize $\Sigma \Delta U_d$, it is necessary again to use the method of Lagrange as in equations 4.10. With respect to any k_d, as in equation 5.5,

$$\frac{\partial \Sigma \Delta U_d}{\partial k_d} = \frac{B_{y_1 d}(1 - r_{y_1 y_1 d})}{2 \sqrt{k_d} \, [1 + (k_d - 1)r_{y_1 y_1}]^{\frac{3}{2}}} - C_1 = 0. \tag{7.5}$$

Letting λ be an unspecified multiplier, and retaining the constraint of equation 7.3, we obtain a series of v equations of the form

$$\frac{B_{y_1 d}(1 - r_{y_1 y_1 d})}{2 \sqrt{k_d} \, [1 + (k_d - 1)r_{y_1 y_1 d}]^{\frac{3}{2}}} - C_1 + \lambda C_1 = 0. \tag{7.6}$$

No algebraic solution for this system of equations has been obtained.

Special Cases

We can treat the equation directly when $v = 2$. Then, from equation 7.3,

$$K = \frac{C_T - C_{01} - C_{02}}{C_1} \tag{7.7}$$

$$\frac{B_{y_1}(1 - r_{y_1 y_1 1})}{2 \sqrt{k_1} \, [1 + (k_1 - 1)r_{y_1 y_1 1}]^{\frac{3}{2}}}$$
$$= \frac{B_{y_1 2}(1 - r_{y_1 y_1 2})}{2 \sqrt{K - k_1} \, [1 + (K - k_1 - 1)r_{y_1 y_1 2}]^{\frac{3}{2}}}. \tag{7.8}$$

This equation involving the single unknown k_1 indicates the optimum distribution of effort between two tests, when other parameters are fixed.

A second special case to be considered is that where all v tests and the related decisions are uniform, that is, $r_{y_1 y_1 d}$, $B_{y_1 d}$, and C_{0d} are the same for all decisions. Then, from equation 7.6, k_d is the same for every decision. From equation 7.3,

$$v = \frac{C_T}{C_0 + kC_1}. \tag{7.9}$$

This permits us to inquire as to the optimum number of tests to be used. Equation 7.4 becomes

$$\Sigma \Delta U_d = v B_{y_1 d} \sqrt{\frac{k}{1 + (k - 1)r_{y_1 y_1}}} - C_T. \qquad (7.10)$$

Substituting for v (using equation 7.9), and maximizing ΔU with respect to k,

$$\frac{\partial \Sigma \Delta U}{\partial k} = 0 = \frac{C_T B_{y_1 d}(1 - r_{y_1 y_1})}{2\sqrt{k} \; (C_0 + k C_1) \; [1 + (k - 1)r_{y_1 y_1}]^{\frac{3}{2}}}$$

$$- \sqrt{\frac{k}{1 + (k - 1)r_{y_1 y_1}}} \; \frac{C_T C_1 B_{y_1 d}}{(C_0 + k C_1)^2}. \qquad (7.11)$$

Simplifying,

$$(1 - r_{y_1 y_1}) \; (C_0 + k C_1) - 2k C_1 [1 + (k - 1)r_{y_1 y_1}] = 0 \qquad (7.12)$$

$$k = \frac{1 - r_{y_1 y_1}}{4 r_{y_1 y_1}} \left[-1 + \sqrt{1 + 8 \frac{C_0 r_{y_1 y_1}}{C_1 (1 - r_{y_1 y_1})}} \right]. \qquad (7.13)$$

This value of k yields maximum utility. The second root of equation 7.13 is ignored because it yields a negative value of k, which has no practical meaning. The optimum v is determined by substitution in equation 7.9.

ADAPTIVE TREATMENT

A similar analysis for adaptive placement leads to a simpler solution. The equation analogous to equation 7.4 is, from equation 5.13,

$$\sum_1^v \Delta U_d = \sum_1^v B_{y_1 d} \left[\frac{r_{y_k y_k d}}{r_{y_1 y_1 d}} \right] - \sum_1^v (C_{0d} + k_d C_1). \qquad (7.14)$$

The method of Lagrange leads to v equations of this form:

$$B_{y_1 d} \frac{(1 - r_{y_1 y_1 d})}{[1 + (k - 1)r_{y_1 y_1 d}]^2} - C_1 + \lambda C_1 = 0. \qquad (7.15)$$

Letting $\mu = \dfrac{1}{1 - \lambda}$, we find that

$$k_d = 1 - \frac{1}{r_{y_1 y_1 d}} + \frac{\mu}{r_{y_1 y_1 d}} \sqrt{\frac{B_{y_1 d}(1 - r_{y_1 y_1 d})}{C_1}}. \qquad (7.16)$$

These equations can be solved for d for any set of tests. If we let

$$D_{y_1 d} = \frac{1}{r_{y_1 y_1 d}} \sqrt{\frac{B_{y_1 d}(1 - r_{y_1 y_1 d})}{C_1}} \qquad (7.17)$$

and recall that $\Sigma k_d = K$ is a constant determined by test costs, we find that

$$k_d = 1 - \frac{1}{r_{y_1 y_1 d}} + \mu D_{y_1 d} \tag{7.18}$$

and

$$\Sigma k_d = K = v - \sum_1^v \frac{1}{r_{y_1 y_1 d}} + \sum_1^v \mu D_{y_1 d}. \tag{7.19}$$

Therefore

$$\mu = \frac{1}{\sum_1^v D_{y_1 d}} \left[\sum_1^v \frac{1}{r_{y_1 y_1 d}} - v + K \right]. \tag{7.20}$$

Denoting any particular d by d',

$$k_{d'} = 1 - \frac{1}{r_{y_1 y_1 d'}} + \frac{D_{y_1 d'}}{\sum_1^v D_{y_1 d}} \left[\sum_1^v \frac{1}{r_{y_1 y_1 d}} - v + K \right]. \tag{7.21}$$

There is one such equation for each of the tests.

These equations may be used to compute the optimum distribution of effort. With w decisions, there are many possible subsets of tests. These equations give a distribution of effort for any set, but do not indicate directly which set is best. Various possible subsets may be compared by calculating $\Sigma \Delta U_d$ after lengths are optimally adjusted, to determine which test is most profitable.

Special Cases

If all decisions are uniform, from equation 7.14

$$\Sigma \Delta U_d = v B_{yd} \frac{r_{y_k y_k}}{r_{y_1 y_1}} - C_T. \tag{7.22}$$

Substituting for v and $r_{y_k y_k}$, and differentiating,

$$\frac{\partial \Sigma \Delta U_k}{\partial k} = \left[\frac{C_T}{C_0 + k C_1} \right] \frac{B_{y_1 d}(1 - r_{y_1 y_1})}{[1 + (k - 1) r_{y_1 y_1}]^2}$$
$$- \frac{k B_{y_1 d}(C_T C_1)}{[1 + (k - 1) r_{y_1 y_1}][C_0 + k C_1]^2} = 0 \tag{7.23}$$

$$\frac{1 - r_{y_1 y_1}}{1 + (k - 1) r_{y_1 y_1}} - \frac{k C_1}{C_0 + k C_1} = 0 \tag{7.24}$$

$$k = \sqrt{\frac{C_0(1 - r_{y_1 y_1})}{C_1 r_{y_1 y_1}}}. \tag{7.25}$$

This is the optimum length for each test in uniform adaptive placement decisions.

REFERENCE INDEX

Ackoff, R. L., ed. (1961). *Progress in operations research*. Vol. I. New York: Wiley. **151.**

Adams, E. W. (1960). A survey of Bernoullian utilities and applications. In H. Solomon, ed., *Mathematical thinking in the measurement of behavior*. Glencoe, Ill.: Free Press. Pp. 151-268. **6, 10, 122, 159.**

Anderson, G. L. (1949). Quantitative thinking as developed under connectionist and field theories of learning. In Esther J. Swenson *et al.*, *Learning theory in school situations*. Minneapolis: Univ. of Minn. Press. Pp. 40-73. **25.**

Anscombe, F. J. (1961). Bayesian statistics. *Amer. Statistician*, 15, 21-24. **154.**

Arbous, A. G. (1952). Tables for aptitude testers. Goldfields, Union of So. Africa: Nat. Inst. for Personnel Res. **294.**

Arbous, A. G., and Sichel, H. S. (1952). On the economies of a prescreening technique for aptitude test batteries. *Psychometrika*, 17, 331-346. **70, 74-75, 82-83, 294.**

Arnoff, E. L., and Sengupta, S. F. (1961). Mathematical programming. In R. L. Ackoff, ed., *Progress in operations research*. Vol. I. New York: Wiley. Pp. 105-210. **162.**

Arrow, K. J. (1958). Utilities, aptitudes, choices: a review note. *Econometrica*, 26, 1-23. **159.**

——— (1963). *Social choice and individual values*. New York: Wiley. **3, 122-123, 159.**

Aumann, R. J., and Kruskal, J. B. (1959). Assigning quantitative values to qualitative factors in the naval electronics problem. *Nav. Res. Log. Q.*, 6, 1-16. **164.**

Bechhofer, R. E. (1958). A sequential multiple-decision procedure for selecting the best one of several normal populations with a common unknown variance, and its use with various experimental designs. *Biometrics*, 14, 408-429. **169.**

Bechhofer, R. E., *et al.* Sequential ranking procedures with special reference to Koopman-Darmois populations. Monograph in preparation. **169.**

Becker, S. W., and Siegel, S. (1958). Utility of grades: level of aspiration in a decision theory context. *J. exper. Psychol.*, 55, 81-85. **159.**

Bellman, R. (1957). *Dynamic programming*. Princeton: Princeton Univ. Press. **168.**

Bennett, G. K., and Doppelt, J. E. (1948). The evaluation of pairs of tests for guidance use. *Educ. psychol. Measmt.*, 8, 319-325. **292.**

Berkson, J. (1947). "Cost-utility" as a measure of the efficiency of a test. *J. Amer. Stat. Assn.*, 42, 246-255. **52, 75.**

Birnbaum, A. (1957). Efficient design and use of tests of mental ability for various decision-making problems. Randolph AFB, Texas: School of Aviation Medicine. **171.**

Birnbaum, A., and Maxwell, A. E. (1960). Classification procedures based on Bayes's formula. *Appl. Stat.*, 9, 152-169. **165, 234-253.**

Blackwell, D., and Girshick, M. A. (1954). *Theory of games and statistical decisions.* New York: Wiley. **6.**

Blau, P. M., *et al.* (1956). Occupational choice: a conceptual framework. *Indust. and Lab. Rel. Rev.*, 9, 531-543. **159.**

Bloom, B. S. (1942). Test reliability for what? *J. educ. Psychol.*, 33, 517-526. **64, 291.**

Blumberg, M. S. (1957). Evaluating health screening procedures. *Oper. Res.*, 5, 351-360. **158.**

Bordin, E. S., and Bixler, R. H. (1946). Test selection: a process of counseling. *Educ. psychol. Measmt.*, 6, 361-373. **131-132.**

Box, G. E. P. (1954). The exploration and exploitation of response surfaces: some general considerations and examples. *Biometrics*, 10, 16-60. **26-27.**

―――― (1957). Evolutionary operationism: a method for increasing industrial productivity. *Appl. Stat.*, 6, 81-101. **181.**

Brogden, H. E. (1946). On the interpretation of the correlation coefficient as a measure of predictive efficiency. *J. educ. Psychol.*, 37, 65-76. **29, 32, 37, 39, 50, 67, 307.**

―――― (1949a). When testing pays off. *Personnel Psychol.*, 2, 171-185. **37, 39, 255.**

―――― (1949b). A new coefficient: application to biserial correlation and to estimation of selective efficiency. *Psychometrika*, 14, 169-182. **33, 39, 278, 307.**

―――― (1951). Increased efficiency of selection resulting from replacement of a single predictor with several differential predictors. *Educ. psychol. Measmt.*, 11, 173-196. **57, 111-113, 141.**

―――― (1959). Efficiency of classification as a function of number of jobs, per cent rejected, and the validity and intercorrelation of job performance estimates. *Educ. psychol. Measmt.*, 19, 181-190. **163.**

Brogden, H. E., and Taylor, E. K. (1950). The dollar criterion ― applying the cost accounting concept to criterion construction. *Personnel Psychol.*, 3, 133-154. **33, 125, 155, 158, 255-256.**

Bross, I. D. J. (1953). *Design for decision.* New York: Macmillan. **6.**

Brown, C. W., and Ghiselli, E. E. (1953). Per cent increase in proficiency resulting from use of selective devices. *J. appl. Psychol.*, 37, 341-345. **32.**

Burt, C. (1961). The gifted child. *Brit. J. stat. Psychol.*, 14, 123-139. **183.**

―――― (1962). Psychological evidence. *Times educ. Suppl.*, Jan. 26, p. 462. **207.**

Cardinet, J. (1959). The use of profiles in differential classification. *Educ. psychol. Measmt.*, 19, 191-205. **110-111, 129.**

Carroll, J. B. (1962). The prediction of success in intensive foreign langauge training. In R. Glaser, ed., *Training research and education.* Pittsburgh: Univ. of Pittsburgh Press. 177.

Chernoff, H. (1953). Locally optimal designs for estimating parameters. *Ann. math. Stat.,* 24, 586-602. 100.

———— (1959). Sequential design of experiments. *Ann. math. Stat.,* 30, 755-770. 169.

———— (1960a). Sequential tests for the mean of a normal distribution. In J. Neyman, ed., *Fourth Berkeley symposium on mathematical statistics and probability.* Vol. I. Berkeley: Univ. of Calif. Press. Pp. 79-91. 169, 170.

———— (1960b). Motivation for an approach to the sequential design of experiments. In R. E. Machol, ed., *Information and decision processes.* New York: McGraw-Hill. Pp. 15-33. 169-170.

———— (1961). Sequential experimentation. *Bull. Int. Stat. Inst.,* 38, 3-9. 169.

Chernoff, H., and Moses, L. E. (1959). *Elementary decision theory.* New York: Wiley. 150, 154.

Christal, R. E. (1963). JAN: a technique for analyzing group judgment. *Tech. Doc. Rep.* 63-3. Lackland AFB, Texas: 6570th Personnel Res. Lab. 269.

Churchman, C. W. (1961). *Prediction and optimal decision; philosophical issues in a science of values.* Englewood Cliffs, N.J.: Prentice-Hall. 151, 160.

Churchman, C. W., and Ackoff, R. L. (1954). An approximate measure of value. *J. Oper. Res. Soc. Amer.,* 2, 172-187. 129.

Cochran, W. G. (1951). Improvement by means of selection. In J. Neyman, ed., *Second Berkeley symposium on mathematical statistics and probability.* Berkeley: Univ. of Calif. Press. Pp. 449-470. 29, 32, 70, 74, 83, 307.

Conrad, H. (1950). Information which should be provided by test publishers and testing agencies on the validity and use of their tests. *Proceedings, 1949 Invitational Conference on Testing Problems.* Princeton: Educ. Testing Service. Pp. 63-68. 35.

Coombs, C. H. (1953). Theory and methods of social measurement. In L. Festinger and D. Katz, eds., *Research methods in the behavioral sciences.* New York: Dryden. Pp. 471-563. 10, 129.

Cronbach, L. J. (1953). *A consideration of information theory and utility theory as tools for psychometric problems.* Urbana: Coll. of Educ., Univ. of Ill. [Mimeo.] [Out of print.] 100, 127, 139.

———— (1955). Processes affecting scores on "understanding of others" and "assumed similarity." *Psychol. Bull.,* 52, 177-193. 21, 62.

———— (1956). On the non-rational application of information measure in psychology. In H. Quastler, ed., *Information theory in psychology.* Glencoe, Ill.: Free Press. Pp. 14-30. 100.

———— (1957). The two disciplines of scientific psychology. *Amer. Psychologist,* 12, 671-684. 177.

Cronbach, L. J., and Gleser, Goldine C. (1957). *Psychological tests and personnel decisions.* Urbana: Univ. of Ill. Press. 224, 237, 254, 273-276.

Cronbach, L. J., and Gleser, Goldine C. (1959). Interpretation of reliability and validity coefficients. *J. educ. Psychol.*, 50, 230-237. **151, 291-303.**

Cronbach, L. J., Rajaratnam, Nageswari, and Gleser, Goldine C. (1963). Theory of generalizability: a liberalization of reliability theory. *Brit. J. stat. Psychol.*, 16, 137-163. **152-153.**

Davies, O. L. (1958). The design of screening tests in the pharmaceutical industry. *Bull. Int. Stat. Inst.*, 36, 226-241. **166.**

——— (1962). Some statistical considerations in the selection of research projects in the pharmaceutical industry. *Appl. Stat.*, 11, 170-183. **158.**

Dear, R. E., and Atkinson, R. C. (1962). Optimal allocation of items in a single, two-concept automated teaching model. In J. E. Coulson, ed., *Programmed learning and computer-based instruction.* New York: Wiley. Pp. 25-45. **174.**

Doppelt, J. E. and Bennett, G. K. (1953). Reducing the cost of training satisfactory workers by using tests. *Personnel Psychol.*, 6, 1-9. **123.**

Dreyfus, F. (1961). Dynamic programming. In R. L. Ackoff, ed., *Progress in operations research*. Vol. I. New York: Wiley. Pp. 211-242. **168.**

Duncan, O. D., *et. al.* (1953). Formal devices for making selection decisions. *Amer. J. Sociol.*, 58, 573-585. **52.**

Dunnett, C. W. (1960). On selecting the largest of *k* normal population means. *J. Roy. Stat. Soc.*, ser. B, 22, 1-40. **191.**

——— (1961). Statistical theory of drug screening. In H. de Jonge, ed., *Quantitative methods in pharmacology*. Amsterdam: North Holland. Pp. 212-231. **166.**

Dwyer, P. S. (1953). *Selection and linear combination of tests in relation to multiple criteria and differential classification*. Washington, D.C.: Dept. of the Army, PRB Res. Note 7. **108, 129.**

Educational Testing Service (1955). Examiner's Manual, Cooperative School and College Ability Tests. Princeton: Educ. Testing Service. Pp. 30-35. **291 ff.**

Edwards, W. (1954). The theory of decision making. *Psychol. Bull.*, 51, 380-418. **6, 128.**

——— (1961). Behavioral decision theory. *Annu. Rev. Psychol.*, 12, 473-498. **159.**

Edwards, W., *et al.* (1963). Bayesian statistical inference for psychological research. *Psychol. Rev.*, 70, 193-242. **153.**

Elfving, G. (1952). Optimum allocation in linear regression. *Ann. math. Stat.*, 23, 255-263. **100.**

Elston, R. C. (1963). A weight-free index for the purpose of ranking or selection with respect to several traits at a time. *Biometrics*, 19, 85-97. **161.**

Evans, R. N. (1953). *A suggested use of sequential analysis in performance acceptance testing*. Urbana: Coll. of Educ., Univ. of Ill. [Mimeo.] **70.**

Federer, W. T. (1964). Procedures and designs useful for screening material in selection and allocation with a bibliography. *Biometrics.* [In press.] **166.**

Ferguson, G. A. (1949). On the theory of test discrimination. *Psychometrika*, 14, 61-68. **138, 276.**

Finch, G., ed. (1960). *Symposium on air force human engineering, personnel, and training research.* Washington, D.C.: NAS-NRC Publ. No. 783. **165.**

Finney, D. J. (1956). The consequences of selection for a variate subject to errors of measurement. *Rev. Int. Stat. Inst.,* 24, 1-10. **187, 188.**

―――― (1958). Statistical problems of plant selection. *Bull. Int. Stat. Inst.,* 36, 242-268. **188.**

―――― (1960). A simple example of the external economy of varietal selection. *Bull. Int. Stat. Inst.,* 37, 91-106. **166, 207.**

―――― (1961). The transformation of a variate under selection. *Sankhyā,* ser. A, 23, 309-324. **191-201.**

―――― (1962a). Cumulants of truncated multinormal distributions. *J. Roy. Stat. Soc.,* ser. B, 24, 535-536. **188.**

―――― (1962b). Genetic gains under three methods of selection. *Genet. Res.,* 3, 56-62. **229.**

―――― (1962c). The statistical evaluation of educational allocation and selection. *J. Roy. Stat. Soc.,* ser. A, 125, 525-564. **166-167, 182-233.**

Fisher, R. A. (1956). *Statistical methods and scientific inference.* New York: Hafner. **154.**

Fiske, D. W., and Jones, L. V. (1954). Sequential analysis in psychological research. *Psychol. Bull.,* 51, 264-276. **71.**

Flood, M. M. (1956). The traveling-salesman problem. *Oper. Res.,* 4, 61-75. **162.**

Frederiksen, N., and Melville, D. F. (1954). Differential predictability in the use of test scores. *Educ. psychol. Measmt.,* 14, 647-656. **175-176.**

Freeman, H. A., *et al.,* eds. (1948). *Sampling inspection.* New York: McGraw-Hill. **75, 326.**

Friedman, L. F., and Yaspen, A. J. (1957). An analysis of stewardess requirements and scheduling for a major domestic airline — Annex A. The assignment problem technique. *Nav. Res. Log. Q.,* 4, 193-197. **162.**

Gaylord, R. H., *et al.* (1951). The relation of ratings to production records: an empirical study. *Personnel Psychol.,* 4, 363-372. **263.**

Ghiselli, E. E. (1960). Differentiation of tests in terms of the accuracy with which they predict for a given individual. *Educ. psychol. Measmt.,* 20, 675-684. **176-177.**

Girshick, M. A. (1954). An elementary survey of statistical decision theory. *Rev. educ. Res.,* 24, 448-466. **2, 5-6, 19, 69.**

Goodman, L. A. (1953). The use and validity of a prediction instrument. *Amer. J. Sociol.,* 58, 503-508, 510-513. **124.**

Greenberger, M. H., and Ward, J. H., Jr. (1956). An iterative technique for multiple correlation analysis. *IBM tech. News Letter,* 12, 85-97. **269.**

Gulliksen, H. (1950). *Theory of mental tests.* New York: Wiley. **17, 135.**

Gupta, S. S., and Sobel, M. (1958). On selecting a subset which contains all populations better than a standard. *Ann. math. Stat.,* 29, 235-244. **168.**

Häkkinen, S. (1958). Traffic accidents and driver characteristics. Dissertation, Univ. of Helsinki. **286-287.**

Harding, F. D., Jr., and McWilliams, J. T., Jr. (1957). Language aptitude tests as predictors of success in a six-month Russian course. *Tech. Note* 57-86. Lackland AFB, Texas: Air Force Personnel and Training Res. Command. **157-158.**

Heermann, E. F. (1963). Univocal or orthogonal estimators of orthogonal factors. *Psychometrika*, 28, 161-172. **180.**

Horst, P. (1949). Determination of optimal test length to maximize the multiple correlation. *Psychometrika*, 14, 79-88. **89.**

——— (1954). A technique for the development of a differential prediction battery. *Psychol. Monogr.*, 68, no. 9. **4, 109.**

——— (1956). Optimal test length for maximum differential prediction. *Psychometrika*, 21, 51-67. **109, 116, 118-119.**

——— (1960). Optimal estimates of multiple criteria with restrictions on the covariance matrix of estimated criteria. *Psychol. Reports Monogr. Suppl.*, 6, 427-444. **162.**

Horst, P., and MacEwan, Charlotte (1956). Optimal test length for maximum absolute prediction. *Psychometrika*, 21, 111-125. **101-102, 105, 117-118.**

——— (1957). Optimal test length for multiple prediction: the general case. *Psychometrika*, 22, 311-324. **117.**

Hull, C. L. (1928). *Aptitude testing.* Yonkers: World Book. **1, 31, 86-87, 136.**

Jackson, J. E. (1960). Bibliography on sequential analysis. *J. Amer. Stat. Assn.*, 55, 561-580. **168.**

Jarrett, R. F. (1948). Per cent increase in output of selected personnel as an index of test efficiency. *J. appl. Psychol.*, 32, 135-146. **32, 34, 274.**

Johns, M. V. (1961). An empirical Bayes approach to non-parametric two-way classification. In H. Solomon, ed., *Studies in item analysis and prediction.* Stanford, Calif.: Stanford Univ. Press. Pp. 221-232. **161.**

Johnson, C. D. (1960). The population control or moderator variable in personnel research. *Tri-Service Conference on Selection Research.* Washington, D.C.: Office of Nav. Res., 1960. Report ACR-60. Pp. 125-134. **176.**

Johnson, N. L. (1961). Sequential analysis: a survey. *J. Roy. Stat. Soc.*, ser. A, 124, 372-411. **168.**

Kao, R. C., and Rowan, T. C. (1959). A model for personnel recruiting and selection. *Management Sci.*, 5, 192-203. **167.**

Keith Smith, J. E. (1961). Stimulus programming in psychophysics. *Psychometrika*, 26, 27-33. **173.**

Kelley, T. L. (1923a). *Statistical method.* New York: Macmillan. **31, 135.**

——— (1923b). A new method for determining the significance of differences in intelligence and achievement scores. *J. educ. Psychol.*, 14, 321-333. **292.**

Kempthorne, O., and Nordskog, A. W. (1959). Restricted selection indices. *Biometrics*, 15, 10-19. **161.**

Knetz, W. J. (1963). *Operational analyses of the Naval Personnel System: Part III. Development of the Enlisted Personnel Simulation System.* Washington, D.C.: Amer. Inst. for Res. **165.**

Koopman, B. O. (1953). The optimum distribution of effort. *J. Oper. Res. Soc. Amer.*, 1, 52-63. **105-106.**

Kossack, C. F., and Beckwith, R. E. (1959). The mathematics of personnel utilization models. *Tech. Rep.* 59-359. Lackland AFB, Texas: Personnel Lab. **165.**

Kuhn, H. W. (1955). The Hungarian method for the assignment problem. *Nav. Res. Log. Q.*, 2, 83-97. **162.**

Lawrence, D. H. (1954). The evaluation of training and transfer programs in terms of efficiency measures. *J. Psychol.*, 38, 367-382. **174-175.**

Lindley, D. V. (1953). Statistical inference. *J. Roy. Stat. Soc.*, ser. B, 15, 30-76. **240, 245.**

——— (1961). Dynamic programming and decision theory. *Appl. Stat.*, 10, 39-51. **151, 168.**

Loevinger, Jane (1947). A systematic approach to the construction and evaluation of tests of ability. *Psychol. Monogr.*, 61, 4. **138, 278.**

Loevinger, Jane, *et al.* (1953). Maximizing the discriminating power of a multiple-score test. *Psychometrika*, 18, 309-317. **99.**

Long, J. A. (1934). Improved overlapping methods for determining the validities of test items. *J. exper. Educ.*, 2, 264-268. **278-279.**

Long, W. F., and Burr, I. W. (1949). Development of a method for increasing the utility of multiple correlations by considering both testing time and test validity. *Psychometrika*, 14, 137-161. **89.**

Lord, F. M. (1955). Some perspectives on "the attenuation paradox in test theory." *Psychol. Bull.*, 52, 505-511. **96, 138.**

——— (1958). The utilization of unreliable difference scores. *J. educ. Psychol.*, 49, 150-152. **152, 291-303.**

——— (1962). Review of H. Solomon, ed., *Studies in item analysis and prediction. Psychometrika*, 27, 207-213. **171.**

Lubin, A. (1961). The interpretation of significant interaction. *Educ. psychol. Measmt.*, 21, 807-818. **177-178.**

Luce, R. D., and Raiffa, H. (1957). *Games and decisions.* New York: Wiley. **240.**

McDaniel, E. D., *et al.* (1961). Grade utility: a new non-cognitive factor in academic prediction. *Educ. psychol. Measmt.*, 21, 621-628. **159.**

Madden, J. M. (1963). An application to job evaluation of a policy capturing model for analyzing individual and group judgment. *Tech. Doc. Rep.* 63-15. Lackland AFB, Texas: 6570th Personnel Res. Lab. **268-269.**

Magwire, C. A. (1953). Sequential decisions involving the choice of experiments. Stanford, Calif.: Stanford Univ. Unpublished technical report. **108, 119-120.**

Mannheim, H., and Wilkins, L. T. (1955). *Prediction methods in relation to Borstal training.* London: H.M.S.O. **158.**

Maxwell, A. E. (1957). Contour analysis. *Educ. psychol. Measmt.*, 17, 347-360. **181.**

Meehl, P. E. (1954). *Clinical versus statistical prediction.* Minneapolis: Univ. of Minn. Press. **21, 148.**

Mendenhall, G. V. (1959). Analysis of differences between language and non-language IQ's of the California Test of Mental Maturity. Hollywood: Calif. Test Bureau. [Mimeo.] **292, 297-298.**

Meyer, D. L. (1963). Response surface methodology in education and psychology. *J. exper. Educ.*, 31, 329-336. **181.**

Myers, J. H., and Forgy, E. W. (1963). The development of numerical credit evaluation systems. *J. Amer. Stat. Assn.*, 58, 799-804. **155.**

Nisbet, J., and Buchan, J. (1959). The long-term follow-up of assessments at age eleven. *Brit. J. educ. Psychol.*, 29, 1-8. **192-193.**

Osburn, H. G., and Melton, R. F. (1963). Prediction of proficiency in a modern and traditional course in beginning algebra. *Educ. psychol. Measmt.*, 23, 277-288. **178-180.**

Overall, J. E., and Williams, C. M. (1961). Models for medical diagnosis. *Behavioral Sci.*, 6, 134-141. **165.**

Paterson, J. J. (1962). An evaluation of the sequential method of psychological testing. Unpublished doctoral dissertation, Michigan State Univ. **171-173.**

Paulson, E. (1963). A sequential decision procedure for choosing one of k hypotheses concerning the unknown mean of a normal distribution. *Ann. math. Stat.*, 34, 549-554. **168.**

Pearson, E. S. (1962). Some thoughts on statistical inference. *Ann. math. Stat.*, 33, 394-403. **153-154.**

Pearson, K. (1931). *Tables for statisticians and biometricians.* Part II. Cambridge: Cambridge Univ. Press. **187.**

Petch, J. A. (1961). G.C.E. and Degree, Part I. Northern Universities Joint Matriculation Board, O.P. No. 10. **216.**

Raiffa, H. (1961). Statistical decision theory approach to item selection for dichotomous test and criterion variables. In H. Solomon, ed., *Studies in item analysis and prediction.* Stanford, Calif.: Stanford Univ. Press. Pp. 187-220. **170-171.**

Raines, G. N., *et al.* (1954). Psychiatric selection for military service. *J. Amer. Med. Assn.*, 156, 817-821. **123-124.**

Rao, C. R. (1962). Problems of selection with restrictions. *J. Roy. Stat. Soc.*, ser. B, 24, 401-405. **161.**

Restle, F. (1961). *The psychology of judgment and choice.* New York: Wiley. **159.**

—— (1964). The relevance of mathematical models for education. In E. R. Hilgard, ed. *Theories of learning and instruction.* Chicago: Univ. of Chicago Press. Pp. 111-132. **174.**

Richardson, M. W. (1944). The interpretation of a test validity coefficient in terms of increased efficiency of a selected group of personnel. *Psychometrika*, 9, 245-248. **29, 32-33.**

Riley, Vera, and Gass, S. I. (1958). *Linear programming and associated techniques: a comprehensive bibliography on linear, nonlinear and dynamic programming.* Baltimore: Johns Hopkins Press. **162, 168.**

Robbins, H. (1960). A statistical screening problem. In I. Olkin *et al.*, eds. *Contributions to probability and statistics.* Stanford, Calif.: Stanford Univ. Press. Pp. 352-357. **154.**

Roche, W. F. (1961). The Cronbach-and-Gleser utility function in fixed-treatment employee selection. Unpublished doctoral dissertation, Southern Ill. Univ. **155, 157, 254-267.**

Roe, A. (1963). *An adaptive decision structure for educational systems.* Los Angeles: Univ. of Calif., Dept. of Engineering. **179.**

Sarbin, T. R. (1942). A contribution to the study of actuarial and individual methods of prediction. *Amer. J. Sociol.*, 48, 593-602. **127.**

Saunders, D. R. (1956). Moderator variables in prediction. *Educ. psychol. Measmt.*, 16, 209-222. **175.**

Savage, L. J. (1961). The foundations of statistics reconsidered. In J. Neyman, ed., *Fourth Berkeley symposium on mathematical statistics and probability.* Vol. I. Berkeley: Univ. of Calif. Press. Pp. 575-586. **153.**

Sechrest, L. (1963). Incremental validity: a recommendation. *Educ. psychol. Measmt.*, 23, 153-158. **154.**

Shannon, C. E., and Weaver, W. (1949). *The mathematical theory of communication.* Urbana: Univ. of Ill. Press. **100.**

Siegel, S. (1959). Theoretical models of choice and strategy behavior. *Psychometrika*, 24, 303-316. **9.**

Simpson, M. G. (1961). An introduction to dynamic programming. *Appl. Stat.*, 10, 32-38. **168.**

Sitgreaves, Rosedith (1961a). Optimal test design in a special testing situation. In H. Solomon, ed., *Studies in item analysis and prediction.* Stanford, Calif.: Stanford Univ. Press. Pp. 29-45. **171.**

———— (1961b). Further contributions to the theory of test design. In H. Solomon, ed., *Studies in item analysis and prediction.* Stanford, Calif.: Stanford Univ. Press. Pp. 46-63. **171.**

Smallwood, R. D. (1962). *A decision structure for teaching machines.* Cambridge: M.I.T. Press. **174.**

Smith, J. W. (1956). A plan to allocate and procure electronic sets by the use of linear programming techniques and analytical methods of assigning values to qualitative factors. *Nav. Res. Log. Q.*, 3, 151-162. **164.**

Smith, N. M., Jr. (1961). Review of C. W. Churchman, *Prediction and optimal decision. J. Amer. Stat. Ass'n.*, 56, 1013-15. **160.**

Smith, N. M., Jr., *et al.* (1953). The theory of value and the science of decision, a summary. *J. Oper. Res. Soc. Amer.*, 1, 103-113. **122, 128.**

Sobel, M., and Wald, A. (1949). A sequential decision procedure for choosing one of three hypotheses concerning the unknown mean of a normal distribution. *Ann. math. Stat.*, 20, 502-522. **94, 168.**

Somerville, P. N. (1954). Some problems of optimum sampling. *Biometrika*, 41, 420-429. **95, 169.**

Stanley, J. C. (1960). Interaction of organisms with experimental variables as a key to the integration of organismic and variable-manipulating research. In Edith M. Huddleston, ed. *Yearb. Nat. Council Measmt. Used in Educ.* Pp. 7-13. **177.**

Statistical Research Group, Columbia University (1945). *Sequential analysis of statistical data: applications.* New York: Columbia Univ. Press. **75, 91, 326.**

Stein, C., and Wald, A. (1947). Sequential confidence intervals for the mean of a normal distribution with known variance. *Ann math. Stat.*, 18, 427-433. **94.**

Stoller, D. S. (1954). Univariate two-population distribution free discrimination. *J. Amer. Stat. Assn.*, 49, 770-777. **247.**

Tallis, G. M. (1961). The moment generating function of the truncated multi-normal distribution. *J. Roy. Stat. Soc.*, ser. B, 23, 223-229. **188, 203.**

Taylor, C. W. (1950). Maximizing predictive efficiency for a fixed total testing time. *Psychometrika*, 15, 391-406. **89.**

Taylor, H. C., and Russell, J. T. (1939). The relationship of validity coefficients to the practical effectiveness of tests in selection. *J. appl. Psychol.*, 23, 565-578. **31, 34, 50-51, 53, 67-68, 75, 124, 287, 291.**

Thrall, R. M., *et al.*, eds. (1954). *Decision processes.* New York: Wiley. **12.**

Thurstone, L. L. (1931). *Reliability and validity of tests.* Ann Arbor, Mich.: Edwards. **31.**

Trouton, D. A., and Maxwell, A. E. (1956). The relation between neurosis and psychosis. *J. ment. Sci.*, 102, 1-21. **247.**

Tukey, J. W. (1960). Conclusions vs decisions. *Technometrics*, 2, 423-433. **154-155.**

van Dantzig, D., and Kriens, J. (1960). Het economisch beslissingsprobleem inzake de beveiliging van Nederland tegen stormvloeden. *Report of the Delta commission.* II, 2, Part 3. **285.**

van Naerssen, R. F. (1963). *Selectie van chauffeurs.* Groningen: Wolters. **155, 157, 160-161, 273-290.**

von Neumann, J., and Morgenstern, O. (1947). *Theory of games and economic behavior.* Princeton: Princeton Univ. Press. **3, 11.**

Votaw, D. F., Jr. (1958). Solution of the quota problem by a successive reduction method. *Oper. Res.*, 6, 56-64. (See also pp. 874-876.) **162.**

Votaw, D. F., Jr., and Dailey, J. T. (1952). Assignment of personnel to jobs. *Res. Bull.* 52-24. Lackland AFB, Texas: Human Resources Res. Center. **129.**

Wagner, H. (1962). Review of R. L. Ackoff, ed., *Progress in operations research.* Vol. I. *J. Amer. Stat. Assn.*, 57, 257-261. **151.**

Wald, A. (1950). *Statistical decision functions.* New York: Wiley. **3, 11-12, 91, 120, 240.**

Ward, J. H., Jr. (1958). The counseling assignment problem. *Psychometrika*, 23, 55-65. **162.**

——— (1959). Use of a Decision Index in assigning Air Force personnel. *Tech. Note* 59-38. Lackland AFB, Texas: Personnel Lab. **269, 270.**

——— (1962a). Multiple linear regression models. In H. Borko, ed., *Computer applications in the behavioral sciences.* Englewood Cliffs, N.J.: Prentice-Hall. Pp. 204-237. **269.**

——— (1962b). Comments on "The paramorphic representation of clinical judgment." *Psychol. Bull.*, 59, 74-76. **180.**

Ward, J. H., Jr., and Davis, Kathleen (1963). Teaching a digital computer to assist in making decisions. *Tech. Doc. Rep.* Lackland AFB, Texas: 6570th Personnel Res. Lab. **160, 164, 268-272.**

Wesman, A. G. (1953). Better than chance. *Test Service Bull.*, 45, 1-5. **32, 67.**

Wesman, A. G., and Bennett, G. K. (1951). Problems of differential prediction. *Educ. psychol. Measmt.*, 11, 265-273. **57, 114.**

Wickert, F. R. (1962). Some implications of decision theory for occupational selection in West Africa. In A. Taylor, ed., *Educational and occupational selection in West Africa*. London: Oxford Univ. Press. Pp. 127-138. **150**.

Wolfowitz, J. (1950). Minimax estimates of the mean of a normal distribution with known variance. *Ann. math. Stat.*, 21, 218-230. **94**.

Young, S. S. Y. (1961). A further examination of the relative efficiency of three methods of selection for genetic gains under less-restricted conditions. *Genet. Res.*, 2, 106-121. **229**.

Young, S. S. Y., and Weiler, H. (1960). Selection for two correlated traits by independent culling levels. *J. Genet.*, 57, 329-358. **203**.

Ziller, R. C. (1957). Vocational choice and utility for risk. *J. counsel. Psychol.*, 4, 61-64. **160**.

ILLINI BOOKS

B-1	Grierson's Raid: A Cavalry Adventure of the Civil War	D. Alexander Brown	$1.75
B-2	The Mars Project	Wernher von Braun	$ .95
B-3	The New Exploration: A Philosophy of Regional Planning	Benton MacKaye, with an introduction by Lewis Mumford	$1.75
B-4	Tragicomedy: Its Origin and Development in Italy, France, and England	Marvin T. Herrick	$1.95
B-5	Themes in Greek and Latin Epitaphs	Richmond Lattimore	$1.95
B-6	The Doctrine of Responsible Party Government: Its Origins and Present State	Austin Ranney	$1.25
IB-7	An Alternative to War or Surrender	Charles E. Osgood	$1.45
IB-8	Reference Books in the Mass Media	Eleanor Blum	$1.50
IB-9	Life in a Mexican Village: Tepoztlán Restudied	Oscar Lewis	$2.95
IB-10	*Three Presidents and Their Books: The Reading of Jefferson, Lincoln, and Franklin D. Roosevelt	Arthur E. Bestor, David C. Mearns, and Jonathan Daniels	$ .95
IB-11	Cultural Sciences: Their Origin and Development	Florian Znaniecki	$2.25
IB-12	The Legend of Noah: Renaissance Rationalism in Art, Science, and Letters	Don Cameron Allen	$1.45
IB-13	*The Mathematical Theory of Communication	Claude E. Shannon and Warren Weaver	$ .95
IB-14	Philosophy and Ordinary Language	Charles E. Caton, ed.	$1.95
IB-15	Four Theories of the Press	Fred S. Siebert, Theodore Peterson, and Wilbur Schramm	$1.25
IB-16	Constitutional Problems Under Lincoln	James G. Randall	$2.95
IB-17	Viva Mexico!	Charles Macomb Flandrau, edited and with an introduction by C. Harvey Gardiner	$1.95
IB-18	Comic Theory in the Sixteenth Century	Marvin T. Herrick	$1.75

Also available in clothbound editions.

IB-19	Black Hawk: An Autobiography	Donald Jackson, ed.	$1.75
IB-20	Mexican Government in Transition	Robert E. Scott	$2.25
IB-21	John Locke and the Doctrine of Majority-Rule	Willmoore Kendall	$1.25
IB-22	The Framing of the Fourteenth Amendment	Joseph B. James	$1.45
IB-23	The Mind and Spirit of John Peter Altgeld: Selected Writings and Addresses	Henry M. Christman, ed.	$1.25
IB-24	A History of the United States Weather Bureau	Donald R. Whitnah	$1.75
IB-25	Freedom of the Press in England, 1476-1776: The Rise and Decline of Government Controls	Fredrick Seaton Siebert	$2.25
IB-26	Freedom and Communications	Dan Lacy	$1.50
IB-27	The Early Development of Henry James	Cornelia Pulsifer Kelley, with an introduction by Lyon N. Richardson	$1.95
IB-28	*Law in the Soviet Society	Wayne R. LaFave, ed.	$1.95
IB-29	Beyond the Mountains of the Moon: The Lives of Four Africans	Edward H. Winter	$1.75
IB-30	The History of Doctor Johann Faustus	H. G. Haile	$1.45
IB-31	One World	Wendell L. Willkie, with an introduction by Donald Bruce Johnson	$1.75
IB-32	William Makepeace Thackeray: Contributions to the Morning Chronicle	Gordon N. Ray, ed.	$1.45
IB-33	Italian Comedy in the Renaissance	Marvin T. Herrick	$1.75
IB-34	Death in the Literature of Unamuno	Mario J. Valdés	$1.25
IB-35	*Port of New York: Essays on Fourteen American Moderns	Paul Rosenfeld, with an introductory essay by Sherman Paul	$2.25
IB-36	*How to Do Library Research	Robert B. Downs	$1.45
IB-37	Henry James: Representative Selections, with Introduction, Bibliography, and Notes	Lyon N. Richardson	$3.50

* Also available in clothbound editions.

IB-38	Symbolic Crusade: Status Politics and the American Temperance Movement	Joseph R. Gusfield	$1.75
IB-39	*Genesis and Structure of Society	Giovanni Gentile, translated by H. S. Harris	$1.95
IB-40	The Social Philosophy of Giovanni Gentile	H. S. Harris	$2.45
IB-41	*As We Saw the Thirties: Essays on Social and Political Movements of a Decade	Rita James Simon, ed.	$2.45
IB-42	The Symbolic Uses of Politics	Murray Edelman	$2.45
IB-43	White-Collar Trade Unions: Contemporary Developments in Industrialized Societies	Adolf Sturmthal, ed.	$3.50
IB-44	*The Labor Arbitration Process	R. W. Fleming	$2.45
IB-45	*Edmund Wilson: A Study of Literary Vocation in Our Time	Sherman Paul	$2.45
IB-46	*George Santayana's America: Essays on Literature and Culture	James Ballowe, ed.	$2.25
IB-47	The Measurement of Meaning	Charles E. Osgood, George J. Suci, and Percy H. Tannenbaum	$3.45
IB-48	*The Miracle of Growth	Foreword by Arnold Gesell	$1.75
IB-49	*Information Theory and Esthetic Perception	Abraham Moles	$2.45
IB-50	Outlawing the Spoils: A History of the Civil Service Reform Movement, 1865-1883	Ari Hoogenboom	$2.95
IB-51	*Community Colleges: A President's View	Thomas E. O'Connell	$1.95
IB-52	*The Joys and Sorrows of Recent American Art	Allen S. Weller	$3.95
IB-53	*Dimensions of Academic Freedom	Walter P. Metzger, Sanford H. Kadish, Arthur DeBardeleben, and Edward J. Bloustein	$ .95
IB-54	*Essays on Frege	E. D. Klemke, ed.	$3.95
IB-55	The Fine Hammered Steel of Herman Melville	Milton R. Stern	$2.95

* Also available in clothbound editions.

Also available in clothbound editions.

University of Illinois Press Urbana, Chicago, and London